DEMYSTIFYING
Kashmir

DEMYSTIFYING
Kashmir

Navnita Chadha Behera

BROOKINGS INSTITUTION PRESS
Washington, D.C.

Library of Congress Cataloging-in-Publication data

Behera, Navnita Chadha.
  Demystifying Kashmir / Navnita Chadha Behera.
    p.   cm.
  Summary: "Traces Kashmir history from prepartition India to the current-day
situation. Provides an analysis of the philosophical underpinnings and the local, bilateral,
and international dynamics of the key players involved in this conflict. Conclusion
focuses on the parameters, players, politics, and prognosis of the ongoing peace process
in Kashmir"—Provided by publisher.
  Includes bibliographical references and index.
  ISBN-13: 978-0-8157-0860-5 (trade cloth : alk. paper)
  ISBN-10: 0-8157-0860-2 (trade cloth : alk. paper)
  1. Jammu and Kashmir (India)—Politics and government. 2. Jammu and Kashmir
(India)—History—Autonomy and independence movements. 3. Azad Kashmir—
Politics and government.   I. Title.
  DS485.K27B395 2006
  954'.604—dc22   2006027991

1 3 5 7 9 8 6 4 2

Cartography by Meridian Mapping
Minneapolis, Minnesota

Typeset in Minion

Composition by Pete Lindeman, OSP Inc.
Arlington, Virginia

Printed by R. R. Donnelley
Harrisonburg, Virginia

CONTENTS

Maps

Foreword

I REMEMBER, AS A CHILD in the 1950s, hearing my parents talk about the Vale of Kashmir as a place of great beauty, halfway around the globe, where World War III might begin. That was during the cold war, of course, when Pakistan had military links to the United States while India, through its policy of non-alignment, was on the wrong side of John Foster Dulles's version of the principle: *if you're not with us, you're against us.* While the cold war is history, the Kashmir conflict is still with us. It could very well have erupted into a nuclear war during the Kargil crisis of 1999, when I was in the State Department and intimately involved in diplomacy on the South Asian subcontinent. Therefore it is with a personal sense of pride, as well as an institutional one, that I welcome having the Brookings Institution Press publish a book of this quality and timeliness.

In the pages that follow, Navnita Chadha Behera has contributed substantially to our understanding about the complex dynamics of this seemingly intractable dispute. The international community has chiefly viewed Kashmir as a territorial dispute—a battleground for wars between India and Pakistan—and, from the late 1990s on, a nuclear flashpoint. Since 9/11 the area has become an important locus for waging the "war on terror." Complicating matters, several post-9/11 terrorist strikes around the world can be traced back to Pakistan, and there are linkages between al Qaeda and Kashmir-focused groups such as Lashkar-e-Taiba and Jaish-i-Mohammed.

Dr. Behera illuminates the Kashmir issue's multifaceted character. The former princely state of Jammu and Kashmir, to give it its proper name, is home to a myriad of religious, ethnic, and linguistic groups. These make powerful demands on the Indian and Pakistani states and now have a growing international presence of their own.

Dr. Behera makes the case that there can be no enduring resolution of the Kashmir conflict without addressing these divergent political demands. As with the former Yugoslavia, merely carving out new states does not necessarily resolve ethnic conflicts. She notes that all instruments of violence (ranging from guerrilla warfare to the threat to use nuclear weapons) have failed to resolve Kashmir. Obviously, all the parties must reach a mutually acceptable and negotiated solution, but so far they have been unable to agree on the nature of the dispute, let alone a particular formula.

One of the many virtues of this meticulously researched book is that it moves from a close examination of Kashmir itself to a careful explication of the policy options open to all parties—Indians, Pakistanis, the Kashmiris, and the international community.

Brookings is especially pleased to add Dr. Behera's book to its growing list of volumes on India and South Asia. Since India's emergence as a major player in geopolitics and geoeconomics, along with Pakistan's evolution as a stable and responsible member of the international community, this region is vital to what kind of century we have ahead of us. And South Asia is of growing importance to Brookings as we seek to become a truly global think tank. Our publication of this book is a mark of that commitment.

STROBE TALBOTT
President

Washington, D.C.
November 2006

Acknowledgments

I WOULD LIKE TO acknowledge the many individuals who provided assistance in the research and writing of this book. I am especially indebted to Stephen Cohen for inviting me to serve as a scholar in residence at the Brookings Institution between 2001 and 2002. It is during this period that the idea for this book was born. Without Steve's enormous patience and encouragement, this book would not have materialized.

Special thanks are due James Steinberg, former director of the Brookings Foreign Policy Studies program, for his support and valuable suggestions on an early draft. The book has gained much from the detailed and meticulous attention of Alexander Evans, Jasjit Singh, Praveen Swami, Surinder Oberoi, as well as comments from Ashley Tellis, Ayesha Siddiqa, Ejaz Haider, Lt. Gen. Talat Masood, and several anonymous readers. I owe a deep sense of gratitude to all of them.

Anisha Kinra, Poonam Kumari, Aditi Singh, and Sonia Huria provided crucial research support, and without Abid's painstaking efforts, I could not have completed the chapter on Azad Kashmir and the Northern Areas. I would also like to acknowledge the contributions of many scholars, journalists, political leaders, and government officials who have shared their insights and debated these issues with me over the years.

At the Brookings Institution Press, Vicky Macintyre painstakingly edited the manuscript, Carlotta Ribar proofread the pages, and Mary Mortensen provided the index. Larry Converse provided assistance with the cartography, typesetting, and printing, Susan Woollen helped to develop the cover of the book, and Janet Walker provided overall support in getting the book to print.

As ever, I wish to acknowledge my husband, Ajay, for his unfailing support and my daughter, Miska, for her little, albeit precious generosities in allowing my "absence" for all those times we should have been together.

DEMYSTIFYING
Kashmir

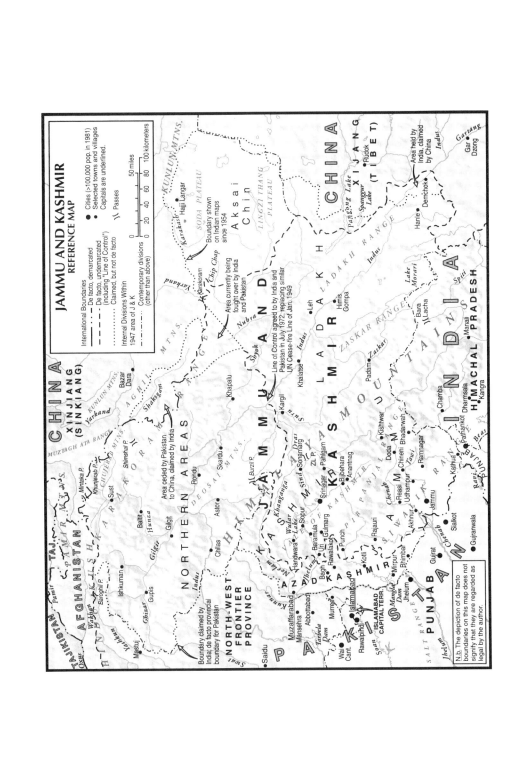

JAMMU AND KASHMIR
REFERENCE MAP

International Boundaries
─··─··─ De facto, demarcated
─·─·─ De facto, undemarcated
(including "Line of Control")
··········· Claimed, but not de facto

Internal Divisions Within
─ ─ ─ 1947 area of J & K
─··─··─ Contemporary divisions
(other than above)

● Cities (>100,000 pop. in 1981)
● Selected towns and villages
Capitals are underlined.
)(Passes

0   20 40 60 80 100 kilometers
0   50 miles

N.b. The depiction of de facto
boundaries on this map does not
signify that they are regarded as
legal by the author.

INTRODUCTION

THIS BOOK IS AN ATTEMPT to redefine the Kashmir conflict by breaking away from conventional assumptions about the basic issues and underlining their many facets. The book questions various stereotypes arising from a skewed Hindu-Muslim understanding of the region's antagonisms and history, which suggests the dispute is rooted solely in the idea that a Muslim-majority state had its fate determined by a Hindu maharaja, that Pakistan—the "homeland" of the subcontinent's Muslims—is incomplete without Kashmir's inclusion, or that India's secular credentials depend on Kashmir's continued accession. By turning a blind eye to the local dynamics of Kashmiri politics in pre-partition India and disregarding the political stakes of the Indian National Congress and of the Muslim League in Kashmir, previous analyses have tended to see Kashmir as an immutable zero-sum test of India's and Pakistan's legitimating ideologies—in which one's validity invalidates the other's—which in turn precludes the possibility of *any* reconciliation.

On the surface, it is easy to see why Kashmir is typically understood as a territorial dispute between two belligerent neighbors in South Asia. Jammu and Kashmir is a former princely state partitioned since 1949, yet still regarded as a homogeneous entity. India and Pakistan control almost half of its territory (a small portion is occupied by China), with both claiming jurisdiction over the whole. The line of demarcation is called the Line of Control (see map 1). Nevertheless, developments in the Pakistani part (made up of Azad Kashmir and the Northern Areas) simply do not figure in the debates on Kashmir, while stories of Kashmiris seeking to break away from the part administered by India distort reality by overlooking the region's complexities. The political construct of a Muslim-majority Jammu and Kashmir state pitted against a majoritarian

Hindu India—or of an Islamic bond cementing the relationship between Azad Kashmir and the Northern Areas with Pakistan—is, at best, misleading.

With its extraordinary medley of races, tribal groups, languages, and religions, Jammu and Kashmir is one of the most diverse regions in the subcontinent. Even its majority community of Kashmiri Muslims is not a unified, homogeneous entity in terms of its political beliefs, its ideological leanings, or the political goals of the decade-long insurgent movement in the Kashmir Valley. There are sharp divisions between those demanding that Jammu and Kashmir become an independent state, those seeking to merge with Pakistan, and those wanting to reconcile their differences with India through constitutional mechanisms guaranteeing their political rights. Nor does the Kashmiri political leadership necessarily speak for the diverse minorities of the state, including Gujjars, Bakkarwals, Kashmiri Pandits, Dogras, and Ladakhi Buddhists. Across the Line of Control, the Northern Areas also presents a rich mosaic of languages, castes, Islamic sects, and cultures, which cannot be subsumed under the overarching category of "Muslim brotherhood" without distorting the diverse political aspirations of the region's residents. It is essential to recognize the deeply plural character of Jammu and Kashmir's society on both sides of the line of control and the political aspirations and choices of its minority communities. The irreducible and homogenizing parameters of ideology and nationalism usually applied in analyzing the Kashmir conflict are clearly at variance with the plural realities and diverse political demands of the region's various communities, ranging from affirmative discrimination to more autonomy, separate constitutional status within India or Pakistan, and outright secession.

The central argument of this book is that the Kashmir conflict revolves around many complex, and multilayered issues, emanating from equally complex causes. Any hope for creating critical political opportunities that will allow the parties to explore ways to find a just, viable, and lasting solution to the conflict depends on deeper insight into these complexities.

The first chapter delves into the history of pre-partition India and seeks to shift the parameters of the Kashmir debate from the ideological to the political domain. As it points out, Kashmir's fate in 1947, including its accession to India and eventual division into two parts, was decided not on ideological grounds but on the outcome of the political battle between the Indian National Congress and the Muslim League. Within the princely state of Jammu and Kashmir, the National Conference, led by Sheikh Abdullah, influenced the course of events at that critical juncture far more than did the Dogra Hindu maharaja, Hari Singh.

Chapters 2 and 3 discuss the key political and military components of India's and Pakistan's Kashmir strategies. For its part, India has pursued a markedly political strategy in the region, although it erred in retreating from its fundamental commitment to provide a federal, democratic, and secular model of self-governance to the people of Jammu and Kashmir. It is now on a corrective course, making amends with constituents who remain alienated from the Indian state. India's leadership does not think militarily about Kashmir, has no offensive military objective to bring Azad Kashmir and the Northern Areas back into Jammu and Kashmir state, and accordingly has no aggressive military strategy in Kashmir. Pakistan, in complete contrast, has not evolved a political strategy for arguing its case on Kashmir. Rather, it has persistently tried virtually every instrument of violence to alter the status quo in Kashmir by force—and has failed in all such attempts. Whether it has learned from its mistakes, due mainly to certain systemic flaws in its strategic decisionmaking institutions, is unclear.

Chapter 4 turns to the terms of reference in the "self-determination" debate over Kashmir, which have departed little from those of the UN Security Council debates of the early 1950s. It traces the historical antecedents of the demand for self-determination, first raised by Sheikh Abdullah in the Dogra reign of Maharaja Hari Singh and now nourished by multiple notions of self-determination among the diverse communities of Jammu and Kashmir state. Chapter 5 focuses on the insurgent movement launched in 1989–90 that transformed the dynamics of the Kashmir conflict. Originally an indigenous, mass movement toward *azadi* (independence), it was taken over by a much smaller, well-armed, well-trained, and committed group of militants—mostly non-Kashmiri—who turned it into a *jihad* and proved to be its undoing. In chapter 6 the spotlight is on the forgotten frontiers of Azad Kashmir and the Northern Areas, and on the instruments, strategies, and dynamics of Pakistan's colonial-style domination of those regions. Here, too, the local populace and its leadership are engaged in a struggle for their constitutional and political rights.

Chapter 7 moves to the international sphere, to examine the implications of the Kashmir conflict there. The analysis closes in chapter 8 with an overview of the four P's of the ongoing peace process in Kashmir: its parameters, players, policies, and prognosis.

CHAPTER ONE

REDEFINING THE PARAMETERS

IN THE HINDU-MUSLIM PARADIGM usually applied to the Kashmir dispute, India's secular credentials are at stake on one side and Pakistan's founding two-nation principle on the other. Thus if India must prevail as a secular entity, what is the point of Pakistan's existence? Alternatively, if the two-nation principle holds, how should India engage with its Muslim population, which more than fifty years after partition is approximately the same as that of post-1971 Pakistan. In other words, if conceived in communal terms, the dispute becomes a zero-sum game. This is not to say that ideological (religious), economic, military, and strategic factors played little or no role in the Kashmir conflict. Rather, political factors were of primary importance.[1] As this chapter shows, those at loggerheads over Kashmir in pre-partition India were political entities, most notably the National Congress and the Muslim League (a political party founded in 1906 to protect the interests of Muslims in British India). Each sought Kashmir's accession, but not as an inalienable part of a future India or Pakistan. Their central concern was the region's strategic location for the geographical consolidation of the two new sovereign states. The communal rationale for including Kashmir emerged almost as an afterthought. It was not until then that Jawaharlal Nehru spoke of Kashmir's importance to establishing the secular basis of the Indian nation-state and that Liaquat Ali Khan claimed Pakistan was incomplete without Kashmir. Thus Kashmir's fate was not decided on ideological grounds; it was an outcome of the political battle fought between the National Congress and the Muslim League, with certain extraneous factors, such as the British army commanders and the raiders' attacks, playing an important role.

Map 1-1. *Pre-Partition Map of India*

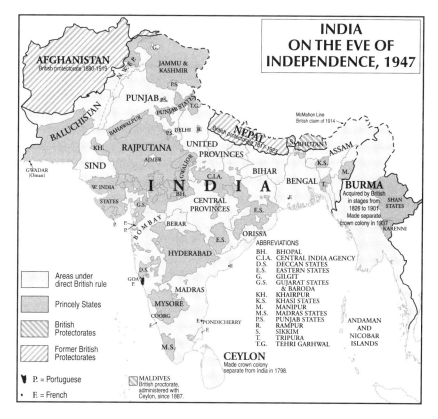

In 1946, when the British decided to partition India, they proposed to carve the state of Pakistan from the Muslim majority provinces in India, with the boundaries to be drawn up by the Radcliffe Boundary Commission. The transfer of power applied only to those areas and provinces that were directly ruled by the British, which constituted about 54 percent of the subcontinent's territory (see map 1-1). The remaining 46 percent was administered by the British through treaties (in many cases, multiple treaties) with the rulers of 564 states, including large kingdoms such as Hyderabad, Jammu and Kashmir, Gwalior, Mysore, and Patiala, and historically important ones such as Udaipur, Jaipur, and Travancore. Many had their own armies, currency, and railways. Under the Cabinet Mission Plan of May 1946, British paramountcy over those states would lapse with Britain's departure, making them independent, although they were urged to join the Indian or Pakistani Dominion through a new federal relationship or other political arrangements.

Princely States: The New Battleground

Britain's departure opened a new battleground for the National Congress and the Muslim League to try to expand the territorial boundaries of the future India and Pakistan, respectively. Significantly, both agreed that the two-nation theory, the deciding principle for the British approach to partitioning India, did not apply—that actually there was no *fixed* formula for apportioning the princely states between the two dominions. The National Congress had agreed to the partition on the condition that the Muslim League and its leader, Mohammed Ali Jinnah, accept the division as a final settlement. There was no question of partitioning the princely states on communal grounds or of determining their accession by that factor. Jinnah had also reiterated that the Lahore Resolution, enunciating the demand for Pakistan, was "only confined to British India," albeit for different reasons. While the National Congress sought not to lose any more territory on the altar of the two-nation theory, the Muslim League courted all the princely states, hoping to persuade them either to accede to Pakistan or to remain independent, irrespective of their Hindu or Muslim character. The two groups also differed in their larger objectives, political calculations, and strategies.

The National Congress's Objective and Strategy

The National Congress's objective was to unify the princely states, bring them into the Indian union, and consolidate India's frontiers. To this end, Nehru and the nationalist leadership of the Congress invoked Indian history, reminding the states of the successive political invasions and internal disintegrations of the past. The political configuration of India before the transfer of power, with its 564 princely states, had made "a patchwork of the country like a crazy quilt," threatening to plunge the subcontinent into chaos. The "ship of Indian freedom," it was feared, could well "founder on the rock of the states."[2]

For the National Congress, India was fundamentally a single entity. Its leaders envisaged and struggled to win *Poorna Swaraj* (complete independence) for both British India and the princely states, which were subject to British suzerainty. People in many of those states enjoyed little political freedom and were economically exploited by their rulers. Nehru was convinced that the feudal princely order was propped up by British colonial power. In his presidential address to the Lucknow Congress in April 1936, he came down hard on autocracy and feudalism:

A free India cannot tolerate the subjection of many of our children and their deprivation of human rights, nor can it ever agree to a *dissection of its body and a cutting up of its limbs.* If we stand for any human, political, social, or economic rights for ourselves, we stand for those identical rights for the people of the States.[3] (Emphasis added)

Since the princes and the British had the same interests, the people in the princely states and the rest of India found themselves struggling for the same freedoms, which gradually became integrated into a single whole, strongly championed by the Congress. The All-India States Peoples' Conference (AISPC), which came into being in 1927, was another strong supporter of the integration of the people's movements in the states and the general anti-imperialist struggle waged by the National Congress. In 1936 Pattabhi Sitaramayya, presiding over the Karachi session, urged that "the states Peoples' Conference . . . be organically related to the Congress and restate its creed linking the responsible government of the states' people as an integral factor of the *Poorna Swaraj* or complete independence of the Congress."[4] The following year the Congress issued the Haripura Resolution declaring that it stood "for the same political, social, and economic freedom in the states as in the rest of India and consider[ed] the states as integral parts of India, which cannot be separated."[5]

The Congress made the rights of people in the states an issue in the settlement of India's constitutional problem. The Nehru Committee Report of 1928 demanded that rulers give their people the right to elect representatives to an Indian Constituent Assembly. In March 1942, after prolonged hostilities, the British sent Sir Stafford Cripps to India with a long-term offer to set up "an elected body charged with the task of framing a new Constitution" giving India dominion status. Two conditions were attached to the proposal: the provinces of the new dominion would have the option to secede from the union, and a treaty would be signed between Britain and the constitution-making body to cover "all necessary matters arising out of the complete transfer of responsibility from British to Indian hands." British paramountcy, Cripps said, would be "automatically dissolved" for states entering the union. However, the crown would retain the means to implement its obligation toward nonadhering states, in which case there would be no change on the questions of British paramountcy and other related matters except with their consent.[6]

After a month of deliberation, the working committee of the Congress resolved to reject the Cripps offer, arguing that it ignored millions of India's residents, treating them as "commodities at the disposal of their rulers." This, said Congress, went against the grain of both democracy and self-determination:

While the representation of an Indian state in the constitution-making body is fixed on a population basis, the people of the state have no voice in choosing those representatives, nor are they to be consulted at any stage, while decisions vitally affecting them are being taken. Such states may in many ways become barriers to the growth of Indian freedom, enclaves where foreign authority still prevails and where the possibility of maintaining sovereign armed forces has been stated to be a likely contingency, and a perpetual menace to the people of the states as well as to the rest of India.[7]

Congress also rejected the British interpretation of the lapse of paramountcy. Nehru agreed that the states should be free to join either the Indian or Pakistani Constituent Assembly, but his government refused to recognize the right of any princely state to independence. On April 18, 1947, addressing the annual session of the AISPC, he declared that "any state which did not come into the Constituent Assembly would be treated by the country as a hostile state." Such a state, he added, "would have to bear the consequences of being so treated."[8] Congress understood the gravity of the situation and accorded utmost priority to securing the accession of states into the Indian union. Consolidation of India's territorial frontier was thus the union's single most important goal, a task undertaken by the Ministry of States Department, led by Sardar Patel.

Congress's strategy had two critical components. The first was the Instrument of Accession, a legal mechanism devised by the States Department that was equally acceptable to both the Congress and the rulers of the princely states. It asked the rulers to accede to the Indian union in only three areas—defense, external affairs, and communications—without any other commitments. Since the first two functions had been handled by the British in any case, the rulers would not be losing any rights that they had previously enjoyed in those areas. From the Congress's point of view, the policy of accession ensured the fundamental political unity of the country and established the necessary political structure that would make India one federation, with the provinces and the states as its integral parts. The second step of the strategy was to support the people's movement in the states and simultaneously negotiate with the rulers. The combination of Nehru and Sardar Patel proved to be very effective in pursuing those apparently conflicting goals. Nehru closely identified with the people's movements and at times even confronted the rulers on behalf of the popular leadership in the states.[9] Addressing the General Council of the States Peoples' Conference at New Delhi on June 8, 1946, Nehru made it "perfectly clear" that in allowing rulers to continue as constitutional heads, "the only ultimate rights we recognize are the rights of the people. Everything else must give way to them. Sovereignty must reside in the people and not in any individual."[10]

For the Congress, the will of the people was the overriding factor in a state's decision on accession to India or Pakistan. Even if it conflicted with the ruler's preference, the will of the people ultimately had to prevail. The princely rulers therefore feared the Congress for undercutting their power. Whereas Nehru carried the stick, Patel offered the carrot, assuring the rulers that it was in their best interest to accede to the Indian union. Doing so, he argued, would enable them to have a direct voice in shaping the policies of the central government. Because of this "masterly handling of the rulers," remarked V. P. Menon, a top government official who worked closely with Sardar Patel, they "soon came to recognize [Patel] as a stable force in Indian politics and as one who would give them a fair deal.... [H]is unfailing politeness to the rulers, viewed against his reputation as the 'Iron Man of India,' endeared him to them and created such confidence that all accepted his advice without demur."[11]

Patel had pulled off a miracle. In less than three weeks, 551 states had acceded to the Indian union. The gigantic proportions of his accomplishment could be judged by the reconfiguration: though partition had robbed India of 364,737 square miles and a population of 81.5 million, the integration of states added nearly 500,000 square miles and a population of 86.5 million (not including Jammu and Kashmir).

The Muslim League's Objective and Strategy

Throughout the 1940s, the Muslim League focused primarily on British India. Its policies with regard to the princely states evolved in two phases, before and after the British conceded to the demand for partition. In the first phase, the Muslim League concentrated on achieving its ultimate political goal—the creation of Pakistan. At this point, it viewed political realities in the subcontinent through a "Muslim lens." Hence it supported "Muslim minority rights, Muslim Princes, and, in the case of Kashmir, the Muslim majority [populace]."[12] Its choice of allies from within the princely states was also influenced by an ongoing hostility between it and the Congress. Before partition, there had been a rapid growth of people's movements in the states, some of which (such as the AISPC) were closely aligned with the Congress before the Muslim League was born. In an effort to court as many enemies of the Congress as possible, the League leaned toward the princes. "Careful to avoid antagonizing the rulers," it hoped to "both weaken the Congress and expose new sources of support for the League's perennially empty coffers."[13]

Otherwise, the Muslim League was unconcerned about states' affairs in general and did not try to intervene in them. For a long time, it merely emphasized its desire for responsible government in the states and did nothing to help the people's movements there. As far back as 1940, Jinnah made clear the Muslim League's policy of not estranging the princes: "If these states willingly agree to come into the federation of the Muslim homeland, we shall be glad to come to a reasonable and honourable settlement with them. *We have however no desire to force them or coerce them in any way*" (emphasis added).[14] He was referring mainly to Kashmir, Bahawalpur, and Patiala in northwest India.

According to the *Dawn,* a prominent newspaper published in Karachi, the Muslim League had "no wish or desire to stir up trouble in the states to indulge in a campaign of misrepresentation or vilification against the Princely Order."[15] Hence in Muslim-majority states ruled by Hindu princes, such as Kashmir and Mysore, Jinnah sought to placate the rulers, since his impression was that they were really going to be "just, fair and sympathetic."[16] In the states ruled by Muslim princes, the League's policy was shaped by their usefulness to its larger game plan. The Nawab of Bhopal, for example, had an important role in the Chamber of Princes, while the wealthy Nizam of Hyderabad was a source of considerable financial support.[17] The Jam Saheb of Nawanagar, being chancellor of the Chamber of Provinces, could provide advice on any constitutional proposals, so long as the princely order did not try to oppose Jinnah.[18] The princely states were thus useful at the negotiating table as well as in undercutting the Congress.

That changed, however, after the British agreed to the establishment of Pakistan. Jinnah then realized that the fruit of all his labor was a "mutilated and moth-eaten" state shorn of eastern Punjab and western Bengal (including Calcutta), which he had rejected out of hand in 1944 and 1946. Having failed to expand Pakistan's territories within British India, he looked to the two groups that held the key to increasing the size of Pakistan: the princes and the Sikh community. Since the violence of communal politics and the suspected orthodoxy of the Muslim League forced the Sikhs out of any proposed Muslim state, the only other way to expand was to include princely states, or at least to limit the number of princely states acceding to India.[19] Therefore Jinnah's new aim was "to prevent the consolidation of India and to balkanize it, if possible" in order to make the differences in size and population between India and Pakistan seem unimportant.[20] As a result, he supported the British proposal for ending their paramountcy, declaring:

> Constitutionally and legally the Indian states will be independent sovereign states on the termination of paramountcy and they will be free to decide for themselves and to adopt any course they like; it is open to them to join the Hindustan Constituent Assembly or the Pakistan Con-

stituent Assembly, or decide to remain independent. In the last case they may enter into such agreements or relationship with Hindustan or Pakistan as they may choose.[21]

Furthermore, "Neither the British government, nor the British parliament, nor any other power or body could compel the States to do anything contrary to their free will and accord, nor had they any power or sanction of any kind to do so."[22]

Jinnah reaffirmed that paramountcy would terminate on August 15, 1947, which would mark the beginning of "the full sovereign status" of the Indian states, and that the ruler of a princely state had an absolute right to accede to either country. The Muslim League was sure it had a win-win strategy, first because Jinnah believed that he had the princely states within the prospective boundaries of Pakistan in his pocket. That was probably why the Muslim League did not initiate serious negotiations to secure their accession to the new Dominion of Pakistan until *after* the transfer of power. Second, the problem of the states was infinitely less important for Pakistan than for India, which had to negotiate with a much larger number of princely states. Furthermore, the most formidable bastions of the princely order were in India, which therefore faced a greater potential danger that some states might declare their independence. In addition, the leaders of the Indian federal government were more likely to be at odds with the rulers of the states than was the case in Pakistan.[23]

If Jinnah's strategy of siding with the rulers and validating their sovereign and independent status after August 15 worked, it would be at the cost of India and not of Pakistan. Discounting both the principles of ideology and geographical contiguity, Liaquat Ali Khan declared on April 21, 1947, that the Indian states would be "free to negotiate agreements with Pakistan or Hindustan as considerations of contiguity or their self-interest may dictate, or they may choose to assume complete and separate sovereign status for themselves."[24] This tactic was "the culmination of the policy of [the Muslim League] which pitted the rulers against the Congress."[25] The battle was truly on.

One of the first Indian states to declare it would become independent and not join the Indian Dominion was Travancore, India's southernmost state, surrounded on three sides by Indian territory. Jinnah had long discussions with the Dewan of the state in late 1947, and the two agreed to exchange representatives. Hyderabad announced it would take a similar course. Jinnah's objective, thinly veiled, was not only to keep as much territory and population away from India as possible by upholding the rulers' right to decide their people's future, but also to foment discord between the Indian union and the states, which would then be bound to seek a closer alliance with Pakistan. Reflecting the official views of the Muslim League, the *Dawn* observed that Pakistan promised to respect the independence and integrity of the states:

> The contrast between the attitude of the Muslim League and Congress in this regard is so striking and the promise of nonintervention by the League so reassuring that we would not be surprised if a number of even non-Muslim states decide eventually either to join the Pakistan Constituent Assembly or to enter into closer treaty relations with Pakistan than with Hindustan. As autonomous members of the Union of Pakistan or as allies of Pakistan, the Indian States, whether Muslim or Hindu, will have a more honourable position than otherwise. As for the Congress threats, we have no doubt that Hyderabad and Travancore will firmly stand up to it and refuse to be bullied, and their example should hearten others who have not yet made up their minds.[26]

Jinnah even tried hard to persuade some Hindu rulers of bordering Rajput states to stay independent and join Pakistan at a later date on terms to be dictated by the ruler. Jinnah, so the story goes, "signed a blank sheet of paper and gave it to Maharaja Hanwant Singh of Jodhpur, along with his own fountain pen, saying, 'You can fill in all your conditions.'"[27] Other Hindu Rajput states, such as Jaisalmer and Bikaner, were also approached. The Nawab of Bhopal, a former president of the Chamber of Princes who was sure to have some influence on the views of other Indian rulers, was offered a governorship. In keeping with its strategy, the Muslim League set aside the principles of contiguity and communal character and accepted the accession of Junagarh, which did not share any border with Pakistan and whose population was 85 percent Hindu.

The Outcome

Thus the battle for the princely states was a deeply political, not ideological, contest fought with no holds barred. On the eve of independence, Jinnah appeared to be on the losing side. Except for Junagarh, Hyderabad, and Jammu and Kashmir, all the princely states contiguous to India, including Travancore, had been persuaded to sign the Instrument of Accession. By contrast, as of August 14, 1947, no ruler had acceded to Pakistan (see table 1-1).[28] The reasons why Nehru and Patel's strategy worked whereas Jinnah's failed have important implications for the situation in Kashmir.

Put simply, Jinnah backed the wrong horse. He failed to recognize that the very existence of the rulers of the states depended on either the support of their

Table 1-1. *States Acceding to Pakistan*

| State | Date of accession | | Language of majority |
	Executed	*Accepted*	
Bahawalpur	October 3, 1947	October 5, 1947	Punjabi
Khairpur	October 3, 1947	October 5, 1947	Sindhi
Kalat	March 27, 1948	March 31, 1948	Brahui
Makran	March 17, 1948	March 17, 1948	Baluchi
Las Bela	March 7, 1948	March 17, 1948	Sindhi
Kharan	March 17, 1948	March 17, 1948	Baluchi
Chitral	October 6, 1947	February 18, 1948	Kowar
Amb	December 31, 1947	December 31, 1947	Pushtu
Dir	November 8, 1947	February 8, 1948	Pushtu
Swat	November 3, 1947	November 11, 1947	Pushtu

Source: Wayne Wilcox, *Pakistan: The Consolidation of a Nation* (Columbia University Press, 1963), pp. 82–83.

people or the protection of one of the dominions—India or Pakistan—that would replace the British, their erstwhile masters. Faced with a growing people's movement, almost every "ruler knew that his inevitable fate lay with the majority and their masters, the Indian National Congress."[29] With British protection about to end, no other option was available. The Congress had announced that any state not joining the Constituent Assembly by August 15, 1947, would be considered a hostile state. The new Dominion of Pakistan was hardly in a position to guarantee their security—as Junagarh, Hyderabad, and Kashmir, the three princely states that held out, would soon discover.[30]

Jinnah's second political failure lay in underestimating India: "The assumption had been that the division of the subcontinent would weaken India more than Pakistan, an illusion as dangerous as an underestimation of the resolve and courage displayed by the army and government of India."[31] There was also considerable faith in the Nizam's ability to defend Hyderabad against a splintered India long enough, at least, for Pakistan to stabilize its territories in the west and east.[32] Jinnah failed to appreciate the stakes involved for India, which viewed assimilation of the states as a sine qua non of national life. For the Muslim League, the states had primarily strategic value, as a bargaining chip in the pursuit of a different goal: namely, the creation of Pakistan and expansion of its boundaries at India's cost.

The peculiar circumstances on the subcontinent before the transfer of power had played to Jinnah's strengths. His negotiating skills had clearly helped him in dealing with the British. He had managed to pull off a feat unprecedented in modern history, which was to create a new state entirely legally. He had not had to lift a gun or even order anyone else to do so, and it is hard to think of anyone else who created a nation without spending even a single day in prison.[33] He used to say that he had created Pakistan "with the assistance of my steno and a typewriter."[34] Jinnah's monumental achievement rested on a combination of talents that constantly frustrated the British: his refusal to compromise and his brilliant ability to grasp and articulate the most complex legal issues. By contrast, in the princely states, where the people's movements had developed a momentum of their own, Jinnah was out of touch with the realities. This was particularly important in Kashmir, which had a record of waging an independent popular struggle against the autocratic rule of the Dogra maharaja, Hari Singh.

The Local Dynamics: Story in Kashmir

The Dogras were a predominantly Hindu people installed as rulers of Kashmir under the Treaty of Amritsar signed in 1846. It awarded the Dogra ruler, Gulab Singh, the territories of Kashmir, Ladakh (up to the Dras River), Gilgit, and Chenab (see map 1-2) for the sum of 750,000 pounds sterling, in recognition of his services to the British crown. Kashmir remained an independent princely state until 1947. As already mentioned, its political affairs are usually viewed through an ideological lens, with the emphasis on the fact that the fate of this Muslim-majority province was dictated by a Hindu maharaja, Hari Singh. That approach is misleading on at least two counts: it tends to regard "Hindus" and "Muslims" as monolithic groups, and it is blind to Kashmir's underlying cultural, ethnic, socioeconomic, and regional affinities, which have often played a critical role in changing the course of Kashmiri politics. The political realities in Kashmir are far more complex, especially in the wake of several radical transformations in the 1930s and 1940s.

Dogra rule was marked by a strong regional bias against Kashmiris and religious discrimination against Muslims. Kashmiris were subjugated and denied the right to possess arms. The lot of Muslims was even worse: they were excluded from state services, the Muslim peasantry and industrial workers were heavily taxed, and trade, business, and banking were monopolized by Punjabis and Dogras. Without access to modern education, Muslims sank into a deep distrust of rule under the Hindu Dogras.

However, polarization in Kashmir was not merely the result of ethnoreligious alignments. It also evolved from the Dogra system of state patronage, which deprived sections of the indigenous population of their political, economic, and religious rights. Kashmiri Muslims complained that Kashmiri

Map 1-2. *Dogra State of Jammu and Kashmir*

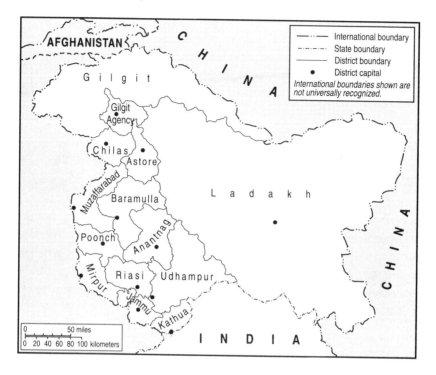

Pandits, the original inhabitants of Kashmir Valley, filled the ranks of the state administration, leaving the predominantly Muslim peasantry and artisan class at the lowest rung of society.[35] Kashmiri Pandits, in turn, grumbled that Dogra Rajputs formed the bulk of the army and that Punjabis had cornered the top posts in the state bureaucracy.

MOBILIZING KASHMIRI MUSLIMS

Kashmiri Muslims were divided into several small groups, each with a limited political agenda. Muslim silk factory workers, for instance, pressed for better working conditions. Educated Muslim youth in Srinagar formed the Reading Room Party to secure better educational facilities and jobs in the state administration, while the Muslim Young Men's League at Jammu was engaged in underground activities to achieve economic and political independence of the state.[36] Those early agitations were limited in their agenda and scope until growing discontent with the Dogra maharaja exploded in a massive Muslim agitation in 1931, which the Muslims called a religious war. It proved to be a turning point in sharpening the external boundaries of the Kashmiri Muslim community in relation to the Dogra Hindus and Kashmiri Pandits, who supported the maharaja. When Maharaja Hari Singh appointed the Glancy Commission to address Muslim grievances, Pandits opposed it vehemently. The Kashmiri Pandit movement, however, soon lost its momentum and ceased to be an independent political force.

Kashmiri Muslims were organized under the All-Jammu and Kashmir Muslim Conference, founded in 1932, which enjoyed the support of the Muslim intelligentsia, clergy, tradespeople or traders, industrial laborers, artisans, and peasants. They demanded a bigger share in the civil services for educated Muslim youth, land ownership, lower land revenue charged to the peasantry, better working conditions for industrial laborers, and recruitment of Muslims into the army. Religious demands included the return of mosques to the Muslim community and removal of impediments to the conversion of Hindus to Islam.

In their quest for support from Indian Muslims, Kashmiri Muslim leaders received a favorable response from Punjabi Muslims, the Ahrars and Ahmadiyas.[37] When Maharaja Hari Singh used force to suppress the movement, Mirwaiz Yusuf Shah (*mirwaiz* is the title of the head of a sect of Kashmir's Muslims) asked Muslims to take up arms and participate in his congregations, to defy the government ban on meetings. Thousands of Muslims armed with spears, axes, hammers, knives, swords, and a few handguns arrived at Ziarat Dastgir Sahib at Khanyar, Srinagar. The maharaja informed the British that an armed rebellion had broken out in Jammu and Kashmir and sought military help.

British intervention demonstrated that the princely states were merely instruments of the colonial power and were being exploited to serve British interests more than that of the maharaja. Realizing that their political emancipation was inseparably linked with the withdrawal of British paramountcy rather than the maharaja's ethnoreligious lineage, Kashmir's Muslims tempered the religious edge to their grievances significantly and emerged as a new secular and regional entity.

Secularizing the Movement: Birth of the National Conference

This trend was abetted by the formation of several local political organizations with a secular, nationalist outlook and socialist objectives—such as the Kashmir Youth League, established in 1936. The labor movement was another important development along secular lines, spearheaded by unions such as the Kisan Sabha (Farmer's Union), Peasants Association, Students Federation, Government Sericulture and Silk Labor Union, Turpentine Labor Union, and Telegraph Employees Union, along with other unions of carpet weavers and *tonga* (horse-driven carriage) drivers with a collective manpower of 100,000, including Muslims, Hindus, and Sikhs. Such progressive and liberal movements helped political leaders, especially the young and popular Sheikh Abdullah, see the conflict in a different light, no longer focusing on its religious roots but rather on the exploitative nature of the state's political and economic structures.

In addition, Muslim support from outside the state had come unstuck owing to increasing cleavages (between Ahrars, Ahmadiyas, and Punjabi Muslims), as well as sectarian differences (between Shias and Sunnis and between Sunnis and Wahabis).[38] Mirwaiz Yusuf Shah turned against Sheikh Abdullah and the Ahmadiyas, for example, while Sheikh Abdullah was in conflict not only with the Mirwaiz but also with the Ahrars and Ahmadiyas. Thus the chasm between the Kashmiri leadership and Punjabi Muslims deepened. Needing a new ally, Kashmir's Muslim Conference turned to the Indian National Congress, which was also spearheading a freedom movement against British colonial rule. With its secular and nationalist leadership, however, the Congress could not support a communally oriented political movement and instead urged Muslim leaders to build a united front and convert the Muslim Conference into a national organization.

The younger Muslim Conference leaders, including Sheikh Abdullah, Maulana Sayeed Masoodi, and Ghulam Mohammad Bakshi, wanted to see the Muslim struggle become a secular movement for political, social, and economic reforms. Sheikh Abdullah, the chief architect of that transformation, laid its foundations in his address at the Muslim Conference's annual session in March 1938:

> We desire that we should be free to set our house in order and *no foreign or internal autocratic power should interfere in our national and human birthrights.* This very demand is known as Responsible Government. . . . The first condition to achieve Responsible Government is the participation of all those people. . . . They are not the Muslims alone nor the Hindus and the Sikhs alone, nor the untouchables and Buddhists alone, but all those who live in this state. . . . We do not demand Responsible Government for 80 lakh Muslims but all the 100% state subjects. . . . Secondly, we must build a *common national front* by universal suffrage on the basis of joint electorate.[39] (Emphasis added)

The National Demand, adopted in 1938, envisaged the institution of a responsible government, universal adult franchise, and minority safeguards. At a special session in June 1939, the Muslim Conference was converted into the All–Jammu and Kashmir National Conference. In 1944, in the Naya Kashmir manifesto, the National Conference went beyond demands for improvements in Muslim welfare to seek a restructuring of the political and economic systems of Jammu and Kashmir state. The Bill of Rights—which stipulated equality of the rights of all citizens irrespective of nationality, religion, race, or birth in all spheres of national life—reached out to all classes of people in the state.[40] A concerted effort was made to enlist the support of large sections of society by incorporating the Peasants Charter, which advocated the transfer of all agricultural land to actual tillers of the soil; the Workers Charter, which ensured basic rights and better working conditions; and the Charter of Women's Rights in the political, economic, social, legal, educational, and cultural spheres.

At the national level, the National Conference coordinated its efforts closely with similar popular political movements elsewhere in the country under the rubric of the All-India States Peoples' Conference. Sheikh Abdullah was fully conscious that "the struggle in Indian States [was] not as much against the Princes as against British imperialism," and that Kashmiris alone could not stand up to the colonial hegemony.[41] Therefore when the Cabinet Mission vested in the princes a state's right to join independent India's Constituent Assembly, the National Conference revolted. Sheikh Abdullah realized that such an eventuality would fragment India and perpetuate the Dogra maharaja's despotism and subjugation of Kashmiris. The National Conference therefore demanded that the Treaty of Amritsar be repudiated, paramountcy dissolved, and Dogra rule liquidated. Sheikh Abdullah described the princely system as an outer flank of British colonialism and the National Conference's Quit Kashmir movement as a logical extension of the Indian struggle for freedom. The annual session of the National Conference in 1945 adopted a wider resolution recognizing the essential unity of India and demanded India's independence and the right of self-determination for cultural nationalities in India.

When Kashmir's Maharaja Hari Singh decided to crush the movement by force, the cadres of the National Conference resorted to demonstrations, which were answered with mass arrests and shootings. Among those arrested were Sheikh Abdullah, Maulana Masoodi, and Sardar Budh Singh, who were tried for sedition and revolt against the Dogra state.[42] Outside the state, Jawaharlal Nehru supported the Quit Kashmir movement and called upon regional councils, *praja mandals*, *lok parishads*, state Congress committees, and other people's organizations in the states to hold meetings and demonstrations to express solidarity with the Kashmiris. He also asked them to raise funds and organize volunteers to march to Kashmir and join the struggle there. However, the Quit Kashmir movement petered out, owing in part to the National Conference's lack of organizational and tactical preparation and in part to the government's determined effort to crush it militarily. Moreover, the National Conference was not the only player in the political arena; it faced competition from the Muslim Conference.

REVIVING THE MUSLIM CONFERENCE

A section of the Muslim Conference leadership, based mainly in Jammu, had strong reservations about the move to secularize Kashmiri politics and vehemently resisted the attempts to fold the party into the National Conference.[43] In its view, reorganizing the Muslim Conference would divide the Muslims. In any case, the Hindus would not cooperate because their interests were tied up with the Dogra government, and the Congress, being a Hindu organization, would never support Muslim subjects in a Hindu state. One of the Muslim Conference leaders, Chowdhary Ghulam Abbas, openly repudiated the principle of national unity, declaring that Hindus and Muslims were two nations and Islam did not admit their integration into a social and political unity. The leaders subsequently agreed to the reorganization, provided that the Muslim agenda remained secure within the folds of the proposed National Conference, with separate electorates and the right to address specific Muslim grievances in political, economic, and administrative matters. Nonetheless, some Muslim Conference leaders and cadres from Poonch, Mirpur, and Kotli chose to break away. They, along with the Azad Muslim Conference, led by Mirwaiz Yusuf Shah, established a local unit of the Muslim League in Srinagar.

Meanwhile, the struggle within the National Conference continued. The more the National Conference stressed secular political goals and came closer to the National Congress, the greater the differences between the secular faction and the supporters of the Muslim identity, who made no bones about their preference for the Muslim League over the Congress at the national level. Chowdhary Ghulam Abbas, for one, claimed that Hindus and Sikhs had been allowed to join the National Conference only to neutralize their resistance to Muslim demands.[44] The two factions continued to spar until the National Conference split on the question of the Pakistan Resolution in 1940. Muslim leaders in the Poonch, Mirpur, and Muzaffarabad districts hailed the resolution and pledged support for a separate homeland for Indian Muslims. They formally broke away from the National Conference in 1941 and revived the Muslim Conference.

The Muslim group characterized itself as the Muslim segment of Jammu and Kashmir society challenging the Hindu Dogra maharaja and aiming to create a Muslim state based on Islamic laws and scriptures. It drew members mainly from the middle and upper middle classes. Territorially, its base in the Kashmir Valley was very limited, although Abbas enjoyed considerable support in the Jammu, Poonch, Rajouri, Mirpur, and Bhaderwah areas.

Among its demands, the Muslim Conference pressed for Muslim representation in the civil service in proportion to Muslim population, restitution of property rights in land, abolition of the laws prohibiting cow slaughter, amendment of the Hindu Personal Law of inheritance, and abrogation of the Arms Act of 1940, which had divested Muslims of their right to possess arms. Furthermore, its members wanted political power transferred to the majority community's political leadership—the Muslim Conference—since Muslims in Jammu and Kashmir would not accept minority Hindu rule. Azad Kashmir (Free Kashmir), the political manifesto issued in 1945, committed the Muslims of Jammu and Kashmir to the Muslim League's struggle for a separate homeland and reiterated faith in "one leader who is Qaid-e-Azam Mohammad Ali Jinnah, one organization which is the Muslim League and one objective, the realization of Pakistan."[45] Under the Cabinet Mission plan, Muslims demanded that seats in the Constituent Assembly represent Indian states on the basis of their population.

The Muslim Conference condemned the Quit Kashmir movement and charged that the National Conference, in collusion with the Congress, was dividing Muslims in order to perpetuate Hindu hegemony in the state. Jinnah dismissed the movement as the brainchild of the "lumpenproletariat, instigated by foreign elements."[46] Later, the Muslim Conference launched its own civil disobedience movement in Jammu and Kashmir, known as Direct Action, in response to an appeal from the Muslim League. With most of the Muslim Conference leaders behind bars, Chowdhary Hamidullah was appointed acting chairman, but activities soon came to a halt because of differences between him and Mirwaiz Yusuf Shah, which came to a head when each expelled the other from the party. From the sidelines, the imprisoned Abbas began sending frantic messages, asking supporters to resume the civil disobedience movement, but instead Hamidullah persuaded Mohammed Ali Jinnah to abandon the agitation. These events put an end to the civil disobedience movement sanctioned by the Muslim Conference, left the party divided, and dealt a severe blow to the little influence the party had enjoyed in the Kashmir Valley.

STRUGGLE BETWEEN SECULAR AND RELIGIOUS IDENTITY OF KASHMIRIS

To complicate matters, the National Conference remained in turmoil along Muslim and Hindu lines, despite the formal separation of the secular and Muslim factions. At issue again were the divide-and-rule policies of the maharaja's government, which had passed a special ordinance introducing two scripts, Devanagari and Persian, in Kashmir's government schools and under the Jammu and Kashmir Arms Act of 1940 prohibited all communities except Dogra Rajputs from possessing firearms. This pitted the National Conference Muslim leaders against their Hindu colleagues.[47]

The two became further estranged when the National Conference's Muslim leaders—Sheikh Abdullah, Maulana Masoodi, Ghulam Mohammad Bakshi, and Ghulam Mohammad Sadiq—began secret negotiations with Jinnah and the Muslim Conference in October 1943, without the knowledge of party president Sardar Budh Singh. Hindu and Sikh members questioned the Muslim League's stand on communal separatism, particularly after Jinnah had visited Kashmir and called for *unity among its Muslims,* indicating that Indian Muslims were in full support of their cause: "With one objective in view, you should establish one platform and one organization and rally round one banner. . . . 99 per cent of the Muslims who met me are of the opinion that the Muslim Conference alone is the representative organization of the State Muslims."[48] Jinnah's speech divided the rank and file of the National Conference deeply. By insisting that Sheikh Abdullah accept Chowdhary Ghulam Abbas's leadership, unite under the banner of the Muslim Conference, and support the Muslim League, Jinnah was asking Abdullah to repudiate every principle and political goal that he had fought for. Abdullah refused to do that and gave up trying to build bridges with the Muslim League. In retrospect, this proved to be a critical development because Jinnah realized that he would not be able to win the plebiscite without Abdullah's support.

It was not just Muslim and non-Muslim leaders who were at odds within the National Conference. Muslims, too, were divided. Conservatives opposed Congress's ideology and promoted the Muslim cause in Kashmiri society. Radicals committed to Congress's ideals rejected any pleas for Muslim precedence in the political and economic structures of the state. Others oscillated between these two extremes, calling themselves Muslim nationalists. Despite serious ideological differences on all sides, the party did not split any further, primarily because the Hindu and Sikh leaders realized that it provided the best available political platform; a better strategy was to exercise their moderating influence and strengthen progressive Muslim forces promoting the secular political cause within the party, rather than to quit and risk being reduced to an inconsequential minority in Kashmiri politics.

The Interplay, the Battle, and the Outcome

As Indian and Pakistani nationalists battled to consolidate their respective frontiers in the run-up to partition, Kashmir began to take on even greater importance. Jammu and Kashmir was not only the largest princely state in India but it bordered on the Union of Soviet Socialist Republics, China, and Afghanistan and was part of the caravan trade route from Central Asia to India. For both India and Pakistan, it was essential to control the state in order to secure defensible borders. Throughout its history, India had been subjected to periodic invasions from the northwest except when it was under Maurya, Mughal, or British rule and its geographical or strategic frontiers extended to Kabul, Kandahar, and beyond.[49] The importance of securing India's northwest frontier was driven home less than ten weeks after partition: Pakistan's very first act, observed V. P. Menon, "was to let loose a tribal invasion through the north-west. Srinagar today, Delhi tomorrow. A nation that forgets its history or its geography does so at its peril."[50]

Pakistan's security rested on military-strategic logic arising from geostrategic concerns. If Kashmir's western flank became an India-Pakistan border, it would lie within a few miles of 300-kilometer lines of road and rail between the key cities of Lahore and Rawalpindi, which also connected the intermediate cities of Sialkot and Jhelum. As General Mohammed Akbar Khan, who led the tribal invasion into Kashmir in 1947, pointed out, "One glance at the map was enough to show that Pakistan's military security would be seriously jeopardized if Indian troops came to be stationed along Kashmir's western borders. . . . We would remain permanently exposed to a threat of such magnitude that our independence would never be a reality."[51] Besides, there was growing unrest in Pakhtoonistan and Afghanistan over the Durand Line, the new border between Pakistan and Afghanistan, which made the North-West Frontier Province a vulnerable spot for the newly created Pakistan. Many of its leaders feared that if Kashmir were conjoined, an already moth-eaten Pakistan would lose its entire northwestern arm.[52]

Kashmir was also important to Pakistan's agricultural economy. Four of the five rivers in West Pakistan (the Indus, Jhelum, Chenab, and Ravi) originated in and across the mountain reaches of Jammu and Kashmir, and the fifth (Satluj and Beas combined) flowed through Punjab, bordering Jammu and Kashmir on its southern flank. Rivers running into West Punjab, which depended on irrigation for its prosperity, also had their headwaters in Kashmir. In the early twentieth century, the British had started constructing an extensive canal system in Punjab, running from the northwestern corner of Punjab toward the southeast. By the late 1940s, it had reached what is now the border region between India and Pakistan. Canal irrigation not only brought prosperity to Punjab but also created a landed gentry, which formed the core of the feudal system in West Punjab in the 1930s and the 1940s and provided most of the civil and military officers of the newly created state of Pakistan.

Thus Kashmir was considered a new source of vulnerability and its accession to Pakistan an "absolute necessity for [its] separate existence."[53] These realities, together with the strategies of the Muslim League and those of Congress, indicate that the ideological rationale for including Kashmir in either of the new states evolved *after* partition. Congress was supportive of the Kashmiris' struggle against the Dogra maharaja and upheld the National Conference's position that the people should decide the political future of their state. As Mahatma Gandhi emphasized, that power was "inherently vested in the ryots," meaning the populace.[54] Right up to August 1947, Congress advised the maharaja to ascertain his people's wishes and accordingly join either India or Pakistan. It just did not want him to declare independence, which would amount to accepting the British (and later the Muslim League's) interpretation of the principle of the lapse of paramountcy and its implications for all princely states, with alarming ramifications for the unity of India. Nehru's argument that Kashmir was needed to establish secular bases for the Indian state had not yet weighed into the Congress's political calculations.

Sardar Patel was content to "leave the decision to the Ruler [and] if the Ruler felt his and his state's interest lay in accession to Pakistan, he would not stand in his way."[55] Patel's right-hand man, V. P. Menon, pointed out that when Hari Singh sought a Standstill Agreement to gain time in reaching a final decision on Kashmir's political status, India did not sign because it wanted to examine the implications of such an agreement, especially in view of the state's "own peculiar problems" arising from the composition of its population. At the same time, it did not press the maharaja to accede, even though the state was by then connected by road with India. Moreover, as Menon confessed, "our hands were already full and, if truth be told, I for one had simply no time to think of Kashmir."[56]

Likewise, Pakistan's interest in Kashmir did not coincide with the myth that it was always an integral part of the conception of Pakistan as a separate nation-state (some even said the letter K in Pakistan's name stood for Kashmir). Jinnah himself refuted this idea and made no such case for Kashmir's accession to Pakistan right up to the eve of partition. At one point in their correspondence during 1944, for example, Gandhi had asked Jinnah why Pakistan was not specified in the Lahore Resolution calling for a separate state: "Does it bear the original meaning—Punjab, Afghanistan, Kashmir, Sind, and Baluchistan—out of which the name was neumonically formed? If not what is it?" He also asked how the resolution proposed to dispose of "Muslims under the Princes." Jinnah replied: "Yes, the word Pakistan is not mentioned in the resolution and *it does not bear the original meaning. The word has now become synonymous with the Lahore resolution.* . . . The Lahore resolution is only confined to British India. This question [of Muslims in princely states] does not arise out of the clarification of the resolution" (emphasis added).[57]

If Kashmir was integral to the very idea of Pakistan, it is difficult to see why the Muslim League and the Muslim Conference did not ask the maharaja to accede to Pakistan until as late as July 25, 1947. On the contrary, they had urged him to declare independence, promising full support. It is not that Jinnah had no interest in Kashmir; he simply took it for granted that the idea of Pakistan had swept over Kashmir as it had over the rest of India.[58] The political situation in Kashmir was very different, however, as discussed earlier.

On the eve of partition, the positions of the key players with a say in Kashmir's future were as follows: the National Conference demanded that the people, not the princes, represent Indian states in independent India's Constituent Assembly. Congress's acceptance of partition, however, shattered the goal of a united India, and its members decided to postpone the issue of accession until the reins of power were transferred from the Dogra rulers to the people, whose motto had become "Freedom before Accession."[59] Sheikh Abdullah's personal choice was unclear. He opposed partition because he did not believe in the two-nation theory, yet he did not want to accede to India because he felt that "Pakistan would never accept our choice, and we would become a battleground for the two nations."[60] As for the idea of making Kashmir an independent state, he recognized that "to keep a small state independent while it was surrounded by big powers was impossible."[61]

The Muslim Conference's strategy was to rely more on cooperation with the maharaja and on May 21, 1947, appealed to him to declare Kashmir an independent state (its outline at partition is shown in map 1-2).[62] Chowdhary Hamidullah, acting president of the conference, had already promised the maharaja "the support and the cooperation of the Muslims forming a[n] 80 percent majority in the state, as represented by this authoritative organization, the Muslim Conference. The Muslims would readily acclaim him as the first constitutional king of a democratic and independent Kashmir."[63] Since Kashmir was a Muslim-majority state, the Muslim Conference reasoned, the maharaja would be forced to hand over (or at least share) state power with the Muslims.

The decision whether to accede to India or to Pakistan put Maharaja Hari Singh in a bind: he would lose either way. Kashmir's geographical, economic, and sociocultural links with both India and Pakistan made the choice difficult enough, but an added, more important complication was that his political future was at stake as well. If the state acceded to India, he would in all likelihood be forced to abdicate and surrender to his political opponents—the National Conference and the Congress—who had been fighting his regime all along, while joining Pakistan would put his own Dogra Hindu community in jeopardy. Consequently, the maharaja favored independence, primarily because it would enable him to maintain his political control and authority over the state. He disregarded the Congress's advice and Britain's cautious warning that independence was not a feasible option. Furthermore, he failed to recognize how vulnerable the state would be to political and military coercion from either dominion. To stall for time, he sought Standstill Agreements with both India and Pakistan, specifying that "all agreements and administrative arrangements as to matters of common concern now existing between the Crown and any Indian States" should continue unless "new arrangements in this behalf are made." In other words, for the time being the central government of each dominion would have no authority over Kashmir's affairs. Pakistan signed. India did not.

The Game: Historical Developments

Within days of the transfer of power from Britain, all equations changed. The maharaja dismissed Prime Minister R. C. Kak, who had apparently been "hobnobbing with Pakistani politicians promising them Kashmir on a platter."[64] He was even reportedly considering a proposal to hold a referendum to decide Kashmir's future. This news discredited Pakistan's calculations completely, which had revolved around the maharaja's cooperation. The suggestion that he might ascertain the popular choice left the Muslim League and the Muslim Conference floundering. They had never sought the people's support on accession since people mattered little in Jinnah's strategy. According to Sheikh Abdullah, Jinnah once said "Let people go to hell," in reply to a Kashmiri activist who had asked whether the people of Kashmir would decide its future.[65] Consequently, neither organization was now sure how it would fare in a referendum. Pakistan then decided to flex its muscles. When the National Conference deputized G. M. Sadiq to "approach the Pakistani Government at the highest level to recognize the democratic rights of the Kashmiri people for self-determination and abide by the sovereign will of a free people, on the question of free association with either of the Dominions . . . it was of no use."[66]

This explains the sudden turnabout in policy of both the Muslim League and the Muslim Conference after August 15, 1947. Whereas their earlier strategy had been to persuade the maharaja to declare independence, they now pressed for accession, which they argued was integral to the very idea of the Pakistani nation inasmuch as Kashmir was a Muslim-majority state. They also decided to attain this goal by force. Organizing the rank and file, the Muslim Conference forged a joint front with Muslim League units across the border in Punjab and the North-West Frontier Province.[67] A revolt then broke out in Poonch against Dogra forces, and armed irregulars from Pakistan gradually infiltrated Poonch, as well as Mirpur and Muzaffarabad. Next, Pakistan cut off all essential supplies entering Kashmir by road and rail, and on October 22, 1947, armed tribesmen and irregular soldiers of its army invaded Kashmir.

If the raiders hoped to annex Kashmir by force, their strategy failed. The Muslim Conference and the Muslim League, led by Jinnah, miscalculated on three counts. First, the maharaja did not buckle under attack and accede to Pakistan. On the contrary, he released the National Conference leaders (including Sheikh Abdullah), sought Indian military help to ward off the Pakistani attack, and in the end acceded to India, after which the Indian government dispatched troops to Jammu to drive out the raiders. In retaliation, Jinnah ordered Lieutenant General Douglas Gracey (acting chief of the Pakistan Army Staff) to attack Kashmir. However, he was forced to rescind his orders when Field Marshal Sir Claude Auchinleck, the last commander-in-chief of the British Indian army (who became supreme commander for India and Pakistan on August 15, 1947), warned him of the "incalculable consequence" of any military action that could be construed as a violation of Indian territory: in case of a war, "western Punjab and eastern Bengal alike would fall like overripe plums into the Indian basket."[68] Jinnah's second mistake was not to recognize the military weakness of Pakistan's army. Third, the Muslim League had clearly overestimated the Muslim Conference's support in Jammu and Kashmir and consequently was misled by developments in Poonch. As mentioned earlier, the Muslim Conference, under Chowdhary Ghulam Abbas, did have strong support in the border areas of Jammu (including Poonch, Mirpur, and Muzaffarabad), which supported accession to Pakistan. The revolt in these areas was directed against the Dogra forces, and the people welcomed the tribal raiders. However, it was wrong to assume that the Poonch revolt would lead to a greater Kashmiri rebellion because people in the Kashmir Valley, the

National Conference's stronghold, had disavowed their *religious identity* long ago in favor of a *Kashmiri identity.*

Jinnah's Muslim worldview and his strategy for mobilizing the Muslims had two other failings. First, the Muslim population of Jammu and Kashmir was not wedded to its religious identity so was not homogeneous in that sense. The Muslim leadership overlooked the fact that the political class's primary allegiance was to Kashmir rather than Islam. Second, the predominant sentiment in the Kashmir Valley was a strong opposition to feudal practices, and the National Conference was fighting that battle.

Pakistan was concerned not so much about being incomplete without Kashmir as about seeing a Muslim-majority state *voluntarily opting* to join India. That would have delivered a body blow to the two-nation theory even before it had planted its feet in the newly created Dominion of Pakistan. The Muslim League was happy to blame a Hindu maharaja for the accession to Hindu India because it would have been far more difficult to explain how a popular Muslim leader like Sheikh Abdullah could have *chosen* to join India or completely repudiate the two-nation theory, which he felt "breathed poison into the amosphere": "My organization and I never believed in the formula that Muslims and Hindus form separate nations. We did not believe in the two-nation theory, in communalism or communalism itself.... We believed that religion had no place in politics."[69] Perhaps that view is what led Pakistan to use force and try to annex the state. The raiders' attack backfired, however, in that it prompted three key players to shift their positions: Maharaja Hari Singh, the National Conference, and the Congress.

First and foremost, it had foreclosed the independence option. Pakistan's coercive tactics had pushed the maharaja into India's arms. The National Conference's position of "Freedom before Accession" was rendered irrelevant, and Sheikh Abdullah and his party decided to throw in their lot with India. Finally, it raised India's stakes in Kashmir considerably and led the Congress, once prepared to accept Kashmir's decision to accede to Pakistan if it so preferred, to drive back the Pakistani forces and do everything in its power to incorporate the state into the Indian union.

Significantly, Kashmir's fate was not yet sealed. In November 1947, Sardar Patel (in the presence of Nehru) virtually offered to swap Kashmir for Hyderabad.[70] This was possible precisely because Kashmir was not yet considered an integral part of the self-conceived notions of either India or Pakistan. India's desire for geographical consolidation dictated the choice, and Hyderabad was far more important than Kashmir from that standpoint. Kashmir had only a tenuous geographical link with India via Gurdaspur, whereas Hyderabad, if

Map 1-3. *Post-1947 Administrative Map of Jammu and Kashmir*

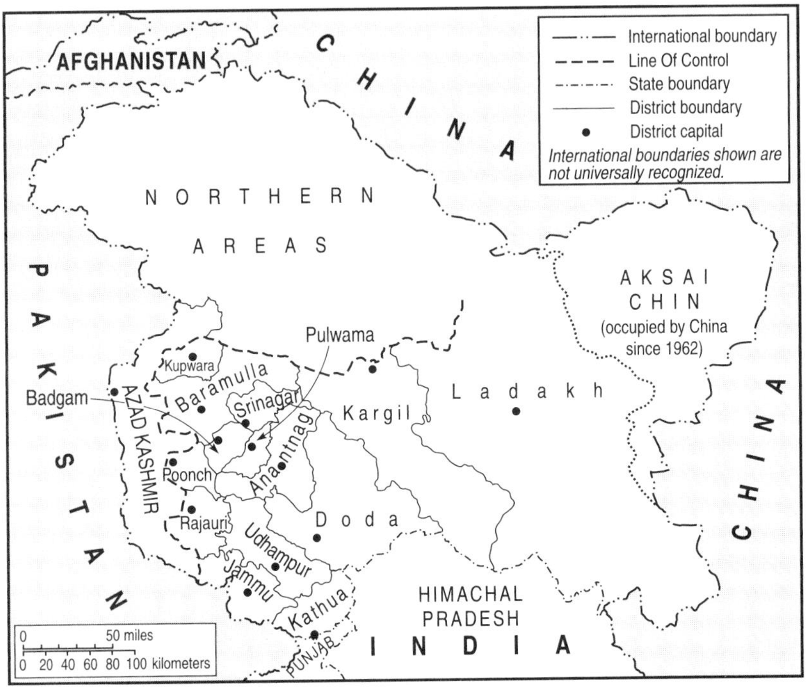

excluded, would have left a gaping hole in the heart of India. Equally significant, Jinnah did not seal the deal despite knowing that the Indian army had driven back the raiders and that the National Conference was not supporting accession to Pakistan. Furthermore, there was not even a remote possibility that Hyderabad would become an independent, landlocked state, surrounded on all sides by Indian territory.

The fighting in Kashmir continued throughout 1948, at which point the role of British commanders became a critical factor, as discussed in chapter 2. The Kashmir issue quickly took on an ideological hue after it was referred to the United Nations. Pakistan's prime minister, Liaquat Ali Khan, started the ball rolling by attributing Kashmir's accession to India's hostility toward Pakistan and its determination to undo the new dominion. He called the accession of Jammu and Kashmir "fraudulent," and said "Pakistan's very existence is the chief casus belli so far as India is concerned."[71] Reversing the accession to India thus became Pakistan's central objective. By then, Indian leaders, especially Nehru, had also begun to see Kashmir in an ideological light, as an essential piece of the secular Indian nation-state. In the wake of the two-nation theory, remarked Mahatma Gandhi, "Muslims all over the world are watching the experiment in Kashmir. . . . Kashmir is the real test of secularism in India."

With the cease-fire declared on January 1, 1949, Jammu and Kashmir was divided into two parts. Almost half of the state—comprising the Punjabi speaking areas of Poonch, Mirpur, and Muzaffarabad, along with Gilgit and Baltistan—joined Pakistan. The other half—including the large Jammu region, the entire Kashmir Valley and Ladakh—went to India. At that point, Kashmir became a permanent bone of contention between the two dominions.

CHAPTER TWO

India's Political Gambit

INDIA'S KASHMIR STRATEGY is deeply political in its character. As explained in the following sections, it has been formulated and institutionalized largely within a constitutional framework. Although New Delhi has now and then strayed from its democratic, federal, and secular commitments to the people in Jammu and Kashmir, over the years the Indian polity has developed a democratic resilience to learn from its mistakes. At the same time, two and a half wars on Kashmir's soil have failed to produce an effective military strategy in the region, owing to a deep-seated defensive outlook and the lack of *offensive* military objectives there.

Political Strategy

Once Jammu and Kashmir joined the Union of India in October 1947, Congress's perspective on the state changed. Its focus shifted from geographic consolidation to shaping the political character of the Indian state, with Nehru as the principal architect. The inclusion of Kashmir was central to Nehru's battle to realize his modernist notion of a secular and plural India. His vision was challenged on two fronts: within, by Hindu nationalism, and without, by Pakistan's two-nation theory, both a form of religious nationalism.

Ever since that theory had led to partition, the Hindu nationalist faction represented by the Jan Sangh and the Rashtriya Swayamsevak Sangh (RSS, a conservative Hindu nationalist organization, whose title translates as National Volunteer Union) had lurked in the background, "waiting for their opportunity to take control of the Indian State."[1] In this context, the voluntary decision of Muslim-majority Jammu and Kashmir to join India strengthened Nehru's hand, supporting his thesis that Indian nationalism was not related to religion: "If the contrary thesis were proved . . . it would have a powerful effect on the communal elements in India, both Hindu and Muslim. That is of extreme importance to us—that we don't by taking some wrong steps in Kashmir create these terribly disruptive tendencies within India."[2] Nehru's offer of a plebiscite should therefore be understood in this wider political context.

PLEBISCITE PUZZLE

Nehru's decision to take the Kashmir issue to the United Nations, his offer to hold a plebiscite in the state, and his subsequent retraction of the offer have been the subject of much debate, with no clear conclusions as to why he changed his mind. In a radio broadcast on November 2, 1947, Nehru promised that Kashmir's future would be decided in accordance with the wishes of the people, through "a referendum held under international auspices like the United Nations." This announcement was in line with Congress's long-held belief that the people and not rulers must select their representatives to the Constituent Assembly, and with the government's general policy after August 15, 1947, favoring the principle that the people should decide their fate in all the states whose future was in doubt. On November 1, 1947, India's first governor-general, Lord Louis Mountbatten, met with the Muslim League's Mohammad Ali Jinnah at Lahore to propose that a plebiscite be held in all three remaining princely states: Hyderabad, Junagarh, and Kashmir. Jinnah refused.[3] In the case of Kashmir, Nehru did not want its accession to be decided by the maharaja unless backed by the National Conference, led by Sheikh Abdullah. Abdullah's position outlined during the Quit Kashmir movement was that the decision rested with the people, not the maharaja. Nehru's plebiscite offer was therefore simply an extension of the government's existing commitment to hold a free and fair referendum. Only a few weeks earlier, Nehru had affirmed that "accession dependent upon the will of people should be the general principle," even though his home minister, Sardar Patel, was opposed to the idea as an "unnecessary complication."[4]

At the same time, Nehru agreed with Sardar Patel that in any case India's sovereignty over Kashmir would be fully established once the maharaja signed the Instrument of Accession. A plebiscite would, however, secure its popular ratification while also deferring to New Delhi's own commitments, Maharaja Hari Singh's desire, and Sheikh Abdullah's public position. Notably, all three were "internal" players. Thus India's proposed contract with the people of Jammu and Kashmir did not imply a "prior Indian withdrawal." Rather, it would exclude *outsiders,* not only the Pakistan-backed raiders but also international powers, except for possibly a "UN presence in Kashmir at the time of the referendum to reassure all concerned of its fairness."[5]

The Indian government favored a very quick plebiscite. According to the original timetable for driving out the raiders, the entire process was to be completed by the end of 1947 but was subsequently pushed to the spring of 1948.[6] The timing was politically significant. The Muslim Conference's only hope of swaying the public toward a union with Pakistan—as the British high commissioner to Pakistan, Sir Lawrence Grafftey-Smith, had correctly reported from Karachi—lay in creating a strong upsurge of communal passion in the Kashmir Valley: "As in the case of the North-West Frontier Province, the massacre of Muslims by Hindus in India may arouse communal sympathies transcending past political affiliations and thereby inflame sympathies for Pakistan which are at present tepid, or non-existent."[7] In that province, a year-long communal campaign to drive out Sikhs, Hindus, and government followers before the referendum succeeded in destabilizing the antipartition Frontier Congress (Khudai Khidmatgars), which was allied with the Indian National Congress (which had won an absolute majority in the Legislative Assembly elections in 1946).[8] To prevent such an occurrence, both Nehru and Sheikh Abdullah wanted a quick plebiscite of the existing electoral rolls.

Why the offer to hold a plebiscite was then retracted has a great deal to do with political circumstances. Nehru's foremost concern was to restore peace and order in the state. This required a military campaign to drive out the raiders and nullify their capacity to coerce people, arouse communal passions, and weaken the nationalist forces (primarily the National Conference). Nehru's objectives were not only to expel the raiders and strengthen the Indian army's position in Kashmir but also to forestall the Pakistan army's formal involvement (although Nehru was convinced from the outset that the raiders had "100% support of the Pakistani authorities") and to strengthen the nationalist political forces led by Sheikh Abdullah, who had organized local Kashmiri resistance before the Indian army arrived in the Valley.[9]

Jinnah's goals were naturally the opposite. His worry, he told Mountbatten, was that "with the troops of the Indian Dominion in military occupation of Kashmir and with the National Conference under Sheikh Abdullah in power, such propaganda and pressure would be brought to bear that the average Muslim would never have the courage to vote for Pakistan."[10] To make matters worse, by December 1947 the Indian army was already gaining the upper hand over the raiders. He therefore sought to secure the withdrawal of the Indian army, bring in Pakistani troops, remove Sheikh Abdullah, and have the two governors-general take over the state administration and arrange a plebiscite under their joint control and supervision. What the raiders had failed to achieve by force, Jinnah tried to attain at the negotiating table. Jinnah and Sheikh Abdullah, as noted earlier, were already deeply divided, not only over pre-1947 Kashmiri politics but also over the fundamental logic of partition. Although Jinnah publicly treated the Muslim Conference as the sole representative of Kashmiri Muslims, he was acutely conscious that Pakistan could not win the plebiscite without Sheikh Abdullah's backing.[11] Since Abdullah had cast his lot with India, the next best option was to discredit him, as Liaquat Ali Khan did, calling him a "quisling and a paid agent to disrupt the Mussalmans of Kashmir" and demanding his removal.[12]

Although the raiders were losing ground on the military front, Nehru was extremely dissatisfied with the "defensive and apologetic" Indian military response to what he described as "not merely a frontier raid but a regular war, on a limited scale, with the latest weapons being used on the part of the invaders."[13] He therefore advocated military strikes on the invaders' bases and lines of communication in the Frontier Province and West Punjab in Pakistan. That increased the risk of an all-out war with Pakistan, yet Nehru was willing to take the risk since "its avoidance," he argued, "had increased our own peril and not brought peace any nearer."[14] In response, Mountbatten strived hard to avoid a war between the two dominions, suggesting the United Nations might help negotiate a settlement. Nehru was at first "adamantly opposed" and resisted Mountbatten's attempts to involve the United Nations *before* expelling the raiders.[15] But Mountbatten persuaded him to reconsider, pointing out that "India had a cast-iron case. He was convinced that the UN would promptly direct Pakistan to withdraw the raiders."[16]

As Nehru later explained, he agreed to go to the United Nations "primarily to avoid the extension of the war elsewhere, i.e., its becoming an all-out war between India and Pakistan. We thought that that would be a dangerous development, bad for India and Pakistan."[17] However, the appeal would be part of a twofold approach: India would also begin "complete military preparations to meet any possible contingency that might arise. If grave danger threatens us in Kashmir or elsewhere on the West Punjab frontier then we must not hesitate to march through Pakistani territory towards their bases."[18] Referring the Kashmir issue to the United Nations proved to be Nehru's biggest blunder. It was no longer just Jinnah and Pakistan-backed raiders that India had to face, but the diplomatic might of the British and later the Americans, who wholeheartedly backed Pakistan. British Commonwealth Relations Officer (CRO) Philip Noel-Baker believed that Kashmir should have acceded to Pakistan, and that Jinnah could not have "planned or designed what in fact has happened."

New Delhi's move to "even provisionally" accept Kashmir's accession was in his opinion a "dangerous and provocative mistake."[19] Within hours, at best days, the tables had turned—not because of any fresh Pakistani maneuvers or dramatic changes in the military situation but largely owing to British intrigue on behalf of Pakistan at the United Nations, which Nehru could not initially fathom. History has yet to judge the British role in perpetuating the communal characterization of the Kashmir conflict as well as in permanently derailing its resolution.

India has never quite succeeded in refuting three misconceptions about the Kashmir conflict that were a direct result of British interventions in the Security Council. First, it was not a Hindu-Muslim conflict in Kashmir. Second, the trouble in Kashmir did not proceed from accession. In fact, the invasion preceded accession. Third, India's commitment to hold a plebiscite was self-imposed; there was nothing compelling it to do so since the signing of the Instrument of Accession would have achieved its desired goal.[20]

On the very day that India approached the United Nations, December 31, 1947, the British launched a well-planned and far-reaching exercise to legitimize the Pakistani version of the dispute, charging that "the conflict was *not*, as India claimed, with tribesmen and others incited and armed by Pakistan but with local insurgents who had rebelled against the maharaja when he acceded to India, whom the Indian army was attempting to crush."[21] Britain's Noel-Baker relentlessly pursued a diplomatic course of action that sought to undo whatever political and military gains India had achieved in Kashmir.

India's appeal to the Security Council (under Article 35 of the UN Charter) focused on Pakistan's aid to the invading tribesmen, claiming that such assistance constituted an act of aggression against India in view of Kashmir's accession to India.[22] The British strategy was to get the Security Council to "simply *ignore* India's complaint of aggression and go straight to the terms of a plebiscite."[23] From India's standpoint, since the infringement of its sovereignty was at issue, the first question for the Security Council to decide was whether India had sovereign rights in Kashmir. If the council upheld the legality of accession, as it was bound to, it would not only have compelled Pakistan to secure the withdrawal of its nationals but also set limits to what the Security Council could recommend, for it could not suggest any procedure that questioned India's sovereignty. Yet this is precisely what happened.

The British proposals, draft resolutions, and "background papers" for allies such as the United States and the president of the Security Council prepared during January and February 1948 took a giant leap and questioned India's sovereign rights over Kashmir. They equated India and Pakistan morally, putting them on the same footing in Kashmir; sought removal of not only the maharaja but also Sheikh Abdullah's government in Srinagar; suggested a practical "takeover" of the Kashmir administration by a UN-appointed Council of Administration; and would allow Pakistan's regular troops to replace Muslim invaders *and* have them police "predominantly Muslim parts of the state" (meaning the Kashmir Valley) while India would be required to withdraw its troops to "predominantly Hindu parts of the state."[24]

This blatantly one-sided and partisan approach embittered Nehru and for decades discredited the United Nations as an impartial institution in the eyes of India's policymakers. Disillusioned and feeling betrayed by the Anglo-American alliance, Nehru denounced Noel-Baker's "*ex parte* conclusions" in an angry telegram to Britain's prime minister, Clement Attlee, and publicly expressed shock that "power-politics and not ethics were ruling the United Nations Organization."[25] As pointed out earlier, Nehru had envisaged a UN presence during the plebiscite only to ensure fair play. Instead, he complained, the UN moves not only encroached upon India's sovereign rights in Kashmir but almost rewarded the aggressor. After Pakistan's foreign minister Sir Zafarullah Khan openly admitted to the United Nations Commission for India and Pakistan (UNCIP) that three of his country's army brigades had been posted on Kashmir's territory since May 1948, the only response that could have assuaged India would have been UN condemnation of Pakistan's aggression, but it never came through.[26]

Subsequent attempts to broker an unconditional cease-fire further incensed Nehru because the order would apply only to India—until then Pakistan had not even admitted having its own army in Kashmir.[27] In a meeting with UNCIP members visiting New Delhi, Sir Girija Shankar Bajpai, secretary-general of the Ministry of External Affairs, emphasized that India's government attached

> the highest importance to the declaration of Pakistan's guilt and, if this guilt were proved, to Pakistan being directed to do what, seven months ago, we had asked the Council that Pakistan should be asked to do. Until this matter was settled, . . . *the offer of [a] plebiscite could not remain open.* If Pakistan wanted a decision by force and that decision went against Pakistan, it could not invoke the machinery of the United Nations to obtain what it had failed to secure by its chosen weapon of force.[28] (Emphasis added)

Although a plebiscite in Kashmir remained India's *official* policy from 1947 to 1954, by late 1948 Nehru was already skeptical of its realization. The first indication came during the UNCIP's visit to New Delhi in July 1948 when

Nehru intimated that he would not be opposed to "the idea of dividing the country between India and Pakistan."[29] Significantly, Sheikh Abdullah concurred, telling UNCIP members in Srinagar that he saw only one solution: "That is the division of the country. If it is not achieved, the fighting will continue; India and Pakistan will prolong the quarrel indefinitely and our people's suffering will go on."[30] Nehru's acceptance of a cease-fire in December 1948—by which time the Indian troops had gained the upper hand, and Muzaffarabad district and rural Poonch could have been retaken—is the clearest indication to this effect. Nehru recognized that the two sides had reached a deadlock, as he mentioned several years later in a note to Sheikh Abdullah:

> It was clear that we would not give in on any basic point, whatever the UN might say. It seemed also clear that Pakistan would not simply walk out and revert to the status quo ante-war. Thus, towards the end of 1948 it seemed to me that there were only two possibilities open to us: (1) continuation of the war in a limited way; (2) some kind of a settlement on the basis of the then existing military situation. . . . I have not mentioned the plebiscite, because it became clear to me then that we would never get the conditions which were necessary for a plebiscite. Neither side would give in on this vital issue, and *so I ruled out the plebiscite for all practical purposes.*[31]

Nehru knew that a substantial number of locals from Poonch, the Jhelum Valley around Muzaffarabad, Gilgit, and adjoining Swat and Hunza were actively involved with the irregulars fighting the Indian army, and he was not keen to bring these people into India against their wishes. Since Sheikh Abdullah's influence did not extend to these areas, Nehru was willing to sacrifice them in order to strengthen Abdullah's position.[32]

From then on, Nehru's strategy in Kashmir turned inward, to his original conception of a plebiscite between the Indian state and the people of Jammu and Kashmir, and thus tried to reach an internal arrangement with Sheikh Abdullah. At the United Nations, India worked mainly to *thwart or stall* any resolutions that had adverse implications for the dominion and to *resist* international pressures for any type of plebiscite with unfavorable terms or proposals of mediation and arbitration backed by the Anglo-American faction (as discussed in chapter 7). The story was not much different for Pakistan. Notwithstanding its public posture, a plebiscite at that historical juncture did not suit Pakistan either.

In reality, neither India nor Pakistan wanted to hold a plebiscite in Kashmir until each was absolutely sure of winning it. As was abundantly clear, each side had its vulnerabilities. One one hand, New Delhi felt it could not trust the United Nations, which was bound to play a determining role in setting the terms of the plebiscite; on the other hand, notwithstanding Noel-Baker's strenuous efforts, Jinnah could not count on support from the Kashmir Valley for accession to Pakistan because his bête noire, Sheikh Abdullah, could not be dislodged from Srinagar. Even Sheikh Abdullah was beginning to appreciate the limits of the National Conference's influence in the state. Contrary to popular belief, in a united Jammu and Kashmir state, Kashmiri Muslims did *not* constitute a majority. Sheikh Abdullah's stronghold lay mainly in the Kashmir Valley. The areas of Poonch, Mirpur, and Muzaffarabad had traditionally supported the Muslim Conference. Furthermore, the National Conference did not have a hold on Gilgit, Hunza, and other northern territories. Sheikh Abdullah became more inclined to accept the partition because it entailed letting go of only those areas whose populace would have remained a thorn in his side and may even have challenged his leadership in the state. Even so, mutual recriminations did not subside: for decades Pakistanis (and later Kashmiris too) blamed Nehru for breaching a solemn pledge made to the Kashmiri people, the world, and the United Nations, while Indians insisted that the fault lay with Pakistan for not vacating Azad Kashmir *first,* as required by the UN resolutions. The plebiscite option had reached a dead end. India's political strategy in Kashmir then took a new course, which evolved in four broad phases.

Masterstroke: Creating Stakeholders in Jammu and Kashmir

The core of Nehru's strategy was to counter the Muslim League's plank of "common religious affinities" with one that championed the political rights of Kashmiris. He sought to create political stakes that would encourage the people of Jammu and Kashmir to stay within the Indian union. This coincided with Nehru's grand strategy of nation building that favored inclusionary over exclusionary means of integration. The key was ethnic accommodation rather than ethnic assimilation or exclusion. Hence he promised to honor the right of self-determination in Jammu and Kashmir, because the security of its future depended on a democratic, federal, and secular India rather than a theocratic and feudal Pakistan.

Nehru's strategy had two critical components. First, in the constant power struggle between the princely monarchy of Maharaja Hari Singh and the mass-based political party, the National Conference led by Sheikh Abdullah, he wholeheartedly supported the popular political forces. Nehru forced the maharaja to appoint Sheikh Abdullah prime minister of the interim government and to transform himself into a constitutional figurehead, allowing

Abdullah to wield the real authority. He also supported Abdullah on various issues, including the merger of Jammu and Kashmir state forces into the Indian army, the creation of a home guard, arming of the Kashmir Valley's Muslims, and criticism of the maharaja for encouraging Hindu communal elements in Jammu. Ultimately, the maharaja was forced to abdicate, and his son, Karan Singh, became the state's first regent. At the same time, Nehru condemned the movement launched in Jammu by the Praja Parishad—a political party based on the RSS Hindu nationalist ideology demanding complete integration of Jammu and Kashmir with India. He wanted to ensure that its "objectionable, anti-social, reactionary and subversive character" and communal leadership did not weaken Sheikh Abdullah's secular support in Jammu and Kashmir.[33]

Second, Nehru pursued the constitutional route to grant Kashmir special status under Article 370 of the Indian constitution, which otherwise had no provisions applicable to the state except Article 1 (bringing it under the territorial jurisdiction of India). In accordance with the Instrument of Accession, the Indian Parliament had legislative power only in matters of defense, foreign affairs, and communications, with residual powers vested in the state, a situation unique to Jammu and Kashmir in the Indian union. Moreover, Kashmir was allowed to retain important cultural symbols such as its own flag and political titles such as *wazir-i-azam* instead of *chief minister* for the elected head of the government, and *sadar-i-riyasat* instead of *governor* for the head of state.

Nehru endorsed the idea of convening a separate Constituent Assembly to determine the future of Dogra rule and to draw up the state constitution. Kashmir's special position was further cemented by the Delhi Agreement of 1952, which abolished hereditary rulership, vested residuary powers in the state, continued special citizenship rights for "state subjects," permitted the state to fly a separate flag alongside the national flag, and, subject to certain restrictions and limitations, extended to Kashmir provisions of India's constitution regarding fundamental rights, emergency powers of the president, and jurisdiction of the Supreme Court.

Nehru had clearly gone a long way in accommodating Kashmiri sensitivities by adapting the Indian constitution to suit their special requirements. This strategy paid rich dividends. Sheikh Abdullah's opening speech to the Jammu and Kashmir Constituent Assembly makes it clear that the nature of the Indian state—which by comparison with Pakistan was far more compatible with the vision of *Naya Kashmir* (New Kashmir), the National Conference's political manifesto of 1944—was what clinched the National Conference decision to accede to India. Abdullah's remarks remain relevant to present-day debates on Kashmir:

The Indian Constitution has set before the country the goal of secular democracy based upon justice, freedom and equality for all without distinction. . . . This should meet the argument that Muslims of Kashmir cannot have security in India where the large majority of [the] population is Hindus. Any unnatural cleavage between religious groups is the legacy of imperialism, and no modern State can afford to encourage artificial divisions if it is to achieve progress and prosperity. The Indian Constitution has finally repudiated the concept of a religious State, which is a throwback to medievalism, by guaranteeing the equality of rights of all citizens irrespective of their religion, colour, caste, and class. . . . In the final analysis, as I understand it, it is the kinship of ideals, which determines the strength of ties between two states.

In commenting on accession to Pakistan, Abdullah noted that Pakistan's "most powerful argument" rests on the tie between itself as a Muslim State and the fact that a large majority of Kashmir's people were Muslims. This argument, he claimed, was "a camouflage . . . a screen to dupe the common man," so as not to see clearly that "Pakistan is a feudal State, in which a clique is trying to maintain itself in power. . . . Religious affinities alone do not and should not normally determine the political alliances of the States." He also questioned the lack of a constitution in Pakistan, which suggested that Pakistan did not "have the confidence of a freedom-loving and democratic people when it has failed to guarantee even fundamental rights of its citizens."[34] In the final analysis, the critical factor that swayed accession in India's favor was not the maharaja's decision to sign the Instrument of Accession but the political conviction of the National Conference's largely Muslim leadership that Kashmir's autonomy would be better protected in a secular and democratic Indian state.

RETREAT: SUBVERTING ITS OWN STRATEGY

India's success with its strategy was short-lived, however. Although the strategy's intrinsic logic was sound enough, New Delhi and Srinagar differed in their interpretations of its underlying principles. Eventually, both turned their backs on their fundamental commitments to create a truly federal relationship between the center and state, institute federal structures within the state, and establish a democratic state for the people of Jammu and Kashmir.

BACKTRACKING UNDER NEHRU

One major weakness of this political relationship was that the two sides differed significantly in their conceptions of Kashmir's autonomous status. India viewed Jammu and Kashmir as a part of the nation and Kashmiris as a subset of its population. Although Nehru was prepared to grant special autonomy to Kashmir, it would not be at the cost of the Indian state. That is why whenever Kashmiri political aspirations clashed with the interests of the Indian union, the latter prevailed. For example, when Sheikh Abdullah opposed the merger of state forces and the Indian army, the center rejected his demand.[35] During negotiations on Article 370 in 1951–52, the National Conference persistently argued that the Jammu and Kashmir Constituent Assembly was a sovereign body independent of the constitution of India, and again the center disagreed. In fact, the center viewed the terms of Article 370 as a temporary provision. Speaking on behalf of the Constituent Assembly, a member of the drafting committee expressed the hope that "in due course, even Jammu and Kashmir will become ripe for the same sort of integration as has taken place in the case of other states."[36] Once Nehru withdrew the plebiscite offer, his goal became closer federal integration. The Kashmiri leadership, on the other hand, sought a co-equal position. Interpreting the Instrument of Accession literally, Sheikh Abdullah envisioned a "division of sovereignty whereby the state would retain complete internal sovereignty."[37] He thus perceived the central government's pressure for closer federal integration as an encroachment upon Kashmir's political autonomy.

Realizing that Kashmiri political aspirations as articulated by the National Conference could not be met within the Indian union, Sheikh Abdullah began exploring the idea of an independent Kashmir. This brought Kashmiris in serious collision with the center. Up to that point, their disagreements had basically been about the *primacy* of the center's identity and the degree of political autonomy that Kashmir could expect as a state of the nation. Kashmir had now gone a step too far: the demand for a sovereign space outside the union challenged India's sovereignty and territorial integrity.

When Sheikh Abdullah turned to the United States and the United Kingdom for support for an independent Kashmir, he overstepped Nehru's foreign policy of keeping India outside the purview of cold war politics. Nehru had already burned his fingers over Kashmir in the international arena with his appeal to the United Nations. In his view, Kashmir's independence was now the worst option for India, which he had categorically ruled out during his visit to Srinagar in May 1953.[38] Above all, Kashmir had become a test case of Indian secularism. India's leaders had never accepted the two-nation theory, and Muslim-majority Kashmir's refusal to join Pakistan had merely served to strengthen India's secular credentials. Once Kashmir became a part of India, however provisionally, it could not break away without putting a dent in the secular rationale of the Indian state, both from within and without. Sheikh Abdullah's secessionist demands threatened to "*empower* Hindu nationalism" by legitimizing its main argument, "that Muslims are essentially disloyal to the country."[39] The demand for independence thus posed a serious threat to India's internal cohesion, autonomy in foreign affairs, and secular credentials. Nehru would simply remove that threat.

On August 8, 1953, Sheikh Abdullah was arrested and imprisoned, and Ghulam Mohammad Bakshi installed in his place. These actions set in motion a gradual dismantling of Article 370 and stifling of its democratic aspirations. Nehru wanted the National Conference to remain an affiliate of the center's Congress and was thus equally responsible for not allowing the democratic opposition to take root in Kashmir.[40] He had concluded that "national interest was more important than democracy and as Kashmiri politics revolved around personalities, there was no material for democracy there. . . . He subordinated the claims of democracy, morality and subnational aspirations to the claims of [a certain conceptualization of] Indian nationalism. In the process, Kashmiris were denied even an accountable government, let alone self-determination."[41]

Bakshi served India's immediate interests by delinking the question of accession from self-determination. He got the state's accession ratified by the Constituent Assembly and instituted closer federal integration with the union. However, the price for Bakshi's policies was a systematic dismantling of all state political and administrative institutions. By relying on personal state patronage to garner political support, Bakshi also managed to divide Kashmiri society into two hostile camps. The benefits of economic development remained confined to a thin, top layer of society and did not trickle down to the masses. It was not so much Bakshi's ideological position on Kashmir's relationship with India that alienated Kashmiris but the particular meaning it acquired under him. In fact, Bakshi was widely identified as "Delhi's man" and not blamed as much as the central government for the political system created by his regime: an undemocratic, highly coercive, and centralized state apparatus with a thoroughly corrupt administration that ruthlessly suppressed all political dissent. As the mass Kashmiri psyche increasingly equated the central government with the Indian state, antigovernment protests became transformed into anti-Indian sentiments. Kashmir's alienation from India had begun.

Abortive Attempts at Rethinking

One incident that pushed things along was the disappearance in December 1963 of Moe-e-Muqaddas (the Hair of the Prophet), Kashmir's most treasured relic. The political movement for the recovery of the holy relic, stolen from its place in the Hazratbal shrine, snowballed into mass protests against the center's local regimes. The state apparatus virtually collapsed, marking the end of Bakshi's regime. In a letter to Nehru, Ghulam Sadiq, an important Kashmiri leader who succeeded Bakshi as chief minister, blasted the myths of India's Kashmir policy, one being that Pakistan had a "wide and firmly rooted" influence on Kashmiri Muslims, and that "from this belief has stemmed a primordial fear of the people." Because of this fear, he argued, "policies were developed that turned a blind eye to the National Conference's corrupt and oppressive regime."[42]

The agitation over the theft of the relic forced Nehru to reconsider the basic premise and structure of India's Kashmir policy. He wanted to make amends by bringing about "a revolutionary change in our viewpoint."[43] Since Sheikh Abdullah remained an important political force, it was first necessary to reach a political accord with him. On April 8, 1964, the state government withdrew the Kashmir Conspiracy Case against Sheikh Abdullah and Mirza Afzal Beg. In response Abdullah conceded that Kashmir had acceded to India in matters of defense, external affairs, and communications but had not surrendered residual sovereignty, and that final accession would depend on a plebiscite. Alternatively, he suggested a negotiated settlement. Nehru welcomed Abdullah's efforts, wedded as they were to "principles of secularism," as opposed to the two-nation theory behind the formation of Pakistan, while also seeking a solution "to live in peace and friendship with Pakistan and . . . put an end to the question of Kashmir. . . . If Sheikh Abdullah can help in bringing this about, he will have done a great service to both the countries. We are prepared to help him in this attempt, but in doing so we must adhere to our principles as well as our basic attitude in regard to Kashmir."[44] In other words, Nehru was open to new ideas as long as they did not compromise Indian secularism and nationalism.

For Abdullah, the solution had to safeguard Kashmiri honor. He suggested a condominium of India and Pakistan over Kashmir, or a confederation with a special intermediate position for Kashmir.[45] The latter was closest to Abdullah's goal of an independent Kashmir. But Pakistan's president, Ayub Khan, shot it down as an "absurd proposal" that would encourage the "forces of disintegration."[46] The prospects of a settlement faded with Nehru's sudden death on May 27, 1964. Abdullah subsequently became more intransigent, refusing to accept the existing constitutional relationship between Jammu and Kashmir and India. He insisted on intervention by Pakistan to guarantee Kashmir's rights, which the state and the central governments found unacceptable. The center, too, reverted to its old policies of interfering in the state's politics to determine who would rule in Srinagar. When Bakshi threatened to dislodge Ghulam Sadiq's government through a no-confidence motion in the state assembly, he was arrested under the Defence of India rules. A misconstrued conception of India's national interests was used as a pretext to subvert the state's democratic institutions.

In a bid to bring about Kashmir's political integration, the ruling National Conference was dissolved and replaced by the Congress. This removed the only secular and possibly pro-Indian platform and left the people with little alternative but to join one of the two remaining camps: the Plebiscite Front (which considered Kashmir's accession to India temporary) or the Congress (widely perceived as an "outsider" or "New Delhi's agent") in the Kashmir Valley. In a letter to Sadiq, historian Prem Nath Bazaz defined the problem succinctly—how to reconcile local with Indian nationalism:

> That leader alone has the chance to survive opposition onslaughts and lead the state people to the goal of democracy as a part of [the] Indian Nation who can, during the transition period, wisely strike a balance between the demands and emotions of the Indians and the aspirations, urges and sentiments of Kashmiris. Only thoughtless people can believe that the aims, inclinations, passions and desires of the two peoples are identical in every respect today; such a notion is misleading and harmful. . . . When last autumn Indian nationalism launched upon an aggressive campaign to demolish the autonomy of the State without the consent of Kashmiris you faltered and acted according to [the center's] bidding.[47]

Sadiq's regime and the central government's short-sighted policies of bulldozing the constitutional and political integration of the state, often through coercive means, defeated the larger objective: which was to emotionally integrate Kashmiris with the rest of the country. To make matters worse, the ruling elite in Srinagar had misappropriated a substantial portion of central aid for the state's economic development. Denied political rights and deprived of a due share in center-aided, state-sponsored economic development, the Kashmiris grew alienated from the Indian state. Seeing their autonomy fast eroding, they were lured toward Abdullah's demand for self-determination and an independent Kashmir. The idea of joining Pakistan, however, still did not find popular support.[48]

In the aftermath of the 1965 war, Sheikh Abdullah stopped pushing for a plebiscite. Instead, he called for a roundtable conference of the representatives of India, Pakistan, and Kashmir, preferably with a mediator, to work out a solution conceding the *substance of the demand for self-determination* while being acceptable to India and Pakistan. It was Pakistan's total defeat in the 1971 war that forced him to give up the Pakistan card as a bargaining tool. Also, Kashmiris seemed to have reconciled themselves to the finality of accession.[49] As Sheikh Abdullah explained, "Our dispute with [the] Government of India is not about accession but it is about *quantum of autonomy.*"[50]

Although the center now enjoyed the upper hand, Sheikh Abdullah's active participation was necessary to bestow political legitimacy on the constitutional integration of Jammu and Kashmir state. Since New Delhi's protégés—Ghulam Mohammad Bakshi, Ghulam Sadiq, and Mir Qasim— together had failed to purge the plebiscite idea from the Kashmiri psyche, the "desirability and *necessity*" of negotiating with Sheikh Abdullah became abundantly clear.[51] As Indira Gandhi shrewdly pointed out, he alone could bring about political and emotional integration with the Indian national mainstream. Indeed, she proved to be more than a match for Abdullah. Under the 1974 Kashmir Accord, Sheikh Abdullah accepted Jammu and Kashmir as a "constituent unit of the Union of India" and was told clearly that Article 370 could not be restored to its original form.[52] Even symbolic political concessions such as changing the title *governor* to *sadar-i-riyasat* and *prime minister* to *wazir-i-azam* were not granted. The central government also rejected Kashmir's plea for permanent special status and instead merely allowed Article 370 to remain on the statute books in truncated form. The promised review of Parliament's laws or any laws or regulations extended to the state after 1953 never took place.[53]

THE DOWNTREND

The accord did not last long. In the bargain struck by Sheikh Abdullah, Kashmir agreed to constitutional integration in return for state power, so as to realize Kashmiris' political aspirations. However, the changing character of the Indian polity and Indira Gandhi's policies, in particular, left little political space for that. Her idea of special status approximated complete subordination.

Nehru's conception of the Indian state and its relationship with subnational identities was very different. Although the federal structure he created subordinated the subnational identities to the Indian state, it recognized the plural realities of a diverse society and gave each segment adequate political space to grow *within* the Indian polity. Mrs. Gandhi's state policies were driven by the much narrower political objective of keeping herself and the Congress Party in power in the face of the growing strength of regional political parties, which were successfully mobilizing linguistic, cultural, and ethnic identities and thereby eroding Congress's base in many states. In her view, accommodating strategies posed a threat to Congress's electoral prospects and to her personal hold on power. Mrs. Gandhi therefore sought total submergence of subnational identities.

Their differing perceptions of the accord, its calculations, and expectations, pushed the Kashmiri leadership and central government even further apart. In Mrs. Gandhi's view, "it provided scope for further application of the Indian Constitution to the state," whereas Sheikh Abdullah considered it "the first step towards restoration of [the] pre-1953 constitutional position of the state."[54] For the next decade and a half, the National Conference and Congress remained in conflict, often mistakenly described as a clash between Kashmir and the central government or between Kashmir and India.

The National Conference, under the leadership of Sheikh Abdullah in the 1977 elections and Farooq Abdullah in the 1983 elections, was bent on preserving the Kashmiri identity and restoring its political autonomy. Like Sheikh Abdullah, Farooq Abdullah considered the elections "a referendum on who should rule Jammu and Kashmir: its own people, or the rulers of New Delhi."[55] They differed, however, in their strategies. Although Sheikh Abdullah accepted that "Kashmir was a part of India and Kashmiris were Indians," he also warned: "If we are not assured a place of honour and dignity in India, we shall not hesitate to secede."[56] It was this rebellious streak that endeared him to the Kashmiris. By contrast, Farooq did not envisage Kashmir's future outside India. Instead of threatening secession, Farooq's strategy was to canvass other corners of India for support. Hence the plebiscite had become a nonissue. Almost everyone polled on whether the plebiscite was an issue in the elections answered no: "People said that the past was dead and they were participating in this election as Indians."[57]

Another critical development of the early 1980s was a growing communalization of the political process both at central and at state levels. Congress had begun painting India as a nation in danger from the so-called antinational opposition and regional parties. With increasing communal and rightist overtones, it emphasized that India's Hindu majority was in danger from antinational Muslim and Sikh minorities and embraced themes that had traditionally belonged to the Hindu chauvinist right. This made the Hindu and Buddhist minorities in Jammu and Ladakh, respectively, fearful of the Muslim-majority Kashmir Valley. Campaigning in the 1983 elections, Mrs. Gandhi told the residents of Jammu that "it was really a part of *Hindu India* and had been neglected by Muslim *Kashmir*."[58] Congress also attempted to foment religious extremism by propping up the Jamaat-i-Islami in the Kashmir Valley in order to undercut the support base of the secular and moderate National Conference.[59]

Sheikh Abdullah and Farooq, too, used religion for political ends. In his campaign, Sheikh Abdullah proclaimed that voting for the Janata Party would mean voting for the Jan Sangh, a champion of Hindu nationalism and a unit of the Janata Party, "whose hands were still red with the blood of Muslims." National Conference leaders administered oaths to the common people on the holy Koran and a piece of rock salt, the symbol of Pakistan in Kashmir, to seek votes. Meanwhile Farooq aligned with Mirwaiz Farooq's Awami Action Committee, a party with pronounced Islamic leanings. Thus in a complete reversal of Nehru's philosophy, religion became legitimized for electoral ends in a political process that had been carefully nurtured as a secular undertaking, opening the floodgates for more conservative and rightist political parties to enter the arena of state politics. More significantly, it propped up Kashmiris' Muslim identity as a counterweight to their secular identity, nurturing extraterritorial loyalties toward Pakistan and, in the long run, posing a serious threat to the Indian state itself.

Farooq Abdullah was never forgiven for the Congress's humiliating defeat at the polls in 1983. Subsequent events—his government in Srinagar was destabilized and arbitrarily dismissed in 1984 by Mrs. Gandhi's regime—shook Kashmiris' faith in the Indian state. Its actions rendered the electoral process meaningless, even dispensable, conveying "the message that even if the people wished to remain within India, they would not be free to choose their own government."[60] Nonetheless, Farooq never felt hostile toward the Indian state. He consistently maintained that Kashmir's accession was complete, final, and irrevocable, and that he was an Indian through and through.

Given a democratic choice between the Kashmiri identity espoused by the National Conference and Islamic ideology, as promoted by the Jamaat-i-Islami, a conservative political party, the Kashmiris gave the former a clear mandate in 1983. The Jamaat party had vowed to bring an Islamic *nizam* (government) into Kashmir, denouncing India as "an occupation force in Kashmir," but its message was totally rejected by the electorate in the Kashmir Valley. It was only when Mrs. Gandhi's regime refused to allow Kashmiri identity independent existence and systematically undermined its political strength that religious identity became uppermost in Kashmiri minds. As Farooq Abdullah aptly remarked, "When Kashmir faces a choice between a democratic and secular India and an Islamic and military Pakistan, it will always choose India. It is only when it faces a choice between a repressive, communal India and an Islamic Pakistan that Islam may become a factor."[61]

The Farooq Abdullah-Rajiv Gandhi accord of 1986, an electoral alliance between the Congress and National Conference, proved to be yet another nail in the secular coffin. Kashmiris had always taken pride in standing up to political pressures from the central government, but Farooq's deal virtually "blocked secular outlets of protest" against the center as well as the state for the prize of power. From 1984 to 1986, the National Conference had projected itself as a party of resistance to the center's domination and painted the Congress as a usurper. When the National Conference joined hands with the Congress, people felt they had been betrayed: "The Accord destroyed the raison d'être of both the parties and forced all types of discontented Kashmiris to seek fundamentalist or secessionist outlets."[62]

In the 1987 elections, the Kashmiri Muslim identity was mobilized by a broad coalition of Islamic groups called the Muslim United Front (MUF), comprising mainly the Jamaat-i-Islami, the Ummat-e-Islami led by Qazi Nissar, and Maulvi Abbas Ansari's Anjunmane Ittehad-ul-Musalmeen.[63] Kashmiri youth formed the bulk of its cadre, many of them from rich peasant or orchard-owning classes and prosperous business groups.[64] The blatant rigging of the 1987 elections and abandonment of constitutional processes proved to be the last straw, persuading the young protagonists that "the bullet will deliver where the ballot had failed." It was in the police control rooms and Kashmiri jails that the first generation of Kashmiri militants was born. Their common refrain was, "We were left with no option but to pick up the gun."[65] Many MUF leaders who contested or campaigned in the 1987 elections later became the chief and area commanders of various militant outfits, a prominent example being Syed Salahuddin, supreme commander of the Hizb-ul-Mujahideen, who had contested the Srinagar elections.

By 1989, therefore, India's political strategy had reached its nadir. The consistent erosion of Kashmir's political autonomy, the successive center-imposed rulers, and the blatant manipulation of the state's electoral processes delivered a body blow to all the principles behind Kashmir's decision to opt for India. Constant undermining of these principles led Kashmiris to believe that they would remain permanently marginalized under the current political dispensation, precipitating the demand for secession that marked the onset of a violent insurgency.

PARADIGM SHIFT: SECESSIONIST MOVEMENT AND THE COUNTERINSURGENCY STRATEGY

In the next phase of the Kashmir conflict, the Jammu and Kashmir Liberation Front spearheaded an underground militant movement to secure *azadi* (independence). It resorted to violence to achieve the immediate political objectives of paralyzing the state apparatus and de-legitimizing the political institutions that had squelched the political aspirations of Kashmiris. Every state institution that could challenge the militants—the police, the paramilitary such as the Central Reserve Police Force (CRPF), and intelligence—was rendered dysfunctional. The militants also halted all political activities by selectively killing prominent workers of the National Conference, the only pro-Indian local political force in the Kashmir Valley. Other political parties, such as the Congress and the MUF, had practically stopped functioning.

The center and state governments initially responded to Kashmiri militancy with utter helplessness, confusion, inertia, and even culpable negligence. New Delhi was aware of the developing situation but "did not quite appreciate the urgency of dealing with it and *militancy was indeed allowed to dig deep roots in the Valley*"(emphasis added).[66] Congress's prime minister, Rajiv Gandhi, was too embroiled in corruption charges to pay attention to Kashmir. Farooq Abdullah's government virtually came under siege when the militants kidnapped the daughter of India's home minister Mufti Mohammed Sayeed on December 8, 1989. The government's mishandling of her kidnapping proved to be a turning point. Its abject surrender in releasing the militants was widely perceived as the ultimate proof that the mighty Indian state had caved in and azadi was around the corner.

In 1990 the underground militant movement erupted into mass processions symbolizing complete rejection of state authority, putting the Indian state on its weakest footing yet. India now recognized the need for a radical shift in its Kashmir strategy. It was no longer a problem of internal "law and order" but of "cross-border terrorism," which required a counterinsurgency strategy.

When the central government appointed Shri Jagmohan governor, much against Farooq Abdullah's wishes, the latter resigned.[67] Brandishing an iron fist, Jagmohan unleashed the coercive arm of the Indian state to eliminate terrorism and force Kashmiris into submission. "The bullet," he believed, "is the only solution for Kashmiris. Unless the militants are fully wiped out, normalcy cannot return to the Valley."[68] So began a long spell of state repression in the form of cordon-and-search operations, and extended periods of blanket curfews in major towns (especially Srinagar) without any provision for essential food supplies, road-block checks with beatings, intimidation, verbal abuse and humiliation, widespread torture, rape, arbitrary detention of scores of youth suspected of being militants, and shootings by the security forces at public processions and in crowded market areas, often in a panic response to the militants' fire. Jagmohan's policy of inflicting "collective punishment on a disloyal population" backfired. He failed to observe a thin though vital distinction between *militants, sympathizers* of militants, and *innocent civilians*. His policy seemed to be, "If you are a Kashmiri, you are a Muslim, you are pro-Pakistani and you have to be dealt with accordingly."[69] This proved to be disastrous; it pushed the populace to becoming anti-Indian and turned the most apolitical Kashmiris into active supporters of militancy.

The broad contours of India's counterinsurgency strategy in Kashmir followed the tried and tested method applied in the northeast and Punjab. This entailed using military pressure to wear down the militants, "wean" the moderates away from the extremists by offering negotiations, and revive the political process initially by pushing through the elections followed by negotiations with separatist groups. These tactics usually culminated in a peace accord with some government concessions relating to the major grievances and some new power-sharing mechanisms.[70] While this had worked effectively elsewhere, it proved to be of limited value in Kashmir.

At the same time, the deployment of army and paramilitary forces warded off the early threat of secession. The euphoria for azadi in the early 1990s had dissipated quickly. India's military response was fierce and fairly successful, at least in the short term.[71] By 1994–95, many ethnic Kashmiri militant groups admitted that they could not defeat the Indian state in a military contest and that guns were after all "not the answer."[72] The broad pattern of militant violence and killings in Jammu and Kashmir from 1988 to 2005 (see tables 2-1 and 2-2) indicates that while militancy was contained, it was far from eliminated. Also, India's military successes did not translate into a safer life for ordinary people in the state. The number of civilians killed by militants grew steadily until the regime of Farooq Abdullah took power in 1996 and again rose sharply in 2002. Though it has declined steadily since then, the absolute number of civilians killed remains very high.

However, exact figures on violence in Jammu and Kashmir are hard to come by. Within the government, such data are generated at three levels: a fortnightly digest published by the Jammu and Kashmir Criminal Investigation Department (CID), data released by the state police based on daily records of First Information Reports (FIRs), and the annual aggregate figures provided by the Ministry of Home Affairs (MHA). Each set is problematic. The MHA provides the most basic information, which is only about the numbers of civilians, security forces, and terrorists killed without any detailed breakdown. In addition, the data released by the police can be misleading. Among the militants killed by the security forces, for example, anybody not immediately identified by his family tends to be listed as a "foreign militant." If recognized after a few

Table 2-1. *Pattern of Militant Violence in Jammu and Kashmir, 1988–2005*

| | Incidents | | | | | | | | | | | |
Year	Attacks on Indian forces	Attacks on others	Explosions	Arson	Abduction	Robbery/ extortion	Inter-Tanzeem clash	Other	Total	Amount looted	Political activists killed	Foreign terrorists killed
1988	6	1	24	118	0	0	0	241	390	0	n.a.	0
1989	49	73	506	334	2	0	0	1,190	2,154	0	n.a.	0
1990	1,098	485	1,164	646	57	23	5	427	3,905	22,691,200	13	0
1991	1,999	321	220	391	100	11	80	0	3,122	6,230,768	8	3
1992	3,413	507	180	564	124	39	139	5	4,971	6,486,563	11	19
1993	2,573	539	238	662	176	50	107	112	4,457	8,357,626	0	97
1994	2,693	619	230	453	237	97	175	80	4,584	13,919,288	7	125
1995	2,253	647	329	570	316	133	169	62	4,479	15,000,071	15	119
1996	1,432	1,025	438	453	377	150	238	111	4,224	3,000,000	69	194
1997	1,116	616	306	277	250	117	223	99	3,004	1,478,970	48	258
1998	1,211	619	332	223	197	81	166	164	2,993	1,091,060	41	394
1999	1,390	660	341	184	140	55	123	45	2,938	2,409,200	49	348
2000	1,560	493	351	60	179	65	102	26	2,836	804,049	28	403
2001	1,994	611	372	100	231	44	95	58	3,505	3,507,740	49	488
2002	1,654	679	255	132	219	56	38	68	3,101	4,351,571	99	516
2003	1,407	478	227	79	232	45	33	74	2,575	2,657,440	34	554
2004	986	539	183	46	168	30	25	79	2,056	11,761,935	40	286
2005	673	378	139	29	109	14	6	55	1,403	892,090	33	206

Source: Praveen Swami, *The Informal War: India, Pakistan and the Secret Jihad in Jammu & Kashmir: 1949–2003* (Routledge, forthcoming).
n.a. = Not available.

Table 2-2. Fatalities and Cross-Border Incidents during Militant Violence in Jammu and Kashmir, 1988–2005

Year	Fatalities								Special police officers killed	Cross-border firing			
	Indian forces	Hindu	Muslim	Sikh	Others	Counter-insurgent militants	Terrorists (including foreign)	Total		Incidents	Security forces fatalities	Civilian fatalities	Total fatalities
1988	1	0	29	0	0	0	1	31	0				
1989	13	6	73	0	0	0	0	92	0				
1990	132	177	679	6	0	0	552	1,546	0				
1991	185	34	549	6	5	0	1,016	1,795	0				
1992	177	67	747	10	35	0	991	2,027	0				
1993	216	88	891	4	40	0	1,584	2,823	0				
1994	220	104	835	11	62	16	1,818	3,066	0				
1995	258	97	1,013	4	47	39	1,545	3,003	0				
1996	241	114	1,175	2	42	131	1,313	3,018	4				
1997	203	64	717	1	58	139	1,282	2,464	13				
1998	230	159	678	1	39	74	1,111	2,292	35	4,314	78	78	156
1999	387	98	684	0	17	104	1,184	2,474	64	4,631	315	58	373
2000	499	132	661	40	9	69	1,808	3,218	70	5,653	114	36	150
2001	577	105	848	18	0	79	2,119	3,746	50	4,153	36	17	53
2002	445	155	803	8	0	16	1,747	3,174	57	5,767	81	74	155
2003	303	89	712	5	1	20	1,526	2,711	54	2,841	29	38	67
2004	302	37	657	1	1	14	964	1,991	50	0	0	0	0
2005	189	54	434	1	0	17	814	1,509	27	0	0	0	0

Source: Swami, *The Informal War.*

days by his family, this is not recorded in the FIR retrospectively but becomes part of the investigation process and may then be available for the *tehsil* (subdivision of a district) records or court proceedings. Therefore a complete set of data can only be generated by compiling the information from the state police, CID, tehsil, and court (district and high court) records and the MHA— a task beyond the scope of this volume. Outside the government, political organizations such as the separatist All-Parties Hurriyat Conference have yet to develop a credible mechanism for systematically collecting such information. This became clear, for instance, from the data provided by the Association of Parents of Disappeared Persons, which indicated that about eighty-four persons disappeared after the People's Democratic Party (PDP) came to power. This was subsequently shown to be only partly correct.[73]

The government's strategy of "weaning" the moderates from the extremists also yielded small and piecemeal gains at best. For their part, the extremists consistently eliminated the moderates for initiating a dialogue with the government or for making any concessions. One of the first leaders to fall victim to the militants' dictates was Mirwaiz Maulvi Farooq, who proved to be a hurdle in the Jamaat's Islamization drive and was not amenable to accepting orders from across the border. His attempts to start a political dialogue with George Fernandes, then minister of Kashmir Affairs, resulted in his death at the hands of the Hizb-ul-Mujahideen on May 21, 1990, which scuttled another such attempt in 1993 by Rajesh Pilot, the minister of state for home in the Congress regime. The brutal killing of Abdul Ahad Guru, a highly respected cardiologist and an ideologue of the moderate Jammu and Kashmir Liberation Front (JKLF), on March 31, 1993, sent a chilling message that breaking ranks with the militants would be punished swiftly. To reinforce this message, Qazi Nissar was killed in July 1994 for his pro-independence sympathies and support for a political dialogue. This move backfired, however, as thousands of Muslims participated in rallies and processions condemning the assassination and publicly denouncing Pakistan.[74]

The central government released prominent separatist leaders, including Yasin Malik of the JKLF in May 1994 and the People's League chief, Shabir Shah, in November 1994, hoping that they would unite the militant factions and prepare the ground for a negotiated settlement. An All-Parties Hurriyat Conference comprising thirty-odd political and militant groups was then formed but given little room to maneuver as the militants openly threatened, "We will liquidate them if they talk of anything other than self-determination under the UN resolutions."[75] The moderates were marginalized within the Hurriyat Conference. Shabir Shah was expelled in 1996 and Yasin was sidelined. The pro-Pakistan Jamaat-i-Islami's chief, Syed Ali Shah Geelani, became the Hurriyat chairman in 1998.

When the Hurriyat failed to deliver a settlement, a group of former militants—including Babar Badar (chief of the Muslim Janbaaz Force), Imran Rahi (deputy chief of Hizb-ul-Mujahideen), Bilal Lodhi (former deputy of the Hurriyat leader Abdul Ghani Lone), and Mohinuddin (chief of the Muslim Mujahideen)—decided to break ranks and hold unconditional talks with New Delhi. The central government responded positively and invited their Forum for the Peaceful Resolution of Jammu and Kashmir for talks at New Delhi.[76] Although the forum's initiative was soon overtaken by the government's decision to hold the Lok Sabha elections, several militant leaders welcomed the initiative, notably the Hizb-ul-Mujahideen's former chief, Ahsan Dar, and the leader of Mahaz-i-Azadi, Mohammad Azim Inqalabi.

Several initiatives by the central government to initiate a dialogue made little headway. Its first such official invitation, issued by Planning Commission chairman K. C. Pant soon after his appointment in April 2001, got no response from the Hurriyat leadership. Syed Ali Shah Geelani demanded that its leaders be allowed to visit Pakistan as a precondition to dialogue. Others, like Abdul Ghani Lone, were more sympathetic to the Pant mission but did not have the organization's backing. Shabir Shah talked to Pant but with no concrete results. On the eve of the state assembly elections in 2002, the center again tried to persuade the Hurriyat to contest elections. The Hurriyat was under tremendous pressure from the United Jihad Council (based in Azad Kashmir) to announce a boycott. The Pakistani leadership had invested heavily in propping up the Hurriyat as the sole representative of the Kashmiris' voice. It naturally equated Hurriyat's refusal to participate in elections with the Kashmiris' rejection of the Indian state. For Pakistan, therefore, the political relevance and legitimacy of Hurriyat would last only as long as it did *not* participate in the elections. When the Hurriyat began to *debate* this issue, the People's Conference leader, Abdul Ghani Lone, was killed to forestall any such move. Nonetheless, a faction of his party did contest the assembly elections, and Ghulam Mohammad Soofi won a seat as an independent candidate from Handwara constituency.

New Delhi then sought to revive the dialogue with the Hurriyat, but the mission, headed by N. N. Vohra, proved to be a nonstarter. His invitation to "all parties interested" in a dialogue in 2003 was dismissed out of hand. Brajesh Mishra, principal secretary to the prime minister, and A. S. Dulat, officer on special duty, did hold a series of covert meetings with top Hurriyat figures.[77] Former union minister Ram Jethmalani conducted a parallel dialogue through his Kashmir Committee, which functioned as a sounding board for new ideas. Rife with ideological differences, factionalism, and personality clashes, however, Hurriyat itself suffered a split in September 2003. Hard-line Islamist Geelani took charge of the breakaway faction. The Muttahida (United) Jihad Council along with the ultraright groups such as the Lashkar-e-Taiba and the Jaish-i-Mohammed decided to throw their weight behind this faction, although it included only one or two Valley-based Kashmiri leaders.[78] The centrist faction led by Maulvi Abbas Ansari included Mirwaiz Umar Farooq, Abdul Gani Bhat, and Fazal-ul-Qureshi. JKLF's Yasin Malik and the Democratic Freedom Party's Shabir Shah distanced themselves from both factions. Later, they formed the Ittehadi Force along with other separatists and the Kashmir Bar Association in order to broker a peace between the two warring groups. That effort also failed.

In a significant departure from its traditional demand for tripartite talks (involving Pakistan), the moderate faction favored a direct dialogue with New Delhi, indicating that the subsequent inclusion of Pakistan was a "matter of timing."[79] However, two rounds of negotiations between this faction and the then deputy prime minister, L. K. Advani, in January and March 2004 brought renewed threats by militants. The Jamiat-ul-Mujahideen warned the moderates "not to kneel at the doorsteps of New Delhi or face being done to death one-by-one."[80] In May, militants killed Mirwaiz Umar Farooq's uncle, Maulvi Mushtaq Ahmad, attacked Farooq's house, and burned down the 105-year-old Islamia School and seminary, run by Mirwaiz-led Anjuman Nusrat-ul-Islam in Srinagar. The moderates quickly retreated, and Ansari stepped down as the Hurriyat chairman. He handed over the reins to Umar Farooq, who announced that the dialogue with New Delhi would be resumed only after reunification of Hurriyat's two factions—a goal that remains elusive.

When Manmohan Singh led the United Progressive Alliance (UPA) to power in New Delhi, the government again offered to hold an unconditional dialogue with separatists but ruled out a specific invitation to any faction of the Hurriyat. Its attempts to reach out to the Geelani faction failed, although the moderates returned to the negotiating table and met the prime minister in September 2005. The talks made little headway apart from a commitment that both sides would meet again to discuss the mechanics of future discussions. In an attempt to put the dialogue on a broad footing, the prime minister sought to engage non-Hurriyat secessionists and held talks with People's Conference chairman Sajjad Ghani Lone and JKLF chairman Yasin Malik in January and February 2006, respectively. All the separatists refused to take part in the first roundtable conference convened by Prime Minister Manmohan Singh in February 2006. Though the Hurriyat expressed willingness to participate in the second roundtable in May 2006 and the UPA government met all its prior conditions, its leaders buckled under last-minute pressure from the militant groups and not only declined to participate but also harked back to the theme of independence for Jammu and Kashmir.

The central government's dogged attempts to initiate a dialogue with the moderates has played a slow, albeit critical, role in gradually opening up the possibility of restoring the legitimacy of the political process and exploring a negotiated solution. In the long run, however, this alone may not deliver peace for two reasons. First, the moderates do not control instruments of violence and have little leverage over the militant groups that do. The Hurriyat is not only divided but is also no longer the *principal* party to the conflict.[81] Its hard-line faction led by Geelani and backed by most *jihadi* groups has described the moderates as "traitors."[82] When the Hurriyat's moderate leaders along with Yasin Malik of JKLF visited Azad Kashmir for the first time in June 2005, ostensibly to consult with and persuade the militant groups across the Line of Control to give "negotiations a chance," the United Jihad Council led by Hizb-ul-Mujahideen chief Syed Salahuddin refused to even meet with them and resolved to continue the jihad in Kashmir. And if they would be open to a dialogue at all, the Hizbul chief and his operational commander, Mohammad Shahnawaz, made it clear that the mujahideen they command must be the "principal interlocutors" with New Delhi and Islamabad.[83]

Second, Hurriyat has been unable to take a consistent stand on key aspects of the dialogue, pertaining to its format, timing, interlocutors, or other participants, as well as its substantive propositions, because it must by and large follow Islamabad's instructions in this regard. Perhaps the only time it held talks with the National Democratic Alliance (NDA) government *without* Pakistan's backing was in 2004, whereupon Islamabad engineered a split in its ranks, followed by militant attacks on the moderates, and projected the Geelani-led hard-line faction as the *real* Hurriyat. Interestingly, when Islamabad shifted its own position and failed to unite the two factions or persuade Geelani to toe the new line supporting the peace process, Geelani was dumped unceremoniously.[84] He was not only deposed as the chairman of the Hurriyat Conference, a position now granted to Mirwaiz Umar Farooq, but also marginalized within the Majlis-i-Shoora (Advisory Council) of Jamaat-i-Islami in Srinagar.[85]

The moderate faction's meeting with Prime Minister Singh in September 2005 took place partly because by then the regime of Pervez Musharraf needed Hurriyat's imprimatur to legitimate its involvement in the peace process as well as to show progress to Musharraf's domestic constituents. Hurriyat refused to take part in the first roundtable held in February 2006, on the grounds that it was attended by people "who do not consider Kashmir disputed," yet it participated in similar discussions in Pakistan in December 2004 that involved the mainstream political parties of Azad Kashmir, which do not dispute Kashmir's accession to Pakistan.[86] Significantly, after President Musharraf held discussions with the visiting National Conference leader, Omar Abdullah, in Pakistan in March 2006, the Hurriyat also fell in line, saying that "the amalgam leaders have no problems sitting with pro-India politicians."[87] Even on substantive issues, Hurriyat has been forced to toe the Pakistani line and has changed its position from demanding self-determination for Kashmir in accordance with UN resolutions—as specified in its (1993) constitution—to supporting Musharraf's proposals for "self-rule." Thus Hurriyat has very little leverage in devising its own agenda. This is also because Hurriyat has avoided seeking a popular mandate from the Valley Kashmiris—a point to be discussed shortly.

The third component of the central government's strategy has been to revive the political process. Initial attempts by P. V. Narasimha Rao's Congress government to hold elections in 1995 met with stiff resistance from across the political spectrum: from the Bharatiya Janata Party (BJP), the Communist Party of India-Marxist (CPI-M) at the center, the National Conference, the Hurriyat and migrant Pandits, and even government officials. The state assembly elections had to be postponed following the Charar-i-Sharif crisis in April 1995, which occurred when the shrine of Sheikh Noordin, Kashmir's most revered saint, was burned down in a clash between security forces and militants. However, the government persisted with its electoral agenda. It decided to hold parliamentary elections in 1996 despite an expected Hurriyat boycott and the complaints of some moderate militant leaders that elections were redundant. Without any meaningful offer of autonomy, the National Conference also decided to lie low.[88] The fear of violence ran high and the political parties grew increasingly apprehensive as the counterinsurgents entered into the electoral fray. The question in all quarters was whether the people would participate. Six parliamentary seats were being contested by 152 candidates. Turnout in the Kashmir Valley was 39 percent, and only 7 percent of the votes cast were invalid, which put to rest media reports of coercion by the security forces. The government seemed to have crossed the Rubicon.

The militants, however, were not assuaged, in large part because of the policies, actions, and strategies of the larger players in the arena—India and Pakistan. The most serious problem with India's handling of the Kashmiri secessionist movement was that it lacked a coherent, consensual, and clearly defined strategy. Ad hoc decisionmaking was the norm. The civil, political, and military wings of the central and state governments were divided and often worked at cross-purposes. Serious dissension arose even within the central leadership as well as between the central and state governments. V. P. Singh's minority government in 1990 was hamstrung by opposing pulls of the left and the BJP. The political initiative of the minister of Kashmir affairs, George Fernandes, clashed with Governor Jagmohan's coercive law-and-order approach.[89] In the Congress regime, Rajesh Pilot remained in conflict with his boss, Home Minister S. B. Chavan, on issues ranging from the appointment of advisers, the Hazratbal siege, negotiations with militants, retention of the Terrorism and Disruptive Activities (Prevention) Act, and the timing of the elections. Governor Krishna Rao was at odds with both Chavan and Pilot and insisted on reporting directly to the prime minister, while the hard-line approach of Home Minister L. K. Advani did not comport with the "peace-making" approach of Prime Minister A. B. Vajpayee in the BJP-led NDA government. Although the BJP and the National Conference were coalition partners in the NDA, they could not agree on initiating a dialogue with the Hurriyat Conference. To add to the discord, the BJP leadership in New Delhi castigated the "healing touch policy" of the coalition government of the PDP and Congress, led by Mufti Mohammed Sayeed, as being "terrorist friendly."

Another serious handicap was the lack of coordination among different wings of the security forces. With Jagmohan at the helm, serious dissension arose in the state police hierarchy between "locals" and "outsiders" (meaning Indian Police Service [IPS] officers from the central cadre), on one hand, and between the Jammu and Kashmir Armed Police (JKAP) and paramilitary forces, on the other.[90] In May 1993, Governor Krishna Rao set up a unified headquarters to coordinate counterinsurgency operations between the security forces, intelligence agencies, and civil departments. Two field headquarters were to be responsible, as usual, for defense against external aggression as well as for antimilitary operations in the state.[91] This arrangement never worked effectively. The paramilitary forces were hesitant to be under the control of the army because the ethos, training, motivation, discipline, style of functioning, and chain of command of the two forces were poles apart and impossible to bridge. The problem was compounded when the paramilitary forces were required to work with the Rashtriya Rifles, a unit practically the same as the regular army.[92] Both indulged in one-upmanship and worked at cross-purposes rather than with one another.

When Farooq Abdullah sought to restructure this unified system and asked the director general of police to head it, the army refused to take orders from the police. The army, with the central government's support, had been demanding overall control of the counterinsurgency operations. India's home minister, L. K. Advani, announced a new "offensive strategy" that would extend the unified headquarters down to the divisional and district levels, which not only failed to resolve the institutional problems but also replicated the power struggles in the existing two headquarters in Jammu and the Kashmir Valley.[93] Also, without the state government's full backing for its own police force—as reflected in the troubled relationship between Farooq's government and the Special Operations Group since 1999 and his successor's decision to disband it—it was impossible to arrive at an effective counterinsurgency strategy.[94] Subsequently, the group underwent several incarnations, in which it was successively known as the Quick Reaction Team, Special Group, and the Commando Force Units of specific districts.

However, the real reason for the military stalemate lay in developments across the border. Since the early 1990s, Pakistan had taken over the reins of the insurgency and directly controlled the supply of men, arms, and weapons to militant groups fighting in the Kashmir Valley. Far-right Pakistan-based militant outfits hostile to a dialogue with India—notably the Lashkar-e-Taiba, Jaish-i-Mohammed, Harkat-ul-Mujahideen, and Harkat-ul-Jihad Islami—had more than adequate local cadres to negate any need for assistance from the Hizb-ul-Mujahideen, the largest indigenous militant group. Despite the cease-fire of 2000 on the eve of the holy month of Ramzan, the violence and civilian casualties increased.[95]

Moreover, the objective of extremist militant groups, the jihadis, seemed transformed from that of seeking Kashmir's liberation to that of bleeding India, which meant they were not amenable to *any* negotiated solution, as discussed in chapter 3. Suffice it to say here that the larger ideological agenda of waging a pan-Indian jihad inspired militant groups such as Lashkar-e-Taiba and Jaish-i-Mohammed to aim at nothing short of India's disintegration.[96]

LEARNING FROM THE MISTAKES: REVERTING TO THE POLITICAL PARADIGM

Slowly but surely, political leaders at the center began to see that a coercive approach to law and order could hold the ground but not win the hearts and minds of the people. Elections were an instrument for enabling the Kashmiris to make their own political choices. The parliamentary elections were the first step in that direction. State assembly elections were held in Jammu and Kashmir in October 1996.

With voter turnout ranging from 15 percent to as high as 60 percent in what most observers described as a free and fair election, the National Conference led by Farooq Abdullah emerged as the key regional political force with an overwhelming two-thirds majority, winning fifty-nine out of eighty-seven seats. More important, for the first time in the postindependence history of Jammu and Kashmir state, the National Conference won in all three regions. A badly divided Congress lost both in the Valley and in the traditional strongholds of Jammu, reducing its strength from twenty-six to seven seats. The BJP increased its seats from two to eight, all in Jammu. But the Kashmiris' vote for Farooq's government was at best qualified support. People had voted against the mounting violence and in favor of replacing the "repressive and bureaucratic" regime with democratic channels for redressing state grievances. The entire spectrum of separatist leaders had boycotted the elections. The slogan of independence had not lost its appeal. The National Conference government faced important challenges: to rejuvenate and rebuild the administrative structure, revive the democratic political processes, regain Jammu and Kashmir's special status while federalizing its own political structure, and, last but not least, tackle the militants. It turned out to be a missed opportunity under a nongoverning regime. Little was done to rebuild the state's ravaged infrastructure, including its schools, hospitals, and bridges. Known as a "nonresident" chief minister, Abdullah and his ministerial colleagues failed to lend a sympathetic ear and ensure a civic, humane, and accountable administration. Several rehabilitation programs for victims of the militancy, the surrendered militants, and the internally displaced community of Kashmiri Pandits simply petered out.[97]

Voter participation declined in the parliamentary elections in 1999, as the public grew more and more disenchanted with democracy.[98] The formation of local bodies or village councils (*panchayats*) and election of their members, which could have made an excellent start, were continually postponed on one pretext or another. Throughout his tenure, Farooq Abdullah refused to open any channels of communication with the Hurriyat or the more moderate elements among the separatists.[99] Attempts by the United Front government led by I. K. Gujral to open talks with the Hurriyat leadership were also scuttled.

Farooq committed yet another blunder by joining hands with the BJP government after the 1998 general elections. The BJP's ideology was anathema to the Kashmiris: its *Hindutva* plank, its commitment to a monolithic sense of nationhood, and its opposition to Article 370 militated against the secular nationalism of the National Conference and its promise to restore the provisions of Article 370. Although the BJP, as part of the National Democratic Alliance, had dropped Article 370 from the coalition government's agenda, the state branch had not renounced it. This not only lowered Farooq's credibility in the eyes of Kashmiris but communalized state politics, especially that of the Jammu region.

Farooq's regime sought to mobilize Kashmiris as part of the Indian nation: "It is only with India that we will progress and our Kashmiriyat survive. Our identity can not survive in any other way. That is my belief."[100] After coming to power, he set up the State Autonomy Committee in November 1996, which in its report of April 1999 upheld the Kashmiri stand on political autonomy and outlined a series of constitutional and legislative measures for restoring its pre-1953 status. It recommended that the president repeal all orders not in conformity with the Constitution Order (as it applies to Jammu and Kashmir) of 1950 and the terms of the Delhi Agreement of 1952. Furthermore, the final settlement arrived at should become an "inviolable" "part of the unamendable basic structure of the Indian Constitution."[101] In principle, the committee proposed a sound and viable political strategy to fulfill the popular urge for self-governance and presented a feasible alternative to the militants' separatist agenda.

But the entire process had been seriously flawed. All members of the State Autonomy Committee, other than its chairman, Karan Singh (who resigned in July 1997 owing to political differences with Farooq Abdullah), belonged to the National Conference, and its deliberations were neither inclusive nor participatory. No critics of state autonomy or leaders of the opposition political parties were represented in the committee, and no formal talks were held with active or former militants or their political representatives, such as the Hurriyat Conference. The issue was not debated seriously in the public forums or media in Jammu and Kashmir. This showed that Farooq had not pursued the autonomy agenda seriously. Rather than treating it as an effective instrument for safeguarding the political rights of the Kashmiris, the autonomy plank was periodically used as a bargaining chip to draw concessions from the central leadership. For instance, the state assembly had unanimously passed a resolution endorsing the State Autonomy Committee's recommendations, but its timing was perceived as Farooq's attempt to scuttle the central government's efforts to initiate a dialogue with the Hurriyat Conference and the Hizb-ul-Mujahideen. The committee's recommendation that the state be restructured into eight provinces along a communal fault line also gave the impression that Farooq was playing politics. Finally, the Vajpayee government's prompt rejection of the committee's recommendations sealed their fate.

Farooq Abdullah was clearly on a weak footing. Anti-incumbency, rooted in the sheer lack of governance, became a key issue in the 2002 assembly elections, which marked the end of Abdullah's dynastic rule. After twenty-seven years in office, the National Conference was voted out of power. The party chief and leading ministerial candidate, Omar Abdullah, also lost his election. Having learned an important lesson, the central government refrained from manipulating the electoral process, and its Election Commission ensured free and fair elections, which were also privately observed by diplomatic staff of several embassies based in New Delhi. Kashmiris in the strife-torn Valley realized once again that their vote mattered and that they could determine their political choices through the ballot box.

Before the elections, politics in the Valley was sharply polarized between nationalist parties such as the National Conference and the Congress, which regarded Kashmir as an integral part of India, and separatist groups, especially the All-Parties Hurriyat Conference (APHC), demanding the right to self-determination via a plebiscite. A new player in the assembly elections, the PDP, sought to acquire the middle ground between the National Conference's pro-India image and the Hurriyat's pro-Pakistan outlook by projecting itself as a secular, pro-Kashmiri party supporting the demand for self-rule. In this way, the PDP tried to appropriate the Hurriyat's political agenda without its secessionist overtones. The National Conference had suffered a serious setback, but with twenty-seven seats, it remained the largest party in the state assembly. More significant, it and the other mainstream parties waged their campaigns from a secular platform without resorting to communal strategies of political mobilization. Those that did, the BJP and the Jammu State Morcha (JSM)–RSS alliance, were dismissed by the electorate.

Also important, the state elections continued to exclude separatist leaders. One reason the Hurriyat had shied away from seeking political legitimacy in the electoral arena was that it lacked a mass base of support. It was also afraid of being purged by militants and was not sure it could win a majority. Unlike traditional political parties, it had no cadre or electoral machinery. To participate in elections involved risks that its members were not prepared to take for fear of being completely marginalized. In an interview to *India Today*, only five hours before his murder, Abdul Ghani Lone had stated that "there is no justification for armed struggle anymore and the militants should stop the violence and start a [political] dialogue," adding that "as a political worker, I am not averse to elections provided New Delhi comes up with legitimate and trustworthy guarantees that elections would be fair and free. If the Government gives this commitment, it can motivate the Hurriyat to take part in the polls."[102]

For their part, Valley Kashmiris rejected Hurriyat's calls for a boycott of the 2004 national elections, the 2005 municipal elections, and the by-elections for three assembly seats in April 2006. In other words, the organization has yet to gain its popular credentials even within the Valley, despite the support individual leaders find in certain parts. Since Hurriyat's inception in 1993, its executive council has never had a single representative from Jammu and Ladakh. Its limited and Valley-centric political horizons were also evident during its first "public" foray into Azad Kashmir in 2005, when it made no attempt to reach out to the local leadership in the Northern Areas. Ironically, soon after its return to the Valley, even the Azad Kashmir prime minister, Sardar Sikander Hayat Khan, questioned Hurriyat's credentials: "How can we accept any decision (on Kashmir) by those who live under compulsions, do not have unity among themselves and are not representatives of all regions."[103]

Nonetheless, a key challenge for the PDP-led coalition government was to start a dialogue with the separatist groups and the militants. As already mentioned, the Mufti's government was committed to a healing touch policy, colloquially called *Goli Nahi, Boli* (Dialogue, Not Bullets). Initially, the state government sought to differentiate between Pakistani nationals who were to be shown "no mercy" and ethnic Kashmiris who were to be treated softly, notably elements of the Hizb-ul-Mujahideen, many of whom had backed the PDP's election campaign in South Kashmir. The state government's decision to withdraw the Prevention of Terrorism Act, release detainees, and disband the ruthless (albeit effective) Special Operations Group of the Jammu and Kashmir police was not appreciated by the central government. The top BJP leaders attacked the Mufti's government for being "soft on the militants." The chief minister sought to make peace with the center by shelving the plans for disbanding the Special Operations Group and by rearresting militants released on bail where the charges were serious.[104] Prime Minister Vajpayee broke the logjam in April 2003, in a speech at Srinagar renewing the peace process. Synergy between New Delhi and Srinagar subsequently improved and was further strengthened by L. K. Advani's dialogue with the Hurriyat leadership. Unlike the National Conference, Mufti Mohammed Sayeed's government supported this dialogue process and even launched a campaign to reopen the road link between Srinagar and Muzaffarabad after a gap of fifty-six long years, as well as to bring about more such openings on the Line of Control.

However, the PDP-led coalition dragged its feet on the home front, especially in streamlining the machinery for civic governance and cracking down on government corruption. It also needed to make a more concerted effort to strengthen legal measures against arbitrary arrests and to rebuild indigenous institutions that could provide social space and mechanisms for reconciliation among the divided communities, such as the Kashmiri Pandits and Valley Muslims.

A singular achievement of the PDP government was the decision to hold statewide municipal elections, after twenty-seven years, and the record turnout at the polls, in total defiance of the militants' call for a boycott. Kupwara and Baramulla, for example, experienced a surprise turnout of 71 percent in town areas and 49 percent overall, which was a dramatic shift from the 2002 assembly elections, when only ninety people cast their votes in Baramulla town. Handwara township recorded a historic 88 percent turnout. Even Sopore, the base of Hurriyat hard-liner Geelani, saw a 26 percent turnout. In South Kashmir, 34 percent cast their votes in Anantnag and 55 percent in the Pulwama district. In Srinagar, voter turnout increased from a mere 5 percent in the previous assembly elections to more than 20 percent, while in Jammu, the level reached 65 percent.

Militants had tried hard to stall the process by killing nearly a dozen election candidates. Subsequently, they shot and killed some elected councilors and forced others to resign. Underlying the high turnout, no doubt, was the desire for basic civic amenities and for visible economic development, but more important, it reflected the belief of ordinary Kashmiris in the legitimacy of democratic politics as an instrument of change. The election results also issued a divided mandate for different political players in the state. The PDP secured a majority in almost all the councils in south Kashmir, and it along with Congress also gained the upper hand in north Kashmir. The National Conference won a comfortable majority in the Srinagar municipality. By contrast, Congress received a major setback in Jammu, despite being the single largest party (with twenty-seven of the seventy-one seats), while the BJP was a close second (with twenty-five seats). Significantly, the small size of constituencies allows every political party to garner many more seats in the municipal elections than in the state elections. A divided mandate has important implications for the peace process in that it requires the participation of players across the political spectrum if it is to succeed.

Despite the changing of the guard at the center, with a new UPA coalition government led by Congress's prime minister Manmohan Singh, there was no radical departure in Kashmir policy. Acknowledging that the Kashmir problem did not lend itself to clear-cut or easy solutions, Singh believed it could be addressed in three basic ways: the government needed to accept the disaffection that large sections of the population felt toward the central government and the mainstream polity; the government's primary task was to reject violence by either side as a means to a solution; and it needed to assert that there would be no second partition of the country along communal lines.[105] During his first visit to Kashmir, the prime minister announced an Rs 24,000 crore plan designed to reconstruct the economy, reform the government, regenerate entrepreneurship, revitalize the institutions of civil society, and redefine the political paradigm and context in the subcontinent. This economic package, he made clear, was in no way largesse: the center would channel a large fraction, Rs 18,000 crores, through the National Hydro Power Corporation to improve the state's transmission and distribution systems. More important, the prime minister took a "calculated risk" and announced that troop levels in the state would be reduced. The government planned to remove one army battalion, numbering 3,000 soldiers, from the Khannabal area of Anantnag district in south Kashmir and another battalion from the Sunderbani area of Rajouri district, along with 1,200 soldiers from Uri, in Baramulla district. In February 2006, India's defense minister Pranab Mukherjee announced the redeployment of a brigade of 5,000 troops to the northeast. Such troop redeployments may not necessarily reduce the number of security forces committed to counterinsurgency duties.[106] Overall, the paradigm shift in democratizing the political process has been a move in the right direction, though its pace and specific dynamics continue to unfold.

Military Strategy

India has no proactive military strategy in operation in Kashmir despite the hostilities there: two conventional wars between India and Pakistan in 1947–48 and 1965; a short war in Kargil in 1999; a continuing military confrontation in Siachin since 1985; several military crises, in 1987, 1990, and 2001–02; and an ongoing proxy war in the Valley. In all these confrontations, India has consistently displayed predominantly defensive and risk-averse behavior in reaction to wars initiated by Pakistan. This pattern arises in part from certain structural variables in India's history that have shaped its strategic outlook. These include past experiences of being on the "strategic defensive," a nonaggressive cultural worldview, Nehru's noncoercive notion of power and his conception of national priorities, and the character of India's decisionmaking apparatus in civil-military relations as well as the doctrinaire thinking of India's armed forces.[107] Above all, India has *no offensive* military objectives in Kashmir. Notwithstanding its declaratory claims on Pakistan-controlled Kashmir, India's armed forces have never been mandated with the task of militarily bringing it back into India's fold. India's objective in Kashmir is to maintain the status quo: to hold and protect what it has.

Wars in Kashmir

Perhaps with the exception of 1971, and after the movement of millions of Bengali refugees from East Pakistan, India has fought mainly defensive wars with Pakistan, all of which have three features in common.[108] First, India did not initiate the wars, but once attacked, its military response has been fierce and successful. Second, India's political and military objectives have been limited to "defending its territorial frontiers," narrowly defined. Third, as a result, the territories won in the 1965 war were returned to Pakistan, restoring the status quo of the cease-fire line established during the first war, in 1947–48, although after the 1971 war India gained about 16, 279 square kilometers of territory while Pakistan gained about 359 square kilometers.[109]

When the raiders attacked the Dogra state of Jammu and Kashmir on October 22, 1947, the maharaja's forces failed to stem the onslaught. Following Maharaja Hari Singh's accession, Kashmir become part of the Indian union and its defense became New Delhi's obligation. Indian troops were subsequently airlifted into Kashmir, much to the surprise of Lord Mountbatten, the supreme commander in Southeast Asia during World War II.[110] The raiders were within 35 miles of Srinagar when the Indian army landed there on October 27. But by November 7, the Indian army had managed to launch a decisive counteroffensive and captured Baramulla within a week. The Indian army then cleared the Valley and secured the high mountain areas of Ladakh. By the end of May 1948, General K. S. Thimmaya had also captured Tithwal on the Kishen Ganga River, and his forces were only 18 miles from Muzaffarabad.

Why India did not take the war into Pakistan remains unclear. Some say that Mountbatten and his British army commanders, especially India's commander-in-chief, General M. C. Roy Bucher, were responsible, and that to protect British strategic interests in Pakistan they made sure India did not extend operations up to the Pakistan border in the Poonch and Mirpur districts. Bucher is said to have leaked the military plans to his colleagues in Pakistan, assuring them that he would not advance beyond specified positions and restraining India's army commanders from taking offensive military action against the adversary.[111] Mountbatten and General Bucher foiled the Indian government's instructions for preparing contingency plans for a counterstrike across the Pakistani border, while prevailing upon Nehru to take the Kashmir issue to the United Nations. Bucher had insisted that a military stalemate was inevitable and even the limited goal of completely removing the raiders was unattainable without carrying the war into Pakistan's territory, an option that was ruled out for fear of precipitating an all-out war. The operations were thus limited to tactical maneuvers: "The strategic objective of pulverizing the adversary's capacity to strike again was never spelt out as a military task."[112]

Until as late as 1951–52, the top rung of India's army brass described the first war with Pakistan as an "internal security operation" and even the official history of the 1947–48 war characterizes it as a "Jammu and Kashmir operation," not as a war.[113] Simply pushing back the Pakistani military had become the goal. That is why the cease-fire line followed no military logic, convenience, or strategic sense of geography. It conceded to the invader whatever territory was not recovered, dividing Kashmir into two parts. According to General S. K. Sinha, who was involved in the Karachi negotiations in 1949, the cease-fire had come as a surprise to the Indian army.[114] Quite early in the peace negotiations, Nehru had suggested formalizing the partition of the state along the cease-fire line.

The 1965 war also followed this pattern. Pakistan sent infiltrators into the Valley to instigate a rebellion followed by regular troops to attack the Indian positions at Tithwal, Uri, and Poonch. Soon thereafter, India launched its first counteroffensive in Pakistan-controlled Kashmir. But when the Pakistani forces, using their geographical and military advantages in Kashmir, threatened the town of Akhnur, the capture of which would have enabled them to seal off the state of Jammu and Kashmir from the rest of India, the Indian army crossed the international border. It launched a powerful attack toward the cities of Lahore and Sialkot in the heart of Pakistan's Punjab province. This was in keeping with the Indian military strategy of "carrying out a holding operation in Kashmir while the main segment of the Indian army would make a determined and rapid thrust further south, towards Rawalpindi or Karachi, to prevent a concentration of Pakistani forces in the principal operational theatre of western Punjab."[115]

Although India's aim was to defend its own territory in Kashmir, its intention in attacking Lahore and Sialkot was perhaps to capture the two cities so as to trade them for Pakistani-held areas or possibly to induce the Pakistanis to withdraw elsewhere. Some military leaders were opposed to limiting the scope of the war or terminating it, wanting to see a more punishing offensive against Pakistan.[116] However, the military was reined in by the prime minister, Lal Bahadur Shastri, who accepted a cease-fire resolution on September 21. Under the Tashkent Agreement, the two sides agreed to stop the war and return to the status quo ante. The Indian army withdrew from a number of strategic positions captured in Pakistan-controlled Kashmir, including the Haji Pir Pass and the town of Tithwal.

The 1971 war between India and Pakistan was fought mainly in East Pakistan, and on India's border with Pakistan in the West, but had serious repercussions for Kashmir. East Pakistan's secession on the grounds of being populated by Bengali Muslims rather than "simply Muslims" put a hole in the two-nation theory. Under the Simla accord, the cease-fire line became the Line of Control, and both sides agreed not to "seek to alter it unilaterally, irrespective of mutual differences and legal interpretations. Both sides further [undertook] to refrain from the threat or the use of force in violation of this Line."[117] India's insistence that Kashmir's future should be decided bilaterally and not under UN auspices appeared to foreclose the plebiscite option.

The confrontation in Siachin is another instance in which Indian forces made the first move, albeit with the intention of maintaining the status quo. Located at an altitude of 20,000 feet, the Siachin glacier falls in an area that was not demarcated under the cease-fire line drawn in the 1949 Karachi Agreement or the 1972 Simla Agreement that converted it to the Line of Control.[118] Both sides claimed Siachin as part of their territory and by end of 1983 had decided to occupy it. The army chief of Pakistan, General Mirza Aslam Beg, acknowledged planning and putting up a proposal to the military regime under Zia-ul-Haq in 1983 "to move into the area next year."[119] The Indian government apparently asked its army to prevent the occupation of Siachin by Pakistani troops. For India, the area was strategically important "simply to ensure that *India was not presented with a fait accompali* like that in Aksai-Chin in the early 1950s."[120] Realizing that well-entrenched defensive positions at such heights could not be dislodged, India decided to airlift two platoons each to Sia la and Bilafond la in Operation Meghdoot on April 13, 1984. Pakistan's army was also getting ready to launch its Burzil force in Operation Abadeel to capture Siachin. It reached Bilfond la on April 24 only to find the Indians firmly entrenched there.[121] The Indian army justified its preemptive move as a means of maintaining the status quo.

Fifteen years later, the Pakistanis moved on Kargil in similar fashion. In the spring of 1999, the Pakistani army attempted to infiltrate regular troops from the Northern Light Infantry and Kashmiri insurgents across a 150-kilometer stretch of the Line of Control and occupied the main mountain peaks in Mushkoh Valley, Batalik, Dras, and Kargil sectors of Ladakh. The intrusion took India's military and intelligence officials by complete surprise.[122] Ill-equipped, poorly prepared, and lacking good intelligence, its army suffered massive casualties in the initial phase. Once the need for greater firepower became apparent, Vajpayee's government used the air force and the Bofors guns to bombard the enemy posts in Kargil, signaling that "all possible steps" would be taken to throw out the intruders. In this case, India's strategy was not just to contain the intruders but also to amass troops all across the 3,500-

kilometer border with Pakistan. The message was clear: "Not only was India preparing to strike hard in Kargil, but if needed it could open other fronts and was willing to risk even a full-fledged war."[123] Its victories in regaining control of the Tololing heights followed by the strategically important Tiger Hill in the Dras sector and Jubar Hill in the Batalik sector demonstrated that Pakistan's positions were not impregnable. At the same time, in a characteristic defensive move, India decided not to cross the Line of Control or bomb the supply lines of intruders in the enemy's rear. This move won overwhelming international support. The crisis ended after Pakistan's prime minister Nawaz Sharif agreed to withdraw from Kargil and to restore the sanctity of the Line of Control. Hostilities ceased on July 11.

UNCONVENTIONAL WARFARE

Since 1990 military engagements between India and Pakistan have moved into the realm of unconventional warfare. Pakistan has waged a low-intensity battle in Kashmir by supporting the insurgents under the protection of its nuclear umbrella. This put India in a quandary. It could not retaliate through conventional or nuclear means because of the unacceptable costs, yet its former defensive strategy would not be effective against Pakistan's proxy war. For India, there was a new strategic logic:

India today, and for the foreseeable future, is unlikely to see its political interests served by either the subjugation or the fractionation of Pakistan. The former option would confront India with the prospect of adding many tens of millions of new Muslims to its already large and relatively poor Muslim population; the latter option would only result in unstable polities and greater discord close to India's border. Since neither of these two possibilities is assessed to be very palatable to New Delhi today, the political imperatives for war at the Indian end are, for all practical purposes, seen to be nonexistent.[124]

Furthermore, India lacks the capability to successfully prosecute a premeditated conventional war of unlimited aims to win a decisive victory over Pakistan. Despite apparent numerical superiority over Pakistan, India's combat power is insufficient to overwhelm Pakistan within the constraints of a short war.[125] If anything, "a conventional conflict would be fought under conditions of near parity, both in qualitative and quantitative terms."[126] The nuclear factor has also restricted India's conventional options. According to former Indian army chief K. Sunderji, "because of nuclear deterrence, the menu of Indian responses to Pakistani provocation in Indian-held Kashmir no longer includes launching a bold offensive across the Punjab border."[127]

India has yet to devise a way to counter Pakistan's strategy of "bleeding India through a thousand cuts." It continues to blame Pakistan for fomenting terrorism in Jammu and Kashmir, yet has been unable to deter or punish Pakistan for doing so. In keeping with its defensive strategic outlook, India has fought this battle too on its own territory—targeting the insurgents and not their foreign supporters. If Pakistan's strategy has been to raise India's costs of retaining Kashmir, India's reaction has been to absorb these costs rather than raise Pakistan's costs: "The Indian leadership's calculation is that it has sufficient domestic resources to absorb the costs of any Pakistani needling without recourse to more provocative alternatives."[128] Thus India is bent on continuing its "reactive . . . effort to maintain peace at the interstate level, even as frantic military operations are conducted domestically. This activity, which has consisted mainly of small-unit operations within Indian territory alone, deliberately precludes cross-border operations of any kind."[129]

Notwithstanding any rhetoric about adopting a "proactive" strategy, New Delhi has shied away from engaging the militants infiltrating from across the borders or undertaking any significant commando operations to strike and destroy their training bases in Azad Kashmir and the Northern Areas. Rather, it has opted for "a static holding of defences [with] a few troops being made available for mobile interdiction of infiltrating columns in the immediate hinterland." Although laudable as a war-avoiding measure, this strategy has passed the initiative "completely into the hands of the insurgents and their Pakistani patrons. The latter dictate the rates of engagement, infiltration, areas to be activated and to what purpose, including methods of initiation."[130]

Such insurgency, many army commanders claim, has never been defeated, which means that India must shift its strategy from combating the elusive insurgents to hitting their sanctuaries, routes of ingress, observation posts, and logistics bases. Without sanctuary, the insurgents would suffer a slow but sure strangulation. Until 1993, their main sanctuaries were in Pakistan-occupied Kashmir and the Northern Areas. These could have been hit by a two-pronged strategy: Pakistani lines of communication that run close to the Line of Control, as in Poonch, could have been raided and limited offensive action undertaken to dislodge Pakistanis from heights in Hajipur, Bogina, and elsewhere. After 1996, however, the insurgents opened new bases in Afghanistan and Pakistan and changed their infiltration routes to the international border in Punjab and Gujarat, as well as the Nepal border with Uttar Pradesh.

Other aspects of India's counterinsurgency strategy—seeking to stop infiltration across the Line of Control and restrict counterterrorist operations to Jammu and Kashmir itself—have also proved inadequate. Indeed, "the problems evident in India's management of the Line of Control a decade ago still persist" as the number of infiltrators continues to far exceed the number of infiltrator arrests, surrenders, and deaths.[131] Moreover, since 1996 relatively few militants have been actually interdicted while attempting to cross the Line of Control. Despite Operation Parakram, launched in the winter of 2001–02, the number of attacks on the security forces and their deaths remained higher than in 1999, and attacks on civilians, and the number killed, rose to levels higher than at any point since 1996.[132] Furthermore, the 700-kilometer hi-tech fence along the Line of Control is not as effective in curbing infiltration as some had hoped as the militants have reportedly been trained in techniques for burrowing below such fences or using other means to cross unmanned sections.[133] As a result, India's insistence on reducing infiltration seems to be misplaced. There are already enough militants and arms inside Jammu and Kashmir to sustain violence at high levels even if infiltration is temporarily choked off. Large surpluses of weapons have also been dumped there for future use. It seems "that *no* level of defensive monitoring of the Line of Control will be adequate as long as Pakistan continues providing military assistance to militant groups in Kashmir."[134]

GETTING OUT OF THE BOX

After the Kargil war, India recognized the strategic importance of being able to conduct operations somewhere between low-intensity conflicts and a full-scale nuclear war. Thus in January 2000 India declared that it would not hesitate to fight a limited war with Pakistan, and that conventional war had not been made "obsolete" by nuclear weapons and "remained feasible."[135] A limited war implies limited political and military objectives, without inflicting excessive hurt at any one time, and actions limited in time, space, and levels of force. Escalation can be a carefully controlled ascent in which political and diplomatic factors, military strategy, and the domestic environment would all play an important part.[136]

The central premise of the new Indian thinking is that any Indian military strategy that could threaten the survival of the Pakistani state would have the potential to transform a conventional war into a nuclear exchange. By contrast, a strategy that would raise the costs of the low-intensity war for Pakistan without approaching any of the dangers just outlined could be fought well below the nuclear threshold. According to some observers, limited wars "demand of

India a new style of war fighting that India has traditionally been uncomfortable with and relatively incapable of. It is a style of war fighting that puts a premium on achieving speedy decision on the battlefield and then terminating offensive action either before the international community intervenes or before the conflict denigrates into attrition."[137] Critics have dismissed it as far too dangerous an approach basically because no planner could promise not to escalate to a higher level, especially in view of Pakistan's determined claims to do precisely that.[138]

With the attack on Parliament on December 13, 2001, India was forced to adopt a new strategy. On December 14, it demanded that Pakistan crack down on the operations of terrorist organizations on its soil and implied that if Pakistan did not respond, India would be compelled to use force. In the biggest military mobilization in its history, India launched Operation Parakram against Pakistan, moving its eastern fleet to the Arabian Sea to join its western fleet. India was conscious of the potential nuclear escalation its troop movements could cause, but there was a growing belief in New Delhi that the time had come to call Pakistan's nuclear bluff.

The political objectives of Operation Parakaram were not clear, however. When asked what the government expected from the war, Prime Minister Vajpayee replied: "Woh baad mein bataayenge" (that will be told later).[139] India initially played its cards well, especially in the international arena. With the "terrorism card" increasingly being employed by other governments—by Israel in Palestine, China in the Xinjiang province, and Russia in Chechnya—India used it deftly to impress upon the international community Pakistan's complicity in sponsoring cross-border terrorism in Kashmir. India's deployment of troops coupled with U.S. diplomatic pressure forced Musharraf to promise not to allow the Pakistani territory to be used for terrorism even in the name of Kashmir. However, with Pakistan refusing to meet India's benchmarks, the BJP leadership found itself running out of options. To do nothing or to blink had increasingly become politically unacceptable, while the military option was not only fraught with the risk of triggering a wider war but might well fall short of achieving the narrow war objectives of destroying the training camps across the Line of Control to send a political message. Such terrorist camps are constantly shifting bases, and limited surgical strikes without occupying the territory would not succeed in permanently blocking the flow of men and arms from Pakistan to India. In any case, this option was never exercised.

Although Operation Parakaram curbed the infiltration levels, it did little to actually improve the tense situation in the state.[140] Ten months later, in October 2002, India unilaterally announced a redeployment of its troops from the border. Its first attempt at forcing Pakistan to end cross-border terrorism had ended inconclusively, although its policy of coercive diplomacy was a bold departure from its previous passive posture on cross-border terrorism. Certainly, India made considerable diplomatic gains in convincing the international community, especially the United States, that Pakistan had been complicit in supporting cross-border terrorism in Kashmir, yet its action ended in a military stalemate.[141] The army's Northern Command (responsible for the Jammu and Kashmir theater) had long argued the need to cross into Pakistan-occupied Kashmir and capture positions that help insurgents slip into Jammu and Kashmir. It also called for a tactical alteration of the Line of Control to ensure that an end to infiltration would be acceptable to the government and even to the world.[142]

Over the years, military power has become a blunt instrument in Kashmir because the political leadership has not been clear about "exactly what results are expected or desired by an active deployment of military force."[143] Although the army foiled the Kashmiris' attempt to secede, it has reached a stalemate in bringing the "law and order," in the Valley, completely under control. Nor has it been able to develop an effective strategic response to Pakistan's proxy war in Kashmir.

To conclude, the strength of India's strategy lies in its democratic resilience, its desire to learn from its mistakes, and its ability to create new substate structures to suit the special political needs of the populace. This alone, however, is unlikely to suffice. Wrecked by prolonged violence, Kashmir is no longer India's internal problem. It has become part of India's Pakistan problem. To fully understand that problem, of course, one must also examine the Pakistani approach to the Kashmir conflict.

CHAPTER THREE

Pakistan:
War-Gaming Kashmir

Where India's political strategy in Kashmir is risk-averse and practically void of military inputs, Pakistan's is quite the opposite. Not yet reconciled to Kashmir's accession to India, Pakistan has war-gamed many scenarios of annexing Kashmir, has experimented with some, and has failed in every single attempt. Yet until recently, its predilection for forcibly changing the status quo in Kashmir does not appear to have diminished or provided space for thinking through a political strategy. Notwithstanding its smaller size and military strength, Pakistan is the revisionist power in South Asia and has, at times, pursued what might be characterized as "rational aggression," that is, "the deliberate, planned conflict or game of ruin" against India, in the calculated hope of relative benefit.[1] Unconventional warfare has, throughout its short history, been a linchpin of Pakistan's Kashmir strategy.

Unlike the Indian leadership, which has paid a heavy price for its political mistakes in Kashmir, the Pakistani establishment has not been held accountable for its military miscalculations in Kashmir. This is due in part to the character and ideology of the Pakistani state and in part to the makeup of its ruling elites. The military establishment has ruled Pakistan for nearly half of its independent existence and has continuously played a predominant role, even when not directly ruling. These systemic flaws in its higher decisionmaking institutions have allowed little room for any critical review of its national strategy.[2] A government that lacks elected representatives of the people in key government departments, particularly the foreign and domestic ministries, "gives the central decision-makers the illusion that they are operating without political limits," as Pakistan's military strategy in Kashmir makes clear.[3]

The First Salvo: The 1947–48 War

Within three months of its creation in 1947, Pakistan supported a tribal invasion of Kashmir and then directly participated in the consequent war with India, which lasted until December 1948. This military confrontation was the first example of Pakistan's willingness to go to war to achieve its objectives in Kashmir, despite the woeful deficiencies of a ragtag army inherited from British India.

In 1947 Pakistan's social, organizational, economic, and political structures were in disarray. Under the terms of the transfer of power, all movable military infrastructure of the former British India had been divided between Pakistan and India on a ratio of 30:70. Because the transfer progressed quite slowly, Pakistan began its statehood in a "militarily vulnerable position."[4] The army was desperately short of officers, many units were far below their sanctioned strength, and most of the military equipment already in Pakistan was obsolete. However, this did not deter Pakistan from starting the war, although Prime Minister Liaquat Ali Khan insisted that formally Pakistan should not appear to have invaded Kashmir. He "thereby formulated a policy that has continued for fifty years: that Pakistan fights for Kashmir by proxy."[5]

Like Liaquat Ali Khan, Mohammed Ali Jinnah, Pakistan's first governor-general, contended that the invasion was a spontaneous act driven by fraternal and religious sympathies. However, several accounts suggest otherwise, especially that of General Mohammed Akbar Khan—known by his nom de guerre, General Tariq—who led the raiders' attack as commander-in-chief of Azad forces.[6] The principal responsibility for the tribal campaign was in the hands of Khan Abdul Qayum Khan, the newly installed Muslim League chief minister of the North-West Frontier Province (NWFP) and himself a Kashmiri from Poonch. Under Qayum's direction, provincial officials ensured the supply of petrol—a scarce commodity in those days—grain rations, and transportation for the tribal invaders.[7] Pakistani officers on leave from the army, were "certainly fighting" alongside the "Azad forces." Although there are no precise estimates of the actual strength of the Pakistani forces, the number of Pakistani army regulars was probably no more that 5 percent of the total strength of the raiders. According to Russell K. Haight, a former American army officer who fought along with them, the real importance of the Pakistani military personnel lay not in their numbers but in their "supply and organizational functions," without which "it would have been "impossible for the Azad Kashmir Government to maintain a fighting force."[8] This established a lasting feature of Pakistan's military strategy in Kashmir, that of "plausible deniability," a striking example of which can be found in a letter from the government of Pakistan to the government of India, dated December 30, 1947: "Pakistani nationals might be fighting in Kashmir but only as private volunteers" or as soldiers on leave "rendering assistance to their kith and kin."[9] In other words, the state refused to accept responsibility for the actions of its citizens. Several weeks earlier, in a meeting with Britain's Lord Mountbatten on November 1, Jinnah had affirmed: "We have no control over forces of [the] Provisional [Azad] Government of Kashmir or the tribesmen engaged in fighting."[10] Yet in the same breath Jinnah stated that if anyone could persuade the Indian army to withdraw, "I will call the whole thing off."[11] Thus it is difficult to believe that the invasion was not Pakistani in origin.

The 1947–48 war also brought to light the influence of "cultural discounting" on Pakistan's decisionmaking processes.[12] This is the belief that one's adversary is culturally inferior and therefore can be defeated despite a strong quantitative advantage. A former Pakistani cabinet minister and columnist, Altaf Gauhar, argues that Pakistan's four wars with India were "conceived and launched on one assumption: that the Indians are too cowardly and ill-organized to offer any effective military response."[13] The image of a weak and divided Hindu foe also appears in General Akbar Khan's account of the war:

In the remotest of our villages, the humblest of our people possess a self-confidence and ready willingness to march forward into India—a spirit the equivalent of which cannot be found on the other side. It may take many generations to create such a spirit. In India, in the absence of homogeneity, a penetration in any direction can result in separation of differing units geographically as well as morally because there is no basic unity among the Shudras, Brahmins, Sikhs, Hindus and Muslims who will follow their own different interest. At present, and for a long time to come, India is in the same position as she was centuries ago, exposed to disintegration in emergencies.[14]

At the same time, Pakistan's political leaders seemed keener to fight the war than its army, which was reluctant "to commit itself firmly in the Kashmir war" and "instead wanted a cease fire and until that could be negotiated wished the tribesmen 'good luck.'"[15] A. H. Suharwardy, a retired Pakistani civil servant, complained bitterly that "many senior officers of the Pakistan Army ... neither bothered nor helped in the least."[16] President Ayub Khan would later write that the war "started as an irregular campaign. Soldiers and officers were out on their own with little direction from headquarters and with considerable responsibility placed in the hands of junior officers."[17]

While the upper echelons of the army were of two minds about the practicality of a military solution in Kashmir, the political leaders fully backed the military option: "If they had been in a position to do so, the Muslim League leaders, with Jinnah's blessings, would have thrown in the army behind the tribal effort."[18] On hearing about the landing of Indian troops in Srinagar, Jinnah had ordered Lieutenant General Douglas Gracey, commander-in-chief of the Pakistan army, to take control of Srinagar airport, despite having only eighteen days of munitions and less than a two-week supply of diesel. It was only when Field Marshal Claude Auchinleck, supreme commander for the Indian and Pakistan armies, warned that such action might have "incalculable consequences," that Jinnah backed down.[19]

The strategic dynamics of the war changed when the British decided that it was essential to contain the Indian forces along the general line of Uri-Poonch-Naoshera for security reasons.[20] An easy victory of the Indian army, particularly in Muzaffarabad, Lieutenant General Gracy pointed out, would almost certainly have turned the tribesmen against Pakistan. Another serious concern, in light of the damage already inflicted on the headworks of the Sutlej and Ravi Rivers, was that India's military offensive might pose a threat to Mangla Headworks, which controlled and supplied water from Jhelum River through the Upper Jhelum Canal.[21]

Pakistan had started the first war on the assumption that the Kashmiri people would support the invading *lashkar* (tribal army) and that the maharaja's forces would be easily subdued. Little if any thought had been given to the prospect of failure or to what might happen if the Indian army forestalled a Pakistani removal of the Kashmiri maharaja. Compared with Azad Kashmir forces, the tribesmen were at an extreme disadvantage: they knew little of Kashmir's mountainous terrain and lacked the full support of the local population.[22] The 1947 war ended in a military stalemate, giving India control over half of Jammu and Kashmir, including its political center—the Valley—and Pakistan the other half. This outcome and the war itself taught Pakistan few lessons, however, as the military confrontation in 1965 made clear.

"Now or Never": The 1965 War

The 1965 war was rooted in the belief that Pakistan's options in Kashmir were running out. Diplomatic negotiations at the United Nations and at the bilateral level had drawn a blank. With the UN resolutions on the plebiscite still in abeyance, Kashmir was being steadily integrated into India. If the situation were to be altered to Pakistan's advantage, it had to be done militarily. In the aftermath of the 1962 border war with China, India had launched a long-term program of reequipping and expanding its armed forces. This program threatened to reduce the military advantages that Pakistan had gained through massive military aid and technologically superior weaponry provided by the United States since 1954. The option of seizing Kashmir militarily in the future seemed to grow dim, and "a 'now or never' mentality gripped the decision-makers in Rawalpindi," guided by the old strategy of resorting to unconventional warfare backed by Pakistan's conventional military might.[23]

To this end, the Pakistan army developed a plan, code-named Operation Gibraltar, to foment a rebellion in the Kashmir Valley. The initial phase involved infiltrating about 5,000 armed men into the area to capitalize on the disturbed conditions in the state and start a mass uprising against Indian rule. The objective was, first, to sabotage military targets and disrupt communications and, second, to distribute arms to the people of the Indian part of Kashmir and encourage a guerrilla movement there.[24] In the next phase, regular Pakistani army troops would move in to seize significant positions in Kashmir, especially in the Valley, in a series of quick, decisive thrusts. Assuming that the first two stages went as planned, the Pakistanis would accomplish all this before the Indian army had a chance to mobilize against them, and the Pakistani leadership could present the supposedly rebellious situation as a fait accompli to the international community, with a call for assistance to the Kashmiris.[25] These measures, it was hoped, would finally settle the Kashmir dispute on terms favorable to Pakistan.

What remained unclear was whether Pakistan wanted to annex Kashmir or "to take such action as will defreeze [the] Kashmir problem, weaken India's resolve and bring her to the conference table without provoking a general war."[26] According to Pakistan's former UN ambassador, Iqbal Akhund, the 1965 war was "planned in a confusion of aims"

> rooted in the belief that Kashmir, lost on the battlefield in 1948 could be won back by diplomatic means.... The venture therefore fell between the two stools of Pakistan's Kashmir policy, the first being to mobilize diplomatic pressures for imposing the settlement laid down in UN resolutions; and the second, to seize important Indian territory and then exchange it for Kashmir.[27]

This "confusion of aims" emanated from seriously flawed assumptions. For one thing, the Pakistanis believed that India's forces were not prepared to withstand an attack, as seemed evident from an attempt to test the mettle of its political leadership and army earlier in the year. Pakistan had conducted a "limited probe" in the Rann of Kutch, in the western Indian state of Gujarat, that met with a slow and weak military response. That, coupled with India's readiness to seek third-party intervention, led the Pakistanis to erroneously conclude that India lacked the stomach for battle and was still reeling from the psychological shock of the disastrous 1962 Sino-Indian border war. In fact, India had deliberately chosen not to divert its major forces to the Kutch front because the terrain favored Pakistan, and in any case the real war seemed likely to come in Kashmir and the Punjab.

Meanwhile, in an atmosphere of mistaken euphoria, Pakistan's army grew "cocky, even truculent."[28] Ayub Khan boasted: "As a general rule Hindu morale would not stand more than a couple of hard blows delivered at the right time and place. Such opportunities should therefore be sought and exploited."[29] To Pakistanis, India appeared to be a disoriented and dispirited nation in the wake of Nehru's death, with a weak and divided leadership. The country seemed well on its way to disintegration. On the contrary, under Prime Minister Lal Bahadur Shastri, "diminutive in size but firm of will," the Indians showed little hesitation in attacking the staging bases of the guerrillas across the cease-fire line.[30] Subsequently, they not only crossed the international border but also refused to panic when the Chinese threatened to intervene. Pakistan's military planners had ruled out any Indian attempt at such a military offensive, especially if it entailed crossing the frontier with Pakistan in both the east and west.[31]

From earlier agitation over the theft of a religious relic (see chapter 2), Pakistan concluded that it had widespread popular support in the Valley. Owing to their own cultural biases, Pakistan's leaders had clearly overlooked one critical factor: there was complete communal amity in the Valley. Hindus, Muslims, Sikhs, and even a small number of Christians mingled together, and the area reverberated with their slogans in praise of God: *Har-Har Mahadev, Allah-o-Akbar,* and *Bole-so-Nihar.* Instead of revolting against India, Kashmiris turned in Pakistani infiltrators and developed considerable animosity against them. General Mohammad Musa Khan grudgingly admitted that "the Muslim population [in the Valley], although by and large willing to help, were unable to co-operate fully."[32]

To relieve the military pressure in Kashmir, Indian troops had crossed the international border and within twenty-four hours stood at the gates of Lahore, which then lay virtually undefended. Pakistan was caught off-balance as "its command structure was hopelessly inadequate to meet the requirements of a shooting war."[33] The army's premier formation, the 1st Armored Division, had one regiment's worth of tanks that were out of commission because of mechanical problems. The total strength of the army was down by two infantry divisions. As one of its colonels observed, an "inexcusable act of gross misconception and miscalculation of the operating factors [had] sent the Pakistan Army into battle with 25 percent of its soldiers on annual leave."[34] Ayub Khan conceded privately that the situation was "catastrophic."[35] A scathing assessment of Pakistan's military performance found "inadequate training at all but unit level, misguided selection of officers for some higher command appointments, appalling command and control arrangements, poor intelligence gathering, and almost unbelievably bad intelligence procedures." All in all, "the Pakistan army was not ready to fight *any* war in 1965, never mind a war against an enemy smarting from previous defeats, anxious for revenge, well-equipped, and with enormous reserves of *matériel*, ammunition, and manpower."[36]

Ayub had also miscalculated the international reactions to the war. He expected the security guarantees against international communism under the 1959 agreement with the United States to apply to a conflict with India. Not only was the United States unwilling to intervene but it also imposed an embargo on arms supplies to both India and Pakistan. This created a fatal shortage of ammunition and spare parts in Pakistan without having a similar impact on India. Pakistan's air force had only two weeks' supply, at wartime rates, of starter cartridges for the engines of its Sabre aircraft, the mainstay of the fighter force. After an eight-day trip to China in March 1965, Ayub and his foreign minister, Zulfiqar Ali Bhutto, had also concluded, *wrongly*, that the Chinese would assist Pakistan in the event of a war with India.

Pakistan had started a war that it was in no position to win. Like the 1947–48 war, it soon wore down to a military stalemate. The army was shaken by the result. There was some plain speaking when the chief of the army staff toured military bases, and morale was badly affected in some units, for which "the inability to take all of Kashmir was a rude awakening."[37] Even after the cease-fire, the official media in Pakistan gave the impression that India had suffered a humiliating defeat. The Tashkent Declaration, which made it clear that the war was a draw, was met with public protests, violent demonstrations, and riots in a number of Pakistani cities.[38]

The Pakistani military establishment has been unable to come to terms with its own flawed strategic assessments and poor battlefield performance against India because no critical review of its mistakes has ever been seriously attempted. When former cabinet minister G. W. Choudhury asked Ayub Khan whether the usual procedure for debating both sides of the issue had perhaps not been followed in deciding to launch the 1965 war in Kashmir, Ayub answered: "Please do not rub in my weakest and fatal point."[39] His successor, Yahya Khan, refused, despite Ayub's orders, to allow an authentic record of the 1965 war to be prepared. Commenting on Pakistan's inability to learn from its own mistakes, one of Ayub's key advisers wrote: "Few people outside the armed forces realize how close Pakistan came to disaster in the 1965 War due to inadequate preparation, facile assumptions and criminal Foreign Office advice."[40] Future generations of Pakistanis will hear a radically different version: "In the 1965 war, Pakistan inflicted ignominious defeats on India on all its fronts and broke its back"[41]

In the absence of a critical review, the mistakes of the 1965 war were repeated on an even bigger scale in 1971, when Yahya Khan got Pakistan into an "un-winnable" war. Given the logistical difficulties of supporting the military campaign in East Pakistan, the Pakistan army was trounced, with India holding 90,000 prisoners of war and Pakistan losing half its territory. Yet the military leadership remained in denial. Testifying before the Hamoodur Rehman War Commission, Yahya justified all his actions, maintaining that he did not consider Pakistan's defeat "a military debacle at all" or see the "surrender of forces in strictly military terms."[42] While Bhutto blamed Pakistan's military failures on the Soviet Union, Yahya insisted that it was "nothing but a treachery of the Indians." Other analyses point to internal mismanagement, the treachery of Bengali leaders, the "overambitiousness" of Bhutto, and the "inept leadership" of General Yahya Khan.[43] Historical scholarship on the cause of the war is also deeply problematic, as in some cases it blames the Bengali Hindu for punishing innocent West Pakistanis "for sins they had not committed."[44] Most Pakistani versions overlook the contribution of Pakistan's deeply flawed priorities, choices, and policies to the East Pakistan crisis. This inability to confront the fundamental mistakes of policy formulation and policy choices continues to haunt Pakistani decisionmaking. As General Pervez Musharraf noted in expressing his firm opposition to putting the people named in the War Commission report on trial: "Something happened 30 years ago. Why do we want to live in history? As a Pakistani, I would like to forget 1971."[45]

Following Pakistan's defeat in the 1971 war and the Simla Accord, which ruled out the use of force by either side to unilaterally alter the Line of Control, the Kashmir issue remained on the backburner until 1989, when Kashmiris rebelled against the Indian government. While the trouble was of India's own making, Islamabad was ready to take advantage of the situation to fulfill its long-standing ambitions in Kashmir. To add to its incentive, Pakistan, backed by the United States, had just won a war in Afghanistan against the mighty superpower, the Soviet Union.

The Afghan Model and the Strategy of Offensive-Defense

With the "Afghan model" in mind, the Pakistan army launched a military exercise, Zarb-i-Momin, in 1989 to test its new strategy of "offensive-defense." As subsequently documented in a restricted paper titled "The Gulf Crisis 1990," the idea was to capitalize on India's political vulnerability in Punjab in the hope that Sikhs would join Pakistan in fighting the Indian army.[46] Furthermore, by taking the war into India's domestic territory, Pakistan "would naturally dampen the enemy's capability to launch an offensive," and the government would have more room to negotiate.[47]

With the marked escalation in militant violence in the Valley in 1989, Kashmir appeared ripe for this strategy. The new mantra of national security was that India could only be contained through an offensive strategy that kept the Indian army embroiled within, notably in Jammu and Kashmir.[48] However, unconventional conflict could still be a viable strategy once Pakistan acquired nuclear capability because New Delhi would presumably find it too expensive to retaliate by means of either conventional or nuclear war. This was possibly

> the *maximum* solution that can provide Pakistan with security without any outside assistance. Each component plays a unique role. Nuclear weapons immunize Pakistan against the worst Indian military depredations imaginable. In Islamabad's calculations, they also provide a degree of latitude that allows for the support of Indian insurgencies as an additional means of whittling down New Delhi's military advantages, which might otherwise be directed against Pakistan. Continued conventional military investments checkmate those Indian military capabilities not encumbered by counter insurgency demands, while simultaneously providing the initial means of resistance should deterrence break down.[49]

The specifics of the Kashmir strategy in this larger game plan were not yet clear. The Kashmiri militants who crossed the Line of Control for arms training during 1988 to 1990 were told that once the "uprising" began, Pakistan would attack to liberate Kashmir.[50] This was the old formula: initiate a war with unconventional means backed by the army's conventional military might. But it was also the formula that had failed twice. Both campaigns in 1947 and 1965 had begun as guerrilla wars that grew into conventional wars in which India's superiority in numbers and armaments brought the conflict to a stalemate.

The indigenous character of the insurgency in the initial phase was a significant departure from past guerrilla campaigns in Kashmir, which had failed primarily because they lacked popular support. In the late 1980s and early

1990s the Valley became a radically different place, with Kashmiris cheering Pakistani cricket teams in matches against India and celebrating Pakistan National Day while mourning on the day commemorating Indian independence. Pakistan was revered as friend, philosopher, guide, and ally in the Kashmiri struggle against India. This along with the military crises in the winter of 1989–90 presented a golden opportunity for Pakistan to attack and liberate Kashmir, but the attack never came about, for both military and political reasons.

In the past, Pakistan was checkmated by India's superior conventional strength. This time, it also had to reckon with India's nuclear capability. The conventional wisdom in Pakistan is that it deterred India from attacking Pakistan in 1990, but a case can also be made for the reverse. Having just won a war in Afghanistan without resorting to conventional forces, the Pakistani establishment appeared to have decided in favor of "a purely guerrilla war strategy."[51] Politically, the Jammu and Kashmir Liberation Front (JKLF), which was at the forefront of the secessionist movement, had advocated *azadi* (independence) and a merger of the two divided parts of Kashmir. Liberation of Kashmir at this juncture would have risked losing what Pakistan already had under its control: Azad Kashmir and the Northern Areas. That necessitated taking control of the militant movement in Kashmir. Pakistan had to "curb the azadi forces, meaning they would not equip them and not send them into the valley. It was decided that the Pakistan army should take over the private camps that had sprung up. Benazir Bhutto, Pakistan's prime minister, addressed a press conference later that month . . . and said that accession to Pakistan was the only option open to Kashmiris."[52] The first set of Afghan and Pakistani militants to go to Kashmir were sent from Jalalabad in the early 1990s by Hizb-e-Islami chief Gulbadin Hekmatyar and were attached to the Hizb-ul-Mujahideen. The new battle cry was: "Hum Jashn-e-Kabul mana chukay, Ab ao chalo Kashmir chalain" (We have celebrated victory in Kabul/Let's go to Kashmir now).[53] Gradually, Pakistan took control of the key levers of the movement—its cadre, training, funds, and weapons.

Jihad as an Instrument of State Policy

The guerrilla strategy had two central features: it strived to maintain a low threshold and to invoke the principle of "plausible deniability," portraying the insurgency as an "intifada" or a "freedom-struggle" to which Pakistan extended only moral and political support.[54] A low threshold meant supplying cadre, funds, and weapons without raising the ante on the conventional military front.

Throughout the 1990s, the Pakistani establishment believed that its strategy—by now, popularly known as *jihad*—was paying rich dividends. According to Pakistani estimates, 600,000 to 700,000 Indian troops were bogged down in Kashmir. The insurgency had caused 61,000 military and civilian casualties—more than in all India-Pakistan wars—and cost the Indian exchequer Rs 45,000 crore.[55] Arun Shourie, a minister in the National Democratic Alliance (NDA) government, concurred: Pakistan's "masterly strategic offensive against India" cost it little while tying down much of India's forces and putting "the severest strain even on the territorial integrity of India" without provoking any retaliatory offensive on Pakistan's territory. "This," he added, "has been quite a success: India has come to accept that Kashmir is a dispute; it has come to accept that Pakistan is an equal party in the dispute; it has come to accept that, if it wants the dispute to be settled, India has to negotiate a settlement with Pakistan."[56] Pakistanis believed that they were turning the heat on India in Kashmir and gaining a strategic hold on its eastern frontiers, where the Taliban—a product of Pakistan's *madaris* (Islamic seminaries; the singular form is *madrassa*) in Pakistan—had marched into Kabul in 1996.

The apparent success of using jihad to achieve Islamabad's national security objectives in Kashmir and Afghanistan had led to an exponential growth of the jihadi infrastructure within Pakistan. It has approximately 40,000–50,000 madrassah institutions with an estimated strength of 1 million to 2 million students. The armed jihadis number about 200,000, which is equal to one-third of the 600,000-strong Pakistani army. Over a million young people, who are drawn to jihad but are not armed, provide further backing to this 200,000-strong force.[57] Significantly, madrassah students are most supportive of an interventionist and aggressive foreign policy for Pakistan. In a student survey about the Kashmir issue conducted in 2002–03, 60 percent of the respondents favored war to free the region from India, and 53 percent supported having jihadi groups fight the Indian Army.[58]

If madaris supplied the labor, wealthy Pakistanis and Arabs around the world supplied the capital. The business of jihad—what the late liberal Pakistani scholar Eqbal Ahmad dubbed "*Jihad* International, Inc."—was becoming increasingly privatized. Eventually, many jihadi groups became financially independent. Besides, the weapons left over from the U.S. pipeline for the Afghan mujahideen were more than sufficient to keep the fires raging for a long time.[59]

As yet, however, jihad had not delivered the ultimate prize—Kashmir. Though ideologically committed and militarized, the establishment in Islamabad was unable to fathom why. Because Pakistanis have always viewed

Kashmiris through an Islamic lens, they have consistently mistaken the latter's "anti-Indian" feelings for "pro-Pakistan" sentiments. Islamabad fails to understand or perhaps refuses to accept the fact that the Kashmiri notion of *azadi* means an independent state and *not* one merged with Pakistan. The independence option was ruled out in Pakistan's game plan.[60]

As mentioned earlier, Pakistan's decision to support only pro-accession militant groups such as Hizb-ul-Mujahideen and later to induct jihadi groups into their cause alienated the Valley Kashmiris. Their disillusionment with Pakistan ran deep—a fact that Pakistani leaders, in characteristic denial, refused to acknowledge. Bereft of popular support, militants could merely inflict pain on Indian security forces but could not secure Kashmir's liberation. By the late 1990s, the insurgency and violence that had peaked in 1994 were on the wane.[61] Finding it increasingly difficult to recruit local Kashmiris, Pakistan was forced to fall back on Pakistani nationals and foreign mercenaries. Another blow was that separatist leaders had begun exploring political options for negotiations. Kashmir had also ceased to be an active issue on the international agenda, while New Delhi had managed to hold three state and national elections in Jammu and Kashmir. Despite an uneven turnout, these elections put a popular government in Srinagar. The possibility that jihad could liberate Kashmir had begun to fade.

The Kargil War

The Pakistan army then decided to up the ante and take greater risks in escalating the conflict. There was a sense in Islamabad that "the freedom to pursue unconventional warfare against India could be expanded into a limited conventional war with a specific political objective."[62] In early 1999, troops of Pakistan's Northern Light Infantry, in the garb of Kashmiri militants, crossed the Line of Control and occupied strategic mountain peaks in Mushkoh Valley, Dras, Kargil, and Batalik sectors of Ladakh. Pakistan's master plan was apparently to block the Dras-Kargil highway, cut Leh off from Srinagar, trap the Indian forces on the Siachin glacier, raise the militants' banner of revolt in the Valley, question the sanctity of the Line of Control (possibly alter it), and bring the Kashmir issue firmly back to the forefront of the international agenda.

Tactically, the Pakistan army's military operation was brilliant. The selection of the area, the timing of the intrusion, the extent of area taken, and the preparedness of the intruding groups indicated detailed planning.[63] Kargil is the only sector on the Line of Control where the Pakistan army has the advantage of higher positions. Its military planners had exposed the Achilles' heel of the

Indian army by catching it napping in a strategically important area. They had struck when India's political leadership was in a state of suspended animation and the country was being led by a prime minister who had lost the support of Parliament.

However, the military operation had no strategic game plan and was based on faulty assumptions. To begin with, the Pakistan army believed that with the capture of the high ridges, the Indian army would find it impossible to dislodge the Pakistanis and would acquiesce, just as Pakistan had done when the Indians seized Siachin glacier in 1984. The onus would be on India to prevent escalation, and Pakistan would lose no territory or strategically advantageous positions. The United States and other Western powers would adopt an "even-handed approach" and refrain from passing judgment on the rights and wrongs of the conflict. Pakistan could, of course, claim, as its foreign minister Sartaj Aziz argued, that it was primarily the "Kashmiri freedom fighters' struggle" and that the Line of Control was not actually demarcated. Invoking the mantra of plausible deniability, Prime Minister Nawaz Sharif told foreign correspondents that the "Kashmiri mujahideen did not start the freedom movement on my orders and they will not stop on my instructions."[64] Another mistaken belief was that Pakistan's nuclear capability would deter a significant Indian response. In other words, if India shifted to an all-out conventional war, the possibility existed that it could turn nuclear and that world powers would then intervene to force a settlement of the Kashmir dispute, thereby internationalizing it.

What General Pervez Musharraf—the military mind behind Kargil—and his team did not anticipate was the ferocity of India's response.[65] Atal Bihari Vajpayee's government unleashed India's artillery and air force to bombard the enemy posts in Kargil. By mobilizing its armed forces into a high state of alert and concentrating its naval power in the Arabian Sea, India signaled that it was fully prepared for a full-scale war.[66] The Indian victories also demonstrated that Pakistan's positions were not at all impregnable. In six weeks of warfare, nearly 700 Pakistanis died. Autopsies of dead Pakistani soldiers revealed the presence of grass in their stomachs, indicating that they had run out of food supplies.[67] Pakistan's nuclear card—a veiled threat that it would "not hesitate to use any weapon in our arsenal to defend our territorial integrity"—backfired. India called its bluff. When Pakistan chose to withdraw under American pressure, "without using any strategic weapons, or even the vaunted Pakistan Air Force, India felt emboldened."[68]

For the first time, Pakistan could no longer deny its involvement in Kashmir, as it had strenuously maintained throughout the 1990s.[69] India strategically released the transcript of an alleged cell-phone call between Pakistan's chief of army staff (COAS), General Pervez Musharraf, and the chief of general staff, Lieutenant General Mohammed Aziz, in which the latter said that the Pakistani army was holding the mujahideen "by the scruff of their neck," and that they could be withdrawn whenever the COAS wanted.[70] Pakistan failed to convince the international community that Kargil was the handiwork of Kashmiri militants. To the United States, it was clear that "the scope and planning of this operation, as well as the equipment, logistics, artillery and communication support necessary to carry it out, all point to the direct involvement of the government of Pakistan, its army and intelligence services."[71] Pakistan's eventual withdrawal confirmed that it was controlling the mujahideen. Moreover, the agreement on modalities of disengagement was backed by a formal appeal to the mujahideen from the Defense Committee of the cabinet—Pakistan's highest decisionmaking body on security matters—to withdraw from Kargil.[72]

Kargil was a diplomatic disaster for Pakistan. The Vajpayee government's position won overwhelming international approval. The world's leading industrial nations, the Group of Eight (G-8), held Pakistan, without naming it, responsible for "the military confrontation in Kashmir," describing "the military action to change the status quo as irresponsible" and asked Pakistan to withdraw its forces north of the Line of Control. They called Pakistan's nuclear bluff by refusing either to intervene in the Kashmir—as distinct from Kargil—dispute or to put any pressure on India to stop the fighting. The European Union publicly called for "the immediate withdrawal of infiltrators."[73] The United States also depicted Pakistan as the "instigator" and insisted that the status quo ante be unconditionally and unambiguously restored. "No progress was possible," emphasized President Bill Clinton, "until Pakistan pulled out its forces from the Indian zone of Kashmir."[74] For its part, China suggested guarded neutrality, urging both Islamabad and New Delhi to defuse the situation. Pakistan's diplomatic isolation was complete. That and the veiled threat of a cutoff of International Monertary Fund (IMF) aid—the lifeline of Pakistan's economy—forced Sharif to back down.[75]

Even Pakistani analysts have argued that, politically and strategically, Kargil was an ill-conceived and fundamentally flawed strategy whose political objectives were not clearly thought through. Maleeha Lodhi, Pakistan's current ambassador to the United Kingdom, called the Kargil decisions "impulsive, chaotic, erratic and overly secretive," arguing that "playing holy warriors this week and men of peace the next betrays an infirmity and insincerity of purpose that leaves the country leaderless and directionless."[76] Kargil revealed not only systemic flaws but also a reluctance to learn from previous mistakes. Just as in

1965 and 1971, the generals did not think through the consequences of their actions. High levels of distrust between the political and military elites also hampered planning. Afraid of leaks, the military went overboard with its secrecy, to the detriment of the decisionmaking process.[77]

Even now the Pakistan army steadfastly refuses to acknowledge that Kargil was a defeat or that Kargil-like operations are unacceptable and a danger to stability in the subcontinent. The issue remains "off-limits" in military circles.[78] Perhaps Pakistan saw Kargil as "yet another tactical operational exchange similar to others along the LOC [Line of Control] . . . where the ante was raised incrementally."[79] Many officers, in fact, believe that they were denied a victory and that "Sharif lost a war in Washington that had already been won in Kargil."[80] As some observers have pointed out, this rationalization of Kargil implies the possibility that Pakistan might be tempted to carry out Kargil-like operations in the future."[81]

More important, the military establishment did not believe real constraints had been put in place against any use of violence in Kashmir and India: "The Kargil fiasco does not appear to have extinguished Pakistan's belief that violence, especially as represented by low-intensity conflict, remains the best policy for pressuring India on Kashmir and other outstanding disputes."[82] Pakistan therefore seems to think its diplomatic and military options for resolving the Kashmir issue are quite limited. Given these constraints, Pakistan argues that one of its few remaining successful strategies is "to 'calibrate' the heat of the insurgency in Kashmir and possibly pressure India through expansion of violence in other portions of India's territory."[83]

Bleeding India through a "Thousand Cuts"

The Kargil debacle had clearly not dented the Pakistan army's faith in the jihad strategy. On the contrary, if jihad had not delivered Kashmir yet, the problem lay not in the strategy per se but in the fact that it had not been exploited to the hilt. If India could absorb the costs of jihadi violence in Kashmir, the argument goes, then extending it to the all-India level would certainly force it to abandon Kashmir. Indeed, "for Pakistan, the *jihad* in Jammu & Kashmir marks the point at which the space between state policy and faith vanish."[84] The sheer intensity of this undertaking is reflected in former army brigadier S. K. Malik's declaration that

terror struck into the hearts of the enemies is not only a means, *it is the end in itself.* Once a condition of terror into the opponent's heart obtained, hardly anything is left to be achieved. It is the point where the means and the end meet and merge. *Terror is not a means of imposing decision upon the enemy; it is the decision we wish to impose upon him.*[85] (Emphasis added)

Jihad was gradually becoming an end in itself, with even more ambitious goals of balkanizing India by accelerating its internal fragmentation. This is not so surprising since many Pakistani elites think that India is an unnatural state, being far larger than other states of the region, and should therefore be reduced in size. This suggestion was first put forth by Chaudhury Rahmat Ali, the inventor of the name "Pakistan," which first appeared in a pamphlet titled *India: The Continent of Dinia* in 1945. It sought to demolish the "myth of Indianism" and to help "non-Indian nations"—Muslims, Dravidians, Akhoots (depressed castes), Christians, Sikhs, Buddhs, and Parsis—establish their sovereignty in the continent of Dinia, an anagram of *India* meaning the "abode of religions."[86] In the days preceding the partition, Jinnah also made desperate attempts to do the same. Two decades later, as war approached in 1971, Zulfiqar Ali Bhutto told one of his confidantes: "Once the back of Indian forces is broken in the east, Pakistan should occupy the whole of Eastern India and make it a permanent part of East Pakistan. . . . This will also provide a physical link with China. Kashmir should be taken at any price, even the Sikh Punjab and turned into Khalistan."[87] In the 1990s, the jihadi leaders adopted this agenda, vowing not to rest "until the whole of India is dissolved into Pakistan." One went further: "We ought to disintegrate India and even wipe India out."[88]

After September 11: Altered Strategic Calculus

The jihad strategy ran into a major roadblock with the devastating terrorist strikes against United States on September 11, 2001, followed by suicide attacks against the Jammu and Kashmir state assembly in October and the Indian Parliament in December 2001. These watershed events changed the rules of the game, perhaps forever. In a speech at the United Nations in 2001, President George W. Bush laid down the ground rules for a state's responsibility for terrorist groups operating inside its borders, with no room for neutrality. This delivered a serious blow to two key pillars of Pakistan's Kashmir strategy. Pakistan could no longer allow jihadi groups to use its territory with impunity, nor could it completely absolve itself of the responsibility for the violence perpetrated by them beyond its borders. The Kashmir issue was suddenly transformed from a question of self-determination to one of cross-border terrorism. More and more key players in Washington, Paris, London, and Moscow conceded that New Delhi had reason to complain of continuing terrorist infiltration from Pakistan to India.

As soon as Washington decided to target al Qaeda and its host, Afghanistan, Pakistan would have to cooperate for political and operational reasons. Faced with a U.S. ultimatum of "you are with us or against us," the Musharraf regime lost little time in forsaking the Taliban and allying itself with the United States. But this created fissures between the Musharraf regime and Jihad Inc. Musharraf alienated many jihadi groups by severing Pakistan's ties with al Qaeda and the Taliban, helping America destroy their bases in Afghanistan, and arresting and handing over the Arab jihadis to the United States. He thus feared a backlash. On its western front, India raised the military ante, ordering full mobilization of its troops, and threatened war unless Pakistan cracked down on the jihadis. The underlying message was that supporting jihad would no longer be a "low-cost option."

Tactical Shifts

Musharraf grudgingly agreed that Pakistan should not allow jihad in the name of Kashmir. However, there was mounting evidence that this concession was a tactical retreat and not the harbinger of a paradigm shift. Subsequently, the Pakistani government released most of the terrorists it had arrested—including top leaders like Hafiz Muhammad Saeed of Lashkar-e-Taiba and Maulana Masood Azhar of Jaish-i-Mohammed—and the jihadi groups continued to operate under new names.[89]

Earlier, too, Musharraf had tried making such tactical distinctions. Before 9/11, his policy had been to curb jihadi power to check growing sectarianism within Pakistan while supporting it across the borders to achieve Pakistan's national security objectives. Ideologically, Musharraf made an effort to gain legitimacy for the concept of jihad by distinguishing between jihad from terrorism, and justifying the former as a legitimate instrument of the Kashmiris' freedom struggle. He told Prime Minister Vajpayee, "You do not expect me to accept cross-border terrorism. This is wrong. There is nothing going on across the border, it is a Line of Control and also there is no terrorism, there is a freedom struggle going on there."[90] After 9/11, he castigated al Qaeda on its eastern borders in Afghanistan but shied away from dismantling the domestic jihadi network geared toward Kashmir's liberation. This explained his regime's desperate attempts to protect its assets by asking such groups to lie low, shift bases to Azad Kashmir, and limit the public appearance of arms and donation boxes that solicited funds for jihad. The military establishment decided to promote the Kashmiri groups rather than the jihadis; asked the cadre of the banned groups such as Jaish-i-Mohammed and Lashkar-e-Taiba to merge into Hizb-ul-Mujahideen, Tehrik-ul-Mujahideen (TuM), and Al Omar; strove to recruit local cadres; and renewed contacts with JKLF members.[91] These fine distinctions were bound to run aground, partly because of the intrinsic dynamics of the jihadi groups, which had developed an independent agenda—as discussed shortly.

The "Ripe Apple Theory"

The fundamental pillars of Pakistan's Kashmir strategy did not change. The military establishment still adhered to the "ripe apple theory": if Pakistan continued to bleed India, it would make India's retention of Kashmir so prohibitive that Kashmir would fall. In other words, the complete failure of war as an instrument to annex Kashmir in the 1947–48 and the 1965 wars, the Kargil debacle, and the discredited jihad strategy had collectively failed to dissuade the Pakistani establishment from planning new war games to take over Kashmir. This became evident from the Musharraf regime's response to India's total deployment of its forces on the border, in the wake of the Kaluchak massacre in May 2002 and the resulting military crisis. Musharraf was "'absolutely confident' that the freedom struggle in Kashmir [had] entered a crucial phase where an Indian military adventurism across the Line-of-Control would trap the Indian army in a Vietnam or Afghanistan-like situation and hasten the freedom process for the Kashmiri Muslims."[92] The Pakistani army had concluded that the military posturing by India might actually push it into a deeper strategic quagmire in Kashmir. As General Musharraf explained:

> We are not only on the defensive. We'll take the offensive into Indian territory. . . . At the moment, if there is anything that they do across the Line of Control, there are thousands, hundreds of thousands of people in Kashmir, Azad Kashmir, our part of Kashmir, who are demanding to be armed. . . . [and] who are telling me . . . [start], we will take Kashmir.[93]

The script had not changed much from Pakistan's first Kashmir venture almost fifty-five years before.

As for the nuclear aspect of Pakistan's strategy, Lieutenant General Javed Hassan, one of the architects of the Kargil war, indicated that "Pakistan [would] not escalate the conflict; it would force India to escalate to a point where Islamabad gets a reason to go nuclear." If India did escalate the conflict, it would have to be "on Pakistan's terms," and "if India's escalation crosses Pakistan's thresholds, it will have cause and justification to escalate to the nuclear level. India will have been shown to have behaved irresponsibly and forced Pakistan to take extreme measures."[94]

The battle plans also revolved around the old formula of using irregulars in conjunction with the armed forces of Pakistan. Newspapers reported the army's decision to deploy a large part of the Special Services Group commandos all along the Line of Control to carry out sabotage and subversion within Kashmir.[95] The militant groups—including Jaish-i-Mohammed, Lashkar-e-Taiba, Hizb-ul-Mujahideen, Harkat-ul-Mujahideen, and al Badr—were directed to dominate strategic areas in border belts and areas south of the Pir Panjal Hills. They were equipped with night-vision devices, sniper rifles, rocket launchers, mortars, grenade launchers, and sophisticated communication systems. Their task would have been to destroy communication links by blowing up bridges and railway lines, disrupting supply lines, and trying to engage the Indian army from its rear in a war.[96] Since the military crisis was defused, the possible outcomes of this strategy remain a matter of academic analysis, but clearly not much had changed within the power corridors of Pakistan's military establishment, at least until the end of 2002.

Peace Process: A Strategic Shift or Another Tactical Turn?

Since then, Pakistan's Kashmir strategy has taken a dramatic turn in returning to the negotiating table and participating in the peace process. The ice was broken during Prime Minister Vajpayee's visit to Islamabad in January 2004. Declaring that "history had been made," General Musharraf promised not to allow the territories under Pakistani control to be used for terrorism.[97] The two countries agreed to resume their dialogue for a peaceful resolution of all bilateral issues, including Kashmir. Despite a change in government in New Delhi, which caused much anxiety in Islamabad, the peace process has been sustained.[98] In fact, buoyed after his first meeting with Prime Minister Manmohan Singh in September 2004, Musharraf has been firing a rapid volley of proposals to resolve the Kashmir issue when just a year earlier he was being called the "mastermind behind Kargil." He has suggested dividing Kashmir into seven geographical regions, demilitarizing a part or all of them (variations of the Chenab formula), having a soft border across the Line of Control, and finally, creating a demilitarized autonomous Kashmir (for the specific details, see chapter 8). The large question, of course, is whether this is a harbinger of a strategic shift or is yet another tactical maneuver.

The reasons for changing course may be telling. On one hand, Pakistan's Kashmir strategy has reached a stalemate. The army has failed to take over Kashmir by force or to use force as a "tactical instrument" compelling India to make territorial concessions on Kashmir. Politically, it has alienated the Valley Kashmiris, who no longer look to Pakistan as their savior and are less willing to do Pakistan's bidding. Pakistan had armed and trained Kashmiri militants but never trusted them as a reliable partner. Islamabad was nervous that the latter would strike a deal with New Delhi, as was evident from a public admission that Pakistan leadership was instrumental in splitting the Hurriyat to forestall its dialogue with New Delhi.[99] Threats to eliminate the Hurriyat leaders and the steady depletion of the Kashmiri cadre in the militant ranks also point in this direction. In other words, Pakistan has *unsuccessfully* exhausted the entire spectrum of violence—from nuclear blackmail to unleashing jihad—in attempting to alter the status quo in Kashmir. Therefore Pakistan seems to have little option but to return to the negotiating table.

On the other hand, one could say that growing pressures, from within and without, have persuaded the Musharraf regime to abandon the jihad strategy, whose fundamental assumptions in the post-9/11 period have started going awry. The same mujahideen who targeted Kashmir after the eviction of Soviet forces in Kabul had—after the fall of Taliban—turned toward Pakistan in search of new agendas. When they found that the government had not only abandoned the Taliban but was also "arresting people indiscriminately, particularly those with beards," many groups, such as Jaish-i-Mohammed led by Maulana Abdul Jabbar, decided to "resist and work against U.S. interests in Pakistan." Their objectives were to "hit out at top government functionaries who are perceived to be pro-American while driving the country towards a state of anarchy."[100] Soon, its "blowback effect" began to hurt the ruling establishment because its corporate interests, being that it was an ally of the United States, clashed with those of the jihadis, who in serving the state in Kashmir also developed "an independent agenda of eventually capturing the Pakistani state."[101] This may be "a bitter pill" for Pakistan's generals to swallow, as some have pointed out, but "the fact is that Kashmir cannot be liberated by force. The 'bleed India' policy, an apparently cheap option for Pakistan, was vociferously advocated for over a decade. This has totally collapsed—Pakistan has bled no less than India."[102]

Furthermore, jihadi culture, sectarian organizations, and their numerous splinter groups, many of which have acquired the status of a "Pakistani al Qaeda," have seeped deep into the body politic of Pakistan.[103] Government officials investigating domestic acts of terrorism soon realized the length and breadth of the canvass available to these people, stretching from a small village in Azad Kashmir to Karachi in one direction, and from Pakistan's eastern borders to South Waziristan in the other. In the Miramshah and Wana areas of Waziristan, hundreds of foreign militants including Arabs, Central Asians, Chechens, and Afghans, as well as members of the Pakistani militant outfits, are reportedly deeply entrenched. Over the years, they have established bases and dens for storing explosive devices, not to mention training centers where militants are taught various tactics, including how to carry out ambushes, raids, and attacks.[104] Pakistan offers a fertile place for hosting them partly because it gives them "access to unlimited manpower and acquiring explosives or weapons of any sort is not a problem" and partly because "they expect to find friends in the government and sympathizers among the people."[105]

At the same time, partnership with the jihadi groups is at cross-purposes with Musharraf's professed goal of ending the sectarian violence and ridding Pakistani society of extremist elements. They all share deep bonds of Islamic ideology, common political targets, training centers, and resources. For example, Lashkar-e-Jhangvi, a sectarian organization recently renamed Jundullah, is working as al Qaeda's strike force. Harkat-ul-Mujahideen al-Aalami, widely believed to be an offshoot of the Kashmiri militant outfit Harkat-ul-Mujahideen, is also suspected of having close operational ties with al Qaeda and was responsible for bombing the U.S. consulate in June 2002.[106] Although the first suicide bombing in Pakistan, on March 17, 2002, targeted an international church in Islamabad, soon the tactic became part and parcel of homegrown organized terrorism and was even directed at the country's top leaders, President Musharraf and Prime Minister Shaukat Aziz.[107] Five abortive assassination attempts on Musharraf—two within a span of eleven days in December 2003—perhaps forced him to rechristen the jihadis "spoilers" in an effort to find a way out of the impasse in Kashmir. "He is serious," a U.S. State Department official noted; "he was born again on December 25th."[108] As one commentator observed:

> Back in 2001, Pakistan's permanent establishment (read army/ISI) was still riding the tiger of jihad and thinking that with the American connection restored, Pakistan could have its cake and eat it. It could carry America's bags in Afghanistan and simultaneously sustain jihad in Kashmir. . . . Having to contend with the real world in the meantime, they are now the wiser. Far from being able to ride and control the *jihadi* tiger, they have found themselves on the receiving end of its menacing snarl.[109]

This was also the lesson emanating from Afghanistan. Pakistan's support for pan-Islamic jihad had turned on its head. The Taliban had accepted the theory of strategic depth on its own terms, implying that Pakistan "provided the ideological strategic depth for Afghanistan."[110] The new strategic context in the post-9/11 world stigmatized terrorism and raised the costs of supporting terror.

Notwithstanding its lavish praise for General Musharraf's contribution in fighting terrorism, the government in Washington is beginning to realize that the jihadi infrastructure in Pakistan was only partly affected after 9/11 and is still capable of harboring al Qaeda, including Osama bin Laden. Most telling are the continuing arrests of top al Qaeda functionaries on Pakistan's soil and the footprint of Pakistan-based jihadi groups from Iraq to California to London.[111] Pakistan is under constant pressure to completely dismantle the jihadi infrastructure. As the core commander, Safdar Hussain, explained, "Military operation in South Waziristan was necessary because in the post-9/11 geopolitical environment, un-administered areas cannot exist in any part of the world, particularly in places such as the Pak-Afghan tribal region, which has been a breeding ground for terrorists participating in the Afghan war."[112] Notably, the Pakistan army has paid a heavy price in fighting this war: it has lost more than 600 men over the past three years. Perhaps that is why the Pakistan army yielded and signed a peace deal with the local Taliban *shura* in September 2006. It ceased the military campaign, freed prisoners, and sent the army back to barracks, and the militants agreed to halt attacks on Pakistani forces and stop cross-border raids into Afghanistan targeting U.S. and Afghan troops. This, in turn, led many U.S. analysts to question General Musharraf's commitment to fighting the war on terror.

The growing gap between Pakistan, almost a "failed state" in some eyes, and a "globalizing India" drove home the point that the strategy of "bleeding India through a thousand cuts" had utterly failed. In 2003 India's economy posted 7.4 percent growth, the second-fastest rate in the world, while that of Pakistan had slid to 3.6 percent and was castigated as the "*Jihadi* rate of growth."[113] Though IMF-approved government policies bolstered by generous foreign assistance have generated a solid macroeconomic recovery, with economic growth climbing beyond 7 percent in 2004 and 2005, there is a widening gulf between the government's idea of economic performance and the harsh economic reality experienced by Pakistan's people.[114]

Overall, Pakistan is clearly in a difficult situation, though this does not necessarily dictate that its establishment should make peace with India at the cost of its core national interests in Kashmir. Immediately after the 9/11 attacks, for instance, Pakistan was in a far more dire condition, yet Musharraf had steadfastly refused to compromise on the Kashmir policy and through sheer tactical maneuvering managed not to do so. This is but one of several reasons why it is difficult to assess whether Pakistan has permanently relinquished the jihad strategy, the foremost being that the jihadi groups are its only leverage against India. Resistance within the army to dismantle these groups may not be "ideological" so much as tactical, in that the extremist forces are viewed "as strategic assets in the ongoing conflict in Kashmir."[115] The pro-militancy lobby argues that it was the armed uprising in the Valley that drew international attention and questions whether it is strategically wise to wrap up the entire militant campaign without any meaningful concessions from New Delhi. In this view, the militant movement should be allowed to simmer in the event that bilateral negotiations fail to deliver a breakthrough.[116] Some also point out the practical difficulties of abruptly jettisoning a policy that has been nurtured for decades: "For 23 years, the Pakistanis were taught that Arabs and Afghans were mujahids. All of a sudden, they want us to unlearn that lesson."[117] The locals had difficulty enough understanding international diplomacy in the fight against the Soviet Union in Afghanistan, let alone the compulsions for Pakistan or President Musharraf to reverse this policy now.

Another cause for skepticism is that the Pakistani establishment, especially Musharraf, makes a deliberately fuzzy distinction between jihad and terrorism. For example, barely three months after promising that Pakistan would not permit its territory to be used for terrorism (clearly in Kashmir), Musharraf reverted to his old position in an address to an *India Today* enclave in March 2004: "There is no terrorism in Kashmir. We think there is a freedom struggle going on. I have said Pakistan will not export terrorism to any other area. I have been saying that all along. I have also clearly been differentiating between what is happening in Kashmir. We in Pakistan don't call it cross-border terrorism. We call it a freedom struggle."[118] He also gave an extremely narrow definition of the Taliban as "the previous Mullah Omar's government, their abettors and supporters," and while he categorically denied they would be allowed in Pakistan, he maintained a conspicuous silence about the domestic jihadi groups. As one commentator observed:

> From the point of view of Pakistan's Islamist militants and their backers in the establishment, *Jihad is only on hold but not yet over.* The major Kashmiri Jihadi groups retain their infrastructure that could be pressed into service at a future date. Afghanistan's Taliban also continue to find safe haven in parts of Pakistan as recently as the spring of 2005. Afghan and American officials complain periodically of the Taliban still training and organizing in Pakistan's border areas but their protests are rejected summarily with rhetoric similar to the one about domestic militant groups.[119]

Pakistan's foreign office, through its permanent representative to the United Nations, has periodically debated the definition of terrorism at the United Nations even though it has ostensibly been a crucial ally in the U.S.-led global war against terrorism.[120] The bottom line is that if the Musharraf regime had made up its mind to *foreclose* the jihad option *of any kind*, as it seems to have done in the case of al Qaeda and that organization's remnants in Pakistan, it would have moved to disarm extremist groups, block their sources of funding, and reduce their potential recruitment to marginalize them in the political process.[121] There lies the rub. In trying to keep out the mainstream political parties, the Musharraf regime has been forced, time and again, to rely on Muttahida Majlis-e-Amal (MMA), an alliance of six Islamic parties, which in turn draws on the vast, deeply entrenched network of more then fifty radical groups. For instance, when elections produced a hung parliament, the state worked frantically to cobble together a multiparty grouping that would elect Zafarullah Jamali as prime minister. These efforts included the ultimately successful wooing of Azam Tariq, leader of the defunct and banned Sunni sectarian organization, Sipah-e-Sahaba. On the other side of the political divide, the leader of Tehrik-e-Jaffria, another banned group, closed ranks with other Islamic parties in the MMA. This explains why the rise of Islamic militancy cannot be assessed in isolation.

Earlier, the establishment required the support of Islamic groups to implement its regional goals (that is, Kashmir policy), whereas now the Musharraf regime, operating in a political vacuum, needs them for its own survival. "Will it be possible," one observer asks, "to muzzle the mullahs when the government itself solicits their support in times of political crisis?"[122] Similar compulsions have led certain quarters within the establishment to steadfastly continue supporting those who have directly challenged the writ of the government, made the country a "soft state," forced it into political isolation, and nearly earned it the status of a country spawning global terrorism, which seemed warranted when the head of the militant Jamiatul Ansar, Maulana Fazlur Rehman Khalil, was released from detention after only a few months. His outfit was rechristened following an American ban on the Harkat-ul-Mujahideen, which had an extensive network and infrastructure in Afghanistan and Kashmir. Khalil's case is not the only one that runs against the government's counterterrorism policy. Earlier, the military government had released Maulana Abdul Jabbar from custody despite charges of organizing suicide attacks within Pakistan.[123]

Without doubt, such a radical transformation in Kashmir policy must be emanating from a broadly based consultative process involving all of Pakistan's important players across the political spectrum. The debate on Kashmir within

Pakistan has only just begun. A growing awareness of the costs of this conflict has led many intellectuals, journalists, and scholars to urge a reappraisal of the Kashmir issue. Although a broad consensus is emerging among political parties on the need to improve relations with India, Musharraf is skating on rather thin ice when it comes to securing support for his specific proposals to resolve the Kashmir issue. A paradigm change in Pakistan's Kashmir policy would require not only a shift in structural imperatives but also a political approach that appears to elude the Pakistani establishment. The following section explains why.

Political Strategy: The Missing Element

Since 1947 Pakistanis have argued, in keeping with the two-nation theory, that the Muslim-majority Dogra state of Jammu and Kashmir belongs morally and ideologically to Pakistan. Yet they have never made a political case for Kashmir's accession to Pakistan nor showcased Azad Kashmir as a successful political story to the Valley Kashmiris. On the contrary, the relationship between the Pakistani state and people in Azad Kashmir and the Northern Areas is an apt illustration of internal colonialism, as discussed in chapter 6. Here, it suffices to say that despite the centrality of the Kashmir issue to Pakistan's ideology, polity, and foreign policy, Islamabad has paid little attention to the social concerns, political aspirations, and political choices of Kashmiris living in areas under their own control. That is mainly because the Pakistani establishment does not even try to understand Kashmir's realities owing to the character of Pakistan's polity, state structures, and ruling elites and their experiences of governing the country largely through nonelective—administrative and military—instruments of control, all of which explain the lack of a political strategy on Kashmir.

The history of Pakistani politics is one of failure to establish enduring and credible political institutions, evolve a functioning constitution, or hold regular and consequential elections.[124] In a period of fifty-five years, Pakistan has had three constitutions, put forth in 1956, 1962, and 1973. In 1985 the military regime of Mohammed Zia-ul-Haq fundamentally altered the constitution with his introduction of the Eighth Amendment establishing a president-dominated executive. That measure was repealed by Nawaz Sharif in 1998. President Pervez Musharraf has now created a new constitutional order through the Legal Framework Order—a capsule of twenty-nine amendments to the constitution passed in 2004 under the Seventeenth Amendment, which the elected Parliament was forced to accept.[125] The newly created National Security Council not only formalizes the military's role in governance but also accords it more weight than the elected representatives of the people. The opposition political parties argue that, at worst, the council will be a tool in the hands of the serving army chief to override the elected parliament and prime minister and, at best, will keep the elected parliament and the prime minister pitched against a coterie of nonelected military chiefs.[126] The institutional balance of power in favor of military bureaucratic forces is thus well entrenched in the state apparatus of Pakistan. Recent national elections were held in 1985, 1988, 1990, 1993, and 1997, but in the state's fifty-nine-year history no elected government has succeeded another—all have been deposed by the military or dismissed by presidential fiat.

Pakistan had no well-developed party organization when it came into existence, and it is still struggling to establish a party-based system of parliamentary democracy. That is partly because successive military regimes have sought to depoliticize Pakistani society by discrediting the political parties and bypassing the provincial bases of their power to place local political processes under centrally directed bureaucratic or military control. This was certainly true of Ayub Khan's model of "basic democracies," which cultivated a new rural constituency for endorsing rather than setting the political and economic agendas of the regime. Similarly, Zia-ul-Haq established a federal advisory council, the Majlis-i-Shoora, which was wholly appointed by the president for a four-year term. Zia declared that elections on a party basis ran counter to the teachings of the Quran and Sunna and repudiated the parliamentary form of government, since they were all based on a Western and therefore non-Islamic model. General Musharraf also followed a top-down approach from the center to the district level, deliberately ignored the provincial authority, and formally entrenched the military at the grassroots level by making elected representatives work under different military committees.[127]

Even during democratic interludes, the power structure was headed by a troika with the president acting as the "eyes, ears, and hands" of the army chief, and the prime minister wielding the least influence of the three. Benazir Bhutto acknowledged as much: "It is obvious that the civilian regime has no option but to permit the armed forces of Pakistan to retain an autonomy, that is neither sanctioned by the constitution nor is in the larger interests of the state."[128] Military rule has created a style of governance that is poorly suited to debate, coalition building, or bargaining, since these factors are alien to military culture. Its penchant for controlling the political process "from above" is captured well in the following remarks by General Musharraf:

> I do not believe in power sharing. I am a soldier and believe in the unity of command. I believe that there should be one authority to run things

rightly. If there are two authorities nothing can be accomplished properly. What I want to say is that in the parliamentary system, the Prime Minister is the Chief Executive of the Country. He will have all the powers. He must run the government with all the authority. However, I want to have power to the extent that he dares not undo what I have said. He dare not violate national interests. He dare not reverse the reform agenda. I want to assure that I will support the prime minister if he practices governance rightly and in the interest of Pakistan. I will back him up. I will strengthen him fully. This is how democracy in Pakistan will function. It cannot allow him to manipulate institutions. Banks, State Bank, nationalized banks were plundered in the past. This will not be allowed. So there is no question of sharing of power.[129]

This is also why Pakistan has not been able to effectively integrate its provinces or distribute resources equitably between the dominant Punjab and the subordinate provinces of Sindh, the North-West Frontier Province, and Baluchistan. Some analysts attribute it to the "political economy of defence," in which the imperatives of state making, especially in guarding it from external and internal threats soon after independence, forced the leadership to invest a large part of the state's meager resources in building and modernizing its armed forces.[130]

The fundamental reason behind East Pakistan's secession in 1971 lay precisely in such policies of the ruling establishment. The Bengalis suffered from an "inner colonialism," a systematic economic exploitation whereby West Pakistan utilized the income generated by the East's jute exports to finance its own development. As a result, between 1959–60 and 1969–70, per capita GDP in East Pakistan grew at a rate of 17 percent compared with West Pakistan's 42 percent. Not surprisingly, Bengali economists began to oppose the "two-nation theory" and the "two-nation economy."[131] The idea of sharing power within a federal constitution, with a Bengali majority in the lower house, was anathema to the civil bureaucracy and the defense establishment. The first military coup by Ayub Khan in 1958 had sought to preempt precisely this possibility by imposing the one-unit scheme that amalgamated all provinces into a new entity called West Pakistan, putting it at par with East Pakistan. The scheduled national elections were stalled by martial law, and when they finally took place in 1970, they ended with Pakistan's dismemberment.

Although East Pakistan seceded, the story is not much different in Sindh and Baluchistan. Hundreds of thousands of hectares of new fertile agricultural land that became available in Sindh in the wake of construction of new barrages on the Indus River were distributed among the top military and civilian officials, mostly the Punjabis, ignoring the local Sindhi peasants.[132] The Sindhis have dropped to a bare majority or less in seven principal cities. Their region has been described as one "in which a peripheral people feel in danger or actually have been swamped: numerically, economically, and culturally, within their own land by newcomers or invaders."[133]

The situation in Baluchistan is particularly volatile, with the Baluch nationalists up in arms against the federal government over development of the Gwadar port and the establishment of new cantonments in the province. The Pakistani establishment's marketing of the province as a prime region for global investment and as a corridor for trade to Central and West Asia without adequate stakes for the locals has added fuel to the fire. The local people and Baluch nationalists are suspicious of the army's agenda, fearing it might reduce them to a minority in their homeland. Baluch political parties have joined hands in an alliance called the Baluch Ittehad. Its two-point agenda is exactly the same as the one professed by the armed rebels: opposition to military garrisons and mega-projects in the province. One of their perennial grievances is that "the province's wealth is being transferred to an already better off Punjab and that the country's armed might is being used for this."[134] Discovered in 1952, five gas wells at Sui at present supply 38 percent of Pakistan's domestic and commercial energy needs, yet only 6 percent of Baluchistan's population has a gas connection. Ironically, these connections came a decade after gas had been supplied all over Pakistan. State sector gas companies are making annual profits to the tune of Rs 84 billion. Until 1991, when the first National Finance Commission was constituted to divide resources among the provinces, these profits were being devoured by the center. Since then, Baluchistan has been the recipient of a meager 5 percent of these profits.[135] The explanation, said Nawab Bugti, a Baluch nationalist leader who was killed in a military operation in August 2006, is that "they think that natural resources are national assets, and we think that they are Baloch assets, and whoever wants to use them must do them through us, not by direct possession." Although Baluchistan is the richest province in terms of mineral resources, it is the least developed in Pakistan. Baluchistan's trading, commercial, mining, and industrial enterprises and local transport are also largely controlled by the Pathans and the Punjabis.

The "Punjabization" of Pakistan is clearly reflected in the highly lopsided pattern of the nation's regional development.[136] Punjab, with its rich soil, ample water resources, and political support from the Islamabad government, has remained the major beneficiary of development activities. As a result, Punjab is becoming prosperous while other provinces are being impoverished.

More than 50 percent of the population of Sindh and Baluchistan live below the poverty line. In terms of human resource development, Baluchistan and NWFP have less than 25 percent literacy. As Nawabzada Baluch Mairi, a prominent Baluch leader, points out, "Today, the Baloch is a slave to the Punjabi colonial system. If Punjabi-dominated Pakistan considers that our struggle for freedom from slavery means disintegration, we don't care. . . . Awareness is increasing in [the] Baloch nation to protect their identity, culture, history, and natural resources and they will emerge triumphant."[137] Sindh also feels severely discriminated against in resource allocations in the recognition of political and economic rights and interests. The water crisis, in particular the issue of the Kalabagh Dam and its proposed proportional sharing by different provinces, continues to be a serious issue.

The centralizing process has met with great resistance in large part because the ethnic composition of the military-bureaucratic oligarchy does not adequately reflect the state's diversities and has therefore alienated those omitted from its ranks. Seventy percent of Pakistan's military personnel are drawn from Punjab.[138] Punjabis are also disproportionately represented in the federal bureaucracy. By contrast, the Bengali majority of the pre-1971 Pakistan population was by and large excluded from military service and poorly represented in the bureaucracy. While the Punjabi-dominated army has always had a strong Pakhtun element, with 25 percent of its cadre recruited from the Frontier Province, the Sindhis, with a 4.5 percent share, and Baluch (not necessarily ethnic Baluch), with a meager 0.5 percent, remain marginalized. Mohajirs who earlier exercised almost complete control of the higher echelons of the federal civil services gradually lost their ground to Punjabis and now exhibit separatist tendencies.

With the perpetuation of a nonrepresentative, administrative mode of governance, political processes have had little chance to develop and the state has grown distant from society. In order to maintain its control over the discontent developing within the provinces, the state resorted to force and coercion. The center's dismal record of dismissing the elected governments in provincial assemblies speaks volumes. Within eight days of partition, Jinnah dismissed Khan Sahib's Congress ministry in the North-West Frontier Province and installed a Muslim League ministry under Khan Abdul Qayum Khan. Seven months later, in another show of force, the chief minister of Sindh, M. H. Khuro, who had opposed the governor-general on the separation of Karachi from the province, was dismissed on charges of corruption and poor administration. The 1973 constitution provided safeguards for provincial autonomy but barely a month later, Zulfiqar Ali Bhutto authorized military operations against the Baluchis on the grounds that they were encouraging a secessionist movement. The governments of Benazir Bhutto and Nawaz Sharif had much the same record.

Pakistan's military and democratic regimes have been ill-disposed toward not only the sociopolitical and cultural diversities of Kashmir and the Sufi traditions of Islam but also their own ethnic and linguistic identities—Bengali, Sindhi, and Baluch. Every Pakistani leader has sought to fashion the state's structures on the premise that the Islamic faith as such was the sole and sufficient condition of its nationhood. It is argued that in a state of Muslims there are no separate ethnic groups. Jinnah wanted to build a strong nation, founded on the idea of one nation, one culture, and one language: "Unity in uniformity was the operational phrase."[139] Jinnah considered provincial identities a "curse" and exhorted his followers "to get rid of this provincialism, because as long as you allow this poison to remain in the body politic of Pakistan, believe me, you will never be a strong nation."[140]

At the time Pakistan became a nation, Urdu was the mother tongue of only 5 percent of the population (mainly of the North Indian immigrants), and Bengali was spoken by 51 percent of the people in East Pakistan. Punjabi was spoken in Punjab, Pushto in the North-West Frontier Province, Sindhi in Sindh, Baluchi and Brahvi in Baluchistan, Pahari and other Kashmiri dialects in Azad Kashmir, and virtually a dozen other languages in the Northern Areas of Pakistan. The Pakistani leadership's decision to make Urdu the lingua franca of Pakistan was bitterly resented by the indigenous peoples of West Pakistan and the Bengalis and in East Pakistan led to language riots and a total rout of the Muslim League in the 1954 provincial elections. Other non-Urdu speakers, especially Sindhis, resented the insensitive manner in which Urdu—a totally alien mode of communication—was being imposed on them. Yet Pakistan's constitution completely overlooks ethnic and linguistic identities and recognizes only religious minorities.[141] Such contradictions between Pakistan's official status as an Islamic nation-state and the realities of its multiethnic society shed considerable light on its Kashmir policy.

Disregarding the Kashmiris' demand for a single independent state, most Punjabi decisionmakers, for example, insist that "Pakistan must support secessionist forces in Indian-occupied Kashmir."[142] They still dance to the tune of "Kashmir *banega* Pakistan" (Kashmir will become part of Pakistan), perhaps because

> keeping the Kashmir dispute alive without going to war over it serves Punjab's interests within Pakistan and in South Asia. It keeps hostility with India intact and provides an important justification for maintain-

ing a huge military machine, which drains the resources that could otherwise be allocated to development projects. The military machine is used as the Punjab's iron hand with which to tighten its grip on the smaller provinces.[143]

Most Sindhi and Baluch leaders are of precisely the same opnion. The late G. M. Syed, who pioneered the Sindhi nationalist movement, saw Kashmir's accession to Pakistan as "unrealistic and dangerous for smaller nationalities in Pakistan" as that "would encourage Punjabis to pursue a more vigorous policy of expansion and, in doing so, they would be more repressive towards Sindhis."[144] Sardar Atalluah Khan Mengal, the former chief minister of Baluchistan, agreed that the Kashmir dispute has been "exploited by the Punjabis to keep conflict alive," and "to keep a huge army intact," which also "gives them clout over the smaller nationalities."[145] Most Sindhi and Baluch leaders believe that the best way to resolve the Kashmir dispute would be to unite the two parts into a single demilitarized and neutral state.

Conclusion

Pakistan's Kashmir strategy is now in a state of flux, though still dominated by a civil-military oligarchy that seems bent on forcibly altering the status quo in Kashmir. Despite some radical changes in the past two years, it is too early to say whether they are far-reaching. Pakistan's rethinking of its Kashmir policy is partly a result of increasing internal and external pressures, a deadly stalemate in Kashmir itself, and the growing awareness of the cost of conflict in Pakistani society. A paradigmatic shift may be difficult to bring about, however, because Kashmir is linked to the structural imperatives of the Pakistani state, whose establishment has yet to acquire the political tools and master the political skills needed to bring about such a transformation.

CHAPTER FOUR

MULTIPLE NOTIONS
OF SELF-DETERMINATION:
JAMMU, KASHMIR, AND LADAKH

THE KASHMIRIS' RIGHT TO self-determination has been debated largely within the framework of the 1949 UN resolutions on holding a plebiscite, which limited the people's choice to joining India or Pakistan. This entailed a singular notion of their right to self-determination that ruled out independence, framed the Kashmir issue as an India-Pakistan conflict, and played down the question of people's "political" rights.

This chapter questions these and other "given" parameters of conventional analyses of the Kashmir dispute that overlook its complex local dynamics. As already mentioned, the Kashmir issue tends to be viewed as an intractable "territorial dispute" between two belligerent neighbors. Hence the secessionist movement of Kashmiris is usually explained from the viewpoint of one side or the other. Indians see it as a "proxy war" being waged by Pakistan.[1] Pakistanis consider it an uprising or "freedom struggle" by Kashmiris.[2] Neither standpoint provides political space for the voices of the people of Jammu and Kashmir.

Furthermore, both perpetuate the fallacy that the two parts of the divided state are homogeneous entities and the Kashmiris a monolithic group. Such an approach overlooks the plurality of the state, with its diverse communities: Gujjars, Bakkarwals, Kashmiri Pandits, Dogras, and Ladakhi Buddhists on the Indian side; and Balti, Shina, Khowar, Burushashki, Wakhi, and Pahari-speaking people on the Pakistan side; as well as Ismaili, Sunni, Shia, and Nur Bakshi sects of Islam in Azad Kashmir and the Northern Areas. Each is struggling to nurture its sociocultural identity, find avenues of social and economic development, and create its own political space. In other words, each community interprets the political rights inherent in the right of self-determination differently.

The deeply plural character of Jammu and Kashmir society is at the heart of the secessionist movement in the state and helps to account for secessionist demands as well as failures. However, past analyses have tended to focus only on the relationship between the Kashmir Valley (rather than all of Jammu and Kashmir) and the Indian state. According to some, that relationship and the resulting political process choked off opportunities for young Kashmiris, who then resorted to violence because they were unable to express democratic dissent in an institutional context.[3] Indeed, India's consistent policy of denying democracy coupled with the systematic subversion and destruction of Jammu and Kashmir's federal autonomy has been directly blamed for the Kashmiri uprising "for self-determination" that erupted in the 1990s.[4] These arguments, however, do not explain why the same processes produced a radically different political response in Jammu and Ladakh, which vehemently opposed the Valley's demand for secession.[5]

Rather, the alienation of ethnic communities and their resulting demands for self-determination are rooted in the organization of the modern nation-state, which revolves around the notion of a single, presumably unified, nation. This principle applied to a plural society governed through electoral democracy is inherently problematic because the "single nation" tends to be identified with the dominant majority. Since the state is the sole repository of political power, that power is exercised by the "majority," leaving the minority communities feeling alienated and marginalized. They therefore try to create alternative sovereign spaces outside the existing state boundaries where they can exercise political power. But without questioning the logic and character of the nation-state, they merely reproduce the hierarchical social and political conditions they sought to escape, giving rise to more demands for secession by smaller minorities and thereby compounding rather than resolving the problem.

The population of Jammu and Kashmir became alienated when interventionist and centralized state structures appropriated its autonomous status. Yet in fighting against those integrative pressures, Kashmiris replicated unitary power structures and thus alienated the people of Jammu and Ladakh. The Kashmiri idea of self-determination in a multiethnic, multireligious, and multilingual society was to call for a plebiscite, as mandated by UN resolutions of 1949, but this is not the approach other communities would take, such as Dogras, Kashmiri Pandits, Gujjars, Bakkarwals, and Ladakhi Buddhists. Although it is essential to understand why Kashmiri Muslims became alienated from the Indian state (see chapters 2 and 5), one should not lose sight of the political aspirations of other communities as well. They had a great deal to do with the failure of the Kashmiris' secessionist agenda in the 1950s and the 1990s and are a critical factor in shaping the future peace process.

Kashmiris began pressing for the right to self-determination even before India's partition, under the authoritarian regime of Maharaja Hari Singh. This marked the first of three phases in the evolution of Kashmir's political character.

First Phase: Masses versus the Maharaja

Kashmiris, led by Sheikh Abdullah, first demanded the right to self-determination in 1945, at which time the National Conference called for basic political rights and a responsible and representative government, as proclaimed in the National Demand of 1938. A vision of how the political and economic systems of Jammu and Kashmir state might be restructured was then formulated in the Naya Kashmir manifesto of 1944. The British decided, however, to vest the state's right to join an independent India or Pakistan's constituent assembly in the princes, with the result that the National Conference abandoned the path of constitutional reform and launched the Quit Kashmir movement, seeking an end to Dogra rule. Reflecting the spirit of the time, Sheikh Abdullah argued that all men and women have a fundamental right

> to live and act as free beings, to make laws and fashion their political, social and economic fabric, so that they may advance the cause of human freedom and progress. . . . [This is] inherent and cannot be denied though [it] may be suppressed for a while. I hold that sovereignty resides in the people; all relationships—political, social, and economic—derive their authority from the collective will of the people. . . . Quit Kashmir is not a question of revolt. It is a matter of right. . . . We, the people of Kashmir, are determined to mould our own destiny.[6]

As a first step, the National Conference demanded that the Treaty of Amritsar, signed in 1846 making Kashmir part of a princely state, be repudiated and that Jammu and Kashmir be given independent sovereign status. This marked a shift from "political" to "territorial" connotations for "self-determination" that became even more pronounced following a raiders' attack and resulting division of the state. Attention then turned from developments within the state to the bilateral arena.

Another important early development was that at its birth in 1939, the National Conference had reached out to all the subjects of Jammu and Kashmir irrespective of their caste, creed, belief, and region in the state. That all-inclusive approach received its first blow in 1941, when the National Conference split and the Muslim Conference was revived. At the same time, regional political alignments cutting across the boundaries of Kashmiri and Muslim affiliations and territorially dividing Kashmir Valley from the Jammu region began to emerge because the political base of National Conference leaders became divided along these lines. Sheikh Abdullah was popular in the Valley, while Chowdhary Ghulam Abbas held sway in the Jammu region. As each attempted to assert his supremacy within the party organization, the two clashed, splitting the party ranks accordingly and eventually causing the National Conference to break up.

The Muslim Conference broke up in much the same way, in this case owing to serious differences between Chowdhary Ghulam Abbas and Chowdhary Hamidullah as well as Mirwaiz Yusuf Shah. Their differences also related to language and religion.[7] Muslims in the Jammu region were mostly Punjabi-speaking and felt closer to Punjabi Muslims than to the Kashmiri-speaking Muslims of the Valley. But the Kashmiri leadership under Sheikh Abdullah had severed its links with the Punjabi Muslims in the aftermath of the 1931 agitation. Moreover, Kashmiris followed an eclectic form of Sufi Islam, whereas the people in Jammu and Poonch were traditional Sunnis. Numerically, the strength of Jammu Muslims came close to that of Kashmiri Muslims.

The implications of the regional fault line in Kashmiri politics did not escape Sheikh Abdullah. Though a secular leader, he recognized that, politically, Kashmiri Muslims remained his primary constituency. Yet at the outset the Kashmiri identity had been built around its *secular* character, including all communities—Muslim, Hindu, and Sikh—and a wider *regional* dimension incorporating *all state subjects* in Jammu and Kashmir. With the gradual loss of support of the Jammu Muslims, Sheikh Abdullah began articulating Kashmiri identity in a *cultural* sense, arguing that the people's right to self-determination in Indian states had a *cultural base.* He therefore sought to have the *cultural*, sociological, and psychological identity of people in the Indian states recognized and their right to frame measures concerning their *autonomous social, cultural, and political identities* entered into the Union of India's constitution. In Kashmir, he explained, the National Conference had accepted the principle of self-determination not only in respect of creed but also within the framework of *culture*, emphasizing the unique and distinct nature of *Kashmiriyat,* which distinguished Kashmiris from people in other regions of the state.

However, the cultural, linguistic, and regional diversity at the local level was sacrificed on the altar of partition, which was anchored in the two-nation theory. Once communal parameters became entrenched in defining the Kashmir conflict, the right to self-determination turned into a plebiscite issue, carried all the way to the United Nations, with attention focused on the timing, conditions, and modalities of holding the plebiscite.[8] At home, attention was riveted on the emerging political relationship between Srinagar and New Delhi. This was a game of high political stakes, so there was little interest in the smaller stories unfolding within Jammu and Kashmir. When Jawaharlal Nehru withdrew the plebiscite offer, however, and sought closer federal integration of the state, fissures began to develop not only between Kashmiris and India but also between the Valley and Jammu and Ladakh.

Second Phase: Growing Schisms and Shrinking Social Base

Sheikh Abdullah's decision to support Maharaja Hari Singh's accession to India was a matter of political conviction. As argued in chapter 2, the leaders of the National Conference believed that Kashmir's political autonomy would be better protected in a secular and democratic Indian state. Since they differed in their conceptions of "autonomous status," however, Sheikh Abdullah revived the debate on the right of self-determination, now incorporating in the concept the state's right to secede: "Under the provisions of international agreement, we can sever our relations with India even today, if we wish to do so. This right is given to our state and not to others."[9] This not only brought him in collision with the Indian state but it also laid bare the simmering regional divisions within Jammu and Kashmir. There was a clear structural problem. The National Conference had sought the status of an autonomous republic in the Indian union to safeguard and nurture the interests of the Kashmiris. But reversing the logic in Jammu and Kashmir, Kashmiris—the majority community—were reluctant to share political power with Jammu and Ladakh.

Iniquitous Division of Power

The Constituent Assembly (dominated by the National Conference) had created a unitary state with a clear concentration of powers in the Valley through disproportionate representation in both the Constituent Assembly and the state assembly. With 45 percent of the state's total population and a land area of 26,293 square kilometers, Jammu was substantially larger than the Valley, which covered 15,853 square kilometers. Yet Jammu had only thirty-two members in the state Legislative Assembly compared with forty-four for the Valley. Also, the Valley returned one member for 73,000 inhabitants, whereas Jammu returned one for 90,000. In parliamentary elections, Jammu returned one member for 1.4 million people compared with one member for 1 million people in the Valley. Ladakh's 95,876 square kilometers constituted 60 percent of the state's area, but with only 2.27 percent of the population and two seats in the state assembly.

Constitutionally and politically, the state had no system of checks and balances. Sheikh Abdullah had painstakingly built a "monolith structure" in a "one-party state," apparently because the people of Kashmir wanted "one organization (the National Conference), one leader (Sheikh Abdullah) and one programme (*Naya* Kashmir)."[10] Parliamentary democracy, resting on the principle of majority rule, was transformed into "Kashmiri rule": Sheikh Abdullah's five-member cabinet had only one representative from Jammu and none from Ladakh. In the first elections for the Constituent Assembly in 1951, forty-five of the forty-nine opposition candidates of the Praja Parishad were rejected on flimsy technical grounds, thereby subverting the democratic process and denying Jammu a voice in shaping the future political system.

Sheikh Abdullah, keen to empower the majority community of Kashmiri Muslims, gave them the jobs and land they had long been "denied," thereby indicating acceptance of the "legitimacy of communal claims."[11] This obfuscated Jammu and Ladakh's regional representation in the civil service because the majority of Hindus in the state government were Kashmiri Pandits. In the struggle between Kashmiri Muslims and Pandits over government jobs, the claims and needs of Dogras, Gujjars, Ladakhi Buddhists, and Ladakhi Muslims were largely ignored.

In a revolutionary program of land reform, the National Conference transferred 800,000 acres of land to 247,000 tillers without any compensation to the owners. Although this program was intended to correct a historical wrong against the peasantry, it was criticized on communal grounds because most landlords in Jammu were Hindus. Since land in Ladakh was the property of the monasteries, the reforms were perceived as an attack on the Buddhist clergy. The program also contained economic reforms, such as the nationalization of the transport industry and state control of trade, but these measures were said to cripple the non-Muslims. These unitary state structures and parochial policies of the National Conference government favored the Valley in political, economic, and administrative matters, leaving Jammu and Ladakh feeling neglected and marginalized, and prepared to seek separation from the Valley.

Jammu and Ladakh: Seeking Separation from the Valley

In Jammu, the exodus of Muslim Conference cadres and the deportation of key leaders after the raiders' attack had left a political vacuum. It was filled by the

Praja Parishad, a party founded by Balraj Madhok on the local organizational base of the Rashtriya Swayamsevak Sangh (RSS). Strongly influenced by Hindu nationalism, the party accused Sheikh Abdullah of trying to Islamicize the administration, especially since he had broken up the Hindu-majority district of Udhampur and was opposed to the rehabilitation of Hindu and Sikh refugees. To add to Jammu concerns, Urdu had become compulsory and the Sanskrit Research Department closed down. Most important, political initiative and power had slipped out of Dogra hands, and it was felt that "agrarian reforms would fundamentally alter the pattern of social organization of the state to their disadvantage."[12] The political tribulations and economic plight of the Jammu Hindus was attributed entirely to the Kashmiri Muslim leaders of the National Conference, particularly Sheikh Abdullah.

The Praja Parishad sought to end Kashmiri domination over Jammu by demanding complete integration of Jammu and Kashmir into the Union of India, which would transfer power from the Valley-based government to the central government. In 1952 it began agitating for changes to this end with the support of the Bharatiya Jan Sangh, the Hindu Mahasabha, the Ram Rajya Parishad, the Punjab Arya Samaj, and some Akali leaders. The Parishad's program called for the abrogation of Article 370, full integration of the state into the Union of India, full application of the Indian constitution, removal of the present distinction between "state subjects" and Indian citizens, complete jurisdiction of the Supreme Court, removal of customs barriers between Kashmir and India, fresh elections to the Kashmir Constituent Assembly, and investigation of corruption in the state administration by an impartial tribunal. It questioned Sheikh Abdullah's motives by pointing to inconsistencies in his logic: "If Sheikh Abdullah hated the Two-Nation theory, and his principles were the same as those of the Indian polity, then where was the ground for not accepting a full accession? Where was the need for a state constitution as distinct from a national constitution?"[13] Jammu reverberated with the popular slogan, "Ek desh mein do vidhan, do nishan, do pardhan, nahin chalega, nahin chalega" (In one country, two constitutions, two flags and two chiefs will not work; will not be tolerated). The urban population of Jammu city, especially its students, was effectively mobilized.

Stressing the unity of the Indian nation, Jan Sangh leader Syama Prasad Mookerjee accused Abdullah of "consciously or unconsciously, . . . creating a new sovereignty for Jammu and Kashmir" and of dangerously "developing a three-nation theory, the third being the Kashmiri nation," after India had already been "torn into two by the two-nation theory."[14] That was indeed the nub of the problem. Sheikh Abdullah was trying to create a Kashmiri *nation*, but its increasingly narrow boundaries could not politically accommodate the people of Jammu and Ladakh, who demanded *their* own right to self-determination.

The Praja Parishad failed to develop into a mass movement, however, owing to its limited social base, especially in rural areas, where the National Conference had already introduced beneficial land reforms for the peasantry. It drew support mainly from Hindu landlords, *jagirdars*, and *sahukars* (money lenders) who had enjoyed a privileged position under the maharaja's rule. By focusing on Hindu-Muslim issues, the Parishad also failed to win over Jammu Muslims who did not support the National Conference but were not in favor of the communal agenda either. It also neglected the small but influential Hindu minority of Kashmiri Pandits in the Valley and the Ladakhi Buddhists who shared its antipathy for Sheikh Abdullah.

Ladakh was equally unhappy and insecure about the transfer of power from the maharaja to a Kashmiri administration. Although Shia Muslims dominated the Kargil tehsil, originally part of Baltistan, Ladakh had a Buddhist-majority population that did not identify with the Kashmiris and felt alienated by the iniquitous power structure and partisan policies of Abdullah's government. Ladakh was particularly anxious to protect its distinct religion and culture. Its *gompas,* or Buddhist temples—which were its life and soul and in need of restoration—had received no financial aid under these policies. Nor were any funds available for rehabilitating the Buddhist refugees of the Zanskar area.[15] The studied indifference of the state government in transferring Zanskar to Leh tehsil was in marked contrast to its willingness to grant Doda the status of a separate Muslim-majority district in the Jammu region. People also resented the Abdullah government's decision to impose Urdu in Ladakhi schools and to discontinue scholarships for children of backward areas and grants-in-aid provided under the Dogra regime for three primary schools run by Shias, Sunnis, and Buddhists. Furthermore, no allocation was made in the first budget for Ladakh's development, which was not mentioned "even once."[16] The region had, in fact, no separate plan until 1961.

Neglected and marginalized within the state structures, the Ladakhi Buddhists felt they needed to make an independent decision about their political future and thus projected themselves as a "separate nation by all the tests—race, language, religion and culture—determining a nationality."[17] They emphasized historical links with the Dogras of Jammu rather than with the Kashmiri Muslims, arguing that the Treaty of Amritsar transferring the maharaja's power was valid for Kashmir Valley alone. Ladakh's relationship with the Dogras was governed by an earlier and separate treaty (resulting from the War of 1834) in which the Valley did not figure. Furthermore, the ties that bound the Ladakhis to the Dogras were now broken, so there was no longer any constitutional link beween the Ladakhis and the state, and they were morally and juridically free to choose their course independent of the rest of the state.[18]

A memorandum submitted to Prime Minister Nehru on May 4, 1949, by Cheewang Rigzin, president of the Ladakh Buddhist Association (LBA), pleaded that Ladakh not be bound by the decision of a plebiscite should the Muslim majority of the state decide in favor of Pakistan. The people sought to be governed directly by the government of India, or to be amalgamated with the Hindu-majority parts of Jammu to form a separate province, or to join East Punjab. Otherwise, they might well consider reuniting with Tibet. In 1952 Kushak Bakula sought federal status for Ladakh, so that Ladakh would bear essentially the same relationship to Jammu and Kashmir state as Kashmir to India, and the local legislature would be the only authority to make laws for Ladakh.[19] Even National Conference members in Jammu and Ladakh sought internal autonomy from Kashmir Valley. Balraj Puri of Jammu submitted an individual memorandum to Nehru in 1950 demanding internal autonomy and devolution of powers to smaller regions. At the same time, the Praja Parishad agreed to call off its agitation provided the principle of autonomy was applied to Jammu and Ladakh.[20]

Initially, Sheikh Abdullah and Nehru agreed to a state constitution granting limited regional autonomy to Jammu and Ladakh. The Basic Principles Committee of the Constituent Assembly was entrusted with working out the details, and a plan was prepared to establish five autonomous regions: Kashmir Valley, Jammu, Gilgit, Ladakh, and a region comprising the districts of Mirpur, Rajouri, Poonch, and Muzaffarabad.[21] However, the plan was soon abandoned. Sheikh Abdullah was not prepared to concede to Jammu and Ladakh those very rights and privileges that he himself had demanded from the Indian state, which were not to be interpreted as a step toward separatism but as a "mutual accommodation of each other's viewpoint":

> After all in a democratic country, the ultimate factor which decided the relationship between various units is the measure of willingness of each of these parts to come closer to each other for the common good of all. History has taught us that false notions of uniformity and conformity have often led to disastrous consequences in the lives of many nations.[22]

When Jammu and Ladakh argued that their status as a federating unit of Jammu and Kashmir state would be a healthy unifying force among different peoples of the state, Abdullah backtracked. He called the Praja Parishad agitation a reactionary and communal revolt by a handful of feudal landlords and parasitic classes and refused to accede to the Ladakhi Buddhists' demand for a central administrator. Prime Minister Nehru appreciated the legitimate grievances of the people in Jammu and Ladakh but subordinated their political aspirations to fighting an older and larger political battle, in which India's secular nationalism was pitted against Pakistan's two-nation theory. He castigated the narrow communal approach of the Praja Parishad movement, fearing that it would undermine Sheikh Abdullah's position, and persuaded the Ladakhi Buddhist leadership not to press its demands because any constitutional or administrative action might weaken India's stand on Kashmir in the UN Security Council.

Problems persisted, however, because Sheikh Abdullah's social support was shrinking. For the first time since 1947, he began differentiating between the "Muslims and non-Muslims of the state":

> It is the Muslims who have to decide accession with India and not the non-Muslims as the latter have no place in Pakistan and because their only choice is India. . . . My main concern and effort has not been to convince the Hindus and Sikhs that their future lay in India but the Muslims who form the majority. It was Muslims who were forced to ponder whether they could rely on the Indian promises and stay within the Indian Union.[23]

His conception of the Kashmiri identity had changed from "the people of Jammu and Kashmir state" to mainly the "Kashmiri Muslims." If the Valley was made a separate state, Sheikh Abdullah was prepared to let go of Jammu and Ladakh. He declared: "If the people sincerely desire to separate and establish a separate *Dogra Desh*, I would say with full authority *on behalf of the Kashmiris* that they would not at all mind this separation."[24]

In a parallel and somewhat mutually influencing process, Jammu and Ladakh sought to break away from what they perceived as Kashmiri rule. They did not identify with the Kashmiri identity or share the state's vision of internal power-sharing structures and relationship with the Indian state. An independent Kashmir dominated by the Kashmiri Muslim majority would have little political space for them. In demanding their right to self-determination, they sought separation from Kashmir Valley and integration with the Indian union. The Praja Parishad approved a plan to partition Jammu and Kashmir state through a regional plebiscite. In Ladakh, Kushak Bakula threatened obliquely that the "longing for a political union with Tibet would become pronounced if Ladakh's entity within India was not respected."[25]

In the end, Kashmiris did not achieve independence; and Jammu and Ladakh did not attain internal political autonomy from the Valley or a complete merger with the Indian union. The principal reason was the fragmented Kashmiri identity, which was due to the plurality of society in Jammu and Kashmir and the resulting internal contradictions in the Kashmiri thesis. The Kashmiris' notion of self-determination was to seek separation from the Indian state, whereas that of Jammu and Ladakh was to seek full merger with the Indian state. If the right of self-determination were granted to both, they checkmated each other. Even Kashmiri Muslims were no longer a cohesive political force. The National Conference party and government were divided deeply on the issue of accession. One group, led by Mirza Afzal Beg and backed by Sheikh Abdullah, insisted that the constitutional relationship with India should not go beyond the Instrument of Accession. The second group, led by Ghulam Mohammad Bakshi and including G. L. Dogra, D. P. Dhar, and Ghulam Mohammad Sadiq, preferred a more comprehensive relationship with the Indian union.[26] Nehru backed the latter, and on August 8, 1953, Sheikh Abdullah was dismissed and subsequently arrested. Thereafter Jammu and Ladakh's demands lost their momentum.

The basic political equations have not changed much since then. In an interesting parallel, much as successive regimes in Srinagar refused to concede political autonomy to Jammu and Ladakh regions, Kashmir's own autonomy was consistently eroded by the central government. And the rapprochement between Sheikh Abdullah and the central government was also accompanied and backed by reconciliation between Jammu and Ladakh regions and the state. At the All-Kashmir State People's Convention in 1968, a more understanding Sheikh Abdullah admitted that "it was fear and suspicions of one region regarding the other which apparently prompted Jammu to opt for merger with India against Kashmiris wanting to join Pakistan" and assured that their regional interests would be safeguarded.[27] The convention had proposed a five-tier constitutional setup of the state with regional autonomy and further devolution of political power to districts, blocks, and *panchayats*. After coming to power, however, Abdullah reneged on creating federal structures and reorganizing the constitutional setup of the state, nor was he willing to share political power by allowing regional autonomy. Political forces in the state were once again divided along regional lines. By the late 1980s, history seemed to be repeating itself, with the forces of separatism again stirring in Jammu and Ladakh and those of secession in the Valley.

Third Phase: Kashmiri Insurgency and
Separatist Agendas of Jammu and Ladakh

The winter of 1989–90 marked the onset of the Kashmiri insurgency, the details of which are discussed in chapter 5, while the Ladakhi Buddhists began their violent agitation for status as a union territory in August 1989. The next few years witnessed a growing communalization of the political idiom, strategies, and goals of various political movements in the state. Where the Kashmiris cast their demand for secession in terms of a Hindu-Muslim divide, especially after the Pandit exodus in 1990, the Buddhists mobilized against the Kashmiris on the basis of a Buddhist-Muslim divide, which they also extended to the Shias of Leh, who are almost all of Balti stock and ethnically similar to Ladakhi Buddhists.

Significantly, the seeds of communalization were planted in the late 1960s when leaders in the Valley sought to undercut the political base of groups demanding regional autonomy by creating alternative political alignments along communal lines. The Congress Party, under Kushak Bakula, had been agitating for the restoration of a direct central administration in Ladakh.[28] To scuttle this movement, Chief Minister Ghulam Mohammad Sadiq promoted a new leadership of lamas by favoring Kushak Thiksey over Kushak Bakula, and at the same time favored the Muslim leadership of Kargil over the Buddhist leadership of Leh.[29] Annoyed by some communal incidents in 1969 and fearful of being relegated to a minority within Ladakh, the Buddhist Action Committee decided to demand the status of a Scheduled Tribe. It also asked that Tibetan refugees be settled in Ladakh, the Bodhi language be made a compulsory subject up to high school, and that Ladakh's political representative be a full-fledged cabinet minister. Apart from the induction of Sonam Wangyal in the cabinet, most of these demands were rejected by the state government on account of strong opposition from the Muslim Action Committee, which feared that such changes would upset the ethnic balance in the region. As a result, the Muslims of Kargil, who were predominantly Shia, began to see their interests inextricably linked to those of Kashmir, even though the vast majority of its Muslims were Sunnis. Sheikh Abdullah's decision to divide Ladakh into two districts in 1979—Leh and Kargil—created yet another communal fault line in Ladakh, between its Buddhist and Muslim identity. This became much more pronounced during the agitation in 1989.

Ladakh: Demand for Union Territory Status

The trouble began with a minor scuffle between a Buddhist and some Muslim youth in Leh market in July 1989, which then snowballed into a violent separatist struggle by the Ladakh Buddhist Association. Its members demanded that Ladakh be given separate constitutional status as a union territory, accusing the "Kashmiri Sunni Muslims" of inciting the local Argon Muslims, who were decidedly in the minority, to "dictate terms" to the Buddhist majority and thereby dominate both the administration and economy. Buddhists also complained that the rich Bodhi language was being suppressed in favor of Urdu, now being imposed on Ladakhi children.[30]

Ladakhis leveled an assortment of other complaints against the Kashmiri Muslims and the Kashmiri-dominated bureaucracy: they were accused of halting development contracts for the construction of buildings, roads, and bridges; of orchestrating the gross underrepresentation of Buddhists in the state services (of the state's 2,900 government employees, only 2 were Ladakhis);[31] and of adopting unrealistic norms for the allocation of plan funds to Ladakh. Between 1987 and 1989, for instance, the state government had received more than Rs 100 crore from the prime minister's Special Assistance Fund, but Leh got only Rs 21 lakh. Under the Jawahar Rozgar Yojna, the Valley was given Rs 7.2 crore, while Leh was given only Rs 20 lakh.[32] More significantly, the systematic dismantling of important forums for Ladakh development (such as the Ladakh Affairs Department), the absence of Ladakhi representatives in Farooq Abdullah's coalition government, and the fact that Buddhists were given only one of Ladakh's four seats in the state assembly reinforced their belief that the Valley was still treating Ladakh "as a colony."

COMMUNALIZATION OF POLITICAL STRATEGY. The Buddhist agitators called for a boycott of the Kashmiri Muslims. Valley traders soon vanished from the Leh market, and their hotels and restaurants were shut down. The machinery of government became paralyzed as Kashmiri officials fled the areas of Leh, Khalsi, Nubra, and Zanskar. Denouncing "Kashmir's imperialism" and "hegemonism," LBA activists called on the local population to "free Ladakh from Kashmir." The LBA president asserted that "the Kashmiri rulers have been systematically eroding the Buddhists' ethnic and cultural identity for the last forty-two years and it can be saved only by making Ladakh a union territory."[33] The social boycott against Kashmiri Muslims was soon extended to the local Muslims, rupturing the centuries-old bonds of amity.[34] For the next three years, the Buddhists avoided Muslim-populated areas and did not enter hotels, restaurants, or shops run by Muslims. Farmers were prohibited from exchanging tools. No interreligious marriages were allowed, and meetings among relatives of different faiths were stopped.

The new generation of Buddhist leaders was playing the same old communal game that Valley-based Kashmiris had instigated to break the unity of the Ladakhi front and scuttle its hopes for regional autonomy by fostering communal consciousness. The aim in this instance was not only to send a message to Ladakh's Muslim minority but also "to gain the ear of the central government."[35] As LBA leader Rigzin Zora admitted, it was "an exercise in arm-twisting . . . [and] was crude, uncivilised and unbecoming of us."[36] Nonetheless, many felt it *necessary* to drive the point home that the local minority (Muslims) should not bank upon the state majority (Sunni Muslims) to dictate terms to the local majority (Buddhists): "It taught them (the Muslims) a lesson as they had allowed themselves to be instigated by forces in the Valley," was the common refrain.

In another tactical move, the LBA sought to build bridges with Hindu nationalist forces in order to win central sympathy for its demands. The Bharatiya Janata Party (BJP) obliged by repeatedly writing to then prime minister Narasimha Rao raising Ladakhi concerns in Parliament.[37] In March 1990, BJP member Ashwini Kumar and others helped organize a national convention on the issue of Ladakhi demands. Five months later, an LBA delegation participated in a BJP convention for the first time, at which Atal Bihari Vajpayee supported the Ladakhis' demand for union territory status after forty-three years of being "denied their constitutional rights." LBA president Thupstan Chhewang urged that the BJP and LBA unite, "for our sufferings are common."[38]

Changing the Goalpost: Demand for an Autonomous Hill Council. Following tripartite talks between New Delhi, Srinagar, and LBA leaders in October 1989, the LBA agreed to a compromise: it would withdraw the demand for union territory status in return for the establishment of an Autonomous Hill Council, along the lines of the Darjeeling Gorkha Hill Council. This arrangement would still provide a mechanism for self-governance by granting Ladakh autonomy in local administration, economy, and planning. However, with a change in the regime at the center, the proposal was shelved until 1991, when the Congress Party returned to power. Now the central government impressed the LBA leadership with the importance of secularizing its political demands and lifting the social boycott of Muslims, which ended in 1992 following talks between the LBA and the Ladakh Muslim Association (LMA). The Buddhists relented because they needed the LMA's support, and the latter acquiesced after the Buddhists agreed that "concessions to Ladakhis should not be given in the name of a communal body."[39] With the formation of a Joint Coordination

Committee drawn from all of the area's communities—Buddhist, Shia and Sunni Muslim, and Christian—the demand for a Hill Council earned support of all the people of Leh. Interestingly, the LBA and the BJP then began drifting apart, partly because the LBA could not join hands with the LMA and simultaneously pursue a communalist stance with the forces of Hindutva, and partly because the center's willingness to establish the Hill Council had reduced the need for opposition pressure on the government.[40]

For their part, Kashmiri leaders strongly opposed the Hill Council and succeeded in deferring its implementation. The center backtracked to avoid "rubbing the Kashmiri leadership on the wrong side" and jeopardizing efforts to restore normalcy in the Valley. Yet it had been precisely this kind of Valley-centric thinking that had alienated the people of Ladakh and Jammu, who believed that the center belittled and disregarded their political aspirations because they had not challenged India's political and security interests or "resorted to the gun" against the state. Although LBA leaders were at pains to explain that they believed in peaceful coexistence and did not approve of violence, they felt they were being forced "to lose our identity and fight for our dues."[41] Angered by the frequent deferments of establishing the Hill Council, Ladakh youth began agitating again in April 1995. P. V. Narasimha Rao's government finally relented, and the Ladakh Autonomous Hill Council Act was enacted on May 9, 1995, providing an autonomous council each for Leh and Kargil, and an interdistrict council to advise them on matters of common interest.[42]

Kargil Muslims were skeptical, however. For one thing, they believed that Buddhist-majority Leh would continue to overshadow Kargil's identity. Earlier, they had strongly objected to the Leh-centric conception of the Ladakh region, which until the 1980s had made Leh the site of all the district headquarters and central government offices. Yet administrators there had done nothing to remedy Kargil's backwardness, lack of an airport, or policies that discriminated against it.[43] In addition, the political equation in Kargil was clearly the reverse of that in Leh. Kargil's inhabitants did not wish to antagonize the Kashmiri leadership, although they did not support the secessionist movement in the Valley. Most of Kargil's leaders across the political spectrum supported the idea of the Hill Council in principle, but they postponed a final decision until the turmoil in the Valley was resolved.

WORKING OF THE AUTONOMOUS HILL COUNCIL. The Hill Council was envisaged as a dynamic instrument for empowering the Ladakhi Buddhist community and for deciding their local development priorities. Some of its functions were to allot, use, and occupy land vested in it; formulate and review the budget and development programs for the district as well as guidelines for implementing schemes at the grassroots level; promote the languages and culture of the area; manage undemarcated forests, canals, or watercourses for agriculture; develop desert areas; plan, promote, and develop tourism; oversee vocational training; and preserve the environment and ecology of the area. The council has extensive rights to levy and collect local taxes and fees of different kinds, including those on grazing, business, transport, entertainment, temporary occupation of village sites, and roads.

After a decade of operation, however, the Hill Council has failed to adequately address local issues. Many elected councilors have found that "their de-facto powers are limited by the state government's attempts to sabotage their work."[44] Soon after the first Ladakh Hill Council started functioning, the National Conference government led by Farooq Abdullah—who had bitterly opposed the council concept—had come to power in Srinagar. It resorted to stonewalling tactics in approving the budget or releasing funds that, in view of the short working season in Ladakh, often made it impossible to implement local projects. All major projects, especially those for generating hydroelectric power, still had to be cleared by the state government, which often did not come through. Moreover, the Hill Council was merely another addition to an already crowded field of political-administrative bodies "characterized by fragmented and overlapping competences among agencies whose agendas and interests vary profoundly."[45] Furthermore, the chief executive councilor who runs the Hill Council on a day-to-day basis often clashes with those higher on the administrative ladder. To complicate matters, a parallel series of constituencies and local bodies with development planning powers already exist under the Panchayati Raj system. Hence administrative powers are dispersed among the Hill Council and other governmental agencies, such as the Desert Development Agency, which commands a vast area classified as "wasteland" and plans development activities related to water management and land conservation. Some development schemes in the border area are also sponsored by the army. There has been no systematic attempt to coordinate the activities of all these groups, let alone the nongovernmental agencies such as the Students Educational and Cultural Movement of Ladakh.[46] It is little wonder that the hopes generated by the creation of the Autonomous Hill Council have been squandered.

REVIVAL OF THE DEMAND FOR UNION TERRITORY STATUS. With a hamstrung Hill Council, the Ladakhi Buddhist leadership kept toying with its original idea of gaining union territory status for Ladakh.[47] The LBA could see that the Regional Autonomy Committee exploring various options for the devolution of powers within the state was making no headway. It was also motivated by the state assembly's unanimous adoption of a resolution seeking restoration of Jammu and Kashmir's pre-1953 status.

In August 2002, Ladakh's Buddhist political leaders turned to a new strategy. Buddhist ministers in the state government and two members of the Legislative Assembly for Leh district resigned from their respective political parties. At the same time, all district units of political parties, including the Congress, the National Conference, and the BJP, were disbanded and reorganized under the umbrella of a Ladakh Union Territory Front (LUTF). Although the LUTF was instrumental in uniting Buddhist political leaders across the political spectrum, it also resurrected the old communal polarizations within and outside the region. Muslim leaders of Leh, for instance, had not been taken into LUTF confidence, though they were invited to join the movement. While stressing they did not unequivocally agree with the demand for union territory status, the local Muslim representatives did not contest the LUTF candidates. Both the LUTF candidates, Rigzin Zora and Sonam (Pinto) Norbu, were thus declared unopposed and elected in the 2002 assembly elections. Notably, this gesture was reciprocated soon after by the appointment of Muslim executive councilor Ghulam Abbas Abidi to the Hill Council.[48]

At the same time, the Shia Muslims of Leh remain wary about union territory status. Having organized themselves into a Ladakh Muslim Coordination Committee, they want wider consultation between all corners of Ladakh before putting forth a collective Ladakhi view on this issue. At the regional level, Kargil remains strongly opposed to the union territory demand. Instead, it accepted the proposal for a Kargil Autonomous Hill Council, whose first elections were held in July 2003. However, communal tensions between the two communities persist.[49] This became evident in a series of communal clashes that broke out in both Leh and Kargil districts in February 2006 over an alleged desecration of the Quran in the village of Bodh Kharbu.

At the national level, the LBA and the Sangh Parivar moved closer again, in part because of important instrumental benefits for both. In fact, the Sangh Parivar has taken a more active interest in Ladakh since 1997, as is evident from the growing presence of the RSS in the region and some major initiatives such as the Sindhu Darshan Abhiyan—a pilgrimage to the Indus River in Ladakh, which first took place in October 1997 and is now held annually from June 1 to 3. Since the Kargil conflict, it has been advertised as "a celebration of national unity and communal harmony and a movement to honour brave jawans (soldiers)."[50] In 1995, the RSS also established a local nongovernmental organization called the Ladakh Kalyan Sangh (LKS) in Hindi and Ladags Pandey Tshogspa in Ladakhi. It was dedicated to *"seva* (service), *sanskar* (values) and *ekta* (unity);' especially social work and education, although its real purpose, according to a local LKS leader, was to "stop the Muslims."[51] While the LUTF might be "willing to share a platform with the Sangh Parivar to promote its agenda for union territory status, the Hindutva's line—which considers Buddhism 'identical' with Hinduism or a mere subset of Hinduism—goes directly against the 'Buddhist pride' agenda promoted by the LBA and the Ladakh Gompa Association, which represents the interests of the monastic establishment."[52] That is probably why Hindutva is likely to have limited appeal in Ladakh.

CROSS-CUTTING POLITICAL AND ECONOMIC STAKES. Communal polarization within Ladakh has not been clear-cut. Local elites of the same community have also engaged in the struggle for political authority because of growing economic stakes. Leh has seen an influx of immigrants owing to its massive tourism earnings—the number of tourists has more than doubled since 1999—and huge flows of funds from military contracts. Because many of the immigrants are affluent Buddhists from the eastern agricultural regions of Leh, the district's Buddhists fear that they will gradually be marginalized. The rich Punjabi contractor class from the plains has also given them tough competition by bagging most of the megasize lucrative contracts.[53] On the political front, the LUTF claimed to speak for all of Ladakh's Buddhists until former LBA president Tsering Samphel broke ranks and announced the rebirth of the Ladakh unit of the Congress in December 2005. This decision betrayed Ladakh's unified fight for union territory status, split the LBA down the middle, and forced its executive out of office.

The stakes have changed in Kargil too. As in Leh, military contracts have given rise to a new contractor class, which finds religion useful to consolidate its influence. Competing with the traditional clerical class represented by the Islamia School is the Imam Khomeini Memorial Trust (IKMT), which is made up of the new trading and business elites.[54] Their political differences became evident in 2002 when the IKMT broke ranks with the Islamia School, which traditionally supports the National Conference, and backed an independent Lok Sabha candidate who had the support of the Congress. The IKMT's candidate lost, but the action heralded the end of a unitary, pro–National Conference Shia order. In December 2003, the Islamia School hit back by winning the first elections to the new Kargil Hill Council. Government legislation in December 2004 that gave voting rights to the four nominated members in the Hill Council was used to dethrone Qamar Ali Akhoon of the National Conference and put the Hill Council under the control of the IKMT-backed Congress leader Asghar Ali Karbalai. Note, too, that development funds now being handed over to the Kargil Hill Council have become a major means of patronage. If, as most people in the region expect, the Line of Control softens to enable trade with Gilgit and Baltistan, Kargil could witness an economic boom that will enable it to break its centuries-old economic dependence on both Leh and Srinagar.

JAMMU'S REGIONAL POLITICAL ASPIRATIONS

After suffering political and economic neglect at the hands of successive state governments, Jammu began making demands again as well. These ranged from a separate state of Jammu to regional autonomy and a regional council. Significantly, the proposals were all rooted in Jammu's regional aspirations, while the religious (Hindu) identity remained dormant.

The Jammu Mukhti Morcha (JMM), a new regional outfit, demanded that Jammu and Kashmir be divided, with one part becoming the separate state of Jammu. It was tired of seeing Valley-dominated state governments favoring Valley residents in state services. The ratio of Valley and Jammu employees in the state secretariat and regional services of Kashmir and Jammu was 99:8 and 99:1, respectively.[55] Although Jammu contributed more than 70 percent of the state's revenue, it received less than 30 percent of budgetary allocations for its development. Of the state's tourism budget, nearly 90 percent was spent on the Valley every year.[56] Among the state's large power projects, only one was installed in the Jammu region, at Chenani.[57] All professional and technical institutions were located in the Valley.[58] In addition, the Dogri language (spoken by fifty Lakh people) was excluded from the Eighth Schedule of the Indian Constitution, while Kashmiri (spoken by fewer than thirty Lakh people) enjoyed constitutional recognition.

For JMM activists, the only way to redress these political and economic regional imbalances and enable Jammu to meet its political aspirations was to make it a separate state.[59] Jammu, it was argued, is already a well-defined natural region, bounded by the Ravi in the south and Pir Panjal in the north and having a distinct cultural and historical identity. However, the JMM failed to mobilize mass support for this cause, in part because the organization is of recent origin and its founders, a group of intellectuals, have confined their activities mainly to processions, strikes, and memorandums to the state and central governments. Many in Jammu dubbed it a product of the central Home Ministry, which propped it up to counteract the Kashmiri demand for inde-

pendence.[60] Another group with thin support outside the intellectual community, the Jammu Autonomy Forum, sought a federal constitution to replace the
unitary setup and revive the old idea of devolving power at the district, block,
and panchayat levels, with safeguards for the ethnic communities in each
region. The JMM lost further support when in its new incarnation—as Jammu
State Morcha (JSM)—it joined hands with the RSS to contest the 2002 assembly elections. The alliance called for a tripartite division of the state into
Jammu, the Valley, and Ladakh and eventually received the support of the BJP
state unit, which had earlier recommended statutory regional councils and
statutory boards. However, its efforts to redress the political and regional
imbalances favoring the Valley at Jammu's cost took on communal overtones
and therefore failed to garner mass support. It did not win a single seat in the
2002 legislative assembly elections.

Although the people rejected the JSM-RSS agenda, these elections paved the
way for a fundamental change in the political equations for sharing power
between the Valley and the Jammu region. Unlike past elections, this one gave
no political party a sufficient number of Valley seats alone to form a government. Furthermore, no *one* political force could speak for the Valley. The
People's Democratic Party (PDP) won sixteen seats but only 25 percent of the
popular vote, compared with 15 percent for the Congress and 24.5 percent for
independents and others. The National Conference had won only two more
seats than the PDP but took 35 percent of the popular vote. With the rise of
truly competitive politics in the Kashmir Valley, no party could form a government without the cooperation of a partner from Jammu. The split in the ethnic
Kashmiri vote between the PDP and the National Conference had worked to
Jammu's advantage as it heralded the trend of coalition politics in the state,
which is characteristically better attuned to the democratic practices of power
sharing.

Though the Congress had won more seats than its alliance partner, the PDP
persuaded Congress's central leaders to allow Mufti Mohammed Sayeed to
occupy the chief minister's post. It argued that a state government led by the
Congress—"the representative of predatory Indian power"—would alienate
the ethnic Kashmiris, and that a regional party was better placed to mobilize
public opinion behind the peace process, which in turn would lead to significant elements of the Hizb-ul-Mujahideen and the Hurriyat Conference to
commit themselves to democratic politics.[61] Despite political pressure from
Congress members of the Legislative Assembly who in their election campaign
had vowed to install a chief minister from Jammu, their party president, Sonia
Gandhi, acceded to the PDP's demand to lead the coalition government.

Although the PDP supported a dialogue with the separatists and had formed tactical alliances with the local Hizb commanders, the latter refused to join the dialogue process. The PDP was also unable to persuade the Hurriyat to contest elections. Nonetheless, at the end of its tenure in 2005, the PDP again fell back on traditional logic, insisting that "an ethnic Kashmiri must be at the helm of power," especially because the ongoing peace process between New Delhi and Islamabad demanded continuity in Srinagar.

Interestingly, the central leadership of the Congress party appeared willing to give in to PDP's demand for an extension in office, but not its state unit. In deference to its primary constituency—that is, Valley-based ethnic Kashmiris—Sayeed's government had done little to address Jammu's demands for a devolution of power. Three more years of PDP rule would have meant political suicide for the state's Congress leaders, who, in an extraordinary rebellion, threatened to resign en masse, thereby forcing its central leadership to claim the office.[62] This not only changed the power relations between the center and state unit of the Congress Party, which refused to submit to Delhi's fiats, but also signaled a fundamental transformation in state politics by installing the first-ever chief minister from outside the Valley and giving Jammu its due in the political calculus of the state. Congress leader Ghulam Nabi Azad, though an ethnic Kashmiri, is from the Doda region of Jammu. Also, for the first time in the political history of Jammu and Kashmir, power has been decided by the balance of elected representation in the state and not by backroom machinations driven by the state's relationship with the Union of India.

Political Assertion of Subregional Identities

The diversity of Jammu and Kashmir's society extends to the grassroots level. This heterogeneity has given rise to several political alignments along linguistic, regional, religious, cultural, and caste lines, which have added new complexities to the state's political landscape.

POLITICIZATION OF KASHMIRI PANDITS

One such alignment has developed among the Kashmiri Pandits, a target of militant Islamists in the early 1990s, when the Jammu and Kashmir Liberation Front (JKLF) imposed an Islamic code of conduct on the Valley.[63] Cinemas, beauty salons, and shops selling liquor and videocassettes were closed, and Hindi movies banned. Muslim women were ordered to wear *burkas* and Hindu women to stop wearing a *bindi*. People in the transport business were no longer allowed to carry unveiled women in their vehicles, while tailors in Srinagar were warned against stitching any Western-style garments that departed from the traditional attire of Kashmiri women and were kept busy making burkas. The Jamaat-i-Islami, in particular, targeted the Pandits as "Kafirs—the Batta, (Infidels—the Pandit) the first symbol of India in Kashmir." A terror campaign was launched through letters, posters, and pamphlets covered with militant proclamations that an Islamic state was being established in Kashmir: "Yahan kya chalega?—Nizam-i-Mustafa" (What kind of law will prevail here?—The Islamic law). Specific warnings were directed at Pandits, "Zalimo, kafiro, Kashmir hamara chhor do" (Ye cruel infidels, vacate our Kashmir), and "Allah-o-Akbar, Mussalmano jago, kafiro bhago, jihad aa raha hai" (Arise and awake Muslims, buff off infidels, jihad is approaching). Ultimatums were issued from mosques, "Agar Kashmir mein rehna hoga, Allah Allah kahna hoga" (If you wish to continue living in Kashmir, you will have to pray to none other than Allah). And death threats appeared in newspapers warning Pandits to leave the Valley posthaste. In an atmosphere of fear and insecurity, the Pandits began a mass exodus in early 1990.[64] Subsequently, the Hizb-ul-Mujahideen and the Harkat-ul-Ansar foreclosed possibilities of their return.

Apart from a short and abortive attempt at leading the Roti agitation in the 1930s, the Pandits had traditionally integrated their linguistic and ethnic identity with that of being Kashmiris. But the exodus from the Valley, followed by a long spell of misery and suffering at migrant camps in Jammu, Delhi, and elsewhere, forced the Kashmiri Pandits to believe that their political interests were separate and different from those of the Kashmiri Muslims and to assert Kashmiri Pandit nationhood. The Kashmiri Pandits provide an important illustration of a community's attempts to reconstruct history in view of its present political interests. Describing themselves as the original inhabitants of the Valley with a distinct subculture of the purest class of Aryans, the Pandits recount episodes of religious, linguistic, and political persecution by Muslim rulers over the past 650 years.[65] Census figures are quoted to indicate that the community is facing virtual extinction: in 1947 the Pandits constituted 15 percent of the Valley's population, which fell to 5 percent by 1981, and after the exodus to 0.1 percent.[66] The Kashmiri freedom struggle in which Pandits fought alongside Muslims against the Dogra regime is forgotten, and the postindependence history is presented as a story of subjugation, denial, deprivation, and unequal opportunities in a state dominated by Kashmiri Muslims. Land reforms had sought to deprive the rural Pandits of landholdings. Others faced discrimination in employment, were denied promotions to higher cadres, were not admitted to professional institutions or universities, and were refused their fair share of financial resources for developmental plans and business ventures. Constitutional guarantees and service rules were allegedly subverted to benefit the Kashmiri Muslims, and quantity and mediocrity were given precedence over quality and academic merit.

According to one Kashmiri publication, Pandits were employed in less than 5 percent of the state services and less than 1 percent of the higher cadres of administration in the Valley, while Muslims monopolized 94 percent of the state services.[67] The problem is that Muslims voice similar complaints, and both sides quote figures selectively to suit their respective arguments. Kashmiri Muslims point to their negligible share in the central services while the Pandits harp on their poor representation in the state services.[68] Successive state governments were also accused of gerrymandering constituencies to deny the Pandits due representation in the state assembly. For instance, the Pandit-majority localities of Rainawari, Habbakadal, and Karan Nagar in Srinagar city were fragmented, reducing them to insignificant parts of the contiguous Muslim-dominated constituencies. Although three Kashmiri Hindus were returned to the assembly in 1957, 1962, and 1967, the number was restricted to only one member in 1972, 1977, 1983, 1987, and 1996.[69]

A new generation of Kashmiri Pandits formed Panun Kashmir (Our Kashmir) to campaign for a separate homeland in the Valley. The "Margdarshan" convention in 1991 adopted the group's homeland resolution, subsequently reaffirmed by 2,000 delegates from fourteen countries attending the World Kashmiri Pandit Conference in December 1993. It demanded

> the establishment of [a] homeland for Kashmiri Hindus in Kashmir Valley, comprising the regions of the valley to the East and North of river Jhelum (Vitasta); the Constitution of India be made applicable in letter and spirit in this homeland in order to ensure the right to life, liberty, freedom of expression, faith, equality and rule of law; their homeland be placed under Central Administration with a union territory status so that it evolves its own economic and political infrastructure; all the seven lakh Kashmiri Hindus, which includes those who have been driven out of Kashmir in the past and yearn to return to their homeland and those who were forced to leave on account of the terrorist violence in Kashmir, be settled in the homeland on equitable basis with dignity and honor.[70]

The proposed homeland area consists of 8,400 square kilometers in parts of Anantnag, Baramulla, Srinagar, and Pulwama districts. It constitutes 4 percent of the total area of Jammu and Kashmir state as it existed in August 1947. The Jhelum River divides the "homeland" from the rest of the Valley. Panun Kashmir vehemently objects to having the area described communally as a "Hindu

Homeland," instead calling it a "Homeland for internally displaced Kashmiris who have faced oppression for centuries. *These people mostly happen to be Hindus.*" It has sought to mobilize international support by projecting its plight as a "holocaust" or "genocide of an ethnic minority" and the movement as "a fight against human rights violations" because "it is their identity, ethos and heritage extending over the millennia that is now being obliterated by the terrorists armed and trained by Pakistan."[71] At home, Panun Kashmir has articulated its demands mainly through strikes, processions, and government petitions. It gains ready recruits from Pandit refugees who have found little solace elsewhere and also has some support from militant Hindu organizations in India, though it has eschewed violence thus far.[72]

Sixteen years of banishment from the Valley have left the Pandit community in disarray. They are deeply divided over basic issues such as whether Pandits want to "return" to the Valley, their number, and the best means to accomplish this objective. The urban, educated Pandits who found jobs and settled elsewhere are unlikely to return to the Valley. This is evident from the fact that despite the state government's legislation to check the distress sales of the Hindu properties, about 85 percent of such properties (including residential houses and agricultural and nonagricultural land) have been disposed of.[73] On the other hand, Pandits languishing in the migrant camps or those not willing to abandon their ancestral lands are keen to return, although precisely for that reason they do not support the idea of the homeland if they are required to abandon the rights and possession of self-cultivated land, homes, and shops in areas that do not fall within its territory. There are generational differences too. While the "older generation [is] pining to go back, the middle generation [is] lukewarm on the issue and youngsters loathe the idea of a native land that is alien to them."[74] The issue is further complicated by the dispute over the number of those displaced in the first place. While most Kashmiri organizations put this number anywhere between 300,000 and 400,000, the total number of registered migrant families is 53,538, of which 31,490 are living in the Jammu region, 19,338 in Delhi, and 2,710 in other parts of the country.[75] Many families are not registered, however, and are staying outside the camps on their own.

Since 1996 successive state governments have committed themselves to ensuring a secure and peaceful return of the Kashmiri Pandits and have announced several relief and rehabilitation packages from time to time.[76] According to Minister of State for Home Sri Jaiprakash Jaiswal, the center has given the state government a grant of 10 crores for the reconstruction and renovation of houses and shrines near Kheer Bhavani and Mattan, where the displaced Kashmiri migrants can be settled temporarily until such time as they can repair their own residences. Construction of 200 more such flats at Sheikhpora in Budgam has been sanctioned, for which the center has released Rs 16 crores thus far.[77] Even so, none of the registered migrant families have returned to the Valley. One problem is that despite a rare consensus among elected state representatives and the separatists (including Hurriyat) on the need to bring the Pandits back, these groups strongly differ on the strategies and specific measures required to secure this goal. Various organizations representative of Kashmiri Pandits are at odds over this issue as well.

Panun Kashmir opposes the very idea of a "phased" return, arguing that this would divide and fragment Kashmiri society. It insists that only the creation of a homeland will make a Pandit return possible. Some in the community think otherwise. The Hindu Welfare Society, for instance, seeks to consolidate the Kashmiri Pandits who have lived in the Valley throughout the insurgency period—estimated to number more than 8,000 families—by persuading them not to leave while asking the government to provide them security and jobs. The Kashmiri Pandit Sabha also believes that the Pandits staying in the Valley should form a nucleus, with a community of displaced Pandits built up around it. These organizations stress the need to quietly prepare the groundwork for their return as publicity of such proposals in the past has been followed by massacres: in March 1997, twenty-three Pandits were killed in Wandhama village (Ganderbal constituency), and in March 2003, twenty-four in Nadimarg village (Pulwama district). Such incidents trigger more migration, making it clear that governments alone cannot provide security to those who wish to return and that it is imperative to initiate a broadly based dialogue with the majority community for this purpose. Kashmiri Pandits, as part of the Kashmir Secular Alliance, discussed this issue with the moderate faction of the Hurriyat for the first time in July 2005. Among the separatists, Yasin Malik of JKLF and Shabir Shah of the Democratic Freedom Party had visited migrant camps in Jammu in the 1990s, while the Mirwaiz-led Hurriyat visited Jammu to meet the displaced Pandit community leaders for the first time in February 2006.[78] Unless various representatives of both communities join with the state government and make a collective effort to ensure the peaceful return and rehabilitation of the Pandit community, its chauvinistic elements may gain ground and in time press for Kashmiri Pandit nationhood.

JAMMU: GUJJARS, PAHARIS, DOGRAS

Gujjars make up the third-largest community in Jammu and Kashmir; they are partly nomadic and mostly Muslims. Their language, Gojri, was the second major language after Kashmiri in the state, though it is not recognized in the state constitution.[79] Gujjars constitute 9 percent of the state's population and are present in the entire state except in Leh and Kargil. Those in Kashmir are concentrated on the mountain slopes and in the valleys of Kukernag, Kangan, Tral, Doru, Pahalgam, Shopian, Kulgam, Handwara, Karnah, Kupwara, and Uri tehsils. In Jammu region, the Gujjars are dominant in the border districts of Rajouri and Poonch, particularly the tehsils of Haveli, Mendhar, Naushera, and Sunderbani. Pockets of Gujjars are also found in Bhaderwah, Doda, Gool, Kishtwar, Kathua, and Udhampur areas.[80]

The Gujjars first gained political prominence when Sheikh Abdullah tried to rope the Muslim-majority districts of Rajouri and Poonch and the Kashmiri-speaking Muslims of Doda into a "Greater Kashmir" in the late 1970s.[81] Indira Gandhi devised a new electoral arithmetic that calculated that the Dogras and Gujjars together outnumbered the Kashmiris, so the Gujjars were cultivated as a counterweight to the Kashmiri Muslims. Initially, the Gujjar identity was promoted through culture, music, literature, and art; on radio programs; and in the state's cultural academy.[82] In 1975 the government established a Gujjar and Bakkarwal Welfare Board, with funds for its welfare schemes earmarked in five-year plans. Education was promoted by opening mobile schools, offering scholarships, and building hostels in Rajouri and Poonch, all of which gave birth to a new literate stratum in Gujjar society. As a result, the Gujjar elite, formerly composed of authoritarian and feudal tribal chiefs and charismatic religious leaders (*pirs*), now includes the new educated members of the professional classes, such as civil servants, journalists, lawyers, and social workers.

Mrs. Gandhi's decision to grant scheduled tribe status to Ladakh prompted the Gujjars to demand the same. But successive central and state governments failed to follow up on their repeated promises until 1991. As a result, Gujjars are now entitled to representation in proportion to their population in the legislature, local self-governing institutions, government services, and professional and technical institutions.

Scheduled tribe status to the Gujjar community provided an impetus for the politicization of the Pahari-speaking people, who felt that the reservation of electoral constituencies for Gujjars would disenfranchise them because they would not be able to elect their own representatives to the Legislative Assembly. The Paharis inhabit the same areas along the Line of Control from Sunderbani up to Uri, Keran, Karnah, on the 500-kilometer-long border of Rajouri and Poonch districts in Jammu, and Baramulla and Kupwara in the Valley. They share the same occupations, customs, traditions, dress, and foods.

The Pahari language is thought to be an offshoot of the Indo-Aryan family of languages and its script is known as Shahmukhi, which is called Naskh in Urdu. Hindko, Kaghani, Karnahi, Pothohari, Hazarvi, Mirpuri, Chhibalvi, and Poonchi are various dialects of Pahari. Although the Paharis are similar to the Gujjars in terms of their social and economic backwardness, they take pains to point out that the Pahari-speaking people form a distinct linguistic, ethnic, and cultural entity.[83] The Pahari language, they also point out, is included in the Sixth Schedule of the state constitution. The articulation of the Pahari identity provides an important example of the "dormancy of religious identity" and "dominance of linguistic identity" as the Pahari Board constituted to formulate their demand for scheduled tribe status includes Rajput Muslims, Kashmiri Muslims, Sikhs, and Hindus of different castes.[84] While their demand for a Welfare Board was accepted in 1989, they have not yet attained scheduled tribe status.

During the Regional Autonomy Committee's deliberations, Pahari leaders proposed the creation of a new Pahari region, separating predominantly Muslim Rajouri-Poonch from Jammu division with an Autonomous Hill Council (AHC), on the pattern of Leh Autonomous Hill Council (see map 4-1).[85]

Pahari grievances touch on familiar subjects in the state: underdevelopment and social and economic backwardness of districts, and the dominance of Jammu district in the share of civil services, public sector undertakings, and important institutions.[86] Pahari leaders argue that with a distinct geography, history, language, culture, and socioeconomic conditions, the region is best suited to have its own Autonomous Hill Council. Another demand for an Autonomous Hill Council has been put forward for the Chenab Valley region, which consists of Doda district, Gool-Gulabgarh tehsil, Basantgarh of Udhampur district, and Lohai Malhar and Bani of Kathua district, along with a scheduled tribe status.[87]

The idea in this case is to divide Jammu and Kashmir state into its four natural regions: the submountainous and semimountainous tract or plane-kandi belt making up the whole of Jammu district, and the plane areas of Udhampur and Kathua districts; the Outer Hill Region, including the districts of Doda, Rajouri, Poonch, and the hilly areas of the districts of Udhampur and Kathua; the Jhelum Valley region (the entire Kashmir Valley); and the Tibetan and semi-Tibetan tracts, including Ladakh and Gilgit. It is argued that since the Chenab Valley region is a distinct and independent region with a rich cultural and historical heritage but is socially, economically, and politically backward, it needs a separate Autonomous Hill Council. Critics view the demands for councils by the Muslim-majority districts of Rajouri, Poonch, and Doda as part

Map 4-1. *Autonomous Hill Councils*

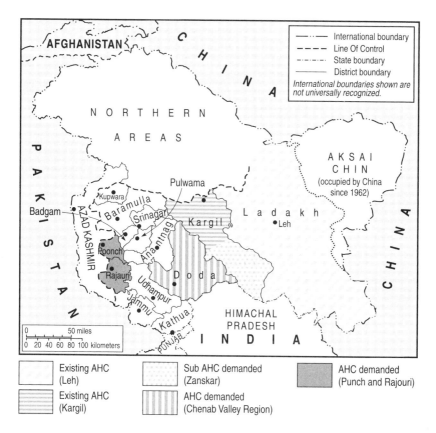

of a larger plan to break Jammu's plural identity and reinforce the communal fault line within the Jammu region.

These claims are in part driven by the desire to undermine the influence of the Gujjar and Bakkarwal leaders in the region, because the latter have traditionally backed the Congress Party. Perhaps that is why the Gujjars do not support the demand for an Autonomous Hill Council for Rajouri and Poonch. While the National Conference could not deliver on its promise of a Hill Council, the PDP sought to make inroads into this region by backing the Pahari demand for scheduled tribe status. However this, too, is unlikely to materialize because Paharis are not recognized as a tribe in the 1931 census of Jammu and Kashmir state; furthermore, they first need to be identified as "other backward castes."[88]

The Gujjars argue that if the Paharis are also given scheduled tribe status, their political advantage will be lost. The state's financial pie for scheduled tribes is not large. All the reserved categories together account for 10 percent of the state cadre. Leh and Kargil get 2 percent each. The Gujjars had been enjoying a 4.5 percent reservation channeled into technical institutions, recruitment, and promotion since 1982, which after April 1991, when they were declared a scheduled tribe, rose to 6 percent. If Paharis are also given scheduled tribe status, that 6 percent will have to be further divided.[89] Furthermore, the government has yet to follow through on its support for Gujjars in technical institutions, teachers' employment, and most important, electoral constituencies. Nonetheless, about 200,000 to 250,000 Gujjars scattered across almost every tehsil of the state know that they will play a key role in shaping the political power equations in the state. According to Mian Altaf, a Gujjar leader from the National Conference, "We can make and unmake governments and any party which fails to recognize this fact will pay the price."[90] By some estimates, Gujjar-Bakkarwal voters can tip the scales in up to a third of the state's eighty-seven assembly constituencies.

Yet another political movement is demanding that the Dogri language, recognized by the Sahitya Academy in 1961, be included in the Eighth Schedule of the Indian constitution. The Dogri Sanstha established in 1944 played an important role in preserving folk literature and Dogri miniature paintings, as well as in performing dramas and *mushairas*. The Dogri Sangarsh Morcha is supported by several literary, social, and cultural organizations.[91] In addition, Jammu's principal political parties have been articulating this demand through processions, demonstrations, and strikes. Despite state support of the Dogri case, it remains to be approved by the central government.

Ladakh: Buddhists and Shia Muslims

In Ladakh, Zanskar's minority Buddhist community of 18,000 feels neglected and discriminated against by Kargil's Muslim-majority administration. The long-standing demand for a monastery, serai, and cremation ground in Kargil town is cited as an example. Kargil leaders, on the other hand, were indignant when Zanskar asked for a separate subhill council at a time when they themselves had not accepted an Autonomous Hill Council for Kargil district. Echoing the LBA's arguments in Leh's context, they emphasized that the "minority [Buddhists] must live according to the [Muslim] majority's considerations and support Kargil's interests."[92] When Kargil accepted the Hill Council in 2003, Zanskar region was allocated three seats on the strength of its population in the district. However, the Zanskar Buddhist Association lobbied for ten seats on the grounds that the criteria for allocating seats should include not only population but also backwardness, topography (Zanskar is virtually inaccessible for nearly eight months a year), and other similar factors.[93] Their demand has not yet been met, however.

Instruments for Balancing Regional Interests

Although the goal of self-governance is equally cherished by all three constituent regions of the state, each sees the concept in a different light. Moreover, the state will be able to acquire more autonomy only if the Valley—the traditional seat of power—is willing to share it with the other regions. Over the past six decades, the state and central governments have developed several instruments for redressing the regional imbalances and debating the issues of regional autonomy.

Commissions of Inquiry

From time to time, the state government has appointed various commissions of inquiry to address these issues. Ghulam Mohammad Sadiq's government appointed the first such commission, headed by P. B. Gajendragadkar, to recommend measures for the equitable sharing of resources among the three regions. Its report acknowledged that the regional identities needed to be taken into account:

> Although the Jammu and Kashmir state has been a single political entity for over a hundred years, it cannot be denied that geographically, ethnically, culturally and historically, it is composed of three separate homogeneous regions, namely Jammu, Kashmir and Ladakh. . . . Even if all the matters were equitably settled . . . there would still be a measure of discontent unless the political aspirations of the different regions of the state were satisfied. In fact . . . the main cause of irritation and tensions is the feeling of political neglect and discrimination, real or imagined, from which certain regions of the state suffer.[94]

The commission recommended setting up statutory regional development boards for the three regions and drawing an equal number of cabinet ministers from Jammu and the Valley, with a full-fledged cabinet minister representing Ladakh and the deputy chief minister representing a different region. A chief minister could come from Kashmir Valley, but Jammu and Ladakh could earn the privilege only by electing the political party of Kashmir's chief minister.[95] After vacillating for a year, the state government appointed boards comprising civil servants and experts. Since these boards were neither statutory nor representative and never functioned, the entire exercise of the commission remained academic.

Sheikh Abdullah, after his release in 1968, debated some of these issues during the two All-Kashmir State People's Conventions—in October 1968 and June 1970—which he organized to ascertain the views of the people and political parties regarding Kashmir's federal relationship with the center as well as interregional relations in Jammu and Kashmir. Abdullah acknowledged that it was essential to give the three regions maximum autonomy to provide their diverse cultures, languages, and religions a sense of participation and belonging and to ensure their emotional integration. Keeping in view "the interests of all regions," the convention proposed to adopt a five-tier state structure under the constitution envisaging regional autonomy and further devolution of political power to districts, blocks, and panchayats. Releasing the constitutional document to the press, Abdullah admitted that "it was fear and suspicions of one region regarding the other which apparently prompted Jammu to opt for merger with India against Kashmiris wanting to join Pakistan" and assured that their regional interests would be safeguarded.[96]

After coming to power, however, he failed to create any of the promised federal structures or to reorganize the constitutional setup of the state, nor was he willing to share political power by introducing regional autonomy. The regions therefore continued to complain of their inadequate share in the state's development allocations. In December 1978, the All-Party Jammu Action Committee formed by the major political parties began agitating for statutory, political, and democratic setups at the regional, district, block, and panchayat level. Abdullah denounced the movement as one "directed against Kashmiris" and spurned any dialogue on the question of "regional imbalances."[97] The government dismissed demands for internal political autonomy on the pretext that the Gajendragadkar Commission had already rejected it, yet at the same time ignored the same commission's recommendation that each region's population, area, specific needs, and potential should be taken into account in determining its share of resources.

Eventually, the government agreed to appoint another commission, headed by Justice S. M. Sikri, to suggest measures for redressing regional imbalances in development allocations, government services, and admissions in professional institutions but declined to consider any constitutional changes to satisfy the political aspirations of the regions. One of the Sikri Commission's major recommendations was that a State Development Board be set up, consisting of the chief minister as chairman and some members of the Legislative Assembly. It devised a new formula for financial allocations to the regions based on their population, area, backwardness, and natural resources; urged the government not to reserve services on the basis of community, caste, or district; and recommended scrapping interviews in admissions to professional institutions. Like its precedessor, the Sikri Commission Report was never implemented.

THE REGIONAL AUTONOMY COMMITTEE

Nearly two decades later, in November 1996, Farooq Abdullah and his National Conference government set up the Regional Autonomy Committee (RAC) to reexamine the issue of interregional relations. In his campaign for the state assembly elections, Farooq had promised regional autonomy for Jammu and Ladakh and subautonomy for ethnic and religious groups in these regions. This appealed to the electorate in Jammu and Ladakh, which, for the first time in the state's postindependence history, overwhelmingly voted for the National Conference party, earning it a two-thirds majority in the assembly. Farooq, however, failed to reverse the historical trend of broken promises with regard to federalizing the state structures.

The entire RAC forum was flawed. It was not a truly representative body because all its members belonged to the National Conference.[98] Opposition leaders had no voice in redrawing the "rules of the game" for internal power sharing. If its objective was to ensure that the National Conference's demands for Kashmir's greater autonomy did not alienate the minorities, it had gone about it the wrong way. Except for Pinto Norbu, a Ladakhi Buddhist, and Mushtaq Bukhari, a Pahari, the most prominent minorities were not represented, including the Kashmiri Pandits, Gujjars, Dogras, and the Shia Muslims (of Kargil). The RAC report, released in April 1999, endorsed the idea of following communal fault lines by recommending that the state be reorganized into eight provinces (map 4-2). It emphasized the ethnocultural, religious, and linguistic homogeneity of Kashmir Valley, yet recommended that it be divided into three new provinces: Kamraz, made up of Baramulla and Kupwara districts; Nundabad, comprising Budgam and Srinagar districts; and Maraz, made up of Anantnag and Pulwama districts. It offered no reasons for the new arrangement, and its recommendations did not take into account the deep political differences between the Kashmiri Muslims and the Kashmiri Pandits. The committee simply disregarded the Pandits' demand for Panun Kashmir without offering an alternative strategy or framework for redressing their grievances and securing their social, cultural, economic, and political rights.

Map 4-2. *Reorganization along Communal Fault Lines as Proposed by the Regional Autonomy Committee Report, 1999*

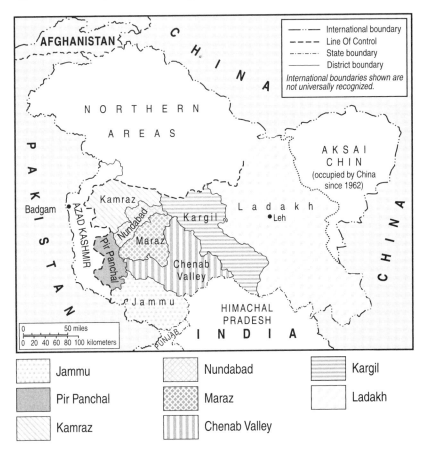

	Jammu		Nundabad		Kargil
	Pir Panchal		Maraz		Ladakh
	Kamraz		Chenab Valley		

The committee rightly questioned the administrative inclusion of Ladakh in the Kashmir region, but instead of rectifying this anomaly by granting Ladakh independent provincial status, it raised an "undisguised communal cleaver."[99] It recommended breaking up the mountainous region into two new provinces consisting of just one district each—predominantly Buddhist Leh and predominantly Muslim Kargil. Ladakh had already been divided into two districts (Leh and Kargil) by Sheikh Abdullah in 1979, a transfiguration that would serve only to sharpen communal and ethnic boundaries. The communal undercurrents of the committee's recommendations were further exposed in its proposed restructuring of the Jammu region into three provinces, along Hindu-Muslim lines. The district of Doda and the single Muslim-dominated

Map 4-3. *Religious Composition of the Proposed Reorganization of Jammu and Kashmir State*

Hindu-majority area   Muslim-majority area   Bhuddhist-majority area

tehsil of Mahore from the adjoining Hindu-majority district of Udhampur would form a new Chenab Valley province. The largely Hindu districts of Jammu, Kathua, and Udhampur would make up Jammu Province. Poonch and Rajouri districts would form the Pir Panjal Province. There was an uncanny resemblance to Sheikh Abdullah's original concept of a "Greater Kashmir," as a comparison of the present and proposed regional setup makes clear. Currently, Kashmir Valley is the only Muslim-majority region with a prominent, albeit small, minority of Kashmiri Pandits; Jammu has a Hindu-majority populace with a substantial Muslim minority; and in Ladakh, the Buddhists outnumber the Muslims (map 4-3). Under the new dispensation, six out of eight provinces (Maraz, Kamraz, Nundabad, Chenab Valley, Pir Panjal, and Kargil) would have a Muslim majority. Apparently, the committee sought to protect only the "Muslim interests" to the total exclusion of other ethnocultural, ethnolinguistic, and ethnoreligious minorities. While it was ready to lean backwards to accept the demand of Jammu region's Muslim minority for separate provincial status, it did not even mention the demand of the Hindu minority in the Valley—Kashmiri Pandits—for a Panun Kashmir, as mentioned earlier. Nor did it take notice of the Zanskar Buddhists' long-standing demand for these areas to be brought under Leh's administration. Likewise, it glossed over the fact that Doda district had a significant Hindu minority alongside its Muslim (58 percent) majority and made no provision for safeguarding the minority's political interests.

These recommendations were far removed from reality because there are no monolithic political groupings of Hindus and Muslims in the Jammu region. Their political affiliations cut across ethnic (Dogra Muslims, Kashmiri Muslims, Gujjars, and Bakkarwals), linguistic (Paharis, Gujjars, Kashmiri, and Dogri), and caste lines, as well as regions. The Jammu Muslims, for example, are in a minority in the Jammu region but form a majority in Poonch, Rajouri, and Doda districts. They do not support the BJP's Hindu politics and a separate state of Jammu, nor are they willing to be assimilated completely into the Kashmiri Muslim identity. At the same time, they do not form a separate and cohesive political group, partly because since the pre-partition leadership of Chowdhary Ghulam Abbas and Allah Rakha Sagar, no political leader has emerged to mobilize them as an independent political force in state politics.

Thus any attempt to superimpose communal boundaries is not only divisive but also bound to fail for two reasons. First, these are political problems and sharpening the communal boundaries will simply not resolve them. For example, the Paharis are spread from Basoli in Kathua to Rajouri and Poonch, on one side, and to Uri and Keran in the Valley. Why, then, does their demand for a Pahari region along the Line of Control exclude areas in the Valley? Also, if the demand is driven by the lack of economic development, one must recognize that the predominantly Hindu hill areas south of the Chenab, in Kathua, have done no better than Rajouri and Poonch. The solution lies in providing a responsive government, rather than in sharpening the communal boundaries. Second, political mobilization along communal lines is bound to limit the social base of the political groups making these demands on the state. And, as argued earlier, without a base of mass support, they are not likely to secure their political demands.

THE ROUNDTABLE CONFERENCES

In February 2006, Manmohan Singh's United Progressive Alliance (UPA) government invited the whole spectrum of political parties, separatist leaders, and political groups for a roundtable conference to collectively deliberate the state's political future. The second roundtable was held at Srinagar in May 2006. This exercise is historically significant for two reasons. First, it directly grapples with the fundamental Kashmir puzzle: that is, who speaks for the people of Jammu and Kashmir? In a significant departure from past practices of negotiating all accords such as the Delhi Agreement (1952) and the Kashmir Accord (1974) with the political leadership of the majority community—the Kashmiri Muslims—which reached decisions *on behalf of* the entire state's populace, New Delhi has, for the first time, provided a political platform where *all* the regions as well as ethnoreligious and linguistic communities can *have a direct say* in the negotiating process. Interestingly, the Valley leadership, the separatists as well as the mainstream political parties, have yet to come to terms with this reality, as is evident from their trenchant criticism of the center's decision to invite seventy-five political parties and groups for the first roundtable and less than half that number to the second conference. While the Hurriyat leader Mirwaiz Umar Farooq characterized it as a "crowded . . . seminar," PDP president Mehbooba Mufti argued that the participants should be exclusive to main significant political parties rather than a huge crowd.[100]

Through the roundtable process, the prime minister has also sought to rejuvenate democratic practices in the state by forswearing the center's personality-driven policy framework of Kashmir. From Sheikh Abdullah onward, "New Delhi saw the leadership of Jammu and Kashmir as corporeal hosts of the State's accession to India."[101] Jammu and Kashmir's future in the Indian union was seen as deriving legitimacy from the influence of often-authoritarian ethnic Kashmiri leaders, rather than from democratic institutions and processes. By entrusting the responsibility of comprehensively reshaping the future contours of the state structures and institutions, including its federal relationships, to the *entire* amalgam of its elected representatives, the UPA government is set to traverse a different path, which can potentially transform the ways political accountability has been understood and practiced in Jammu and Kashmir. Unlike past dialogues, in which a dominant political party in Srinagar only had to get Delhi "on its side," the roundtable process requires local players to "listen to each other," engage in coalition-building by reconciling their divergent interests and perspectives on a whole gamut of issues, and, most important, holds them accountable to their electorate for their stand on these issues as well as their performance in office. The working groups established during the second roundtable conference, for instance, will force the National Conference and the PDP to spell out and reconcile their differing notions of autonomy and self-rule. This exercise would become even more complex if the separatists were to join the roundtable process. Meanwhile, all the roundtable participants have to collectively ponder over the steps needed to persuade the separatists to come on board and at the same time debate the ramifications of their persistent refusal to do so. All parties will also have to reach a common understanding on the kind of relationship they envisage with the other part of Kashmir across the Line of Control and what structures or mechanisms need to be established for that purpose.

Second, the roundtable breaks new ground in establishing an integral linkage between federalizing the state structures at the center-state and the intrastate levels. The historical record shows that Srinagar always got away with not devolving to Jammu and Ladakh the extraordinary political powers it sought from New Delhi precisely because the two sets of processes have been traditionally de-linked. The state's special status enshrined in Article 370 of the Indian constitution stands in stark contrast to the unitary character of its internal structures outlined in the state constitution. The next critical milestone—the Kashmir Accord—was also conspicuously silent on federalizing its intrastate structures and exclusively addressed Kashmir's relationship with the Indian state. That is probably why Sheikh Abdullah could easily backtrack on the commitments he had made regarding the reorganization of the constitutional setup of the state, as discussed earlier. His successor, Farooq Abdullah, was no different, as became evident from the National Conference government's decision to unanimously pass the resolution seeking restoration of the pre-1952 status based on the State Autonomy Committee's recommendations while those of the Regional Autonomy Committee remained on paper. By concurrently addressing the federal relationships at the center-state and intrastate levels, the roundtable process is perhaps best placed to persuade the Valley leaders to rethink their political and constitutional equations with Jammu and Ladakh, as indeed with other minority communities in the state.

This also suggests the center needs to assume a new mantle in reshaping the interregional relationships within Jammu and Kashmir. In the past, central governments shied away from supporting Jammu and Ladakh's pleas for regional autonomy or even sacrificed their claims on the altar of India's "national interests," which they mistakenly believed could only be protected by *siding with* the majority community of Kashmiri Muslims. While New Delhi did not hesitate to dismiss several state governments in the same "national interest," it never criticized Srinagar for consistently failing to keep its promises on power sharing with Jammu and Ladakh. Through the roundtable conference, however, the UPA government is proactively nudging various local stakeholders into collectively exploring ways to bring the different regions in the state together, while recognizing their distinct identities. To this end, the working groups will have to debate and recommend the best instruments— regional councils for Jammu, the Valley, and Ladakh or district councils or a stronger panchayati raj system at the village levels. They must also consider how best to address the ethnoreligious mobilizations seeking a separate home- land for Pandits, a separate Jammu state, union territory status for Ladakh, or Autonomous Councils for other subregions in the state.

The roundtable is undoubtedly a valuable exercise, although it is too early to predict the outcome of its deliberations. Its fundamentals are in the right place, and it appears to be learning from its own experiences. The lack of a spe- cific and focused agenda in the first roundtable was, for instance, rectified in the second conference, which established five working groups to discuss vari- ous complex issues more systematically (box 4-1).

The UPA government also made an earnest attempt to bring the separatists on board, especially the moderate faction of the Hurriyat, by meeting all its prior conditions: namely, that the process include only major parties, that it be preceded by separate negotiations with the prime minister, and that the formal invitation be delivered by the government itself rather than the covert ser- vices.[102] Each of the demands was met. The Hurriyat, however, still chose to stay away.

This shows that the roundtable process faces some formidable challenges. First, it needs to address separatist concerns and, as argued earlier, reckon with the possibility that these groups may not join this process at all. The UPA gov- ernment may find it increasingly difficult to continue a separate high-level dialogue with the Hurriyat without compromising the legitimacy of the roundtable process. The challenge is to consider their viewpoints in working out a blueprint of the state's political future without allowing Hurriyat a veto over the whole process. A second serious snag is that New Delhi has no clear overall plan in mind for Kashmir. Beyond espousing the general maxim that maximum political autonomy must be conceded to Jammu and Kashmir, the UPA government, like the NDA government that preceded it, has yet to spell out precisely what political and constitutional concessions it is willing to offer to strike a new political deal with the people of the state. The third and perhaps most difficult task is to reverse the increasing and deepening communalization of Jammu and Kashmir's polity and society. The whole spectrum of develop- ments in the arena of high politics—Islamization of the *azadi* plank; religious cleansing of the Valley, resulting from the eviction of the Pandit community;

Box 4-1. *Working Groups Established by the Second Roundtable Conference in May 2006*

Group 1: Confidence-Building Measures across Segments of Society in the State

The group will evolve measures to improve the condition of people affected by militancy; schemes to rehabilitate all orphans and widows affected by militancy; issues relating to the relaxation of conditions for persons who have forsworn militancy; an effective rehabilitation policy, including employment for Kashmiri Pandit migrants; consideration of issues relating to the return of Kashmiri youth from areas controlled by Pakistan; and measures to protect and preserve the unique cultural and religious heritage of the state.

Group 2: Strengthening Relations across the Line of Control

The group will recommend measures to simplify procedures to facilitate travel across the Line of Control; increase goods traffic; expand people-to-people contact, including the promotion of pilgrimage and group tourism; and open up new routes such as Kargil-Skardu, among others.

Group 3: Economic Development

The group will develop a strategy that ensures balanced economic development and employment generation and balanced regional and subregional development within the state.

Group 4: Ensuring Good Governance

The group will consider effective measures to increase responsiveness, accountability, and transparency of the administration; strengthen local self-governance; effectively monitor development programs; institute zero tolerance for human rights violations; strengthen the right to information; provide adequate security to all segments of society, particularly the minority communities.

Group 5: Strengthening Relations between the State and the Center

The group will deliberate matters relating to the special status of Jammu and Kashmir within the Indian Union; methods of strengthening democracy, secularism, and the rule of law in the state; as well as effective devolution of power among different regions to meet regional, subregional, and ethnic aspirations.

militants' inroads into the Muslim-dominated districts of the Jammu region and the series of Hindu massacres; the RAC's proposed internal restructuring of the state into eight provinces, carved along a Hindu-Muslim axis; the PDP's flirtation with the Islamic symbols during the 2006 assembly by-elections; the changing political alignments, particularly the coming together of the LUTF, Panun Kashmir, and JSM, backed by the RSS and the VHP—all point in the same direction and, with dire forebodings.

It is important to keep in mind that political mobilization in the state has taken place along religious, ethnic, linguistic, and regional lines. To recognize or superimpose only the communal fault line is both a flawed and potentially dangerous approach. It would not only strengthen the divisive forces within the state but would also legitimize the changing relationships forced on the communities—the Muslims and Pandits of Kashmir, Buddhists and Shia Muslims of Ladakh; and Hindus and Muslims in Doda district—at the household, *mohalla,* and village levels—and in the long term may lead Pakistan to renew its claim on Kashmir on the grounds of the two-nation theory. Prime Minister Singh has committed the roundtable process to two important principles: self-rule and regional federalism. Its litmus test would be to realize these political goals *without* privileging or rewarding communally organized political mobilizations in the state.

Conclusion

The deeply plural character of the Jammu and Kashmir polity makes it imperative to devise instruments and processes for restructuring the rules of the game so as to ensure that power sharing is inclusive. This is necessary not only for reasons of equity and legitimacy but also to "make it work" in the long term. To judge by the historical record, no movement in the state has succeeded in achieving its objectives unless it was inclusive in its political character and social base and unless it represented the political interests of *all* groups, as distinct from those in the *majority.* This explains the failure of the Kashmiris' secessionist agenda in the 1950s as well as the 1990s. They demanded the right to self-determination in the name of "the people of Jammu and Kashmir" but campaigned on behalf of only the majority community: Kashmiri Muslims. The minority social groups, in fact, sought autonomy from the Kashmir Valley. The collective and consistent opposition of the state's linguistic, regional, and religious minorities checkmated the Kashmiri Muslims' demand for secession. Likewise, the most important reason for the failure of Jammu's political demands—ranging from regional political autonomy and a regional council to a separate state—has been the lack of mass support in the region. The Ladakhi Buddhists have not succeeded in securing union territory status for Ladakh because the idea is bitterly opposed by the Kargil Muslims, who make up nearly half of Ladakh's population. The alternative political goal of an Autonomous Hill Council was achieved only after they persuaded Ladakhi Muslims to support their demand. The story of the Kashmiri Pandits is no different. This shows that Kashmir's "self-rule" or autonomy from New Delhi will be acceptable to different cross sections of society only if it is viewed as part of a broader process of devolving power to the regions.

CHAPTER FIVE

AZADI TO JIHAD:
THE DOOMED INSURGENCY

THE KASHMIRI INSURGENCY OF 1989–90 transformed the dynamics of the Kashmir conflict, infusing it with a greater degree of militancy and compounding its complexity. Initially, the insurgency was an indigenous underground movement of young people calling themselves the Jammu and Kashmir Liberation Front (JKLF) before developing into a mass movement for azadi (independence). In its second phase, the uprising split along two lines, one pressing for secession and the other for accession to Pakistan. It was then appropriated by a much smaller, well-armed, well-trained, and committed group of militants—mostly non-Kashmiri—who added a new dimension to the Kashmir problem, turning it into a jihad.

In all three phases, there was a "marked ideological continuity of thought and practice" among the militant groups, from the JKLF and Hizb-ul-Mujahideen to Lashkar-e-Taiba and Jaish-i-Mohammed.[1] The discussion of each phase focuses on the main trends, but the dominant voice must not be misconstrued to mean the *only* voice.

The Liberation Struggle: An Underground Campaign

The Kashmiri youth who spearheaded the secessionist movement were nationalists at heart. There is almost no documented information on their precise socioeconomic composition, but various accounts point to a reservoir of educated, unemployed youth, largely of the petty bourgeoisie comprising artisans, orchard-owners, and small businessmen who had not been affected by the 1950s land reforms.[2] Significantly, this generation was already removed from the struggle for independence that preceded partition, so the solidarity between Kashmiri and Indian values of that period seemed to have faded from

memory. Instead, they were caught up in the heady sweep of contemporary lib-
eration activities, including the dismantling of the Berlin Wall, overthrow of
Romania's tyrannical rule, and alluring calls for freedom among the Central
Asian republics nearer home. The average Kashmiri was very conscious of the
"malleability of borders" and the birth of new nations taking place all around.
Two other critical factors were the growing influence of Jamaat-i-Islami's ideology in the Valley and the resurgence of transnational Islam in the wake of the
Iranian revolution, the Palestinian intifada, and the mujahideens' success in
driving the Soviet Union out of Afghanistan.[3]

Although their understanding of Kashmiri nationhood and the right of
self-determination was more or less in keeping with Sheikh Abdullah's traditions, these young upstarts denounced his legacy for having surrendered the
plebiscite demand for the prize of power in 1975.[4] They also adopted radically
different means to achieve their political objectives. Sheikh Abdullah had
fought his battles through political and constitutional avenues. Even the independence option was floated before the Drafting Committee of the
Constituent Assembly of Jammu and Kashmir state in 1952. The JKLF, on the
other hand, charged that the state's political institutions—controlled by New
Delhi—were the very ones responsible for stifling Kashmir's popular aspirations. Force was therefore necessary to de-legitimize each of these political
institutions, halt all political activities, paralyze the state apparatus, and thereby
transfer people's allegiance and loyalty to themselves.

Every opportunity was seized to meet these objectives. Violent demonstrations erupted over issues ranging from a hike in the power tariff to the
publication of Salman Rushdie's *Satanic Verses*. A systematic campaign was
launched in 1988–89 to replace state-sponsored events with an alternative cal-
endar of public events. *Bandhs* (shutdown strikes) were organized on Indian
Independence Day and Republic Day, and a "civil curfew" (as opposed to a
government-ordered one) was imposed with a ceremonial burning of the
Indian flag, while Pakistan's Independence Day was celebrated with fanfare.
Accession Day, October 27, was denounced as the "day of occupation," and
Nehru's birthday, November 14, was observed as a *yome-i-siaht* (black day).
The young secessionists took pains to commemorate the death of JKLF
founder Maqbool Bhatt, while remembering Sheikh Abdullah's death as a
yome-i-nijat (day of deliverance). In a symbolic gesture, signs bearing the
name "India" were removed from establishments such as the State Bank of
India, Air India, Indian Oil, Bharat Petroleum, and Indian insurance companies. People were ordered to transfer money from Indian banks to the Jammu
and Kashmir Bank. The militants' writ ran large: even public offices tacitly

followed their order to observe Friday instead of Sunday as a holiday, and almost everyone, including the state-owned Srinagar Corporation, complied with its curfews and blackouts.

The militants also made a concerted attempt to monopolize the instruments of violence by attacking police stations in Srinagar with impunity and killing police officers in a particularly barbaric manner.[5] These killings played havoc with the morale of the police force. Its members now became stigmatized as "traitors," were ostracized by society, and forsaken by their senior officers, who did not mourn their colleagues' deaths or accord them any state honor. Attacks on the Central Reserve Police Force and on intelligence officials followed in quick succession.[6] The militants were clearly targeting the institutions responsible for the state's internal security.

With political institutions unable to function, all political activities came to a halt. Militants selectively killed prominent workers of the National Conference, the only pro-Indian force in the Kashmir Valley. They issued an open ultimatum to its local cadre in August 1989, demanding that it publicly dissociate itself from the party. The response was so great that an organized declaration to this effect appeared in the Kashmir daily *Aftab*. Other parties such as the Congress and the Muslim United Front (MUF) became rife with internal dissension and their politicians increasingly disillusioned: "We are not relevant at all. No one talks to us. No one listens to us. You are all up against an idea, which is supported by the gun and believed by the people."[7]

When the militants called for a boycott of the Lok Sabha by-elections in November 1989, a large number of polling officers (about 5,000 according to one estimate) refused to perform their duties, and government school buildings used as polling stations were set on fire. A "civil curfew" was imposed on polling day and a coffin placed outside the polling booth in Baramulla, with a placard stating, "It is for the first man who casts his vote." The administration did nothing. Official estimates of the voting level in Anantnag and Baramulla were 5.11 and 5.47 percent, respectively, while the local media put it at 2 percent. In some polling booths, no votes were cast. Having discredited the political parties and nullified the electoral process, the militants were now on the center-stage of state politics.

Valley Kashmiris took pride in the militants' exploits because the "boys" had somehow restored Kashmir's pride: "People have realized that the secular, nationalist parties are all lies. They are not in power to help the *quam* (community) or *awaam* (people); they are here only for self-aggrandizement and for power." By contrast, the insurgents "were prepared to die for Kashmir," as they demonstrated from the outset with their well-planned strategy.[8] At this point, another player appeared in the wings. Although Kashmiri separatism began as an internal impulse, Pakistan was quick to capitalize on the situation. It did so by playing the "Kashmiri card," as distinct from the "Muslim" or "Islamic card," to show its empathy for the militants. Opinions differ, however, regarding the timing of Pakistan's organizational and armed support to militants. According to Hasim Qureshi, a JKLF leader, they were approached by Pakistani military representatives as early as 1984 with an offer to help prepare for the new phase of "Kashmir's liberation." Amanullah Khan, the JKLF's chief, has indicated that the JKLF "started political planning in 1986 and continued till the end of 1987," and operations began in July 1988 with some boys originally from Kashmir Valley trained in Azad Kashmir "actually fighting" and "training others."[9] Some considered Pakistan an ally, while some saw Azad Kashmir as an extension of their homeland.[10]

Otherwise, there is little information about the inflow of arms and trained youth from across the border. The capture of the first Kalashnikov in the Valley met with a sense of disbelief, as the state floundered to organize a response.[11] Its weak political or administrative leadership helped the militants consolidate their position. When the besieged government of Farooq Abdullah decided to release JKLF militants in exchange for the kidnapped daughter of Union Home Minister Mufti Mohammed Sayeed in December 1989, there was a mass upsurge. The streets of Srinagar were filled with victory processions of jubilant crowds demanding "azadi."

Cry for Azadi: The Mass Movement

With Farooq Abdullah's resignation and Governor Shri Jagmohan's attempts at suppression, as discussed in chapter 2, the movement exploded. The governor's massive crackdown and the Gawkadal incident, in which a large number of unarmed civilians including women and children were killed, transformed the underground militant siege into a popular mass movement.[12] Kalashnikovs replaced black flags and the "boys" became "mujahideen" overnight. Processions became commonplace in the Valley, each joined by several thousands of people demanding azadi, marking the total collapse of state authority.

With the JKLF at the forefront, other militant groups were soon joining in the activities, among them the Allah Tigers, People's League, and Hizb-i-Islamia. Ashfaq Majid Wani, Hamid Sheikh, Yasin Malik, and Javed Mir led the JKLF in the Valley, while Amanullah Khan, its chairman, was based at Muzaffarabad. They jointly devised the military strategy. Azad Kashmir supplied weapons, operated training camps, and provided sanctuary. Amanullah Khan and Javed Mir openly admitted smuggling weapons across the Line of Control to militant ranks in the Valley.[13] Sardar Abdul Qayum, president of Azad Kashmir, described it as the "base camp of the Kashmiri freedom struggle."[14]

Militant operations in the Valley were confined largely to urban areas. A favorite tactic was to shoot security personnel in crowded areas, provoking retaliation and the killing of innocent civilians. Every new "martyr" merited a *namaz-e-janaza* (funeral prayer) from the *mohalla* (colony) mosque, which inevitably led to more shootings, more martyrs, and more mobs, all feeding a vicious circle. Beyond holding security forces at ransom, however, the militants had no long-term strategy to force the Indian state to withdraw from Kashmir. The success of their strategy in paralyzing the administration throughout 1988–89 depended on the fact that the state was unable to mount an effective response. A naive belief that "the Indian state had lost the will to govern" strengthened the hope that once the "uprising" started, Pakistan would invade India to secure Kashmir's liberation.[15] Both were grave miscalculations. Pakistan did not attack, and India did not hand over azadi on a platter. Once the Indian state unleashed its iron fist, the militants, bereft of an effective counterstrategy, were no match for India's massive military power. The real threat to the Indian state emanated not from the militancy but from the mass processions symbolizing complete rejection of state authority. It would be charitable to characterize the mass rallies as a product of the militants' strategy. They were more in the nature of spontaneous outbursts. In fact, militants themselves were overwhelmed by the massive response and were unable to purposefully and effectively harness it for achieving azadi.

That support, the JKLF found, existed in every quarter of the Valley: among intellectuals, trade unionists, peasants, students, and even government employees.[16] Some sections of the Mirpur district of Azad Kashmir, as explained in chapter 6, were also keen supporters of an independent Kashmir. The movement did not even need a charismatic leader to fire people's imagination, "only a spark to ignite their reaction"—Jagmohan easily fulfilled that function.[17] His policy of inflicting "collective punishment on a disloyal population," as discussed in Chapter 2, provided the spark that turned the populace against India and the most apolitical Kashmiris into active supporters of militancy.[18]

Kashmiris devised new social norms and sanctions for justifying political violence. A concerted effort was made to jettison the image of a docile and smiling Kashmiri who had always feared authority with a new valorous one who was not afraid of making the supreme sacrifice of his life. The people marching in the mass processions set the pace. A young man on Srinagar's streets observed: "Everyone here is prepared to die. We have only two choices, to die or to be liberated." The popular slogan "Jo kare Khuda ka khauf, Utha le Kalashnikov" (All God-fearing men should pick up the gun) reflected the Kashmiri mood. Having a mujahid in the family became a status symbol. Families and peer groups competed for the chance to cross the border for arms training. Women and children often provided human shields for armed militants. Children carried placards saying "Indian Dogs Go Home" or "Mujahideen Qaum Zindabad." A new vocabulary of violence depicted militants as "freedom fighters" and security personnel as "occupation forces." Curfews were described as "martial law," and *kabar-i-shaheed* (martyrs' graveyards) became "places of pilgrimage."[19]

Contemporary political practices were applied to justify the Kashmiris' use of violence. State violence provided an easy justification, especially since Kashmiris did not have a history of valiantly resisting hordes of foreign rulers. Nor did traditions and folklore have a reservoir of stories eulogizing heroic conquests and victories against the enemy. When the "Kashmiri" component of the past did not help, many also looked to Islam for a new rationale. Islam's sanction of violence was used to defend the Kashmiri political and militant struggle for "justice." "Jihad" (holy war) did not figure in the militants' political vocabulary, although they had begun referring to themselves as mujahideen.

While the Hizb-ul-Mujahideen is generally credited with injecting Islamic formulations into the movement, the JKLF was already using such themes in its mobilization strategies and public discourse. Its organizational resources were used by the Jamaat-i-Islami cadre, and in turn, the former used the Friday *namaz* (prayer congregation) at the Jama Masjid to mobilize public support.[20] Popular slogans such as "Azadi ka matlab kya, La Illahililillah" (Freedom means the rule of Islamic law) and "Hum kya chahte hain—Nizam-i-Mustafa" (What do we want—Islamic law) used Islam and independence interchangeably. In its official manifesto, the JKLF demanded that Jammu and Kashmir, as it existed before 1947, should be united as "one fully independent and truly democratic state" and advocated equal political, economic, religious, and social rights for all citizens irrespective of race, religion, culture, and sex.[21] However, it had a distinct Islamic flavor in seeking to establish a system of *Islamic democracy,* safeguarding the rights of minorities as prescribed in the Quran and Sunna, and an economy of *Islamic socialism.* In fact, "the practice of the JKLF's politics through the late 1980s and early 1990s was at a considerable distance from its stated [secular] position."[22] JKLF was the main force behind the expulsion of the minority Pandit community, with many of its cadre implicated in the brutal killings of Kashmiri Pandits. This dealt a serious blow to the secular fabric of the Kashmiri identity.[23] The Hizb-ul-Mujahideen carried this agenda of creating a communal divide to other parts of the state, especially the Muslim-majority areas of the Jammu region.

Changing Gears: Liberation to Accession with Pakistan

In mid-1990 the JKLF began losing its power, partly because its top leaders had been killed or imprisoned and partly because it was becoming marginalized by its patron, Pakistan. Where Pakistan was concerned, the "Kashmiri card" had served its purpose and, if allowed to reach its logical conclusion, might back-fire, especially since the JKLF's goal was "independence and re-unification of the divided Kashmir and *not* accession to Pakistan." Consequently, Pakistan decided to "curb the *independence* sentiment" in the Valley (see chapter 3). Thus several pro-Pakistan outfits were raised as rivals to the JKLF, first under Benazir Bhutto and then during Nawaz Sharif's regime.[24] My own interactions with the Valley-based leadership of the JKLF between 1995 and 1997 confirm this point.

Between 1990 and 1993, an assortment of groups mushroomed in the Valley.[25] Most were splinter organizations "based in particular localities, enrolling few followers and habitually moving in and out of alliances and mergers with other groups."[26] They included Ansaullah Jammu and Kashmir, Muslim Janbaaz Force, Harkat-ul-Islam, Yalgar-i-Haidar, Al Madad, Shaheed Farooq Islamic Tigers, Shaheed-e-Farooq Force, Al Barque, Kashmir Freedom Movement, Harkat-ul-Jehad Islami, and Lashkar-i-Mujahideen. The most important new player was the Hizb-ul-Mujahideen (Army of the Holy Warriors), which emerged as Pakistan's favorite protégé, on which it lavished funds, arms, and recruits. At that point, however, the youth's allegiance to any particular group did not matter. The only goal in focus was *"Jao Hind"* (to get rid of Indian rule), by any means necessary and under whatever ideologies might serve to ride the mass movement. Later, tactical considerations became paramount. Several members of the Hizb admitted that "their allegiance to the organization has more to do with access to weapons and training than with a commitment to Hizb's aim of acceding to Pakistan."[27]

The Hizb-ul-Mujahideen and its parent political party, the Jamaat-i-Islami, sought to shift the terms on which the liberation struggle was being waged. The Islamists began reworking the political discourse by redefining the problem:

the *Muslim Valley*, they intoned, was waging an *Islamic movement* against the *Hindu Indian state* in order to accede to *Islamic Pakistan*. Islam, not Kashmiri nationalism, and accession to Pakistan, not an independent Kashmir, were now presented as the solution to the Kashmir question. The Jamaat-i-Islami's ideologue, Syed Ali Shah Geelani, played a key role in recasting the political discourse with an aim to discredit and displace the JKLF's agenda and to provide a religious rationale for advocating Kashmir's accession to Pakistan. Geelani placed the Kashmiri struggle within an Islamist paradigm.[28] He was bitterly opposed to an independent Kashmir based on secular nationalism because nationalism, according to Islam, was rooted in religion.

Geelani believed that the Muslim worldwide *ummat* is a monolithic ideological community, cemented by *aquida* (common belief) and *iman* (faith), which does not discriminate by color, race, language, caste, tribe, or family. Territorial nationalism, he insisted, is a "poisonous philosophy" that the "enemies of Islam"—the foremost being "various western philosophies"—have deliberately sought to infect Muslims with in order to divide and weaken them.[29] Islam, said Geelani, makes a clear distinction between *watan dosti* (love for their country), which it allows, and territorial nationalism or *watan parasti* (nation worship), which it clearly forbids.[30] Writing to Pakistan's prime minister Nawaz Sharif in June 1993, Greelani stated that Jamaat-i-Islami and Hizb-ul-Mujahideen "were the most reliable groups supporting the ideology of Pakistan" and labeled the nationalists "enemies of the *jihad*" and foes of Pakistan. He cautioned that assistance to such groups was a grave threat "to Pakistan's stability and existence."[31] Geelani's criticism of territorial nationalism therefore had a limited purpose: to justify Kashmir's accession to Pakistan on religious grounds.

On the one hand, Geelani insisted that all Muslims are part of one nation—Muslim ummat. On the other hand, he invoked a statist paradigm, positing that India and Pakistan are nation-states. Jihad, for instance, is introduced as an Islamic concept to justify political violence: "Whenever or wherever the laws of Islam are held out for insult and the religious rights (of the Muslims) are trampled upon, *jihad* becomes a binding *farz* (obligation) for all Muslims." Such a situation, he said, prevailed in Kashmir, and that is why jihad had to be waged there—with the participation of all Muslims, "who should now stand up determinedly and assist their Kashmiri brethren."[32] Interestingly, he was conspicuously silent on the question of whether Indian Muslims should be a part of the Muslim ummat and the jihad in Kashmir. The rationale for jihad is also couched in a statist paradigm that implicates India in the deaths of many thousands of Kashmiris because it denied them their right to self-determination and brutally suppressed their struggle. This is the same "Kashmir versus India" framework employed by the JKLF.

Note, too, that the jihad is directed at the Indian state and its agents, and not against Indians or Hindus per se; also that its objective is limited: namely, to free Kashmir from Indian rule. After the liberation of Kashmir, the mujahideen have no intention of intervening in India's internal affairs, and Jamaat-i-Islami would "like to see India as free, prosperous and peaceful."[33] Criticizing certain unnamed Kashmiri militant groups for spreading anti-India hatred, Geelani says that "emotional slogans such as 'Crush India!' are neither realistic nor do they reflect the spirit of Islam."[34] This, however, runs counter to Geelani's generic notion of irreconcilable differences between the Hindus and Muslims, who are considered to be members of two different nations despite living in the same territory. In a pamphlet titled *Masla Ka Hal* (The Solution of the Problem) issued in 1992, Geelani said:

> To advocate that one Muslim *quam* [read "Kashmiri"] be kept apart from the rest would be against the very definition of a *millat* (people) whose communal identity is based only on *kalima tayyiba* (one creed) [There is no God but Allah and Mohammad is the Prophet of Allah], especially so when the group shares common ideological, cultural and communal relations with a neighbouring (Muslim) group [read "Pakistan"] as well as a common border.[35]

Geelani clearly considers Kashmiri Muslims to be members of an all-encompassing "Muslim *millat*" that shows little regard for the state's ethnic or linguistic minorities. He also sweeps under the carpet cultural differences between the Sufi Islam of Kashmir and Sunni Islam practiced in Pakistan. In this way, he justifies Kashmir's accession to Pakistan as being in the ummat's interests. At the same time, he reverts to the nation-state framework to explain the Pandit exodus from the Valley, which he insists was instigated by the Indian authorities in order to project the Kashmiri struggle as an "Islamic terrorist movement" and thereby discredit it in the eyes of the West.[36]

Geelani would bring Kashmiri Pandits back into the Valley, but this, too, is puzzling. First, bearing in mind the immutable differences between Hindus and Muslims in his worldview, the only bonds between Kashmiri Pandits and Kashmiri Muslims would be their Kashmiri heritage or the fact that they both belong to the same "territorial" or "ethnonational" state—a problematic position for Geelani to accept. Second, the suggestion clashed with the Hizbul's game plan of "Muslimizing the Valley" to facilitate accession to Pakistan. Moreover, the Pandit exodus was more or less complete before the latter came to dominate the Valley in 1992–93. The Hizbul, along with Harkat-ul-Ansar and Al Jehad, were instrumental in foreclosing any possibility of the Pandits' return. Salahuddin, the Hizbul chief, warned the Pandits against returning to the Valley because "they had sided with the 'enemy'(the Indian government)" and thus "would not be allowed to return until they had proved themselves to be . . . part and parcel of their movement by making their own contribution."[37] He also threatened to auction the properties of Kashmiri Muslims unless they returned immediately.[38] Similarly, the Hizb-ul-Mujahideen's operations in Doda and later Rajouri and Poonch during 1994–95 were designed to polarize the Hindu and Muslim populace there.

The Hizb-ul-Mujahideen was a large organization having a well-equipped, disciplined, and highly trained cadre with considerable combat experience in Afghanistan.[39] Its front organizations included the Jamiat-ul-Tulba, the student wing, and the Dukhtaran-e-Millat (Daughters of the Faith), the women's wing, which also ran the Islamic Relief Committee and the Islamic Blood Bank. Inspired by the "Afghan model," the Hizb-ul-Mujahideen's strategy was to make the economic, military, and political costs of retaining Kashmir too prohibitive for India. This had two components: to raise military costs by tying down large numbers of the Indian army in the Valley; and to extend the area of operations to other parts of the state, particularly the Doda, Rajouri, and Poonch districts of the Jammu region. Its network spread out to rural areas, which served as good hideouts, and village madaris were a valuable source of militant recruits. Their military tactics included hit-and-run strikes with sophisticated weapons, and by late 1991–92, they were creating "liberated zones" in some pockets of Baramulla, Srinagar, and Anantnag districts. While the JKLF made Azad Kashmir its base camp, the Jamaat-i-Islami organized open camps throughout Pakistan for recruiting mujahideen and collecting funds for the "Kashmiri jihad." They recruited in the Valley as well because since the 1970s they had systematically established madaris implanting a Sunni Islamic culture and literature and about 2,500–3,000 mosques teaching the Quran and Hadith (interpretation of Islam).[40]

The Hizb-ul-Mujahideen mobilized its cadre in the name of Islam and introduced the highly emotive term "jihad"—interestingly, coined in the Urdu and not Kashmiri language—to justify political violence. A popular slogan of Hizb-ul-Mujahideen was "Na guerrilla jang, na quami jang: al jihad, al jihad" (It is neither a guerrilla war nor a national war: it is a holy war). To become a "mujahid," one had to be a "conscious young man who believes in Islam and is ready to sacrifice his life and property for *Nizam-i-Mustafa*. . . . A young man who is prepared to leave his home, his birth place for *jihad* without any compensation and devotes his life for *jihad* and Islam . . . [with one important condition] . . . [H]e must never have been a part of [an] anti-Islamic movement or connected with pro-India activities."[41]

The motivational literature mobilizing the cadre used symbols and metaphors of Islam extensively. Carefully selecting militant strands of Islamic history, allusions were made to the heroic deeds of the Prophet Mohammed. For example, "Badr," signifying the Prophet Mohammed's spectacular victory over Arab pagans of Mecca, was invoked to eulogize Islamic heroism, and exhortations to violence for another jihad were skillfully woven into references to the Prophet's teachings. "Kashmir's song of freedom" carried the same message: "We will bring Islamic revolution in Kashmir. Both the old and the young are ready to lay down their lives. . . . The history of the battles of Badr and Uhud is going to be repeated. Victory is with us. And *we will usher in Islamic revolution in Kashmir*."[42] Several leaders used Islamic fables to mobilize the people, to persuade them that jihad and.martyrdom would "secure freedom" from India.[43]

Although the Islamist appeals had significantly altered the militant movement's discourse in establishing an alternative school of thought and a proaccession lobby, it was precisely because of the required strict adherence to Islamic ideology that the Hizbul found it difficult to expand its social base and lacked popular support in the Valley. Kashmiri Muslims who had supported the Hizb-ul-Mujahideen in "the fight against India" were soon alienated by pure Islamic beliefs, which considered Kashmiri practices of offering prayers at Sufi shrines and *pirs' mazars* (graves of Sufi saints, revered by Kashmiris) to be idolatrous. Also, the ideological gulf between the JKLF's goal of independence and the Hizb-ul-Mujahideen's demand for accession to Pakistan divided the militant ranks sharply and helped fragment the movement.

Jihad-i-Kashmir: A Pan-Islamic Agenda with an All-India Outreach

With the Hazratbal siege and surrender of JKLF militants in April 1993, the insurgency took a new course. It became increasingly difficult for the Hizb-ul-Mujahideen to recruit members of the Kashmiri cadre. Attributing this to fatigue, Pakistan decided to push more Afghan veterans, Pakistani nationals, and foreign mercenaries into the Valley. This trend gathered momentum in 1996, when the Taliban marched into Kabul.

Hizb-ul-Mujahideen, which had earlier replaced the JKLF, was in turn being marginalized by Pakistan-based entities. Notably, its parent organization, Jamaat-i-Islami, had also "undergone political eclipse in Islamabad after 1996,"

in favor of the Deobandis.[44] With them and the Taliban came a new conception of jihad. After the Pakistani army took over military bases in Afghanistan,
including al Badr, it gave them to the Deobandis, al Qaeda, and the like, but
that was not all—it also handed over the Kashmir struggle, which had thus far
been managed by the Jamaat. However, some attribute this move to realpoli-
tik rather than ideological commitment to the cause:

> The military switched to the Deobandis and the extremists simply
> because they were more effective on the battlefield. Besides, there was a
> larger pool of recruits, their ideology was simpler and they were far more
> effective in creating transnational links from Afghanistan all the way to
> Kashmir and beyond in Saudi Arabia and Central Asia. If the military
> was motivated ideologically, it would have vested its fortunes in the
> Jamaat because of the party's clearer and more coherent vision of an
> Islamic state.[45]

Important Deobandi jihadi organizations operating in Kashmir include
Harkat-ul-Ansar (later renamed Harkat-ul-Mujahideen), Harkat-e-Jihad-i-
Islami, al Badr, and Jaish-i-Mohammed. Lashkar-e-Taiba is the most
prominent jihadi organization of Ahl-e-Hadith persuasion. There are differences among and within Islam's two schools of thought on the meaning,
purpose, and means of carrying out jihad. Many organizations of the Ahl-e-
Hadith sect support only "greater jihad," which calls for self-purification. They
consider militant jihad a "lesser" struggle, which, in the case of Kashmir, can
only be justified if "the oppression of the Kashmiri people will be alleviated and
an Islamic state will be established there. . . . However, when it is evident to any
sensible person that our struggle will not yield the above results, why should
we waste our resources and energy there?"[46]

At the other end of the spectrum is Jamaat-al-Dawa and its military wing,
Lashkar-e-Taiba, which considers militant jihad "absolutely obligatory." It vows
to do *jihad* until certain objectives are achieved:

> Muslims should fight as long as a dispute persists; it is obligatory for
> Muslims to fight till Allah's kingdom is established in the world; and till
> they finish all governments by infidels and extract *jeziya* [tax] from them;
> if oppression is going on in any part of the world, Muslims should fight
> it till it is removed; if any infidel kills a Muslim, we should fight to avenge
> it; if any nation perpetrates a breach of contract against Muslims, it is
> obligatory to fight with that nation; when any nation takes an aggressive
> posture on Muslims, we should fight in self-defence; if the infidels

encroach upon any part of a Muslim land, it is obligatory to fight them and restore it.[47]

Such differences also permeated the Deobandi jihadi organizations. While Jamiat Ulema Islam was committed to helping Harkat-ul-Mujahideen, Harkat-ul-Jihad Islami, and Jaish-i-Mohammed in "all possible ways," others felt that jihad in Afghanistan and Kashmir did not pass the test of sharia.[48] Some leaders of Tablighi Jamat argued that "*jihad* is not permissible at all in Afghanistan and Kashmir."[49]

Nonetheless, dominant jihadi organizations of both schools of thought practice militant jihad and share a pan-Islamic agenda, which has shaped their political discourse. The proponents of a transnational Islamic identity define the *millat* as the world's entire Muslim population. Their self-professed goal is to establish a grand Islamic state stretching across the Middle East, Kashmir, Pakistan, Afghanistan, Iran, and Central Asia, similar to the Islamic Caliphate of medieval times.[50] The Harkat-ul-Jihad Islami manifesto, for instance, states that "the prime purpose of this Jamaat is dominance of Islam all over the world. . . . [W]e will never rest content until we attain a threefold objective: freedom of all occupied Muslim areas, complete protection of all Muslim minorities and the regaining of Islamic glory." It offers to serve as "a second line of defence of each Muslim country."[51] Likewise, the Lashkar-e-Taiba declares: "We have taken an oath! . . . Be it Israel or India, America or Russia, U.K. or Serbia, we shall fight against the infidels. We shall not stop *jihad* in the way of God."[52]

As more and more mujahideen became available from the Afghan front, they began to demonstrate a new puritanism in regard to the local Kashmiris as a result of their Deobandi, Ahl-e-Hadith, or Wahabi beliefs. In their worldview, the armed struggle in Kashmir is but one stage of a wider, indeed global, jihad. Kashmir is not a territorial dispute between India and Pakistan, not even a clash between cultures, but nothing less than a war between two different and mutually opposed ideologies: Islam and *kufr* (disbelief). On one hand, Muslims of this persuasion dismiss any attempt to apply a statist paradigm to Kashmir's realities. On the other hand, Geelani and others have argued that Muslims cannot live harmoniously with Hindus without their own religion and traditions coming under a grave threat, thereby necessitating the separation of Kashmir from India.[53] He stops short of following the rational corollary of his argument—that Indian Muslims cannot live as citizens of secular India either. For Lashkar's spiritual head, Hafiz Muhammad Saeed, separation is essential because "the Hindus have no compassion in their religion."[54] Hence it is the duty of Muslims to wage jihad against the "Hindu oppressors." Saeed declares:

"In fact, the Hindu is a mean enemy and the proper way to deal with him is the one adopted by our forefathers . . . who crushed them by force. We need to do the same."[55] The old idea of a "Hindu-Muslim divide" stands revived.

With the induction of Pakistan-based jihadi organizations, the Kashmiri component—its cadre, ideology, and political goals—became eclipsed. For them, the Kashmiris' independence struggle and the right of self-determination are irrelevant:

> The slogan that Kashmiris should decide the future of Kashmir has given rise to an evil, which was distorting the Islamic identity of the present movement and reducing it to a mere democratic movement. From [the] Islamic viewpoint, the people's opinion has no importance. God and the Prophet's (Peace Be upon Him) law is the supreme one and should be obeyed. Barring this, no group and no individual can decide everything.[56]

Lashkar's Saeed concurred: "The notion of the sovereignty of the people is anti-Islamic. Only Allah is sovereign." Its slogan, "Jamhhoriat ka jawab, grenade aur blast" (Demands for democracy will be met by grenades and bomb blasts), captured this worldview.[57] Kashmiriyat was debunked because Islam does not recognize territorial nationalism, arguing that the only real ideology is the ideology of the Islamic Caliphate, transcending race, gender, and territorial boundaries.[58]

The key militant groups (see box 5-1) also split along a new dividing line, that of Kashmiri versus non-Kashmiri cadre and leadership. Yasin Malik refused to play second fiddle to Azad Kashmir's leadership of the JKLF and in 1995 parted ways with Amanullah Khan, asserting that the "movement cannot be run by remote control as Khan was doing" from Azad Kashmir.[59] Seven years later, Hizb-ul-Mujahideen met the same fate when the Pakistani-based leadership decided to expel Abdul Majid Dar and other Valley-based commanders (Zafar Abdul Fateh and Asad Yazdani) for favoring a dialogue with the Indian government. The bulk of the midlevel command in the Hizb-ul-Mujahideen's south and central Kashmir divisions threw their weight behind the expelled leader. Zafar Fateh remarked: "Hizb is not anybody's handmaiden. . . . Those who are sitting across [Pakistan-occupied Kashmir] cannot claim to be representatives of Kashmir and the organization as they have no understanding of the ground situation."[60] Another Hizbul leader, Sayedani, also admitted that militant groups such as Lashkar-e-Taiba, Jaish-i-Mohammed, and Harkat-ul-Mujahideen should work under local groups as "they have no role in the policy-making of militants."[61]

The Hurriyat Conference became fragmented as well. When it split in 2003, Mirwaiz Umar Farooq demanded that the Muttahida (United) Jihad Council, the Muzaffarabad-based conglomeration of militant groups, should stop interfering in the Hurriyat's affairs.[62] Abdul Ghani Bhat, former Hurriyat chairman, fumed: "We never thought a symbol of political unity would be broken up by its mentor." He told a team of Pakistani journalists visiting Srinagar in November 2004 that he had torn up an earlier will in which he had expressed a desire to be buried in Pakistan.[63]

The jihadi groups' ideological beliefs, organizational networks, training camps, and sources of funding and recruitment had acquired a predominantly Pakistani character, as is evident from box 5-1. Some complained that the Pakistanis had become too intrusive and were treating all of Pakistan as a "base-camp" for jihad. Funerals of Pakistani militants killed in Kashmir were given widespread publicity, names of the *Shuhada* were displayed prominently at national conventions, and officials and ministers were encouraged to attend militant congregations such as the ones organized by Lashkar-e-Taiba at its headquarters outside Lahore in Muridke.[64]

In Kashmir, insurgent attacks increased in number and intensity, becoming more lethal. An attack on the Border Security Force camp at Bandipore on July 31, 1999, was the first militant attack in Jammu and Kashmir directed against a major security force base. By the end of January 2000, there had been another twelve attacks on heavily guarded security force establishments, including the 15th Corps army headquarters at Badamibagh, the army divisional headquarters at Baramulla, and the Jammu and Kashmir Special Operations Group (SOG) headquarters at Srinagar, as well as other high-value targets such as the state secretariat and the state assembly. This reflected a new high-risk strategy by a new generation of militants with more experience, better training, and greater firepower.[65] The militants also changed their tactics from clandestine terrorist assaults to open confrontations with the security forces, engaging them in fierce gun battles. Lashkar-e-Taiba was the first organization to carry out suicide attacks in Kashmir. It claimed to have carried out more than fifty suicide missions against security forces, while the Jaish-i-Mohammed, which followed its example, was supposedly responsible for thirty such missions since 2001.[66]

More significantly, in the new game plan, jihad in Kashmir was a mere first step toward a larger pan-Indian jihad. Once again, its seeds were sown early. The Hizb-ul-Mujahideen chief, Syed Salahuddin, had announced back in 1993, "We want to hit India economically . . . and strike in every nook and corner."[67] The confiscated diaries of its top Valley commander and one of its best strate-

Box 5-1. *Key Militant Groups*

JAISH-I-MOHAMMED (JM)

Ideological affiliation: Deoband.
Organizational network: Punjab 68; Sindh 17; North-West Frontier Province (NWFP) 9; Baluchistan 3; Azad Kashmir 3. Total 100.
Training camps and important madaris: Punjab 8; Sindh 6; NWFP 4; Baluchistan 2; Azad Kashmir 1; and Khanpur, Kehrorika, Chechawatni, Shujaabad. Total 25.
Sources of funding: Its fundraisers regularly visit mosques and foreign countries for funds. Despite the ban, it was able to raise Rs 1–1.5 crores from the sale of hides of sacrificed animals. Al-Rasheed Trust and Al-Akhtar Trust also provides funds to JM.
Sources of recruitment: It gets members from government schools and colleges and madaris. The majority of its recruits come from Punjab, especially Multan, Bhawalpur, and Rahim Yar Khan; Waziristan, Peshawar, Naoshara, and Kohat in NWFP; and Karachi and Shikarpur in Sindh.

HARKAT-UL-MUJAHIDEEN (HUM)

Ideological affiliation: Deoband.
Organizational network: Punjab 9; Sindh 2; NWFP 6; Baluchistan 1; Azad Kashmir 3; and Jhelum, Kot Adoo, Bhawalpur, Ahmadpur Sharqia, Banno, Batgram, Taimergrah, Chitral, Sawabi, Sawat, Sakardoo, Simahni, Bagh Rawalkot, Kundal Shahi, Kotli, and Abbaspur. Total 38.
Training camps: It had four training camps in Afghanistan, in Barij, Ghand, and Kabul. The Manshera camp in Pakistan is temporarily closed. This is the biggest camp, which can train 700 militants at a time. One camp at Muzaffarabad in Azad Kashmir is still functioning.
Sources of funding: Its fundraisers regularly visit mosques and foreign countries for funds from Pakistanis living abroad and sheikhs of some Arab states. It also raises funds from Pakistani mosques in cash and in kind during harvest. Despite the ban, it was able to raise Rs 7 lakhs from the sale of hides of sacrificed animals.
Sources of recruitment: The majority come from Punjab, especially Multan, Gujarawalan, Rahim Yar Khan, Khaniwal, Multan, Dera Ghazi Khan, and Jhang; in NWFP, from Dera Ismail Khan, Noshahra and Kohat; and Gilgit. It also draws large numbers of youth from Karachi.

HARKAT-UL-JIHAD ISLAMI (HUJI)

Ideological affiliation: Deoband.
Organizational network: Punjab 8; NWFP 3; and Marri, Kahota, Bhawalpur, Waah Cantt., Chaar Sadda, Sawaat. Total 17.
Training camps: During the Taliban regime, it had six camps in Kandahar, Kabul, and Khost. It also has a Mahmud Ghaznavi camp, Kotli, in Azad Kashmir.
Sources of funding: Funds come from the public in Pakistan and the sale of arms to smaller jihadi groups. Its fundraisers in foreign countries are also very active.
Sources of recruitment: The majority of its recruits come from madaris, mainly from Punjab and the NWFP.

Jamaat-Al-Dawa/Lashkar-e-Taiba (LT)

Ideological affiliation: Ahl-e-Hadith.

Organizational metwork: Punjab 30; Sindh 7; Azad Kashmir 2; and Jhelum, Kabirwala, Kehrorpacca, Tonsa, Moro, Shehdadpur, Dadoo, Jafarabad, Badain, Jaam Nawaiz Ali, Obaaro (Ghotaki), Rawalkot, Bhamber, Kotli, Wailamgarh, and Muzaffarabad. Total 55.

Training camps: After the closure of camps in Afghanistan and Manshera, only five LT camps were working: Tayyaba, Aqsa, Ummul Qura, Abdullah bin Masood, and Markaz Muhammad bin Qasim. It also has ten madaris.

Sources of funding: Funds are collected within Pakistan and abroad. About Rs 20 crores were collected in 2001 as follows: External Affairs, 2 crore; profit of Dar-al Andalus, 80 lakhs; Students' Department, 35 lakhs; hides of sacrificed animals, 2.5 crore; Department of Women, 70 lakhs; Department of Peasant and Labor Wing, 45 lakhs; miscellaneous, 6 crore. It also gets contributions from Arab states. Saudi Arabia, in particular, and its units in European countries send substantial contributions to the jihad fund every year.

Sources of recruitment: It has a wide network of recruitment in Pakistan, which is concentrated in Sindh and southern Punjab. Among LT's 1,106 mujahideen killed in Kashmir, 365 were from Sindh.

Hizb-ul-Mujahideen (HM)

Ideological affiliation: Jamaat-i-Islami.

Organizational network: Punjab 18; NWFP 2; Azad Kashmir 2; and Bhawalpur, Kamaliya, Der, Chitral, Hazara Division, Karam Agency, Rawalkot, Bagh, Kotli, Palandir. Total 32.

Training camps: It had a training camp in Khost province of Afganistan, which was occupied by al Badr. In Pakistan, its camps are distributed as follows: NWFP 5; Boniar 2; Thanda Pani (Abbotabad) 1; Balakot 1; and Chitral 13. In Azad Kashmir, two camps are near Muzaffarabad and one in Ankyal sector.

Sources of funding: According to its 2001 annual report, 7,200 collection boxes throughout Pakistan collected Rs 237,680 that year. After 9/11, most of these were removed. It receives a big share of funds from Jamaat-i-Islami, which has set up several allied forums for this purpose, including the Kashmir Fund, Kashmir Security Fund, Al-Khidmat Foundation, Martyrs of Islam Foundation, and Islamic Mission of the United Kingdom.

Sources of recruitment: Human resources are provided by Islami Jamiat Tulba, Jamiat Tulba Arabiya, Jamaat-i-Islami, National Labour Federation, and Shabab Milli.

Al Badr Mujahideen

Ideological affiliation: Deoband/Jamaat-i-Islami.

Organizational network: Punjab 11; Sindh 1; NWFP 4; and Tehsil Chatyana, Tehsil Gojrah, Tehsil Kamalia, Malakand, Der, Charsadda, Kotli, Bagh, Chham Sector, Karam Agency. Total 26.

Training camps: Its camps are located in the jungles of Kolsh Valley, on the east of Pakkal Valley, near Manshera. Earlier, it had three camps in Afghanistan, but these were captured by Harkat-ul-Mujahideen.

Sources of funding: It has devised new means of collecting funds, such as *jihadi mushaira* (poetry sessions on jihad), military exhibitions, and demonstrations. It also receives funds from several big industrialist groups in Karachi and raised Rs 9 lakhs from the sale of hides of sacrificed animals in 2001.

Sources of recruitment: Madaris of Deobandi and Jamaat-i-Islami schools of thought.

Source: Rana, *A to Z of Jehadi Organizations in Pakistan.*

gic minds, Ali Mohammad Dar, provided details of possible new courses of action throughout India.[68] In 1998 the Hizb-ul-Mujahideen openly declared its intention to take the "war against India outside Jammu and Kashmir" and to "move towards Delhi."[69]

The Lashkar chief, Saeed, had earlier announced that "the *jihad* in Kashmir would soon spread to entire India. Our mujahideens would create three Pakistans [Kashmir, Junagarh and Hyderabad] in India." In a subsequent interview with the Urdu-language newspaper *Takbeer*, he made the progression from Kashmir to India explicit: following the liberation of Kashmir, "Indian Muslims should be aroused to rise in revolt against the Indian Union so that India gets disintegrated."[70] As the jihad in Kashmir progressed, "the notion of this conflict as a first battle in the war for the defense of Islam throughout India has been increasingly translated into action."[71] The December 13, 2001, attack on the Parliament House in New Delhi confirmed that the war in Jammu and Kashmir had transcended its geographical boundaries.

Kashmiri Voices: On the Margins

In time, the jihadis' agenda marginalized the local Kashmiri insurgency. People strongly resented having their political movement hijacked by Islamic warriors who had no respect for the religious beliefs of Sufi Islam and who debunked their political goal of azadi. They were disillusioned with the increasingly fragmented and criminalized militancy, which had turned into a lucrative profession. Furthermore, militant factions had begun turning their guns on each other, and new recruits entering the fray were driven more by the glamour and power of the gun than by ideology. Many militants extorted "donations" from people (particularly from businessmen), while others abused womenfolk and carried out contract killings. The jihad gun had backfired. The mujahids who had been worshipped as war heroes and garlanded by women and children when they came seeking shelter were unwelcome visitors. They were now feared and had lost all affection and respect. Kashmiris, both the populace and its leaders, sought to regain control over the movement and reclaim its discourse concerning Kashmiri concerns, values, beliefs, and political aspirations.

Popular Resistance

People collectively resisted having Islamic ideology imposed on them and often defied the militants' strictures on centuries-old Kashmiri practices and festivals. They clashed with militants in Aish Mugam, for example, when the latter tried to prevent the local villagers from celebrating the *urs* (anniversary of the birth or death of a saint) of Baba Zainuddin Rishi.[72] At the Zain Shah Sahib near Gulmarg, more than 20,000 peasants assembled in defiance of the Hizb-ul-Mujahideen to observe the festival of lights heralding the sowing season in the Valley. In this case, some innocent lives were lost.[73] The Charar-i-Sharif tragedy in 1995 exposed the contempt and disrespect of Afghan mercenaries for the Kashmiri shrine of a rishi who had always cautioned against religious beliefs dividing the people.[74] In time, Kashmiris mounted public protests against the militants. In one such incident, 5,000 women reportedly demonstrated against the slaughter of a Pandit family in April 1992.[75] In another, in the Rainawari area of Srinagar, where in 1991 a group of women had stalled security forces trying to set up a bunker, the following year local people helped a paramilitary force set up office in a building previously occupied by the JKLF.[76]

In 1993 a hue and cry arose following the kidnapping of Nahida Imtiaz, daughter of National Conference member Saifuddin Soz. Even JKLF leaders appealed for her release, whereas only three years earlier they themselves had carried out a similar kidnapping. In May 1994, a crowd of 2,000 people foiled a similar attempt, when militants tried to kidnap Yasmeen, daughter of National Conference leader Ali Mohammad Sagar. This, too, met with public disapproval. At times, the reaction was violent, as when local Muslims hit militants with bats for shooting two Hindu shopkeepers in downtown Srinagar.[77] However, the militants still continued with their repression, and the fear of the gun became all-pervasive. At the same time, the tide had turned.

REDEFINING THE MOVEMENT

The people's resolve to defy militants' dictates induced separatist leaders to try to transform the movement into a popular struggle for the political right to self-determination. Shabir Shah, after his release from detention in 1994, charted a secular course that made it "not a fight between one and the other religion but a war between oppressed and oppressors" and thus redefined the Kashmiri movement:

> We demand [the] right of self-determination to make it unambiguously clear to India that *we are a quam, a respectful and courageous identity* with a determination to march in step with others in the comity of nations. We are not a herd, which can be pushed around by India or Pakistan. . . . We will lay down our lives but will not permit any division of the state by the people in Islamabad or New Delhi.[78] (Emphasis added)

Mirwaiz Umar Farooq, who is ideologically a Deobandi, also remained faithful to his local roots, calling the struggle "not an Islamic movement but a movement of Kashmiri people, whether they were Muslim, Hindu or Sikh. Whosoever lives in Kashmir, this movement is for his rights."[79] For the first time since it got under way, the secessionist movement was being defined in an inclusive fashion. Its leaders had recognized the need to broaden the social and political base of the movement. Shabir along with JKLF leader Yasin Malik, who was released in May 1994, tried building bridges between Kashmiri Muslims and Pandits. However, their efforts to secularize the movement were scuttled by the Jamaat-i-Islami within the Hurriyat Conference. Yasin was condemned for the un-Islamic practices regarding observing fasts, while Shabir's stand on involving the Kashmiri Pandits, Ladakhi Buddhists, and people of Jammu ultimately led to his expulsion in 1996.

The Hurriyat along with other militant leaders protested the prevailing "gun culture" and favored exploring political options. Ghulam Nabi Bhatt, younger brother of Maqbool Bhatt, argued that "the gun cannot get us *azadi*. The solution lies in talking across the table." This view was echoed by JKLF leader Javed Mir: "We can hold talks with the centre provided they centre around independence. *The gun after all is not the answer.*" Amanullah Khan agreed: "I would be a fool if I thought we could shunt out Indians only with the gun. . . . The fight is also political and diplomatic." Azim Inqalabi appealed that the "time was ripe for shedding the gun culture and taking an active part in the democratic struggle." Hurriyat leader Abdul Ghani Lone, barely five hours before being killed, had publicly asked the jihadi groups to leave Kashmiris alone.[80]

A KASHMIRI CRITIQUE OF PAKISTAN'S ROLE

The romantic vision of the "promised land of Pakistan" had faded quickly. Pakistan's support for the right to self-determination had come with a rider— *Kashmir had to support accession to Pakistan.* An independent Kashmir was ruled out. In July 1994, the Hizbul put Qazi Nissar to death for his proindependence sympathies, and the people's alienation from Pakistan took a new turn. Thousands of Muslims joined in rallies and processions condemning the assassination and publicly denouncing Pakistan. The popular slogan "Jo mangega Pakistan, Usko milega kabristan" (Whosoever demands Pakistan shall be put into a grave) captured the public mood.[81]

One who was respected across the political spectrum, Mohammad Azim Inqalabi, stepped up to sharply attack Pakistan in a publication titled *Quest for Friends Not Masters,* which presents a lucid and forceful exposition of Kashmiris' growing disillusionment and anger.[82] According to Inqalabi, the early generation of Kashmiri militants who crossed the Line of Control to get arms training were let down. They were led to believe that once the insurgency was under way, Pakistan would attack India to liberate Kashmir—a promise that was never fulfilled: "Your humiliated mothers and sisters in Kashmir have a reason to question your sincerity."[83]

Addressing the Legislative Assembly of Azad Kashmir in June 2005, JKLF leader Yasin Malik made it clear that the Azad Kashmir leaders had to take maximum blame for the death of 80,000 Kashmiris.[84] He and many other militant leaders, including Inqalabi, had come to realize that Pakistan was systematically undermining every militant group that did not toe its proaccession line. Inqalabi loudly criticized the "persistent appeals in the name of Islamic brotherhood, aggressiveness and parochialism" that were "allowed to be the pith and marrow of the strategy to uproot and replace the established leadership of Kashmir." It was their "hypocritical political posture" that "gave birth to reactionary nationalist slogans" and that needed "to revert from aggressive aggrandizement to brotherly cooperation" in the service of liberation. He lambasted Pakistan for Islamicizing the Kashmir movement when "Kashmiri Muslims . . . [have] kept struggling for centuries against the alien rule just to safeguard their mystic Muslim culture based on the universal principles of love, brotherhood and philanthropy. Kashmiri Muslims are averse to the trends of aggrandizement and assimilation. Attempts to browbeat them or bribe their conscience will simply boomerang."[85] Citing East Pakistan's example, Inqalabi warned Pakistan to change its overbearing "colonial" approach toward Kashmir and to "bear in mind that Kashmiris cannot be subjugated by a system which failed to keep the sovereignty and identity of Pakistan intact in 1971." What Kashmir needed to retain its distinct cultural identity, he emphasized, were "*friends, not masters.*"[86]

While Kashmiris' anger against India had not lessened, their disillusionment with Pakistan also ran deep. Since Pakistan controlled key levers of the militant movement, every militant outfit that did not serve Pakistan's interests was systematically marginalized. JKLF leaders had failed to see through Pakistan's game plan and miscalculated gravely in relying solely on Pakistan for funds, arms, and training. By the time the goal of azadi caught the people's imagination, the JKLF had been eclipsed by the pro-Pakistan Hizb-ul-Mujahideen. When the latter began to lose momentum and failed to recruit Kashmiri militants in large numbers, they too were superseded by foreign mercenaries of the Harkat-ul-Ansar. Gradually, all militant groups realized that Pakistan did not have the military wherewithal to risk a full-scale war with India to liberate Kashmir—or any intention of doing so.

Many believed that Pakistan was using Kashmir merely as a pawn with which to "bleed India." During the Kargil crisis, a tame Pakistani withdrawal after supporting a protracted operation evidently designed to inject life into the insurgency had a profoundly demoralizing effect on the rank and file of the militant groups. The Kashmiri perception of "their protector buckling under international pressure without securing any reciprocal obligations to safeguard the Kashmiri interests" confirmed their worst fears that Pakistan would not go to war with India over the Kashmir issue.[87] A Hurriyat leader's remark, "First we were excluded, then betrayed," spoke volumes. In the aftermath of the 9/11 attack on the United States, the Pakistani establishment's decision to jettison its protégé, the Taliban, and support the U.S. attack on Afghanistan reinforced such impressions.

The Stalemate

The secessionist movement seemed doomed from the beginning owing to its internal contradictions. Politically, the Kashmiri Muslims' demand for azadi was checkmated by other communities in Jammu and Ladakh, and Kashmiri Pandits in the Valley, as explained in chapter 4. Militarily, the ideological divide between those seeking independence and others supporting accession to Pakistan depleted the limited but vital resources of the militants. The JKLF enjoyed popular support but lacked the manpower and weapons; the Hizb-ul-Mujahideen had a well-trained and armed cadre but little public sympathy. Without mutual support, both failed.

The movement also lacked a coherent and effective military strategy. Militant violence was most effective in 1989–90. At the peak of militancy in 1990, there was a naive belief that the Indian state would soon "withdraw," granting Kashmir independence, or that Pakistan would attack India to liberate Kashmir. Both rested on false assumptions, so neither materialized. The militants were overtaken by the mass processions demanding azadi. The real threat to the Indian state was not so much the Kashmiri militant struggle as it was the mass demonstrations that symbolized the people's total rejection of state authority. The Indian state has had considerable experience in successfully tackling insurgencies in the northeast and Punjab but has rarely faced mass movements demanding secession. When the militants failed to channel the mass demonstrations in service of their cause, or sustain them, the battle was half lost.

None other than its patron, Pakistan, quickly neutralized the military might of the JKLF. Devoid of new weapons, cadres, and funds, the JKLF was no match for the massive military power of the Indian state, especially when it was being marginalized from within by the Hizb-ul-Mujahideen. The latter had highly disciplined cadres and better firepower but could not persuade people in the Kashmir Valley to pursue their goal, which was to join Pakistan. The average Kashmiri militant was driven more by economic and political frustration and a deep-seated sense of taking revenge against the perceived oppression than by ideological zest. Religion was simply not an important motivating factor; Kashmiris never considered themselves holy warriors.[88]

Subsequent criminalization and degeneration of the militant ranks left the people disillusioned and caused the gun to backfire. The introduction of foreign mercenaries whose agenda had no room for the Kashmiris' political goals delivered a body blow to the movement. Denuded of local character and support, the foreign militants could at best wage guerrilla warfare, as they did and are doing, and bleed the Indian state. This changed after 9/11 as Pakistan came under growing international pressure to curb its activities. As discussed in chapter 3, initially the Musharraf regime sought to deflect this pressure by focusing on al Qaeda and differentiating between terrorism (on its eastern borders, in Afghanistan) and the so-called freedom struggle (on its western borders, in Kashmir). It tried to protect the homegrown extremist groups because of their strategic value in securing Islamabad's national objectives in Kashmir. Though the situation changed when many of these groups decided to side with al Qaeda and turned against their mentors, the Musharraf regime has not yet pulled the plug on the jihadi groups operating in Pakistan. And, notwithstanding Islamabad's position on the ongoing peace process, these groups are not likely to be amenable to *any* negotiated solution of the Kashmir problem. They have debunked the dialogue process and resolved to continue jihad.

The Hizb-ul-Mujahideen might follow a different path for two reasons. First, the military character of the insurgency is changing, turning into a war of attrition. Sustaining the momentum of militant operations has not proved to be easy for the Hizbul, especially after the dismissal of its Valley-based commanders and killing of other top commanders such as Ghulam Rasool Khan, Ghulam Rasool Dar, Saif-ur-Rehman Bajwa, and Arif Khan in less than a year. Second, pressure is growing from within. Many of the 2,000 to 3,500 Hizbul cadre living in Azad Kashmir's training camps are reportedly keen to return home. Significantly, the demand for an amnesty for them was articulated by the mainstream political parties at the second roundtable conference held at Srinagar in May 2006. Prime Minister Manmohan Singh agreed to review the cases of all detainees, including, he said, "the cases of those who crossed after violating our laws and who are now anxious to return home."[89] He also announced rehabilitation plans for children who have been victims of terrorism as well as families of those terrorists who have been killed in police action. If these schemes, especially the amnesty offer, were to be implemented successfully, the Hizbul leadership might face more pressure from its cadre to reach a negotiated settlement to avoid a depletion of its ranks. Its midlevel commanders, however, would be loath to give up the gun because they have profited from the extortion economy that has flourished in Jammu and Kashmir during the past decade and understand that war pays larger cash dividends than peace.

Hizbul's top leaders also have little incentive to join the dialogue process because much like the Hurriyat, they recognize that the expected rewards—political power in Srinagar (with or without independence)—will not be handed over on a platter by New Delhi, or for that matter, be acquiesced to by mainstream political players within Jammu and Kashmir. In any future political equations, all the players will have to contend with the democratic calculus of the state, but the separatists, as argued earlier, are ill equipped to fight that battle. That is probably why the Muzaffarabad-based faction of the Hizb-ul-Mujahideen seems to be in turmoil, as is evident from the contradictory signals it has been sending ever since Islamabad decided to join the peace process. An agitated Hizbul chief, Syed Salahuddin, vowed in May 2003 that if "Pakistan cracks under foreign pressure, the supreme *jihad* council intends to run its activities independently of it."[90] He described the Srinagar-Muzaffarabad bus as a "cosmetic step," but when the first bus rolled, he warned that no one should target it. Before President Musharraf's visit to New Delhi in April 2005, the Hizb-ul-Mujahideen again issued a cease-fire offer, but when Mirwaiz Umar Farooq asked him in June to support the peace process, the former's plea was totally dismissed. He derisively told the mirwaiz that "being invited to the Delhi *Darbar* or visiting Pakistan was possible only because of the sacrifices of militants" and claimed that no political process could succeed without being backed by a vibrant militant movement. Salahuddin made it clear as to who calls the shots: "We will keep a close watch on the political and diplomatic activities and will support any attempt that is aimed at solving the dispute in accordance with the right to self-determination of the people of Kashmir," as defined in the original UN resolutions.[91]

A year later, in March 2006, the Salahuddin-led United Jihad Council (UJC) staged an unprecedented hunger strike in Muzaffarabad against the "betrayal of the *jihad* in Jammu and Kashmir by President Musharraf."[92] Hizbul's political ideologue, Syed Ali Shah Geelani, had also publicly questioned Musharraf's credentials, saying that the latter "had no mandate to propose a solution unacceptable to the people of occupied J&K," though he is marginalized within the

Majlis-i-Shoora of its parent political party, Jamaat-i-Islami.[93] In May 2006, Hizbul's emissaries warned Mirwaiz Umar Farooq that Hurriyat's decision to participate in the second roundtable conference would make their leaders targets for attack. "The sacrifice offered by the Kashmiris," an earlier UJC statement had asserted, "demand[s] that common people and Mujahideen should get united and take the struggle to its logical conclusion." The Hurriyat buckled and called for the "political, diplomatic and military fronts" of the "Kashmiri resistance" to work "in unison." [94]

There is a military and political deadlock: "The militancy cannot throw out the army and the army cannot eradicate the militancy. Because of this, there has to be a political solution."[95] On that front, too, Kashmiris realize that they cannot secede forcibly, yet they have the power to deny political legitimacy to Indian rule unless their political aspirations are addressed. Pakistan knows it cannot liberate Kashmir by force, but continuation—at best, calibration—of the jihadi violence remains its only card to ensure a place at the negotiating table. Indian leaders realize that they have warded off the threat of secession, but peace will remain elusive without Pakistan's consent and Kashmiris' approval. The insurgency has reached a total stalemate.

CHAPTER SIX

AZAD KASHMIR AND
THE NORTHERN AREAS:
THE FORGOTTEN FRONTIERS

AZAD KASHMIR AND THE NORTHERN AREAS—the Pakistani part of
Kashmir—are conspicuously absent from the debates on Kashmir. These
mountainous regions are enveloped in multiple and overwhelming *silences*—
"intellectual silence" reflected in a striking absence of literature; the
international community's "silence" in selectively focusing its attention on the
Kashmir Valley; "silence" of the Pakistani polity, which in its yearning for Kashmir has cared little about the region's people; and the "silence" of India, which
seems to have completely turned its back on these areas since 1947–48.[1] Dis-
covering the "other" Kashmir is clearly not easy, though a persistent attempt
may explain why Pakistan has sought to keep its own part of Kashmir under
wraps and essentially *outside* the definitional domain of the Kashmir conflict.
The story of Azad Kashmir and the Northern Areas that emerges from these
shadows is a classic example of "intrastate colonialism."[2] Notwithstanding its
name, Azad (Free) Kashmir, the governance structures created therein and in
the Northern Areas by the Pakistani state have replicated some basic features
of classical colonialism: political subjugation and disenfranchisement, systematic economic exploitation, and cultural negation—ordained by significant
degrees of coercion.

 Pakistan has used the territories, resources, and people of Azad Kashmir and
the Northern Areas to achieve its internal and external national objectives.
Militarily, the territories have served as a launching pad for all ventures of
Pakistan's army to annex the Indian part of Kashmir. Politically, their symbolic
value lay in their very existence, inasmuch as Pakistan could convincingly
argue that "an alternative formula other than integration within the Indian
Union presented itself to the Kashmiris across the cease-fire line."[3] Strategically,
Pakistan has traded parts of the Northern Areas to cement a long-lasting mil-

itary and nuclear relationship with China. Kashmir's river system and the Mangla Headworks have proved to be the backbone of agriculture in Punjab—Pakistan's largest, richest, and most powerful province—and one of the largest sources of hydroelectric power for the entire country.

However, the people of Azad Kashmir and the Northern Areas have gained little in return for all the services rendered to the Pakistani state. Azad Kashmir had to wait for more than two decades, until 1970, to be granted its right to the adult franchise. The Northern Areas have fared much worse: its people have struggled for forty-seven years to exercise their basic civil right to vote, which they did for the first time in October 1994. Ambiguities about the constitutional and legal status of the Northern Areas have fostered typical colonial conditions whereby all civil and legal rights reside in the Pakistani state and none in the people. For example, Pakistan has administrative rights over the people, by way of collecting taxes and making laws and enforcing them, whereas the people have no individual rights to choose the administrators or challenge their decisions by way of their own legislative assembly or representation in the federal parliament because constitutionally they are *not* part of Pakistan.

In its system of governance for these territories, Pakistan has gone beyond the colonial tactics of "co-opting" traditional elites of local *mirs* (rulers) and *biradaries* (clans) to create a whole new genre of *nonlocal* ruling elites comprising Punjabi-Pushtun bureaucrats, businessmen, and military personnel, who have monopolized the top rung of the power structures in Azad Kashmir and the Northern Areas. If Azad Kashmir has been made the "*mandi* (market) of Pakistan's Punjab," the local communities in Gilgit and Baltistan have become a minority in their own land owing to a systematic and large influx of Pushtuns, irreversibly changing its demographic profile.[4] Furthermore, Pakistan has resorted to classical colonial methods of "divide and rule" by injecting sectarianism into the Northern Areas, so that the latter's political demands for civil and political rights can be undercut and dismissed by generating Shia-Sunni divisions. This chapter highlights the political, economic, and cultural dynamics of Azad Kashmir and the Northern Areas in an attempt to bring these "forgotten frontiers" firmly back on the agenda for understanding the Kashmir problem.

The first challenge in this mission is how to address the "intellectual silence" on Azad Kashmir and the Northern Areas. Many authoritative texts on Pakistan do not give much attention to these areas or discuss their peculiar administrative and constitutional relationship with Pakistan as a whole.[5] Research scholars and international aid agencies alike have been denied access to these territories. At best, their movements in the border regions are severely restricted because these are said to be "sensitive areas." The same reasons are

given to explain why information on these areas is routinely excluded from virtually all public statistics, including census data. Some books in Urdu written
by Azad Kashmir officials and political leaders have been published in recent
years, but most of this literature is difficult to obtain, even in Azad Kashmir and
Pakistan, and has never been absorbed into the general literature on Kashmir.
Media reports dwell mainly on Kashmir Valley and related topics, such as
refugee camps or militant activities in Azad Kashmir. It is as if "the Northern
Areas as a whole have fallen through a black-hole."[6] The following analysis
should therefore be read with such constraints in mind.

Political Subjugation

Pakistan has politically subjugated these areas through various institutional
mechanisms, bureaucratic structures of authority, rigged electoral processes,
and military rule.

AMBIGUOUS CONSTITUTIONAL STATUS

Both Azad Kashmir and the Northern Areas are a constitutional enigma. One
reason is the muddy partition of the former Dogra state, Jammu and Kashmir,
following war between India and Pakistan. Over the years, Pakistan has consciously chosen to maintain such ambiguities in their constitutional and legal
status as an effective tool for politically subjugating these areas.

Azad Kashmir is azad (free) in name only. Its status was never defined in
standard international legal terms by the Azad Kashmir or Pakistan governments, or by the United Nations. According to a 1948 resolution of the United
Nations Commission for India and Pakistan (UNCIP), Azad Kashmir is not a
sovereign state or a province of Pakistan, but, "pending final solution," is a
designated territory and "administered by the local authorities under the sur-
veillance of the Commission."[7]

The first president of Azad Kashmir, Sardar M. Ibrahim Khan, proposed
that Pakistan "give full-fledged recognition to the Azad Jammu and Kashmir
government and accept it as the only legal and constitutional authority on
behalf of the people of J&K." He advised Mohammed Ali Jinnah to accept the
Instrument of Accession from the territory's government and "treat Jammu &
Kashmir as a legally and constitutionally acceded State to Pakistan."[8] This was
rejected partly because Jinnah, being a legal mind, realized that without
Maharaja Hari Singh's signature on the Instrument of Accession, it would have
no legal validity or, as argued earlier, he simply expected Kashmir (that is, the
Valley) to fall any time. When the raiders were pushed back by the Indian

army, Pakistan pitched hard to get recognition for the Azad Kashmir government through the UN Security Council. Writing to UNCIP chairman Sir Zafarullah Khan, who was also Pakistan's foreign minister, Jinnah

> stressed that the struggle for the liberation of Kashmir was initiated by Azad Kashmir, now represented by the Azad Kashmir government, and that the Government is [a] *necessary party to any settlement of the Kashmir question.* . . . As had already been explained to the Commission, *political control over the Azad Kashmir forces vests in the Azad Kashmir government,* and it is the latter Government alone that has the authority to issue a cease-fire order to those forces, and to conclude terms and conditions of a truce which would be binding upon those forces.[9] (Emphasis added)

This did not work. The UNCIP's position, outlined to Sir Zafarullah, was steadfast and clear: "By 'local authorities' we mean the Azad Kashmir people though we cannot grant recognition to the Azad Kashmir Government." This was apparently the commission's way of dealing with "the *de facto* situation" while recognizing that "the State of Jammu and Kashmir still exists as a legal entity. We have to respect its sovereignty."[10] Since a de jure recognition was not forthcoming, the Pakistan government took steps to consolidate its de facto control over territories under its occupation. Nehru was not alone in reaching a judgment by 1948 that a plebiscite was an uncertain bargain and might not materialize at all. The best course, concluded the Pakistan government, was to establish the Ministry of Kashmir Affairs, headed by a Joint Secretary, which it did in 1948. Until the early 1970s, this office may well have been "the best claim to being the real head of the Azad Kashmir government."[11]

The Karachi Agreement of 1949, signed with this "local authority" or provisional government of Azad Kashmir, brought the Gilgit Agency, later designated the Northern Areas, under the Pakistan government's direct control. As part of this agreement, the provisional government also handed over matters related to defense, foreign affairs, and negotiations with the UNCIP to Pakistan. Since then, the Pakistan government has never seriously sought de jure recognition for the Azad Kashmir government. This, it may be argued, was not simply because the idea had drawn a blank in the UN debates, for its resolute pursuit of the plebiscite option had met a similar fate. Rather, it was because the government realized that all its immediate objectives were being met with de facto control over the territories. Note that the Northern Areas is the only part of Pakistan whose status is not specified in the constitution. While Kashmir is referred to as a disputed territory, the Northern Areas is not even mentioned in the relevant schedule in the constitution. Nor does it have an autonomous or constitutional status of its own. Furthermore, the geographical borders of Pakistan as spelled out in all the constitutions of Pakistan—1956, 1962, and 1973—did not include the Northern Areas.

In October 1947, the Muslim officers and men of the Dogra state army and the Gilgit Scouts revolted against the maharaja and liberated the state from Dogra rule, establishing an independent government on November 1, 1947. It remained a republic for exactly seventeen days under a provisional government headed by Shah Rais Khan. It then formally requested accession to Pakistan and handed power over to Pakistan's first political agent, Sardar Mohammad Alam, without demanding guarantees regarding the future of the area. Pakistan took over the administration but did not announce the accession of these areas to Pakistan. Meanwhile, Jinnah was still eyeing the Indian part of Kashmir and unsure of winning the plebiscite without Sheikh Abdullah's support. The Northern Areas were then declared part of the disputed territory of Jammu and Kashmir state so that in case of any future plebiscite in Kashmir the votes of this region would play a decisive role.

Notably, this was done without seeking the will or consent of the people or local rulers of the area. Instead, their "president was expelled and appointed a civil services officer," and their "army chief, Colonel Khan[,] was demoted to lieutenant!"[12] Nor did they have any say in reaching the 1949 Karachi Agreement, which hived off more than 28,000 square miles of Gilgit and Baltistan from Azad Kashmir that comprised only 4,000 square miles. This agreement was signed by Mushtaque Ahmed Gurmani, minister without portfolio, the government of Pakistan, and the Azad Kashmir government, represented by its president, Sardar M. Ibrahim Khan, and head of the All-Jammu and Kashmir Muslim Conference, Chowdhary Ghulam Abbas. However, the Muslim Conference had no political presence whatsoever in the Gilgit Agency. In the post-1947 period, only Abbas had visited that region in order to popularize the Muslim Conference. Although his visit "was officially sponsored, . . . it did not bear any fruitful result."[13]

Over the years, Pakistan's government has chosen to interpret the constitutional and legal status of the Northern Areas as appropriate for the issue at stake. In the case of a plebiscite, successive governments have maintained that these areas are part of the disputed territory of Jammu and Kashmir state, as specified in the UNCIP resolutions. For all other administrative and political purposes of establishing the Pakistani state's authority as well as for changing its territorial boundaries—internally and externally—these areas have been treated as part of Pakistan, *not* Azad Kashmir. At the same time, Pakistani governments have not granted the fundamental rights of the people of the Northern Areas for the past fifty-nine years on the plea that they are *not* part of Pakistan, as specified in its constitution.

The tactical nature of including Gilgit and Baltistan in the "disputed" Jammu and Kashmir state became clear in the early years when, despite the Karachi Agreement's clear recognition that they were a part of Azad Kashmir, the writ of Muzaffarabad was never allowed to run there. The Karachi Agreement itself was repealed by the Azad Jammu and Kashmir Government Act of 1970, which in turn, was rendered redundant by the Azad Jammu and Kashmir Interim Constitution Act of 1974. On the recommendation of a Northern Areas Committee set up in 1971, the Pakistan government brought changes in the Northern Areas' administrative and internal territorial arrangements. Long separated from Azad Kashmir, they were formally hived off and directly administered from Islamabad along the lines of the Federally Administered Tribal Areas in the North-West Frontier Province. The Gilgit and Baltistan agencies were converted into Gilgit and Baltistan districts. A new district known as Diamer consisting of the subdivisions of Astor, Chilas, and Darel/Tangir was created in December 1972. The then prime minister, Zulfiqar Ali Bhutto, visited the Northern Areas in September 1974 and announced the abolition of the Hunza state and creation of two new districts known as Ghanche, consisting of the Khaplu and Kharmong subdivisions in Baltistan and Ghizr. Later, the Ghanche and Ghizr districts were abolished and merged with the districts of Baltistan and Gilgit, respectively.

Continuing the process of integrating the Northern Areas into Pakistan, Islamabad next included them in Martial Law Zone-E, established in 1977 by General Zia-ul-Haq, who had assumed power in a military coup. In April 1982, he nominated three members of the federal Majlis-i-Shoora (advisory council) from the Northern Areas, and in July, Zia publicly stated that while "Kashmir has been a disputed issue, . . . so far as the Northern Areas are concerned, we do not accept them as disputed" but as "an integral part of Pakistan."[14] In 1985 General Zia-ul-Haq formed a committee of nine federal secretaries to examine the status of the Northern Areas. The committee suggested several options, the most notable being to make the Northern Areas the fifth province of Pakistan, give it the status of a Federally Administered Tribal Area (FATA), merge it with Azad Kashmir, or amalgamate it with Punjab or North-West Frontier Province (NWFP). General Zia shrewdly chose to make the region a de facto province of Pakistan, and eventually a de jure one.[15] Since then, no Pakistani government seems to have "officially" revisited the issue and hence the principle of de facto control endures.

The constitutional and legal status of the Northern Areas has been a long-standing bone of contention between Islamabad and successive Azad Kashmir governments. Muzaffarabad has viewed the government's move to assume direct administrative control over the Northern Areas as "a continuation of the British colonial policy of divide and rule."[16] In 1972 the Azad Kashmir Legislative Assembly passed a resolution demanding the return of the Northern Areas, which had been taken over "temporarily" by Pakistan under the Karachi Agreement. Islamabad simply ignored the resolution. A writ petition made to the Azad Jammu and Kashmir High Court by Malik Muhammad Miskeen and others in October 1990 demanded that the Northern Areas, being Kashmiri territory, be merged with Azad Kashmir.[17] Rejecting the Pakistan government's plea that Muzaffarabad had no jurisdiction "outside" Azad Kashmir, the High Court admitted the petition and in a judgment delivered on March 8, 1993, stated:

> The Northern Areas are and have been part of the state of Jammu and Kashmir as it existed before and on 15 August 1947; the Northern Areas are part of Azad Jammu & Kashmir and are to be construed and acknowledged as such; the detachment of the Northern Areas from the rest of Azad Jammu & Kashmir is tantamount to the violation of the Resolutions of the UN Security Council of 30 March 1951 and 24 January 1957; and, the state subjects residing in the Northern Areas have been deprived of the benefits of fundamental rights enshrined in the Interim Constitution during the past without lawful authority. These rights are admissible and exercisable by them.[18]

The court directed the Azad Kashmir government to immediately assume administrative control of the Northern Areas and asked the government of Pakistan to assist the Azad Kashmir government in this task. The Pakistan government then appealed to the Supreme Court, contending that the "issues raised were basically political in nature and hence not amenable to discussion and judgment before a court of law."[19] It further argued that the High Court of Azad Jammu and Kashmir lacked jurisdiction in this matter as it could not issue a writ to the government of Pakistan. On September 14, 1994, the Supreme Court ruled that "the Northern Areas are part of Jammu & Kashmir state but are not part of Azad Kashmir as defined in the Azad Kashmir Interim Constitution Act, 1974."

The Pakistan government then argued that even the Supreme Court has no jurisdiction over the Northern Areas. This statement was issued by way of an official response to a petition in the Supreme Court by a group called the Al

Jihad Trust, challenging the validity of Pakistan's occupation of the Northern Areas. The government's statement noted that Parliament "has by law yet to admit into the federation Northern Areas on such terms and conditions as it thinks fit." In its official defense before the Supreme Court, the government argued that "Pakistan exercises de facto sovereignty over Northern Areas," that it "has exercised a continuous effective occupation of the Northern Areas for the past 50 years," and that through this period "there has been an effective and continuous display of state authority."[20] Amir Hamza Qureshi, founder of Gilgit-Baltistan Jamhoori Mahaz, cites a writ petition (No. 862/1990) filed in the Lahore High Court that was dismissed on the grounds that

> in terms of Article 1(2) of the Constitution of Islamic Republic of Pakistan, Northern Areas does not form part of Pakistan [but is] linked with the main Kashmir issue which is under consideration in the UN for the last 50 years. Till decision of this dispute Government is administering Northern Areas in accordance with the Provisions of United Nations Commission on India and Pakistan (UNCIP) resolution. *Grant of constitutional status tantamount to unilateral annexation of Northern Areas with Pakistan which will be against Pakistan's stand on Kashmir issue in international fora.*[21] (Emphasis added)

In effect, the Pakistan government has taken the stand that until Kashmir's final status—held in abeyance for the past fifty-nine years—is resolved, it cannot grant constitutional status to the Northern Areas and thereby constitutional rights to its people because that will compromise Pakistan's stand at the United Nations. So in the name of seeking the right of self-determination for the people of the "other" Kashmir (that is, the Indian part), Islamabad continues to sacrifice the fundamental rights of Kashmiris living in areas under its own control. This, of course, as acknowledged by the Pakistan government itself, does not interfere with its powers to exercise complete state authority in these areas, which, as argued in the next section, has turned into an imperialistic relationship.

Reincarnation of the "Princely System": The Pakistani Bureaucracy in Command

In the chequered evolution of Azad Kashmir's political status, one constant has been the supremacy of the Ministry of Kashmir Affairs (MKA) set up in 1948. Notwithstanding the changing form of government—basic democracy (1960), presidential form (1971), and parliamentary system (1974)—the ultimate authority has always been vested in the MKA. One reason is that Islamabad has never followed the basic democratic principle of the separation of executive and legislative powers and thereby ensures that the legislature will remain firmly under the executive thumb. Another instrument Pakistan used to exercise control was to assign virtually all top civil and police administrative posts to Pakistan officials "on deputation" from Islamabad.

The first ordinance, titled the "Rules of Business of the Azad Kashmir Government, 1950," was enacted on December 28, 1950, to serve as the basic law for Azad Kashmir. It vested full executive *and* legislative powers in the "supreme Head of the State," a position that was entrusted to the "supreme Head of the Azad Kashmir Movement," that is, the Muslim Conference Party.[22] The supreme head was given the power to appoint the president and other members of the council of ministers, who would be collectively responsible to him, as well as the chief justice and other judges of the Azad Kashmir High Court, who would hold office "at his pleasure." All legislation required the approval of the supreme head. This position, as Sardar Ibrahim, the first president of Azad Kashmir, soon realized, was "anomalous" because it was the MKA, which, in some ill-defined way, was supposed to "assist in the *appointment of the leaders of Azad Kashmir.*"[23] How such a prerogative could coexist with a democratic electoral process was not specified. Both Sardar M. Ibrahim Khan and Chowdhary Ghulam Abbas criticized these institutions and sought assurances that they would not override popular sentiment within Azad Kashmir. Later, however, Ibrahim admitted that these became "the main cause of difference between the leaders of Azad Kashmir" and "led to the disintegration of the Azad Kashmir Movement to a very large extent."[24]

The "basic facts of life in Azad Kashmir" were clearly reflected in the new "Rules of Business" promulgated in 1952. They vested full power in the joint secretary, MKA, rather than the supreme head of the Muslim Conference. Nominally, Azad Kashmir was run by the president, who held office "at the pleasure" of the General Council of the Muslim Conference, but since that body operated under the supervision of the joint secretary, there was no doubt about the ultimate source of authority. In 1958 the Rules of Business were amended again, with full powers now being vested in a "chief adviser" rather than the Joint Secretary. But because the chief adviser was appointed by and in real terms was responsible to the MKA, this was a change in form, not in fact.[25]

During much of this period, Kashmir affairs were in the hands of a middle-rank Pakistani bureaucrat who behaved like a "viceroy," insisting that the president of Azad Kashmir "come humbly to the Pakistani capital and request an 'audience' with the Joint Secretary."[26] A former president of Azad Kashmir described the system as a "government of Azad Kashmir, by the Pakistanis, for Pakistan."

In 1974 Azad Kashmir got its first interim constitution, set up by Zulfiqar Ali Bhutto's government, which provided for two executive forums: the Azad Kashmir government in Muzaffarabad and the Azad Kashmir Council in Islamabad. The latter is essentially the new *avatar* (form) of the MKA in that it provides for an overarching, all-powerful bureaucratic authority. The council is presided over by the prime minister of Pakistan and includes six other federal ministers—constituting a majority—and the prime minister of Azad Kashmir, with six Azad Kashmir members elected by its assembly and the minister of Kashmir affairs as the ex officio member. The constitution listed fifty-two subjects, virtually everything of any importance, under the jurisdiction of the council, described as the "supra power" by the Azad Kashmir High Court. Paragraph 156 of its historic judgment stated: "No legislation could be placed before the Council (of Ministers) for its approval without obtaining the advice of the Chief Adviser. In case of difference of opinion, the legislation was not to be given effect without prior consultation with the Ministry of Kashmir Affairs."[27] Its decisions are final and not subject to judicial review. The constitution, under Article 56, also empowered the federal government to dismiss any elected government in Azad Kashmir irrespective of the support it might enjoy in the Legislative Assembly.

From the outset, Azad Kashmir's leaders bitterly and publicly complained about the MKA. Sardar Ibrahim criticized the ministry for having "played havoc with the [Azad Kashmir] movement and had it finally liquidated to the satisfaction of all bureaucrats in Pakistan."[28] Four decades later, little had changed: "It [MKA] is like hell. It is the worst example of bureaucracy. . . . It has not served Kashmiris at all. It has always divided and made them fight among themselves."[29] The extraordinary powers of the Pakistani bureaucracy can be judged from the fact that if its members happen to clash with the elected representatives of Azad Kashmir, the latter must give in. For instance, when the chief secretary, Amanullah Khan Niazi, fell out with the incumbent president, K. H. Khurshid, it was ultimately Khurshid who was ousted and detained for some months in Rawalpindi jail.[30] Again in 1991, when Prime Minister Raja Mumtaz Hussain Rathore alleged the elections had been rigged by the federal government and declared them null and void, the minister for Kashmir affairs, Sardar Mehtab Khan Abbassi, charged that those actions had been unconstitutional and unwarranted and dismissed Rathore's government, while Rathore himself was brought to Islamabad by the military and detained for thirty days under the Maintenance of Public Order Ordinance. At critical moments, Muslim Conference leaders have denounced their own governments and the constitutional status of Azad Kashmir as a "bogus" "Pakistani creature" without real independence. In doing so they have risked arrest and imprisonment by the Pakistani authorities. Yet on release and on finding themselves still popular within Azad Kashmir as a result of such radical behavior, they must still accept power under conditions and in a context determined by Pakistani national interests.[31]

Unlike Azad Kashmir, the Northern Areas does not even have a façade of self-governance because of its ambiguous constitutional status. When the Pakistan government sent Sardar Mohammad Alam there as its first political agent in November 1947, one of his first acts was to impose the Frontier Crimes Regulations (FCR) on the entire Gilgit Agency, including Baltistan and the subdivision of Astore. The FCRs are similar to the Criminal Tribes Act promulgated by the British during the colonial rule, which required members of tribes to report to the local police station once a month and keep the police informed of their movements. From 1947 to 1972, the FCRs denied inhabitants of the Northern Areas their basic civil rights. In 1950 control of the Northern Areas was transferred to the Ministry of Kashmir Affairs, although the office of Political Resident for Gilgit and Baltistan looked after the actual administration. This arrangement continued until 1952, when the joint secretary, Kashmir Affairs Division, was given the additional post of Resident of the Northern Areas. In 1967 a separate post of Resident of the Northern Areas was created, with headquarters at Gilgit, which permitted an autocratic style of rule in that the office combined the powers of head of the local administration, high court, commissioner under the FCR, and provincial and revenue commissioner. There being no separate legislative body in these areas, the resident also exercised legislative powers in consultation with the government of Pakistan.[32]

In 1972 Prime Minister Zulfiqar Ali Bhutto abolished the centuries-old Jagir system and kingdoms of Hunza and Nagar, and scrapped the harsh Frontier Criminal Regulations. Thereafter the Northern Areas was divided into three districts—Gilgit, Baltistan, and Diamer—each headed by a deputy commissioner functioning under the commissioner for the Northern Areas, but basically administered by Pakistan in ad hoc fashion. There were no laws defining its governance system and relationship with Pakistan, although an advisory council was established under the jurisdiction of the MKA, but it, too, operated haphazardly, as its members and functions varied from one period to another.[33] This arrangement remained in place for two decades, until 1994. In other words, in the forty-seven years since they came under Pakistan's control, the people of the Northern Areas had no right to vote. They had no elected assembly, or even a municipal council, and no representation in the Federal Assembly (though the territory was granted limited "observer status" for a while during General Zia-ul-Haq's military regime).

Much like Azad Kashmir, the Northen Areas is governed by the Pakistan government, primarily through the Ministry of Kashmir Affairs and Northern Affairs (KANA) based in Islamabad, which exercises supreme control in all matters. It is empowered to impose and withdraw the laws and rules of Pakistan or to frame separate rules for these areas. The executive head of the Northern Areas is the KANA-appointed chief commissioner, who is answerable to the federal government alone. KANA's minister also heads the Northern Areas Council, which is effectively devoid of any powers. It cannot form a government, it cannot legislate, and it has no say in the administration. The council meets at the minister's behest and cannot be convened by its members. No bill passed by the council can become law unless it is approved and signed by the chief executive. The council's only duty, as one cynic put it, "is to receive dignitaries from Pakistan."[34] In 1994 the Human Rights Commission of Pakistan carried out a special study of the situation in the Northern Areas and arrived at a scathing assessment:

> The people of NA have no say in who governs them; the democratic rights of the people have been tied to a cause; a Pakistan civil servant legislates for the Northern Areas and influences all the executive and judicial acts; sometimes arbitrary laws are applied while important ones are not extended, according to convenience; the Northern Areas council has no legislative powers at all; the Judicial commissioner and subordinate courts are not free; the people have no fundamental rights whatsoever; executive acts, however arbitrary, can not be judicially reviewed; the election commissioner is not independent and is vulnerable to pressures; and, the administration has failed to control sectarian clashes due to mis-management and acquiescence to pressure.[35]

Local people perceive it as an alien administration. The status of the Northern Areas is described as that of a "colony forgotten all about by the uncaring coloniser."[36]

Owing to KANA's role in the Northern Areas, all instruments of internal security are controlled by non-locals. Pakistanis man the civil, police, and security services. The Gilgit Scouts, which was the Northern Areas' only local paramilitary force, with a history dating back more than a hundred years, was disbanded in the 1970s because of its sympathies with the locals. In 1971 an organization called the Tanzeem-e-Millat (TM), led by Johar Ali Khan, had demanded that the FCR be repealed and the basic rights of the locals be recognized. When their agitation took a violent turn, the area deputy commissioner, A. R. Siddiqui, ordered the Gilgit Scouts to open fire on the agitators, but they refused. As a result, they were disbanded by Pakistan's Prime Minister, Zulfiqar Ali Bhutto, much to the disappointment of locals: "The Gilgit Scouts was the only credible law-enforcing agency from pre-partition times. Northerners generally resent the undoing of this centuries-old institution."[37] This group was replaced by the Chitral Scouts, another import from the neighboring province, NWFP. The contrast between these two law-enforcing bodies toward the local agitations came into sharp relief in June 1996, when Chitral Scouts opened fire at youth gathered to seek employment with the newly created paramilitary force, the Northern Scouts. This force is dominated by Pushtuns of the NWFP, and its headquarters are located in Dir district of the NWFP's Malakand division.[38]

This extreme bureaucratic control makes the governance structures in the Pakistani part of Kashmir seem like a "continuation of the 'old princely system' under British rule," with Islamabad in the "viceroy" role and locals keeping the traditional biradari system in place.[39] Islamabad has, however, gone beyond the colonial practices of co-opting the old elites composed of mirs and biradaries by introducing a new layer of *non-local* elites of every stripe—religious, linguistic, cultural, and regional—to rule these regions. These are chiefly Pakistani bureaucrats, businessmen, and military personnel. In the Northern Areas, for example, all important officers who assist the chief executive, including the chief secretary, the inspector general of police, the judicial commissioner, and the chief of public works, are Pakistanis who are invariably Punjabi or Pushtun bureaucrats. Equally important, in Shia-dominated Gilgit and Baltistan, the entire top layer of the bureaucracy has always consisted of Sunnis, many linked directly or indirectly with sectarian and militant organizations in other parts of Pakistan. Mohammad Yahya Shah, chief convener of the Hunza-Nagar Movement, has lamented: "We were ruled by the whites during the British days, but we are now being ruled by the browns from the plains."[40] Bureaucratic control over the Northern Areas has led to a growing client class of traders and smugglers mostly from down-country. Called the Silk Mafia, this class operates in cahoots with customs and administrative officials to monopolize trade from China in prohibited items such as silk fabric, firecrackers, and industrial chemicals that can be used in explosives. In the last Northern Areas Legislative Council (NALC) elections held in November 2004, many of these traders entered the political echelons of power by contesting elections as independents. Most such candidates represented nonpolitical elements with business interests in the Chinese trade, while "some had also received 'non-performing' bank loans that could be leveraged by Islamabad to control them."[41] Even before official results were announced, nine out of ten independents who won their elections joined the Pakistan Muslim League (Quaid-i-Azam) Party, backed by the military regime in Islamabad. The judicial system, too, is subservient to the bureaucracy and has failed to check the growth of a client class that has prospered in local politics and trade in recent years. Local traders have, as a result, suffered gradual erosion in their margins in recent years.

Similarly, Azad Kashmir's local officials can never aspire to become an inspector general of police, chief secretary, or finance secretary. Such officials are always "lent" by Pakistan, and some offices even abolished, such as the public service commission in Azad Kashmir. Moreover, the "old guard" of the Muslim Conference has been sidelined by new militant forces influenced by the increasing Islamic sensitivity in Pakistan and the long insurgent movement in the Kashmir Valley. As explained in chapter 3, jihadi forces in Azad Kashmir are expanding and moving toward Deobandi and Ahl-e-Hadith beliefs, overshadowing the "old," indigenous, and secular elements such as those represented by the JKLF. Despite a ban on their activities, many of these militant outfits got a new lease of life after helping relief and rehabilitation operations following the earthquake of October 2005.

The people of the Northern Areas are also excluded from the judicial process. There is only one, and final, court of appeal, which is under the supervision of the judicial commissioner, and no possibility for appeal in the Supreme Court. The commissioner himself has no writ jurisdiction, probably because the people continue to be denied fundamental rights in the constitution of Pakistan, and is not completely free from the executive. His annual confidential report is written by the secretary of KANA, which also makes all decisions regarding the appointment and transfer of the subordinate judges. However, in a landmark verdict on May 28, 1999, the Supreme Court of Pakistan censured "the dictatorial and colonial system at work in Gilgit and Baltistan, where the chief executive, the minister of Kashmir Affairs, appointed by the government of Pakistan, enjoys more powers than even the British Viceroy did before partition."[42] The court directed the government to take administrative and legislative steps to enforce the fundamental rights of the people in the Northern Areas, namely, to allow them to be governed by their chosen representatives, and to have access to justice, among other things for the enforcement of their fundamental rights under the constitution of Pakistan. The court questioned on what basis the people of the Northern Areas could be denied these fundamental rights inasmuch as they are citizens of Pakistan "for all intents and purposes," and thus may "invoke any fundamental rights" as well as be liable for "taxes and other levies competently imposed."[43] Following the judgment, the Nawaz Sharif government announced a "package" providing for an appellate court and more seats on the council, now renamed the Northern Areas Legislative Council. A new legal framework was drawn up granting the NALC powers to legislate on local matters and impose taxes. The first elections to the NALC were held after General Pervez Musharraf came to power in November 1999.

Most of these changes are of a semantic nature, however. Despite several name changes—from the original Northern Areas Advisory Council of 1971 to Northern Areas Executive Council in 1994 and Northern Areas Legislative Council in 1999—the basic structure of the Northern Areas administration remains the same. The federal minister of Kashmir affairs continues to be the area's chief executive, and the chief secretary implements all decisions of the federation of Pakistan. Not surprisingly, the system is a failure: "You cannot devise a political system for the Northern Areas without first clarifying its constitutional status. Are we an autonomous region like Azad Kashmir, or are we a province of Pakistan? As things stand, we are neither one nor the other."[44]

On November 26, 2000, the Musharraf regime announced that it was delegating financial and administrative powers to the NALC and increasing the annual budgetary allocation for the area from Rs 60 million to Rs 1 billion. Just before the NALC's second elections in November 2004, the government announced another new package, which increased the number of NALC seats from twenty-nine to thirty-one, increased women's seats in local bodies by 33 percent, and promised a Rs 500 million outlay to be disbursed, in the words of one nationalist leader, "to the NALC members ostensibly for development but actually to buy their loyalties."[45] Despite such gestures, the feudal character of the power structures, rigorously controlled by the Pakistani bureaucracy, remains untouched. Without any meaningful delegation of financial and administrative powers, the local population continues to be at the mercy of the bureaucracy, without a president, prime minister, parliament, or courts, and no right to cast votes in Pakistan or in Azad Kashmir: It is "like a no-man's land," laments one leader. "We are the last colony in the world."[46]

CURBING POLITICAL FORCES BY MANIPULATING ELECTIONS AND IMPOSING MILITARY RULE

Despite the bureaucratic stranglehold on the power structures, political forces in these territories, especially in Azad Kashmir, have asserted themselves from time to time. Their ways of resisting pressures from Islamabad cannot be discussed without first examining the establishment's instruments of control and coercion. The principal means of control has been to manipulate elections, dismiss any government in Muzaffarabad that is not compliant, and control the government's purse strings. Another effective approach, military regimes in Islamabad have found, is simply to suspend all political activities.

Following these practices, the Pakistani establishment has dismissed and installed governments of Azad Kashmir at will. Many observers consider Sheikh Abdullah's dismissal by the Nehru government a prime factor in the alienation of Kashmir Valley from the Indian State, little knowing that across the cease-fire line such events were almost a fact of everyday life: Azad Kashmir's first government, under Sardar M. Ibrahim Khan, was also dismissed in 1953. From 1953 to 1962 Islamabad sacked three governments in Muzaffarabad, those of Khan Abdul Qayum Khan, Colonel Sher Ali, and Mirwaiz Yusuf Shah. Even before Pakistanis installed their first military regime, Islamabad placed Poonch and parts of Mirpur under martial law when widespread disturbances erupted in 1955 following the publication of the Kashmir Government Act.

Upon taking the reins of power in Islamabad in 1958, Ayub Khan banned all political activities in Azad Kashmir. K. H. Khurshid, the then leader of the Azad Kashmir's government, had initially received assurances from the federal government that the provisions of Ayub Khan's Basic Democracy ordinance would not be extended to the region. In 1960, however, the electoral activities of the Muslim Conference were indeed curtailed, and new union councils were set up as envisaged by the Basic Democracy initiative. Direct interventions into the affairs of Azad Kashmir were furthered through the Basic Democracy provisions of the 1962 constitution. In 1963 the Ministry for Kashmir Affairs was transferred from the Ministry of Home Affairs to the presidential secretariat, under the direct authority of Ayub Khan. In 1964 K. H. Khurshid, the first president of Azad Jammu and Kashmir (AJK) to assume office through Ayub Khan's Basic Democracy system, was dismissed because he began asserting himself, pressing to have Azad Kashmir part of the Indus Water Treaty—a treaty he had earlier opposed.

Both civilian and military regimes treated the Azad Kashmir governments with equal disdain. Under the emergency clauses of the 1974 constitution, a presidential system had replaced the parliamentary system. That year, Prime Minister Z. A. Bhutto dismissed Sardar Abdul Qayum's government (elected in 1970), and in short order his successor, General Zia-ul-Haq, used the same tactic. On August 10, 1977, Zia dissolved the Azad Kashmir legislative assembly and dismissed the cabinet, installing Brigadier General Hayat M. Khan as president and signaling the arrival of a military form of government. In July 1979, General Zia ordered the suspension of all political activities.[47] During his regime (1977–85), the Northern Areas became a separate division under martial law, designated Zone E (Zones A–D being the four provinces of Pakistan), even though martial law had not been declared in the state of Azad Jammu and Kashmir. Under earlier regimes, martial law did not apply in the Northern Areas. On October 31, 1980, President Hayat Khan announced that a Council of Ministers and a Majlis-i-Shoora (Advisory Council), elected on a non-party basis, would be set up along the same lines Zia was introducing in Pakistan.

Political activity resumed when Sikandar Hayat took over as prime minister and Sardar Abdul Qayum became president after an election in June 1985—which, however, was restricted to "registered" parties, thus disqualifying the Pakistan People's Party (PPP). After Zia's death in August 1988, the expectation was that Benazir Bhutto would organize a new coalition government in Azad Jammu and Kashmir, but she chose to focus on rebuilding the PPP's base and renew ties with the various biradari political factions. Of course, she did not hesitate to interfere in Azad Kashmir affairs in support of her party's local branch and also imposed strict limits on Pakistani financial assistance.[48] However, Benazir Bhutto allowed the AJK government to stay in power, the first to complete its tenure since 1947, and to hold elections in 1990.

In the June 1990 elections, the Legislative Assembly elected PPP leader Raja Mumtaz Hussain Rathore as the new prime minister and Chaudhury Sultan Mohammed as the new president. But in August, Benazir was dismissed in Islamabad, and Prime Minister Ghulam Mustafa Jatoi reconstituted the Azad Kashmir Council by appointing five new Pakistani members. Two days later, in a joint session of the council, the assembly reelected Muslim Conference leader Sardar Abdul Qayum as the president of Azad Kashmir by a vote of 32 to 23. In an attempt to forestall Islamabad's move to ease him out of office, Mumtaz Rathore called for sudden elections on June 9, 1991. But contrary to his expectations, his party won only two seats, whereas the Muslim Conference won thirty-two of the forty elected seats. Rathore alleged massive rigging by Islamabad and refused to accept the electoral verdict, declaring that Azad Kashmir would not be treated like a "colony" and threatening to launch an armed agitation. Many independent observers agreed that the results were so one-sided that the entire exercise appeared highly suspect.

The timing of these elections was politically significant. For one thing, the insurgency in the Valley was at its peak. For another, Pakistan's attempts to internationalize the Kashmir issue and growing cross-border movements among the Kashmiris had focused widespread attention on developments in Azad Kashmir and the Northern Areas. With the blatant manipulation of the 1991 elections and arbitrary dismissal and arrest of Prime Minister Rathore, large-scale demonstrations erupted in protest. The PPP termed this an "act of abduction," and Benazir Bhutto, then in the opposition, said that the Kashmiris had become alienated "to such an extent that they want independence."[49] One Azad Kashmir leader remarked caustically on the similarity between occupied Kashmir and the so-called liberated territory: "There the Indian army is launching aggression against the Kashmiri freedom fighters demanding the right to vote. And here in the liberated territory, the army is arresting the Prime Minister."[50] Even a Pakistani general, Saleem Zia, was persuaded that the "Pakistan government should desist from interfering in the internal politics of Azad Kashmir, as it did in the recent past. When a bureaucrat from Pakistan can arrest the Prime Minister of Azad Kashmir, how does one expect the world to attach any importance to the pronouncements of Azad Kashmir government?"[51]

The tables were turned in the 1996 elections. When Sardar Abdul Qayum Khan's ruling Muslim Conference was virtually wiped out in Azad Kashmir, Nawaz Sharif, leader of the opposition, alleged that Benazir's government had rigged the elections. While the PPP and its allies bagged thirty seats, Qayum's party could only collect five. Ironically, on the eve of the polls for the Azad Kashmir Legislative Assembly, Premier Benazir Bhutto had proclaimed: "Come and see what real democracy is. Come and distinguish between free elections and a farce, between freedom and slavery," with an obvious reference to the parliamentary elections held in the Kashmir Valley.[52] However, immediately after polling began, Sardar Qayum accused Islamabad of massive rigging, and by noon his party's candidates for the twelve refugee seats in Pakistan had announced a boycott. Nawaz Sharif even accused Benazir of perpetrating a farce not very different from the one played out in Indian-held Kashmir during the recent Lok Sabha elections.[53]

Next in the line of succession was General Pervez Musharraf, who overthrew Nawaz Sharif's government in 1999 and was not in the least hesitant about interfering in the affairs of Azad Kashmir's government. For example, he forced the ruling Muslim Conference to nominate Major General Mohammad Anwar Khan, former vice chief of the general staff (VCGS) who had been prematurely retired from the army so that he could run for president. By that time, the Pakistani military had established itself as the ultimate arbiter in Pakistani politics. That was also true for Azad Kashmir. For instance, when the rivalry between the two factions of the ruling Muslim Conference led by Sardar Qayum and Sardar Sikandar Hayat reached a crisis point in February 2004, the resigning finance minister sought arbitration. He turned not to the president of Azad Kashmir but to the general officer commanding the 12th Corps at Murree, Major General Wasim Ashraf.

The Pakistan army oversees not only the fortunes of political forces active in Azad Kashmir but also the civil administration, which it has virtually decimated. Its failings were all too evident during a massive earthquake in Azad Kashmir in 2005, which killed more than 55,000 people and left 2.5 million people homeless.[54] One reason for the administration's weak response was that Muzaffarabad was very close to the epicenter of the earthquake, and its buildings and infrastructure were literally buried in the rubble. The army was the only organized force with the manpower and equipment to step into the administration's shoes—but it was found wanting. Its first priority was to secure the strategic heights along the Line of Control, where many of its forward lines had been wiped out, and thus it was feared that India could easily occupy "strategically important peaks that had been left unattended."[55] Hence the army spent almost the entire first two to three critical days—when thousands of people trapped under rubble could have been saved—rushing in reinforcements from Lahore. That is why the army's rescue and relief teams took three days to reach seriously affected towns such as Muzaffarabad, Balakot, and Garhi Habibullah and another couple of days to put its command-and-control system in place. Access to comparatively remote areas in the Lipa and Neelam Valleys took nearly two weeks.

The resulting administrative vacuum was filled by militant outfits with well-equipped training and logistical facilities in the region. Lashkar-e-Taiba, operating under the name Jamaat-al-Dawa, spearheaded the rescue and relief effort, removing the debris from collapsed buildings and providing first aid to the injured within two hours of the earthquake. It claimed to have deployed 10,000 volunteers, including 1,000 doctors running a field hospital at Muzaffarabad. It was also one of the first organizations to reach out to the rural areas through river-raft and mule-train service carrying supplies and medicine to the mountains. Other militant groups involved in the relief work included Hizb-ul-Mujahideen, Harkat-ul-Mujahideen, Rehreek-ul-Mujahideen, al Badr, Hizbul Tehrir, and Tehrik Nifaz-e-Shariat. Among the banned outfits, Jaish-i-Mohammed (renamed Khuddam-ul-Islam) was working under the aegis of the Al-Rahmat Trust, while its splinter group, Jamaat-ul-Furqan, resurfaced with a new identity, Al-Asr Trust. The Karachi-based Al-Rashid Trust and Al-Akhtar Trust also used the quake as an opportunity to revive their organizations.[56] Significantly, the army, the federal government, and the Azad Kashmir government acknowledged and appreciated the rehabilitation work undertaken by these outfits perhaps because their own efforts were found wanting. As a result, whereas the army was criticized for placing its security interests above the lives of thousands of people, the militants were considered "saviors."

Colonization of Resources, Territories, and People

Pakistan's primary reason for seeking to include Kashmir within its boundaries, some argue, is not ideological affinity, but the area's indispensability for securing Pakistan's frontiers—militarily, strategically, and economically. Indeed, Pakistan's record is one of systematically exploiting Kashmir's resources and territories to achieve its national objectives, often at tremendous cost to the people living in those areas. Expropriation of their water resources provides the starkest example. In a speech to the UN Security Council in 1950, Pakistan's foreign minister, Sir Zafarullah Khan, openly admitted that Kashmir's water resources are central to Pakistan's survival:

> The three rivers beginning at the top of the map—the Indus, the Jhelum and the Chenab, which flow from Kashmir into Pakistan, control, to a very large extent, the agricultural economy of Pakistan itself. . . . If Kashmir were to accede to India, this supply is liable to be cut off altogether. This is not an idle apprehension on the part of Pakistan. . . . millions of people would be faced with starvation and extinction. . . . Therefore, to think in terms of Pakistan without Kashmir as an independent country is a complete fallacy.[57]

Mohammed Ali Jinnah once described Kashmir as the jugular vein of Pakistan, but its resources are certainly not benefiting the local people. A case in point is the Mangla Dam, completed in 1968, which has the capacity to generate 1,000 megawatts of power. This dam supplies 65 percent of Pakistan's electricity needs and so far has contributed more than Rs 100 billion to its development. Mangla Dam also serves as the principal water-storage reservoir for the entire canal system in the West Punjab. Thus it plays a critical role in Pakistan's economy. And it has brought Pakistanis throughout the country tremendous benefits: cheap electricity, year-round irrigation, and security from flooding. Yet the people living immediately upstream of the dam have had to bear the brunt of its environmental costs.[58] The Mirpuris have seen much of their most fertile agricultural land and the district's two market towns, including the old town of Mirpur itself and Chaomukh, disappear under 100 feet of the lake's water. The construction of the dam displaced at least 20,000 families, many of whom were forced to migrate, for the most part to Britain.

Through their remittances, the large pool of Mirpuri migrant workers has contributed significantly to Pakistan's national finances in foreign exchange. At their peak in the early 1980s, remittances provided well over 50 percent of the country's foreign exchange earnings and even today are contributing close to that figure.[59]

The Mangla Dam has also had an adverse effect on the local infrastructure, especially on transport and communications. While infrastructural damage is an inevitable consequence of such projects, the government of Pakistan could have made amends at a tiny fraction of the overall costs, but Islamabad chose to cut corners, as was only too obvious to the Mirpuris. Although the dam contractors built a first-class road around the southern (and originally sparsely populated) shore of the newly formed lake, the long and winding road around the densely populated northern shore, which provided the remainder of the district with its only access to the plains, was built to a much lower standard and was not completed until some years after the water had risen. And it was more than a decade before a bridge was finally constructed across the Poonch River to Tehsil Dadial, which the rising waters of the dam had turned into an isolated peninsula inaccessible to vehicular traffic.[60]

Many Mirpuris deeply resented the lack of consideration for their contribution to Pakistan's economy. No serious effort was made to stimulate economic and infrastructural development in Dadial Tehsil, Mirpur district, or in Azad Kashmir as a whole. And although large sums had indeed been spent on the Mangla project, its beneficiaries were most definitely not Mirpuri. The benefits of Mangla's electricity were felt in Lahore, and even in Karachi, long before power lines began to be installed in rural Mirpur.[61]

More important, the level of royalties paid to the Azad Kashmir government for the Mangle Dam's benefits has been disputed between Islamabad and Muzaffarabad for years. Political leaders have raised this issue from time to time, pointing out that Islamabad pays royalty to the NWFP government for Terbela Dam, and on top of that it charges double the electricity tariff from Azad Kashmir than in Pakistan.[62] Another bone of contention is that the cost of the dam is being passed along to the taxpayers. Local people have been demanding that the costs be borne by Punjab, since it has been the main beneficiary of the dam. Azad Kashmir's authorities also complain that the Water and Power Development Authority (WAPDA) operates and maintains the distribution network in the four provinces, while their own government is forced to spends Rs 250 million a year on the operation and maintenance of its own network.

Another contentious issue is that the height of the dam is being raised, but it is for the benefit of the people of Punjab, not the people of Azad Kashmir.

On August 6, 2001, the president of the Jammu Kashmir Liberation League (JKLL) and former chief justice of the Azad Jammu and Kashmir High Court, Abdul Majeed Malick, said there was no justification for raising the level of the Mangla Dam: "The people of Mirpur should not be disturbed once again and if there is a water crisis in Pakistan, then the federal government should construct the Kalabagh Dam (outside the Azad J&K)." He disputed WAPDA's claim that only 40,000 people would be displaced as a result of the extension and that about 100,000 people would be displaced and two tehsils of district Mirpur would be submerged. He pointed out that the people of Azad Kashmir, who were displaced by the original construction of the dam in the 1960s, had not received any relief so far, not to mention the alternate land in Punjab that had been promised to them.[63] In total disregard of the local opposition, the Ministry of Water and Power, WAPDA, and Azad Kashmir's government signed an agreement to allow the height of the Mangla Dam to be raised by 30 feet. That will raise the height of the Mangla reservoir by 50 feet, giving it an increased capacity of 3.1 million acre feet of water. The agreement proposes to compensate Azad Kashmir for raising the height of the dam and includes the sum of Rs 29 billion for the resettlement of the displaced locals.

According to economists from the All-Parties National Alliance, the Northern Areas should also receive a sum of Rs 1,470 crore a year in royalties from using the water resources of the Indus River. Instead, Pakistan gives the area only Rs 225 crore, which will do little to help improve its practically nonexistent infrastructure or rampant unemployment.[64] Although the Indus River originates from the Northern Areas, its royalty is paid to NWFP.

Both Azad Kashmir and the Northern Areas are heavily dependent on Islamabad for financial support. In 2002–03, for example, Azad Kashmir was awaiting federal transfers amounting to a deficit of about Rs 2,680 million. In the next budget, the amount provided went up to Rs 2.28 billion. In most years, only a small proportion of the budget is devoted to development. From a total outlay of Rs 13.2 billion, the Azad Kashmir budget allocates only Rs 3.8 billion for the crucial task of development. Nondevelopment expenditure, estimated at Rs 9.3 billion, makes a major claim on the budget. The story in the Northern Areas is not much different. Between 1960 and 1999, Rs 5.4 billion was allocated for the development of the Northern Areas. Of this amount, Rs 3.3 billion was actually used. Similarly, from 1990–91 to 2000–01, Rs 8.3 billion was allocated for the Annual Development Program (ADP) of the area but the amount used up to December 2000 was Rs 6.8 billion. Thus over a period of forty-one years the Northern Areas have received Rs 13.7 billion for development, of which Rs 10.1 billion has been utilized. Both regions are also excluded from the budgetary process, which is entirely in the hands of the federal government, from the preparation to the allocation of resources. Moreover, the budget is passed not by the elected assembly, but by the Azad Kashmir Council. Although its development projects are made and approved locally, they have to be cleared financially by Islamabad before being passed.

As the foregoing discussion suggests, Azad Kashmir and the Northern Areas are poorly developed. Landholdings are small and fragmented, ranging in average cultivated area from 0.57 hectare in Baltistan to 0.93 hectare in Diamer. Only 0.96 percent of the 69,480 hectares of land in the Northern Areas is under cultivation; the rest lies barren. Per capita landholding is about 0.124 hectare. In Azad Kashmir, the total area under cultivation is about 170,787 hectares, about 12.8 percent of the total, and per capita landholding is only 0.159 hectare. About 91 percent of the population lives in the rural areas and is dependent on forests and agricultural land for its livelihood. With the population increasing at the rapid rate of 2.7 percent a year, the natural resource base is being depleted beyond sustainable levels. Despite reforestation programs, the net loss in forest covers due to commercial and illicit felling of trees ranges from 6,000 to 8,000 hectares annually.

Likewise, the Northern Areas has suffered total neglect except for the efforts of the Aga Khan Rural Support Programs and other nongovernmental organizations that have initiated some micro-development programs. The area has no university and no professional colleges, and no industry. The local people draw their subsistence from tourism and service in the armed forces. Government service is another means of livelihood, but the natives joining the civil service are paid 25 percent less than personnel from other provinces posted in the Northern Areas on deputation, which causes great resentment among the locals. While the Mirpuris from Azad Kashmir have been able to migrate in large numbers to Western countries, this avenue is not open to people of the Northern Areas since they require an exit visa from the Pakistan government for going abroad, which is difficult to obtain.[65]

Pakistan has clearly used the Northern territories to secure its strategic national objectives. When Pakistan ceded the Shaksgam area (5,800 square kilometers) of Baltistan to China in 1963, for instance, the agreement recognized that the Northern Areas was a disputed part of Jammu and Kashmir state, but neither the Azad Kashmir government nor the northern leadership had been consulted on the matter and had absolutely no say in the negotiation of the agreement.[66] Pakistan, however, continues to reap rich dividends from it. The Karakoram Highway from Xinjiang province of China, constructed with Chinese help and completed in 1978, has proven to be of tremendous strategic significance for transporting M-11 missiles and Chinese nuclear equipment to Pakistan.

On its western frontiers, Pakistan's every single war plan for annexing Kashmir (see chapter 3) has used territories of Azad Kashmir and the Northern Areas as the launching pad for conventional military attacks as well as for the infiltration of soldiers and militants. The Pakistani army has used mainly three routes for these purposes, all from its part of Kashmir: the Akhnoor sector along the Jammu-Kathua road for conventional military attacks; infiltration routes to the Kashmir Valley via Baramulla; and the Kargil Heights, which were occupied in 1999 in an attempt to cut off Ladakh via Skardu. Having a free Kashmir, albeit with a client regime, has made it easier for Pakistan to effectively apply its dictum of "plausible deniability," as explained in chapter 3. During the 1990 crisis, when belligerent statements from both India's and Pakistan's leaders raised the specter of war, Islamabad sought to distance itself from the actions of Azad Kashmir. Pakistan's foreign minister, Sahadzada Yaqub Khan, argued that Islamabad was not necessarily responsible for what happened in that area.[67] When Sardar Qayum's government announced a fund to support the cause of "freedom-fighters," Benazir Bhutto remarked: "If the Chief Minister of a particular province or the opposition party chief says that we are going to raise funds for freedom-fighters, what does a democratic government do? . . . We have counselled restraint. . . . but it cannot just arrest the opposition" and described the charges about the training camps in Pakistan as "preposterous."[68]

In one instance, Islamabad's denial of its involvement in movements across the Line of Control backfired. This happened in 1999, during the Kargil crisis, when Islamabad secretly deployed the Northern Light Infantry troops in the guise of Kashmiri mujahideen. Pakistan's army was unable to openly acknowledge their deaths and compensate their families. Of the 300 officers and men who were killed in the conflict, a majority belonged to the NLI from the Northern Areas. Pakistan reportedly refused to accept the bodies of its own soldiers killed in battle and in June 1999 surreptitiously sent back the bodies of over 500 soldiers from the area and buried them without any military honors.[69] When it learned of the situation, the local populace was up in arms because the Pakistan army and government were prepared to accept the bodies of Punjabi soldiers but left the Kashmiri soldiers to rot in the mountains of Kargil. The resentment only mounted after people saw television images of Indian army jawans going to great lengths to recover their soldiers' bodies and give them proper Islamic burials.

In August 1999, in the aftermath of the Kargil crisis, the Northern Areas became the scene of violent confrontations between locals and militants belonging to the Lashkar-e-Taiba in Skardu, which led the Pakistan army to clamp down on these areas. Similar disturbances were also reported from Shigar, northeast of Skardu and Rondu, and west of Skardu on the Skardu-Gilgit road.[70] The people had grown very bitter about the militants getting all the credit for doing nothing while the NLI took heavy casualties. Some nationalist leaders of the Northern Areas also accused the Pakistani army of trying to weaken the NLI in terms of its composition and deployment. At present, eleven of the fifteen NLI regiments are deployed in various cantonments of Pakistan and Azad Kashmir by bringing them down from Gilgit-Baltistan, so their composition is easily changed. Among Gilgitis and Baltis, separation within all NLI Units is ensured so as to divide them permanently.[71] They are now recruited as either Gilgitis or as Baltis in these regiments, along with Punjabis, Kashmiris, and Pathans. Furthermore, after the Kargil crisis, only the KANA class was recruited from Gilgit and Baltistan, in which the share of the Northern Areas is only 2 percent as compared with 7 percent for Azad Kashmir. On the whole, the Pakistani establishment's disregard for the honor of Shia soldiers of the NLI was part and parcel of its negation of the ethnocultural, religious, and linguistic diversities of the Northern Areas.

Negation of Ethnoreligious, Linguistic, and Cultural Diversities

Pakistan has always viewed Kashmir as part of a unified Islamic brotherhood. Its central argument has been that Islam is more than a sufficient link between the people of Kashmir and Pakistan and that the plural character of Kashmir society is unimportant. This reasoning gives rise to an erroneous understanding of the sociocultural and political dynamics of these areas.

The Northern Areas is a rich blend of culture, religions, and languages that have evolved over the centuries. Muslims themselves are not uniform either, with four separate denominations: the Ismaili, Sunni, Shia, and the Nur Bakshi sects. The Nur Bakshis (a group professing beliefs slightly divergent from the Shias) are present in northern and northeastern regions of Baltistan, while Shias may be found in central, southern, and western parts of Baltistan. Shia territory also includes areas west of the Rondu Gorge, namely Haramosh, Bagrot, and some parts of Gilgit and Nagar. Historically, Hunza was also under Shia influence, but at present only the village of Ghanesh remains a Shia enclave. The rest of Hunza is Ismaili. Sunnis are to be found in Gilgit, Tangir, and Darel.[72]

Shias account for 60 percent of Gilgit's population and Sunnis 40 percent. In Baltistan, the proportions are 96 percent Shia, 2 percent Nur Bakshi, and 2 percent Sunnis. Astor has a 10 percent Sunni population. The population of

Chilas and Darel/Tangir is entirely Sunni, while in Hunza, Punial, Yasin, and Ishkoman it is entirely Ismaili. The rising trend in sectarianism exists largely between Sunnis and Shias, although relations with the Ismailis are also becoming polarized.

The population of the Gilgit region has, for centuries, been organized into four castes—Shin, Yashkun, Kamin, and Dom. The Shins consider themselves ritually cleaner than all other castes and treat the goat as their sacred animal, while the cow is abhorred. The Yashkuns (landowners) and Kamins (formerly craftsmen but now mostly poorer farmers) are thought to be probable descendants of an aboriginal population. The Doms, mostly acting as minstrels for rulers or village communities, are latecomers into the region from the south. In addition, other caste-like groups have emerged over the years. These include the Ronos (families of foreign origin who produced the wazirs) and Sayyids in high positions (persons who claimed descent from the Prophet of Islam); Gujjars are perhaps at the lowest rung, forming the depressed socioeconomic classes.

The Northern Areas show the greatest variety of languages in the whole of Pakistan. The people of Yasin and Ishkoman speak Shina, Khowar, Burushashki, and Wakhi. Gilgit is home to a variety of Shina dialects, although Burushashki is the language of communication in some places. Shina is also spoken throughout Diamer and most of areas of Ghizar. Burushashki is the main language of Hunza, but Domaaki is spoken in some pockets. Wakhi is spoken in the upper part of the Hunza Valley and in some villages in Ghizar. Balti is spoken by the entire population in Balistan. In Chilas and the Indus Valley below Chilas, Shina and Kohistani are the predominant languages.

Azad Kashmir has a very diverse population on the western slopes of the Pir Panjal, which has little in common with the Kashmiris of the Srinagar Valley. Historically, this region was one of the most overwhelmingly Muslim parts of the territories of the maharaja of Kashmir, in contrast to Jammu, where Hindus have always been in the majority, and the Valley, which had a Kashmiri Pandit minority. To the west of the Pir Panjal, a tiny Hindu and Sikh minority could be found in the region's few small market towns before partition, but subsequently they all fled to India. Though Azad Kashmiris are overwhelmingly Muslim, they have few cultural connections with the Valley: "they are best seen as forming the eastern and northern limits of the Potohari Punjabi culture which is otherwise characteristic of the upland parts of Rawalpindi and Jhelum Districts."[73]

The Pakistani establishment has used the Islamic ideology or the rallying cry of "Muslim brotherhood" mainly for political ends, which has forced it to often pursue contradictory goals in Azad Kashmir and the Northern Areas. So, for example, Islamabad has sought to impose an ideological uniformity "from above" in Azad Kashmir by making it an ideological state with all its concomitant implications; in the Northern Areas, it has deliberately sown the seeds of religious sectarianism, rupturing the centuries-old ties among the Shia and Sunni communities, so as to prevent a unity among them from making any political demands on the Pakistani state. Different mechanisms have been deployed to this end. In Azad Kashmir, constitutional provisions have formally institutionalized Islam, while in the Northern Areas the establishment has done this more surreptitiously through a systematic violation of the state-subject definition and has attempted to change the demographic profile of that area by bringing in Sunni Pushtun population, mainly from the North-West Frontier Province, as well as by promoting a Wahabi Sunni version of Islam in Shia-dominated areas.

In Azad Kashmir, Article 3 of the Interim Constitution Act (1974) declared Islam to be "the state religion" and disqualified non-Muslims from election to the presidency. More important, the act bars from elective office any person "propagating any opinion or acting in any manner prejudicial or detrimental to the ideology of the State's accession to Pakistan." The oath of office for the president, prime minister, speaker, or a member of the Legislative Assembly or Council of Azad Kashmir incorporates a clause stipulating, "I will remain loyal to the country and the cause of accession of the State of Jammu & Kashmir to Pakistan." The JKLF and Jammu and Kashmir People's National Party (JKPNP) have for years been disqualified from contesting elections because of their refusal to take this oath. Those seeking public employment or enrollment in educational institutions must also uphold this ideology. Bureaucrats and other government employees suspected of disloyalty to the official ideology are routinely dismissed from their jobs.[74] Under General Zia-ul-Haq's Islamization drive in the 1980s, fervently followed by the Sardar Abdul Qayum–led Muslim Conference, such thinking seeped deep into the body politic of Azad Kashmir. A spurt in mosque building and the establishment of madaris financed with Saudi funds marked a shift toward a more orthodox public culture.

Pakistan has violated the "state-subject definition" with impunity in the Northern Areas. Introduced by the then Dogra ruler in 1927, the law bars outsiders from purchasing land in Jammu and Kashmir state. As a result of Pakistan's concerted drive to change the demographic balance of the Northern Areas, the 80 percent Shia majority of 1947 has been whittled down by Punjabi and Pushtun immigration to just 55 percent today.[75] The timing of this policy, however, continues to be a matter of debate. Although the Pakistan government suspended the state-subject law as early as 1952, some scholars attribute it to Z. A. Bhutto's policies of encouraging the *ulemas* (religious preachers). [76] Others believe it was initiated by General Zia-ul-Haq after the success of the Islamic revolution in Iran in 1979, in order to counter the growing sectarian consciousness of the Shias and their demand for political and economic rights on par with the Sunnis. His regime encouraged and facilitated the migration of Sunnis from other provinces and the Federally Administered Tribal Areas (FATAs) and resettled Sunni servicemen in the area. There was also a rapid settling in of "trading classes," mostly from Punjab and NWFP, who soon accounted for more than 60 percent of the economy of Gilgit and Baltistan and were purchasing land and expanding their businesses so vigorously that locals predicted "one day they will throw us out."[77] Even small industries and transport in the region are controlled by nonlocal people, creating a sense of acute insecurity among the local Shias and a sense of antagonism between the locals and outsiders.[78] Muzaffar Ali, the general secretary of the Northern Areas High Court Bar Association, lamented:

> The government is instigating violence to suppress our genuine demands. . . . The state-subject rules remained enforced in Indian Kashmir after 1947 while we blundered by getting integrated without adequate guarantees into Pakistan for the sake of Muslim brotherhood. We have ended up without a Constitution, representation, even without civil or judicial rights as are available to our Pakistani brothers.[79]

Gilgit-Baltistan National Alliance has also called for restoration of the "state-subject law."

The Sunni influx into the Northern Areas has had a lasting impact in destroying the centuries-old traditions of harmonious coexistence among Shia and Sunni communities, particularly in Gilgit. Until the 1960s there was no sectarian problem. The majority of the population of Gilgit consisted of Shias and Barelvi Sunni Muslims, who believe in revering the Pirs and the Sufi saints. Barelvis would freely attend Shia *majlis* (religious gatherings), and some would also give *sabeel* (complimentary milk) to the participants of Shia *julus* (processions) during the holy month of Muharram in Gilgit. Sunni scholars would deliver speeches in such processions. The trend in sectarianism started to surface in the mid-1970s. Several Pakistani analysts have argued that over the years authorities in Islamabad have apparently been instigating Shia-Sunni clashes in the area to keep the population divided.[80]

While the Bhutto government began the process by according greater importance to the ulemas, sectarianism took root during the Zia regime. He used Saudi funds to not only marginalize the more tolerant Barelvi tradition but also to undercut the Shias, especially in the Northern Areas, where they were in the majority. This was done by encouraging and facilitating the migration of people from other areas of Pakistan to the Northern Areas, and even assisting the anti-Shia Sunni extremist organization Sipah-e-Sahaba Pakistan (SSP), then known as the Anjuman Sipah-e-Sahaba, to establish its presence in the area. These organizations, in turn, started a large number of madaris to impart religious education to the local Sunnis in the Deobandi-Wahabi ideology. With extremely low literacy rates in the Northern Areas (14 percent) and few schools—between 1947 and 1995 there were 600 primary schools spread over an area of 28,000 miles—the madaris became not only the main center for the education of local children but also the breeding ground of extremism.

Influences from outside the Northern Areas also fueled religious intolerance. The Islamic revolution in Iran and the Iran-Iraq war widened the Shia-Sunni cleavage in Pakistan. Saudi Wahabi organizations and Iran used Pakistan as a playground to spread, finance, and support their respective faiths when militant Sunni organizations such as Sipah-e-Sahaba Pakistan and Sunni Tehrik had the implicit patronage of the state. Shias responded by forming the Tehrik-e-Nifaz-e-Fiqha-e-Jaffria, later renamed the Tehrik-e-Jaffria Pakistan (TJP). These organizations have subsequently spawned even more sectarian and violent offshoots such as the Sunni Lashkar-e-Jhangvi (LJ) and the Shia Sipah-e-Mohammad Pakistan (SMP).[81]

On the political front, this led to growing demands from the Shia community for the creation of an autonomous Shia state, to be called Karakorum Province. In 1985–86, the Gilgit and Baltistan Bar Association publicly demanded that the Northern Areas be made the fifth province of Pakistan, or be given a local government on the Azad Kashmir model. The result was a fierce crackdown by the Zia regime that in May 1988 produced one of the worst examples of anti-Shia carnage. A huge *lashkar* (army) of 80,000 Sunni extremists annihilated Shia villages, including Jalalabad, Bonji, Darot, Jaglot, Pari, and Manawar. Even their livestock were slaughtered:

> The number of dead and injured was put in the hundreds. But numbers alone tell nothing of the savagery of the invading hordes and the chilling impact it has left on these peaceful valleys. . . . Today, less than two years later, Gilgit is an arsenal and every man is ready to fight. In March 1996, when the administration raided homes in Gilgit town to seize weapons, one was reminded of Karachi and Beirut, not Shangri-La.[82]

These were followed by violent anti-Shia incidents in 1990, 1992, 1993, and 2001. State complicity in encouraging religious sectarianism is evident from the fact that "despite more than 300 sectarian killings since 1988, nobody has ever been punished even for a single one."[83] Until recently, the violent activities of the Sunni extremists were directed only against the Shias. However, in 2004 the Sunni extremists also started attacking the Ismailis and the schools run by the Aga Khan Foundation in the Northern Areas and the adjoining Chitral area in protest against the examination system, projected as secular and anti-Islam. This kind of violence gained momentum after the Muttahida Majlis-e-Amal (MMA) campaign against the Aga Khan Foundation in the rest of the country. In the Northern Areas, especially Gilgit, their charity institutions have come under attack regularly in recent years after being targeted by the radical religious elements waging jihad in Kashmir.

Since July 2003, the Northern Areas have also been witnessing violent protests against Islamabad's decision to introduce the Islamiat curriculum in educational institutions. Shia community leaders argue that Islamiat textbooks have been deliberately distorted to promote sectarian hatred. Distortions are said to be present not only in Islamic studies but also in the textbooks of other subjects, such as Urdu, history, English, and even in drawing books. Agha Ziauddin Rizvi, prayer leader at Gilgit's Imamia Mosque, stated: "I do not advocate elimination of Islamic Studies from the curriculum but I want them purged of all controversial and inflammatory material." Textbooks were said to "hurt the religious sentiments of not only the Shias but also the Sunni-Barelvis."[84] As a government official admitted, this is because the machinery at the Curriculum Wing is strongly biased against the Shia faith and has been hijacked by a powerful ultra-Islamist lobby that follows the Wahabi school of thought. The government of Pakistan promotes this tradition, practiced by the Saudis, which has no tolerance for the Shias. The controversial textbooks, for example, have been written by a panel of four authors—Saeedullah Qazi, Abdul Sattar Ghouri, Shabir Ahmed Mansoori, and Iftikhar Ahmed Bhutta—all of whom are Sunni and Deobandi by belief. That is why, one Shia scholar points out, biases are bound to prevail.[85]

Voices "From Below": The "Subaltern"

Although colonial domination "from above" is strongly apparent in Azad Kashmir and the Northern Areas, this does not mean that there are no independent voices "from below." Since 1947 people of both these regions have asserted themselves from time to time to demand their constitutional, political, and economic rights. Piecing together these strands of their history is equally important because it opens up the possibility of alternative futures for them. "It would be wrong," as one observer writes, " to assume that . . . Azad Kashmir has become just another part of Pakistan. It remains different, with different aspirations. To ignore these aspirations, as local and national leaders have discovered, is to risk political oblivion."[86] Signs of independent thinking within the ranks of the Muslim Conference leadership are evident right from pre-partition days when it was considered to be a rank follower of the Muslim League. At no point in history did the Muslim Conference "merge with the League or come to see themselves first and foremost as Pakistanis, even when the Pakistan army came to the fore in the Kashmir war after May 1948."[87] C. Hamidullah Khan, the acting Muslim Conference president, believed that, should the maharaja commit himself to an independent state, Muslim Conference members "would lay down their lives" for such an entity. Even Yusuf Shah, the mirwaiz who in 1947 drew more than 10,000 people to Srinagar to hear him extol the virtues of an Islamic Pakistan, would be referred to by Jinnah as a "rotten egg" and soon after the liberation in 1949 would come to support calls for an independent state of Kashmir, free of any association with Pakistan.

Other Muslim Conference leaders criticized Pakistan's policies as well, especially as they affected Kashmir. Sardar Ibrahim Khan, for instance, lambasted the Pakistani leadership for having committed the "blunder" of accepting the accession of Junagarh to Pakistan: "Pakistan had no business to accept its accession . . . this was a gamble which lost Pakistan, her legitimate claim on Kashmir."[88] Another blunder, he pointed out, was committed in 1948 when Patel offered Liaquat Ali Khan an agreement on Kashmir with Hyderabad acceding to India and accused Ghulam Mohammad, the then finance minister of Pakistan, of scuttling the deal. "Pakistan's mistakes were many," Ibrahim ruefully concluded.[89]

In the early years after the formation of the Azad Kashmir government, leaders in Muzaffarabad strongly resented the overarching authority of the Ministry of Kashmir Affairs, which forced elected representatives to submit to the bureaucratic structures of authority, thereby undermining their legitimacy as well as political status. Sardar Ibrahim frequently called upon the Pakistani leadership to take note of the provisional relationship between Azad Kashmir and Pakistan, valid only until a time when the entire Kashmir dispute would be resolved. He kept open the option of an independent Kashmir. The call for some form of direct action in favor of a "united and independent" Kashmir had surfaced as early as 1953, when C. Hamidullah Khan called for a renewal of the struggle for Kashmir. That declaration caused some embarrassment for the

Pakistanis, since the meeting of the Muslim Conference was broken up by riot police.[90] These efforts culminated in the formation of the Kashmir Liberation Movement (KLM) in 1958, with K. H. Khurshid as acting aecretary. Its attempts to cross the cease-fire line brought it in confrontation with the Pakistani authorities. Firoz Khan Noon—the last prime minister of the old Pakistan regime—warned the KLM that force would be used to retain the integrity of the cease-fire line and promptly put Chowdhury Ghulam Abbas, one of the most outspoken of the old guard, into a Pakistani prison. Even after the military takeover in 1958, Sardar Abdul Qayum followed his predecessors in organizing fresh crossings of the cease-fire line in 1961 while also pursuing Ibrahim's earlier attempts to seek international recognition for Azad Kashmir. He set up groups of armed volunteers "who were committed to the 'struggle' to 'liberate' Indian-held Kashmir, not for Pakistan but for a separate Kashmiri state."[91]

The Simla Agreement of 1972, which converted the cease-fire line into the Line of Control and virtually abandoned the plebiscite resolutions in favor of bilateral negotiations, appeared to many to be acquiescing to a de facto partition of the Jammu and Kashmir state. This led to widespread disturbances throughout Azad Kashmir and brought about the resignation of Sardar Qayum's government in 1973. Since then the Azad Kashmir leadership's persistent attempts to bring the Northern Areas back into the fold of Azad Kashmir and the jubilation that followed the ruling of the Azad Kashmir High Court in 1992 show that "the flame of independence still burns, to the discomfort of a new generation of Pakistani leaders."[92] When a group of Indian journalists visited Azad Kashmir in October 2004, it was an eye-opener for many: they found out that there are strong undercurrents for a state independent of India and Pakistan in many parts, from Mirpur to Gilgit: "Notwithstanding a sizeable pro-Pakistan constituency," one observer noted, 'Azadi' is the popular slogan."[93] He noted that while people acknowledged Pakistan's role in helping Kashmir struggle for self-determination, the majority believed that an independent Kashmir is the only solution. As one Kashmiri remarked, "We consider both India and Pakistan illegal occupants."[94]

When one takes into account the local diversities in Azad Kashmir, the picture becomes even more complex. It should not be surprising, then, that there is little unanimity among the Azad Kashmiris on what it means to be a Kashmiri, for example. People's commitment to Kashmir has arisen for different reasons and "consequently gives rise to a very different set of objectives."[95] The Suddhans, for instance, remember with pride their early rebellion against the maharaja's forces, yet their fond hope is that Kashmir will become part of Pakistan.[96] The Mirpuris, on the other hand—even though they differ little in cultural and linguistic terms from the Potohari population on the far side of the Jhelum River in Pakistan proper—"now *feel* themselves to be very different from other Potohari Punjabis" and regularly assert that "they are Kashmiris, and by that token *not* Pakistani."[97] As already mentioned, Mirpuris deeply resent Pakistan's disregard for them, having not only overlooked their interests but unabashedly exploited their environmental resources at a great cost to the locals. By defining themselves as Kashmiris and not as Pakistanis provides "Mirpuris with a powerful means of both expressing and legitimizing their grievances."[98] Hence there is a great deal of enthusiastic support both within the district itself and even more so among the overseas Mirpuri diaspora for the prospect of a Kashmir that would be entirely independent of both India *and* Pakistan. Their motto is "Kashmir Azad banega" (Kashmir will become independent). At the same time, it is important to understand that they have adopted this position "not so much as a result of a clear and positive commitment to the cultural distinctiveness of the Kashmir region as a whole, but rather as a consequence of their strong sense of disillusionment about the way in which Pakistan has treated them."[99] Another important aspect of their political disposition is that neither the Suddhan tribals nor the Mirpuris are prepared to accept the inevitable domination of the better-educated and numerically stronger "hatos," as they contemptuously refer to the Kashmiris of the Valley, in case Kashmir is united.

Compared with the political activities in Azad Kashmir, those in the Northern Areas were much more low-key in the early decades after partition. The earliest development of political parties there can be traced to 1957, when the Gilgit League was launched by Mirza Hasan to speak for the rights of the people of the region. In the early 1960s, the Gilgit and Baltistan Jamhoori Wahaz, started by Fazlur Rahman of Ponial, demanded the return of the Northern Areas to Azad Kashmir. Then in 1963 the Gilgit and Baltistan Students Central Organization was formed with the aim of spreading awareness among the students, though later it extended its activities to champion the rights of the people of the region.[100] The Tanzeem-e-Millat's activities in the 1970s for the abolition of FCRs has already been noted. In the 1980s, sectarian organizations such as Sipah-e-Sahaba Pakistan and the Tehrik-e-Jaffria Pakistan came to center-stage in politically mobilizing the people. It was only in the mid-1990s that the federal government first allowed political parties of Pakistan, and significantly *not* that of Azad Kashmir, to extend their activities to the Northern Areas. This led the Pakistan People's Party, Pakistan Muslim League, and the Muttaheda Quami Party, an offshoot of the Mohajir Quami Movement, to open branches in the Northern Areas.

More important and politically significant has been the growth of local organizations that have been at the forefront of articulating popular aspirations of the Northern Areas, especially since the mid-1990s. In 1992 the Balawaristan National Front (BNF) was created as an umbrella body for political groups in the Northern Areas. Other organizations include Jammu and Kashmir People's National Party, which is also active in Azad Kashmir, the Gilgit-Baltistan United Action Forum for Self-Rule, Balawaristan National Students Organization, Baltistan Students Federation, Karakoram Students Organization, and the Northern Areas Students Association. The All-Parties National Alliance (APNA) was formed in 2001 with the aim of organizing the masses of Jammu and Kashmir, including Gilgit-Baltistan, for the independence of Jammu and Kashmir. Its chairman, Wajahat Hussain Mirza, said that, "like the people of Held [that is, the Indian part of Jammu and Kashmir] and Azad Kashmir, we are also a party to the Kashmir dispute," so the Northern Areas should be given representation in any future talks on the Kashmir issue. The Gilgit Baltistan National Alliance was formed on a two-point agenda of attaining provisional constitutional rights and self-rule on the pattern of Azad Kashmir until the final settlement of the Kashmir dispute and representation for the people of Gilgit and Baltistan in any future negotiations on the Kashmir issue.

The popular support base of most such groups, however, remains to be established. Much like the Hurriyat Conference in the Kashmir Valley, they have either not contested the elections for the Northern Areas Legislative Council—two have been held thus far, in 1999 and 2004—or, as in the case of BNF, have not won any seats in the 2004 elections. Nor have they organized any mass political protests against Pakistan's arbitrary rule that may have captured world attention. Political resistance to Islamabad's rule is, however, beginning to be articulated in an organized manner, albeit on a small scale. In the past few years, many "nonofficial functions" organized on November 1 to commemorate the day marking the end of the Dogra regime have turned into occasions to denounce the ambiguous constitutional status of the Northern Areas and its mode of governance, at times violently. APNA, for instance, organized a "black day" on April 29, 2003, which is the day the Karachi Agreement was signed in 1949, sealing the fate of the Northern Areas. The Balawaristan National Front also observed Pakistan's golden jubilee as the "black jubilee."[101] Otherwise, most of their activities remain confined to taking up their cause with the UN Human Rights Commission and other UN organizations in order to make the international community aware of their plight and bring instances of the violation of the human rights of the people of the Northern Areas to the attention of international human rights organizations.

They can do little else, in part because political activity within the Northern Areas remains severely repressed. Abid Ali, general secretary of BNF, indicates that "the Pakistan government is not allowing us to work. You cannot imagine the kind of repression we are facing."[102] More than 150 political workers and leaders of Balawaristan, including its chairman, Abdul Hamid Khan, are facing death sentences on charges of sedition.[103] Many groups have remained underground because any overt expression of political will, even peaceful protests, will result in arbitrary arrests and long jail terms. Even peaceful demonstrations by Gilgit students struggling against high unemployment have been brutally crushed. The Northern Areas' only weekly newspaper, *Kargil International*, was proscribed for publishing "subversive and seditious" materials and "instigating people against President Musharaf and maligning his personality." Copies of its July–August 2004 issue were confiscated and its managing editor and publisher, Ghulam Shehzad Agha, who is also president of a nationalist organization, the Gilgit and Baltistan United Movement, was arrested.[104] On January 2, 2005, leaders from Gilgit and Baltistan attended a seminar organized by Gilgit and Baltistan Thinkers Forum and unanimously declared their objective was to seek freedom from Pakistan's occupation. Pakistani agencies were quick to act: after the seminar. Wajahat Mirza, chairman of APNA and organizer of the event, received a number of threatening phone calls.[105] The BNF leadership alleged that the killing of Agha Ziauddin Rizvi, imam of central Imamia Mosque Gilgit, on January 8, 2005, was also not sectarian in nature, but the handiwork of Pakistani agencies that want "to dilute the unity of all the sects for the freedom of their motherland" and "create disunity in the region by killing the important persons of all the sects, so the joint struggle of the nationalists of all the sects for their future fate could be derailed."[106]

A more interesting development, with potentially more far-reaching political significance, is the BNF's attempt to fashion a new common identity—Balawaristan—for the people of the Northern Areas. In its definition, the term "Balawaristan" refers to

> that area of the former state of Jammu and Kashmir which is now under the illegal occupation of Pakistan, consisting of Gilgit Baltistan. Balawaristan has a population of some two million, consisting of Shias, Sunnis, Ismailis and Nur Bakhshis. It has an area of 28,000 square miles . . . Pakistan has illegally ceded some 2,500 square miles of the territory of Balawaristan to China in the Shoomshall Hunza area.[107]

The BNF leader, Nawaz Khan Naji, claims to have introduced this new ideology that "we are neither Pakistanis nor Kashmiris. That the people from Ladakh to Chitral have a separate identity, status, ideology, entity, that we have our own languages, culture, race, geography, and common economy, but we have never had a separate status." He further argues that all who lived there before the Pakistani occupation "belong to the same nation" and need a common name. "In the past, the area was known as Bala, which means high. The people were called Balawar, or highlanders. That is why we call the area from Ladakh to Chitral, Balawaristan."[108]

Its historical origins indicate that *Boluristan* was the name used in Chinese, Korean, and Arab accounts, including that of a Chinese traveler, Hieun Tsang. During the reign of Abbasid Caliph Mamum (A.D. 813–833) Muslims had conquered Kashmir, Tibet, and the Northern Areas and in their inscriptions referred to the Northern Areas as *Boluristan*. This is also mentioned in the accounts of Muslim historians, including that of Alberuni and of the Tarikh-i-Rashidi of Mirza Haider Dauglat, who conquered Kashmir for Akbar in 1586, which is when Kashmir first became part of India. In a reinterpretation of the pre-independence history of these areas, it is argued that although the region was under Kashmiri rulers from 1850 to 1947, its people constantly fought to expel the Dogras from Gilgit and Baltistan and finally succeeded in 1947. Their attempts to redefine the ethnocultural boundaries of Balawaristan are noteworthy. For instance, Gilgit and Baltistan's cultural and historical relations with Ladakh and Tibet are emphasized. And at home, despite their "social" differences, they "respect" Prince Karim Aga Khan, who is the spritual leader of Shia Imami Ismailia, which make up 20 percent of the region's population. At the same time, it is argued, "we don't have any contact with him as far as our political struggle is concerned," because "we don't believe in religious involvement or interference in this regard."[109]

As for the future of the Northern Areas, the BNF has presented a manifesto for a sovereign and independent republic of Balawaristan, which includes Gilgit, Baltistan, Chitral, Kohistan, and Ladakh. The BNF is careful to point out that while all these regions are seeking self-rule, the inclusion of Chitral, Shhenaki Kohistan, and Ladakh in Balawaristan would depend on the voluntarily expressed political will of their respective indigenous populations.[110] Their foremost objective, however, is to participate in the ongoing peace process and to find a seat at the negotiating table for deciding the future status of the Northern Areas. BNF chairman Nawab Naji insists that "we are the fourth party to the dispute. India, Pakistan, Kashmir and us. We will decide our area's future. They will not impose any solution on us, which we will resist."[111] During the interim period, BNF advocates autonomy for the Northern Areas, an arrangement under which only certain important portfolios should lie with the central government.

Traditionally, three options have been outlined for deciding the political future of the Northern Areas. First, the territory should be recognized as a province. Second, it should become an autonomous entity similar to Azad Kashmir. Third, the region should be amalgamated with Azad Kashmir on an equal footing in terms of power-sharing mechanisms. Most members of the Shia community want the Northern Areas to become a fifth province of Pakistan. They claim that historically they were never a part of the state of Jammu and Kashmir and had no cultural links with it. The people of the Northern Areas have themselves liberated their homeland from the Dogras, and any question of joining Kashmir simply ended there. They insist that the region "acceded to Pakistan and the papers of accession were signed by the Quaid-e-Azam himself."[112] Qurban Ali, heading the Northern Areas People's Party, in step with popular opinion dismisses the notion that the Northern Areas is a part of Kashmir: "We cannot be bracketed with Kashmir. Our aspirations are different. We gave our decision long ago. We are part of this country. We should be granted rights provisionally through an amendment in the constitution, and this means a provincial status as was decided by the cabinet in 1973."[113] The people of Baltistan, who are predominantly Shia, are also in favor of the Northern Areas becoming a separate province of Pakistan, though their more immediate concern is that administratively they should be separated from Gilgit and made a division in their own right. The Tehrik-e-Jaffria was the only party to have openly voiced this demand in the last NALC elections. The PPP leadership assured voters that reforms would eventually lead to a provincial status for the area. The Muslim League, meanwhile, adopted an ambiguous attitude by talking about a constitutional solution, "according to the wishes of the people."

On the other hand, the Sunnis in the Northern Areas, particularly in the Diamer district, want the Northern Areas to be merged with the state of Azad Jammu and Kashmir, for if combined with Sunni Kashmir, they would become a majority whereas at present this is not the case. It is also claimed that the creation of a fifth province would harm the Kashmir issue and joining with Kashmir now would enable them to fight in the jihad, which is their religious duty. The small population of the Northern Areas, they argue, does not render the creation of a separate province a particularly viable option. The only political parties with any influence that favor accession to Kashmir are the Jamiat Ulema-e-Islam, which make their presence felt through the Tanzim-i-Ahl-e-Sunnat wal Jamaat and the Jamaat-e-Islami.

In conclusion, to exclude Azad Kashmir and the Northern Areas in the debates on Kashmir is problematic because these areas constitute a critical piece of the jigsaw puzzle called the "Kashmir conflict." That conflict cannot be fully understood or resolved without involving the local leadership and people in the peace process. The lesson of experience is the same as in the Indian part of Kashmir: that is, deploying monolithic communal parameters to understand the realities of Jammu and Kashmir is not only inappropriate but also yields a politically misleading analysis. The various communities living in different parts of the state across the dividing Line of Control have different political aspirations that *must* be addressed in order to arrive at a lasting peace.

CHAPTER SEVEN

THE INTERNATIONAL ARENA

DESPITE BEING IN THE INTERNATIONAL limelight since 1948, Kashmir has been of little urgent and direct *material* concern to the major global powers. Their Kashmir policy has consistently been embedded in their overall South Asia policy, which in turn has been shaped by their global strategic interests. During the cold war, Kashmir did become embroiled in the East-West conflict for a time and continued to figure on the international agenda afterward from the standpoint of averting a fourth war on the subcontinent. After 1998 the specter of a nuclear war loomed large as well. With the devastating 9/11 terrorist strikes against America, the Kashmir conflict entered into the realm of the "war on terror" and was no longer perceived simply as a by-product of a movement for self-determination. Neither of these factors has done much to reduce the conflict, however. As this chapter demonstrates, international players have had limited leverage in this regard throughout the critical phases of Kashmir's history.

Britain: The Imperial Broker

Both India and Pakistan hold the British—the departing imperial power—responsible for generating the Kashmir conflict as well as for making it an intractable issue. From India's standpoint, Britain's culpability lay in its doctrine of the "lapse of paramountcy," as discussed in chapter 1. By giving the princely rulers a choice as to whether to become independent, the British opened a Pandora's box, with Kashmir at the center of the problems that ensued. When Governor-General Lord Louis Mountbatten pressed Prime Minister Jawaharlal Nehru of India to approach the United Nations, the Kashmir issue took on international dimensions, which, along with partisan diplomacy exercised by Britain's UN representative, Sir Philip Noel-Baker, left generations of Indian policymakers wary of *any* third-party involvement in the Kashmir conflict. Significantly, Pakistanis considered Mountbatten the villain as well for his role in the Radcliffe Commission's decision to grant the Muslim-majority Gurdaspur tehsil to India, thereby creating the sole geographical link between Jammu and Kashmir state and India.[1] Mountbatten's personal friendship with Nehru and his biases against Mohammad Ali Jinnah were another sore point. Some also feel that he should have advised the maharaja to accede to Pakistan.[2]

Up to the end of 1947, Britain was the only overseas power with a significant involvement in the Kashmir conflict. It was the principal trader, investor, and supplier of weaponry for both India and Pakistan. With its officers at the helm of two armies on the subcontinent and Lord Mountbatten as governor-general, Britain was in a unique position to influence the course of the Kashmir conflict in its early phase. Britain was also largely responsible for shaping the attitude of the Western powers and thus the international context of the conflict. Britain's foremost priority was to protect its own strategic interests. Throughout the nineteenth century, Britain's imperial strategy was focused on defending the Indian landmass by controlling the entry points into the Indian Ocean through a ring of naval bases. By the late 1940s, this strategic picture had begun to change with the growth of air power and Western dependence on oil. The defense of the Middle Eastern oil fields and the sea lanes from the Gulf thus became a high priority for Western countries.[3]

In July 1946 the U.K. Chiefs of Staff Committee concluded that while it would be ideal if both India and Pakistan could be drawn into military cooperation with Britain, "the area of Pakistan is strategically the most important in the continent of India and the majority of our strategic requirements could be met, though with considerably greater difficulty, by an agreement with Pakistan alone," especially since air bases in the North-West Frontier of Pakistan were close to the Gulf region.[4] Pakistan also had naval bases and military power available in the event of a Russian threat via Afghanistan. Furthermore, Britain's relations with the "whole Mussulman bloc" would be jeopardized in the absence of close ties with Pakistan. London had also assumed from the outset that a future Pakistan would seek an alliance with Britain, whereas Nehru clearly wanted India to break its ties with the British Commonwealth.[5] At the time of partition, the British government tried to appear even-handed and nonpartisan in its policy toward India and Pakistan, but its own strategic interests in the Middle East, particularly its stand on Kashmir, soon dictated its position on South Asian affairs. This became clear during the UN Security Council debates on Kashmir.

Battleground: United Nations

In the early phase of the UN deliberations, the British worked behind the scenes to bring Western countries around to its own viewpoint on the Kashmir issue. Both the superpowers—the United States and the former Soviet Union—showed little interest. The U.S. acting secretary of state, Robert Lovett, declared that the United States was already overcommitted globally and should avoid choosing to support the interests of India over those of Pakistan, or vice versa. He also felt that U.S. involvement might attract Soviet interest, making it harder to resolve the Kashmir dispute.[6] At the same time, the United States deferred to Britain in political and strategic issues pertaining to South Asia. For its part, the Soviet Union stayed clear of the Kashmir issue until 1952 and abstained from voting on it, although its official stand portrayed the dispute as an Anglo-American plot. Communist China also avoided taking sides, seeing that Pakistan and India were Asian states and neighbors. Like Moscow, Beijing maintained that the Kashmir issue was a creation of U.S. and British imperialists who wanted to transform Kashmir into a U.S. colony and military base. China had little faith in the instrumentality of the United Nations and urged India and Pakistan to negotiate directly.

With its significant knowledge of the subcontinent as the imperial broker between the two dominions and with the presence of British officers in their armies, Britain was in a position to influence developments at the United Nations. It decided to move cautiously, however, in view of the critical situation in Palestine, so as to "guard against the danger of aligning the whole of Islam against us, which might be the case were Pakistan to obtain a false impression of our attitude in the Security Council."[7] Through its UN representative, Sir Philip Noel-Baker, Britain decided to champion Pakistan's cause and decisively influenced the course of discussions in the Security Council in a manner that worked in Pakistan's favor. For example, the Security Council brushed aside the question of Pakistan's involvement in the tribal invasion of Kashmir and focused on seeking a cease-fire linked with arrangements for a plebiscite. At Pakistan's request, it also sought to enlarge the scope of the discussion beyond the Kashmir question by considering "the entire India-Pakistan question" and bringing in Hyderabad and Junagarh.

The Security Council deliberations on Kashmir in early 1948 revolved around four interrelated issues: the control of Kashmir's administration during the plebiscite (Pakistan wanted this in UN hands, whereas India insisted that Sheikh Abdullah remain in charge); the nature and pace of the withdrawal of Indian and Azad Kashmir forces; India's desire to label Pakistan an aggressor; and Pakistan's wish to condemn the overall treatment it received from India. Noel-Baker succeeded in securing Western support for the Pakistani position on three of these issues: Pakistan would not have to take effective action to stop the invaders into Kashmir until a formula was found to resolve the dispute that was acceptable to Pakistan, the Abdullah government would have to be replaced by an "impartial" interim administration, and the United Nations should not merely observe the plebiscite but actually hold it under UN authority.[8]

For reasons of alliance solidarity, the United States was prepared to offer the maximum possible support to Britain, although there were subtle differences in their approach. Noel-Baker's proposals would have placed Kashmir under effective UN control pending a plebiscite and permitted the induction of Pakistani troops into the state with a status similar to that of the Indian army. In 1948 U.S. officials were prepared to recognize the legal validity of Jammu and Kashmir's accession to India, but Secretary of State George Marshall expressed "grave doubts" about the use of Pakistani troops in Kashmir, which, he pointed out, would make it difficult to reach a compromise solution acceptable to India.[9]

Noel-Baker's initiatives had also exceeded the British cabinet's recommendations. Prime Minister Clement Attlee had "approved a pro-Pakistan tilt in general terms but not the detailed and totally one-sided proposals advocated by Noel-Baker at the UN."[10] Although Attlee summoned Noel-Baker to London and in a policy review issued a new set of instructions, the damage could not be fully undone. The outcome was a Security Council resolution adopted on April 21, 1948, setting up the United Nations Commission on India and Pakistan, which did not go as far as Noel-Baker's original draft but nevertheless remained unacceptable to India. Nehru, as pointed out in chapter 2, was angry that the United Nations had failed to condemn Pakistan as the aggressor and seemed to be treating the two countries as equal parties to the dispute. In a letter to his sister he charged that the "USA and UK have played a dirty role."[11]

As the cold war deepened, dividing lines sharpened. The United States, fresh from the Korean War and concerned about a more aggressive Soviet posture in the oil-rich and strategically vital Middle East, which was also militarily weak and politically unstable, became interested in Pakistan's possible role in the defense of the region.[12] The British had suggested a Middle East Defense Organization (MEDO), a British-led military group to be headquartered in

Egypt with mainly Arab members, but perhaps including Pakistan. While the United States was skeptical of MEDO's feasibility, it supported the basic idea of Pakistan participating in the defense of the Middle East as a "better bet than India." Nehru, it argued, appeared to be angling for Indian hegemony over a neutral bloc of countries in Southeast Asia and the Middle East. Yet "neutralism contradicted the fundamentals of 'collective security,' a euphemism to describe American strategic interests since the coming of the 'cold war' to Asia in 1949." Therefore Nehru had to be dealt with "firmly and patiently" and Pakistan treated "as a friendly country."[13] This marked the beginning of a polite British and American rivalry in South Asia. While the U.S. State Department, at the insistence of the British Foreign Office, shied away from giving Karachi a territorial guarantee, U.S. embassies in the Middle East were instructed in June 1951 "to use every appropriate occasion" to bring Pakistan closer to the Middle East.[14]

For its part, Pakistan ardently courted both the United Kingdom and United States and was prepared to play the "Cold War version of the Great Game between imperial Russia and British India." As early as September 11, 1947, Jinnah had stated that "the safety of the North West Frontier [is] of world concern and not merely an internal matter for Pakistan alone." He believed the Russians were behind the Afghan call for Pushtunistan and were trying to stir up fresh communal troubles in both India and Pakistan.[15] Pakistan's leaders had "little hesitation in exchanging base rights, treaty commitments, and its UN votes for U.S. weapons and Washington's political support for its claim over Kashmir."[16] Prime Minister Liaquat Ali Khan, for instance, not only endorsed the U.S. position on North Korea but also backed U.S. demarches to other Arab countries in the Middle East.

Nehru, on the other hand, rejected the bloc politics and was unwilling to play the global balance-of-power game. He was keen to chart an independent course through India's policy of nonalignment. Quite apart from Kashmir, the United States and India found themselves at odds on many foreign policy questions, particularly international control of atomic energy, Palestine and the creation of Israel, and the Indochina conflict. Nehru was aware of the U.S. intent to strengthen Pakistan as a rival to India, because "Pakistan was easy to keep within their sphere of influence in regard to wider policies, while India was uncertain and possibly not reliable."[17]

Since the Kashmir question was a central and vital political issue for India, Nehru decided to dig his heels in and "not give an inch. He would hold his ground even if Kashmir, India and the whole world went to pieces."[18] What had toughened India's position was the apparent impatience of and pressure from powerful elements in the Western countries to get India to accept proposals for a plebiscite, administration, and demilitarization put forth in 1949 by UN Security Council president, General A. G. L. McNaughton (see box 7-1). Nehru had already turned down an earlier appeal by President Harry Truman and Prime Minister Clement Attlee to submit their differences to arbitration. Both India and Pakistan rejected Owen Dixon's 1950 proposal for partitioning Jammu and Kashmir, and a subsequent plan for demilitarization also ran aground.[19] Interestingly, none of the parties involved supported the idea of an independent Kashmir. The main concern, apart from further balkanization of British India, was that Kashmir's political and economic weakness as well as its strategic location would invite communist interference and fuel further regional instability.

UN deliberations had produced an unsatisfactory outcome for all the players. The United States, concerned more about its global interests than about Kashmir's fate, sought Pakistan's participation in the Middle East's defense but refused to resolve the Kashmir dispute on Pakistan's terms or to meet its demand for a "territorial guarantee" against an Indian attack. Although the United States and Britain were unable to deliver Kashmir to Pakistan, their support for Pakistan in the Security Council was considerable enough to alienate India. Through delay and noncooperation, India thwarted Anglo-American pressure to accept a solution on unfavorable terms, but it felt trapped by the UN resolutions on holding a plebiscite in Kashmir. Though Pakistan had the support of extraregional powers, it could not alter the status quo in Kashmir either.

Between 1948 and 1957 the Security Council debated the Kashmir dispute eighteen times, to no avail. What it had secured (largely because of British pressure) was a cease-fire and a guarantee from both India and Pakistan that they would not resort to arms to resolve the issue. From the earliest UN efforts, every interlocutor recognized the limitations of the organization in resolving the issue. Successive mediation attempts also ended in a deadlock. The only way out was to ask the principal players to take the initiative themselves.

The Cold War, the Global Game, and Kashmir

India and Pakistan began direct negotiations on Kashmir in 1953. The United States, continuing to exercise influence through its bilateral channels and keen to avoid another war between the two, decided to make a fresh effort toward a settlement, this time outside the UN framework.

Box 7-1. *Early UN Proposals for Resolving Kashmir*

McNaughton Proposals (1949)

WITHDRAWAL OF FORCES

—Pakistan's regular forces to withdraw from the state of Jammu and Kashmir.
—India's regular forces not required to withdraw. They would remain for security and maintenance of law and order on the Indian side of cease-fire line (CFL).
—Disbanding of local forces, including armed forces and militia of the state of Jammu and Kashmir and Azad forces.

ADMINISTRATION

—Administration of the Northern Areas by "existing local authorities" under UN supervision.

DEMILITARIZATION

—The agreed program of demilitarization via withdrawal of forces, preparatory to the plebiscite, to be accomplished to the satisfaction of the UN representative.

PLEBISCITE

—As per the terms of the UNCIP resolution of January 5, 1949, to be supervised by the plebiscite administrator.

U.S.-PAKISTAN MILITARY ALLIANCE AND ITS IMPACT ON KASHMIR

"Dividing the state," Secretary of State John Foster Dulles wrote in a memorandum to President Dwight D. Eisenhower, "is the only solution that seems to have practical possibilities."[20] Nehru readily agreed that partition might be a better approach and suggested that the cease-fire line, with minor modifications, would provide a reasonable basis for dividing the state. However, Pakistan strongly opposed the idea. Since Kashmir was not the most important issue weighing on his mind, Dulles did not press the proposal.

Dulles's overriding concern at the time was to determine to what extent governments in the Middle East and South Asia were ready to line up with the West against communist aggression in the Far East. Pakistan's leaders, unlike

Sir Owen Dixon Plan (1950)

PLEBISCITE

—Two alternatives were proposed: (a) to hold plebiscite by sections/areas and allocate each section according to the result of the vote therein; (b) to concede some areas that were certain to vote for accession to India and some to Pakistan and by which, without taking a vote therein, they should be allotted accordingly and plebiscite should be confined only to the uncertain area—that is, the Kashmir Valley.

Frank Graham Proposals (1951)

WITHDRAWAL OF FORCES

—On Pakistan's side, tribesmen or Pakistani nationals and Pakistani troops to withdraw.
—On the Indian side, "bulk" of troops to withdraw.
—Large-scale disbandment and disarming of Azad troops.
—Withdrawals or reductions of the Indian and state armed forces.

DEMILITARIZATION

—Demilitarization program to be drawn up by the two governments and their military advisers, meeting under UN auspices. Any differences would be settled by the UN representative, whose decision would be final.

PLEBISCITE

—The plebiscite administrator to be appointed by the government of India not later than the final day of the demilitarization period, who would supervise the plebiscite.

those of India, said the things that Dulles wanted to hear about the dangers of communism. They stressed their allegiance to the anticommunist cause and Pakistan's desire to join the free world's defense team against a possible Soviet invasion "through the mountain passes of Central Asia aimed at reaching the warm waters of the Arabian Sea. The proposed response was an expanded Pakistani army properly equipped for the task of blocking the Soviets."[21] Dulles was impressed and made up his mind to recruit Pakistan into the *cordon sanitaire* that he was determined to erect around the perimeters of Soviet and Chinese communist power. He and Vice President Richard Nixon were also keen to contain India, lest its nonaligned policies become a model for others in Asia. Nixon regarded India and the United States as rivals for influence in

Asia and argued that it would be "a fatal mistake to back down on the aid package solely because of Nehru's objections; such a retreat would risk losing most of the Asian-Arab countries to the neutralist bloc."[22]

Focusing on its global interests rather than Kashmir, the United States decided to provide arms to Pakistan. This derailed India and Pakistan's bilateral negotiations on Kashmir, although Pakistan believed that its enhanced military strength would force Nehru's hand, persuade India to drop its "intransigent attitude," and thus improve, not set back, the prospects for a settlement.[23] Nehru, on the other hand, feared that the move would bring the cold war "right next to our doors" and make Pakistan more reluctant to resolve the Kashmir problem.[24] Kashmir did not even enter the picture for the United States, which saw military aid to Pakistan as a way to marginalize Nehru.[25] He, in turn, perceived it as a tactic to "bring such overwhelming pressure on India as to compel her to change her policy of non-alignment," or "completely [outflank] India's so-called neutralism and . . . thus bring India to her knees."[26] But it had the opposite effect. Nehru ruled out a plebiscite, asserting that the election of a constituent assembly in Kashmir in 1953 had served the purpose, and further balloting was unnecessary. The bilateral talks collapsed. Furthermore, India's foreign policy began turning in the direction of the Soviet Union, though initially only diplomatically rather than militarily, to counterbalance the U.S.-Pakistani alliance. Kashmir was firmly embroiled in the cold war.

Meanwhile, the Soviet Union broke its silence in Security Council deliberations, charging that "the West intended to transform Kashmir and Pakistan into [a] military springboard against the USSR and new China."[27] Once Pakistan decided to join the Western alliance, Moscow began to support India's claims over Kashmir. In December 1955, Soviet president Nikita Khrushchev categorically stated that the people of Kashmir themselves had decided to become "one of the states of the Republic of India." Thereafter, Moscow consistently identified Kashmir as "an inalienable part of the Republic of India" and supported India in all Security Council meetings on the Kashmir issue. In 1957 and 1962, when Pakistan brought the issue back to the Security Council, the Soviet Union, at India's behest, vetoed the UN resolutions.

By the mid-1950s, Beijing's position on the Kashmir dispute had begun to diverge from that of the Soviet Union. The Chinese government adhered to its neutral stand and refrained from conceding that Kashmir belonged to India. This cautious Chinese stand was part of Beijing's South Asia policy, which in turn fell in line with its strategy of counter-encirclement in response to U.S. strategy in the region. In Beijing's view, Washington was attempting to encircle China by establishing a network of alliances such as the South East Asia

Treaty Organization (SEATO) of 1954, which facilitated American military presence in Japan, the Philippines, Taiwan, South Korea, Thailand, Laos, and Pakistan.[28] To counter this threat, China planned a close alliance with the Soviet Union. In South Asia, it forged close links with India but was careful not to alienate Pakistan. For example, the Chinese media rarely subjected Pakistan to direct public criticism for its membership in SEATO, which was otherwise perceived as targeting China. While Beijing's position of keeping out the "foreign arbitrators" and observers pleased India, its neutral stand on Kashmir "was most probably motivated by the assumption that by doing so, Beijing could prevent Pakistan from further aligning itself with the United States."[29]

The 1962 Sino-Indian War and U.S. "Activist" Policy on Kashmir

The Sino-Indian war of 1962 changed the strategic calculus of South Asia. India was forced to abandon nonalignment, at least temporarily, and to seek military assistance from the United States and United Kingdom, which rushed in military shipments. Washington urged Pakistani President Ayub Khan to reassure India by making a significant friendly gesture, "for example, [by] breaking off in a public way his own negotiations with the Chinese about the border."[30] Ayub spurned the overture, objecting strongly to American arms shipments to India. He downplayed the seriousness of the conflict, describing it as a "limited border affair," and urged Washington to take advantage of the situation to press the Indians to settle the Kashmir dispute. Although President John F. Kennedy was reluctant to "give this to him," the Kennedy administration decided to see what it could do to resolve the Kashmir dispute.[31]

Washington sent a high-level team headed by Averell Harriman to the subcontinent. The British dispatched a parallel mission led by Commonwealth Relations Secretary Duncan Sandys. They came to discuss India's arms requirements but also succeeded in persuading the Indian government to reopen negotiations on Kashmir. Ayub also readily agreed to negotiate with India, realizing that a plebiscite was not the best way to settle the dispute and that Pakistan could not expect to receive all of the Kashmir Valley.[32] Despite the high risk of failure and Harriman's pessimistic assessment of the chances of successful negotiations, Kennedy agreed to use U.S. influence in support of talks between Pakistan's Zulfiqar Ali Bhutto and India's Swaran Singh.

On the eve of the talks, Pakistan announced a provisional accord with China demarcating the boundary between Pakistan-controlled Kashmir and China. The news created a furor. U.S. officials feared that the accord would badly damage, if not wreck, the Kashmir talks. They were also upset that Pakistan had disregarded warnings about consorting with China. Equally angry, Indian officials regarded Ayub Khan's action as a contemptuous rejection of Nehru's request that Pakistan refrain from cooperating with China while India was in difficulty. Nonetheless, negotiations proceeded on schedule, continuing for six rounds between December 27, 1962, and May 16, 1963. After reiterating their traditional positions, the two sides seriously discussed the basis for drawing an international boundary through Kashmir. India's idea was to transfer to Pakistan the entire occupied area west and north of Kashmir Valley and also adjust the cease-fire line so as to give it even more area. Pakistan, however, proposed to allot India only a sliver of territory in Jammu and to claim the entire Valley and all of Ladakh. That would have left India with less than 3,000 square miles of the state's total area of 85,000 square miles. Pakistan also insisted that sovereignty over the entire state be transferred to itself, conceding to India transit facilities for some time so as to move its troops to Ladakh. This was so much beyond the maximum that India could concede that the discussions soon floundered. American officials blamed mainly the Pakistanis, warning that "the sympathy that Pakistan has enjoyed from other governments on Kashmir in the United Nations and elsewhere would be dissipated" if the talks failed completely.[33] Despite President Kennedy's urging, Pakistan failed to improve upon its territorial offer. Although he was now pessimistic that the talks could be salvaged, Kennedy approved the release of a U.S.-U.K. paper outlining "elements of a settlement" "giving both India and Pakistan a 'substantial position in the Vale'; ensuring access through the Vale for defence to the north and east (i.e. India's defense of Ladakh); ensuring Pakistan's interest in the headwaters of the Chenab river; ensuring some local self-rule in the Vale and free movement of people to India and Pakistan; and enhancing economic development efforts."[34]

New Delhi protested that this step upset the pace of negotiations and that the concept had been worked out with Karachi behind India's back, following a bureaucratic mix-up that had put the paper in Pakistan's hands before India received it. In a sharp letter to Kennedy on April 21, 1963, Nehru stated: "I am convinced that these ill-considered and ill-conceived initiatives, however well-intentioned they may be, have at least for the present made it impossible to reach any settlement on this rather involved and complicated question."[35] Pakistan, too, rejected the proposal to partition the Kashmir Valley.

In a last-ditch effort, in the sixth and final round of talks on May 15–16, 1963, Dean Rusk and Sandys proposed the idea of mediation. Nehru accepted the idea in principle but Ayub and Bhutto were less than enthusiastic. In exasperation, the United States informed Pakistan that it could not help alter the status quo on Kashmir if Pakistan rejected mediation. Moreover, it refused to subordinate its "strategic interests in Asia" to the settlement of Kashmir.[36] Bhutto eventually accepted but imposed conditions that the Indians were certain to reject. The U.S. State Department finally dropped the mediation proposal, and the talks ended in failure.

The United States clearly had limited leverage on both sides of the Kashmir dispute. The basic equations had not changed. For both India and Pakistan, the stakes in Kashmir were too high to accept a settlement except on their own terms. India seemed willing to make the status quo permanent rather than accept less favorable terms, while Pakistan considered partitioning the Valley "suicidal" and "a settlement with dishonor."[37] Washington was open to any solution but could not find a formula that was acceptable to both India and Pakistan. Harriman recognized that Pakistan's price for forming a joint front with India against the communists was a Kashmir settlement on acceptable terms. "The rub," he conceded, "was that terms acceptable for Pakistan were unacceptable to India."[38] Resolving the Kashmir dispute had proved to be one of the Kennedy administration's "more difficult problems," as the president himself admitted.[39]

In its frustration, Washington procrastinated on the question of long-term military assistance for modernizing India's armed forces. However, New Delhi found Moscow eager to help. This marked the beginning of a long-term arms-acquisition relationship between India and the Soviet Union, bringing a new player into the South Asian arena.

The 1965 War and the New Peacemaker: The Soviet Union

When yet another war erupted in 1965, it was now Pakistan that turned to the United States for military help, which it sought under the 1959 U.S.-Pakistan bilateral agreement and the aide-mémoire of November 6, 1962.[40] Washington considered India's attack across the international border a very serious development, but it also pointed out that Pakistan had triggered the crisis by infiltrating large numbers across the cease-fire line into Kashmir.[41] The Johnson administration suspended military and economic aid to both Pakistan and India.

Pakistan then sought Chinese help. After the 1962 war, China had given up its neutral stand on Kashmir and threw its full support behind Pakistan, although it hoped to see the problem resolved, "in accordance with the wishes of the people of Kashmir as pledged to them by India and Pakistan"[42] In a secret meeting on September 19–20, 1965, Zhou reportedly told the Pakistanis that China was prepared to put pressure on India in the Himalayas "for as long as necessary" but stressed that Pakistan "must keep up the fighting even if [its troops] have to withdraw to the hills." However, Ayub wanted "a quick-fix to force the Indians to the negotiating table. Ayub had never foreseen the possibility of the Indians surviving a couple of hard knocks, and Bhutto had never envisaged a long-drawn-out people's war."[43]

The best the United States could offer in pressing Pakistan to accept a cease-fire was to agree to the need for a Kashmir settlement. President Lyndon Johnson, however, refused to commit to any particular solution and at the same time warned Ayub that he would assume collusion if Pakistan rejected the cease-fire and the Chinese moved militarily against India. Pakistan felt bitterly let down and betrayed by its ally, which had become disillusioned itself. With the Vietnam War at its peak, the United States had lost interest in the subcontinent.

The Soviet Union then stepped in to mediate between India and Pakistan. Premier Alexei Kosygin invited Ayub and India's prime minister, Lal Bahadur Shastri, to the Soviet Central Asian city of Tashkent to forge a postwar settlement. The British and Americans encouraged the Soviet Union to attempt a reconciliation. As Secretary of State Dean Rusk explained: "If they succeeded in bringing about any détente at Tashkent, then there would be more peace in the subcontinent and we would gain from that. If the Russians failed at Tashkent, at least the Russians would have the experience of some of the frustration that we had for twenty years in trying to sort out things between India and Pakistan."[44] In the end, the Soviet Union did little more than persuade the warring parties to return to the status quo before the 1965 war.

THE 1971 WAR, SIMLA AGREEMENT, AND ECLIPSE OF THE KASHMIR ISSUE

The U.S.-Pakistani relationship underwent a sudden, if short-lived, revival in 1971 as a result of a dramatic shift in U.S. global strategy under the Nixon administration. In an effort to restructure the global balance of power, President Richard Nixon decided to open relations with China and asked for Pakistan's help in this regard. This led to the famous U.S. "tilt towards Pakistan."[45] India responded to the emerging U.S.-China-Pakistan alliance by entering into a semi-military treaty with the Soviet Union. It also decided to defy the United States in the Bangladesh crisis. Both the United States and China made threatening noises but shied away from direct military intervention to save Pakistan from disintegration.

India, the dominant power of the war, then moved to reach a bilateral understanding with Pakistan in what became known as the Simla Agreement, which called for a peaceful resolution of the two countries' differences. However, India and Pakistan placed different interpretations on the accord. India felt that it abrogated the UN resolutions as a point of reference for resolving the Kashmir dispute and that the Line of Control rather than the UN cease-fire line could be adopted as the more or less permanent border. In Pakistan's view, the Simla Agreement did not replace the UN resolutions or make the Line of Control a *permanent international* border.[46] Guided by these differing interpretations, both sides continued to press their respective claims whenever the opportunity arose. However, outside powers assumed that the Kashmir dispute was either "solved" or on the way to resolution as a result of the Simla Agreement and moved it out of the international limelight.

The Post–Cold War Era

Paradoxically, the Kashmir conflict reignited just as the cold war was winding down. With the support of their former benefactors dwindling, India and Pakistan found their strategic calculations in disarray. Pakistan no longer had frontline status in a U.S. war against Soviet occupation of Afghanistan. In any case, its alliance with the United States was now shaky because it had crossed the "red line" by making nuclear weapons. In October 1990, a troubled Washington decided to end economic and military aid to Pakistan, which had averaged $650 million a year in the 1980s.

India, too, lost its chief strategic ally when the Soviet Union withdrew from Afghanistan and moved its global strategy in a new direction, to focus on collaboration with the United States and later integration with the West and to end hostility with China. In 1993 Russian foreign minister Andrei Kozyrev, contrary to President Boris Yeltsin's assurances, downgraded relations with India by adopting a policy on nuclear nonproliferation and Kashmir strictly in line with that of the United States and its allies.[47] Additional pressure came from China, through its "policy of containment of India and encirclement by proxy." Notwithstanding the Sino-Indian engagement since 1988, China continued to supply nuclear missile technology, components, and materials to Pakistan and over the years channeled 90 percent of its arms sales to countries bordering India.[48] India thus had its back to the international wall when the Kashmir insurgency erupted in the early 1990s.

Kashmir Insurgency and the Nuclear Flashpoint

By that time, the United States no longer supported a plebiscite in Kashmir.[49] China emphasized a negotiated bilateral settlement.[50] And Germany's foreign minister Klaus Kinkel, during his visit to Pakistan in 1992, stated that the UN resolutions had been "overtaken by later events and new realities."[51] Britain's foreign secretary Douglas Hurd agreed that they had become "part of the background."[52] World capitals seemed hopeful that the Simla Agreement would put the Kashmir issue to rest.

Even the United Nations itself, in the words of Secretary General Kofi Annan, regarded its Kashmir resolutions as "obsolete."[53] When it was suggested that Kashmir be removed from the forum's agenda since the issue had not come up for discussion in three decades, it was retained only at Pakistan's hectic insistence.[54]

THE HUMAN RIGHTS AGENDA

During the early 1990s, Kashmir figured in international forums primarily from the standpoint of human rights abuses in the Valley. Pakistan raised the issue not only before the United Nations but also before the Non-Aligned Movement (NAM), the Commonwealth Heads of Government Meeting, and the Organization of Islamic Countries (OIC). Severe criticism from international as well as domestic human rights organizations initially put the Indian government on the defensive, but eventually the Kashmiris' plank of self-determination found little support even among OIC members, and by 1993–94 Pakistan found the tables turned.

As the Indian government improved its human rights record and opened the Valley to diplomats and the foreign press, reports out of the region began focusing on Pakistan's armed support to Kashmiris, the induction of foreign mercenaries into Kashmir, and the increasingly pan-Islamic character of the militancy. These developments caused consternation among many who considered themselves victims of international Islamic terrorism. In early 1990 Washington warned Pakistan that it ran the risk of being declared an official supporter of terrorism, and in 1993 Pakistan landed squarely on the terrorism watchlist.[55]

Thereafter human rights complaints against India petered out, as Pakistan was persuaded by "Islamic" Iran and its "friend and ally" China not to move forward with any resolution against India before the UN Human Rights Commission (UNHRC) in Geneva. China's own track record on human rights and civil liberties was being criticized by the West, especially in view of activities in Tibet and growing Muslim separatism in Xinjiang Province. It did not want to encourage this trend by voting in favor of a Pakistani resolution on human rights violations in Kashmir.[56] In 1994 even the OIC Contact Group decided to drop the resolution on Kashmir in the UN International Security Committee for lack of support among its members.[57] When Pakistan lobbied for a resolution that would have enabled a fact-finding mission to investigate the situation in the Valley, forty-five of the UNHRC's fifty-three members abstained from voting. The abstentions included the United States, whose vote was most crucial for Pakistan.[58]

Beyond expressions of sympathy, the much-anticipated international support for the Kashmiri cause did not materialize in the aftermath of a sea change in international thinking about such conflicts. Afghanistan had degenerated into a civil war between factions of mujahideen, and by 1995–96 the Taliban's imposition of medieval anarchic practices had brought home the dangers of Islamizing Kashmiri society. The breakup of the Soviet Union and Yugoslavia and the resulting ethnic conflicts made world leaders wary of disturbing international boundaries and creating new states. The Kashmir conflict thus disappeared from the international agenda, and the key players by and large felt it could be resolved through a bilateral dialogue between India and Pakistan. If they adopted a "managerial approach" at all, it was with the limited objective of averting a fourth war between India and Pakistan, especially in view of the potential for a nuclear conflict.

CRISIS MANAGEMENT IN KASHMIR

Since the onset of Kashmiri insurgency in 1990, India and Pakistan have been embroiled in four "military crises," including a short war in Kargil in 1999. The increasing frequency of such crises in a nuclearized South Asia revived international interest in Kashmir as a "nuclear flashpoint" and the root cause of tension in the subcontinent.[59] With the specter of nuclear war hanging over this dispute, international involvement in Kashmir became geared toward crisis management.

The United States, in particular, has played an increasingly assertive role in managing and resolving each such crisis, including the earlier quasi-nuclear crisis of 1984–85 and the Brasstacks crisis of 1987–88. In 1984 U.S. ambassador Dean Hinton assured President Mohammed Zia-ul-Haq that Pakistan would be notified immediately of any signs of an imminent Indian attack.[60] During the Brasstacks crisis, when Indian and Pakistani military moves and countermoves under the guise of annual military exercises created a particularly dangerous situation on the border, the United States provided "good offices to both sides, reassuring each that the intentions of the other were benign, but that mistakes or misjudgment could happen and had to be averted."[61]

The turmoil in Kashmir Valley in 1989–90 coincided with Indian and Pakistani winter military maneuvers. Although no heavy armored equipment was involved, these activities generated belligerent statements from Islamabad and warnings against misadventure in Kashmir from New Delhi. As the situation across the Line of Control grew more volatile, some observers believed that Pakistan was readying its nuclear weapons for deployment, although others saw no direct evidence of such a move.[62] Either way, the first Bush administration was sufficiently alarmed to make every effort to avoid further escalation. Washington received tacit permission from the highest political level in India and Pakistan to confirm that neither side had begun such deployments provocatively. The respective U.S. ambassadors to Pakistan and India, Robert Oakley and William Clark, conveyed the results of these verifications to Islamabad and New Delhi, assuring each that no major military movements were taking place.[63]

Early on in the crisis, the State Department had carried out some low-level discussion about how Washington might play a more active role in settling the Kashmir dispute, but "crisis prevention" soon jumped to a dominant position on the diplomatic agenda. The Bush administration dispatched a mission headed by Robert Gates to the subcontinent, "to address the immediate possibility of miscalculation and inadvertent escalation to war, not the long-term political problems besetting the Indo-Pakistan relationship."[64] After considering various dimensions of a potential conflict there, the mission concluded that Pakistan would be "the loser in every scenario." Furthermore,

> in the event of a war, Islamabad could expect no assistance from Washington; Pakistan must refrain from supporting terrorism in Indian-occupied Kashmir, avoid military deployments that New Delhi could interpret as threatening and tone down its war rhetoric; both sides needed to adopt Confidence Building Measures that had already been discussed, so that this crisis would be more speedily defused and future ones prevented; Gates offered U.S. intelligence support—based on its own "national technical means" to verify a confidence-building regime involving limitations on deployment near the border—if both India and Pakistan concluded such an agreement and were to withdraw their forces from near the border.[65]

In other words, it would be to neither side's advantage to go to war, although the impact on Pakistan would likely be more disastrous. Even if India won, the long-term costs would greatly exceed any short-term benefits. The Gates report helped calm tempers on both sides of the border. Other countries counseled restraint as well. The Soviet Union, in concert with the United States, urged both countries to reduce tensions. Beijing also called for caution, although its major concern was that instability in Kashmir could encourage Islamic militancy in its Xinjiang Province. In early May, Japan's prime minister, Toshiki Kaifu, pressed for negotiations. By end of May 1990, the crisis had been defused.

The Kargil war of 1999 was the first military confrontation in a nuclearized South Asia, and arguably the first real war between two nuclear states. Although nuclear weapons were not used, nuclear capability unquestionably permeated the conflict, and there were reports that both India and Pakistan may have alerted or deployed nuclear weapons and delivery systems at the time.[66] This crisis brought about a "paradigm shift" in the way India and the United States engaged each other in regard to Indo-Pakistani disputes, particularly those over Kashmir.[67] President Bill Clinton held Pakistan responsible for nuclear brinkmanship, demanded that it restore the status quo ante, and emphasized there was no room on a nuclearized subcontinent for the kind of military antics that Pakistan had initiated in Kargil.

As Indian casualties mounted, India informed the United States that it might be compelled to escalate its operations.[68] Deeply concerned about this prospect, Clinton obtained a formal condemnation of the armed intrusion from the G-8 countries that pointedly demanded "full respect" for the Line of Control. He then dispatched the commander-in-chief of the U.S. Central Command, General Anthony Zinni, to Islamabad on June 23 to urge Pakistani leaders to call an end to the Kargil operations. Zinni received "fairly clear" assurances from his interlocutors that the insurgents would be withdrawn from the Indian side of the Line of Control.[69] When Pakistan questioned the reality of the Line of Control and attempted to link its withdrawal from Kargil to negotiations with India on the Kashmir dispute, the Clinton administration insisted that Pakistan's withdrawal be unambiguous and unconditional.

In return for Pakistan's pledge to take "concrete steps . . . for the restoration of the Line of Control in accordance with the Simla Agreement," Clinton promised to personally encourage "an expeditious resumption and intensification" of Indo-Pakistani détente, "once the sanctity of the Line of Control has been fully restored."[70] Spokespersons for the Clinton administration took pains to emphasize that its major concern in brokering the agreement was "the immediate crisis," in other words, Kargil, not the Kashmir dispute. The United States also garnered support from Saudi Arabia to nudge Islamabad into swallowing the bitter pill of a unilateral withdrawal. During the height of the Kargil dispute, China reportedly rebuffed Pakistan's former prime minister, Nawaz Sharif, when he visited Beijing to seek political support in the ongoing conflict.[71]

Kargil produced a rough consensus not just in Washington but more broadly in the West that "the peace of the region would be more secure if the border question were settled along the line which has separated Indian and Pakistani forces for fifty years."[72] While there was considerable international sympathy for the plight of Kashmiris and hope that their aspirations would be met in any eventual solution, the West objected to Pakistan's desire to detach Kashmir from India. In a speech to the Asia Society on March 14, 2000, Secretary of State Madeleine Albright reaffirmed U.S. opposition to changing the territorial status quo in Kashmir through the use of force, emphasizing that "nations must not attempt to change borders or zones of occupation" in this manner: "And now that they have exploded nuclear devices, India and Pakistan have all the more reason to restart a discussion on ways to build confidence and prevent escalation.[73]

President Clinton elaborated on the new approach during his visit to the region in March 2000. He distanced the United States from the concept of self-determination for Kashmiris, reiterated that there could be no military solution to the dispute, and emphasized the need for a peaceful dialogue between the two countries. In a powerful appeal to the people of Pakistan, Clinton warned that "this era does not reward people who struggle in vain to redraw borders with blood."[74] He also made it absolutely clear that the United States had no desire to see a disintegration of India in the name of Kashmiri self-determination.[75]

Since Kennedy's days, no U.S. administration has been prepared to take the risk or to spend the political capital necessary to bring about a resolution of the Kashmir conflict. Nor have any blueprints of a solution emerged from the State Department. The influential think-tank community of Washington endorsed this hands-off approach throughout the 1990s in the belief that the dispute was "not ripe for final resolution" and hence that diplomacy to this end was "bound to fail."[76]

In keeping with the traditional American position, the George W. Bush administration has pressed for bilateral negotiations as well as deeper relations between India and Pakistan. In addition, it has continued Clinton's legacy of seeking engagement with India, in recognition of its important "role in the regional balance": "There is a strong tendency conceptually to connect India with Pakistan and to think only of Kashmir or the nuclear competition between the two states. But India is an element in China's calculation and it should be in America's too. India is not a great power yet, but it has the potential to emerge as one."[77] By contrast, Pakistan was thought to be "on the edge of fulfilling the classic definition of a failed state."[78] Because of Pakistan's political instability, entrenched Islamist extremism, and nuclear weapons status, the United States felt compelled to do all it could to prevent a violent collapse of the nation.

KASHMIR AND THE "WAR ON TERROR"

The devastating terrorist strikes against the United States on September 11, 2001, and the Bush administration's subsequent declaration of "war against terror" transformed the strategic landscape of South Asia. As soon as Washington decided to target al Qaeda and its host, the Taliban regime in Afghanistan, Pakistan's cooperation became necessary, for both political and operational reasons. Pakistan was then given a list of "nonnegotiable" demands, to which General Pervez Musharraf responded by joining hands with the United States.[79] With that decision, Pakistan's diplomatic isolation ended almost immediately, and the nation again became America's "frontline ally."[80] On the other hand, Washington responded with "silence" to India's offer of support after 9/11, including the use of Indian military facilities. India became apprehensive, suspecting that the United States, in order to keep Musharraf happy, would pursue double standards in its fight against terrorism.

A Jaish-i-Mohammed suicide attack on the Jammu and Kashmir state assembly building, killing thirty-eight people on October 1, 2001, highlighted the dangers. Secretary of State Colin Powell and Secretary of Defense Donald Rumsfeld rushed to the region to calm tempers. New Delhi's patience ran out following another, more audacious, suicide attack on the Indian Parliament on December 13, 2001, dubbed "India's own 9/11." New Delhi threatened war unless Pakistan reined in the jihadi groups operating from its soil. India moved roughly half a million soldiers—including three armored strike corps—to parts of Punjab, Rajasthan, and Gujarat bordering Pakistan. Islamabad responded by mobilizing its own armor and 300,000 army troops to the adjacent border areas of Punjab and Sindh.

India, Pakistan, and the United States were obviously operating from different strategic calculations regarding the "war against terror." India's actions reflected a "compellent strategy," partly aimed at getting Washington to apply pressure on Islamabad to stop supporting jihad in Kashmir and India proper.[81] India felt encouraged in this regard by President Bush's post-9/11 doctrine of "targeting terrorists *and* the states that support them." For its part, Islamabad expected Washington to support its militant insurgency in Kashmir as a reward for its military and intelligence operations in the war in Afghanistan. In a public address to the nation on September 19, Musharraf gave five reasons for assisting in that war: to secure Pakistan's strategic assets, safeguard the cause of Kashmir, prevent Pakistan from being declared a terrorist state, prevent an anti-Pakistani government from coming to power in Kabul, and enable Pakistan to reemerge as a responsible and dignified nation.

America feared that a war over Kashmir would divert attention from "Operation Enduring Freedom." Moreover, Pakistan's support was vital if al Qaeda and the Taliban were to be prevented from fleeing Afghanistan. With troops mobilized along the border with India, however, Pakistan would have fewer soldiers to deploy in the hunt for extremists in western Pakistan. Washington was also concerned about the doomsday scenario of Pakistan's collapse, which would pose a number of problems, including the possibility that Pakistan's nuclear weapons might fall into extremists' hands. Its limited objective, therefore, was to avert a war in South Asia.

At this point, the United States formally acknowledged for the first time the link between Kashmiri terrorist groups operating in Pakistan and those in the state, and it put pressure on Musharraf to proclaim that Pakistani soil would not be used to export terror to any part of the world. However, as argued in chapter 3, this was a tactical move that called on the jihadi groups to lie low for a time. The crisis bubbled up again in May 2002 when terrorists attacked an Indian military base at Kaluchak in Jammu, killing thirty-four people, including innocent women and children. In a swift response, Atal Bihari Vajpayee told the Indian army to prepare for a "decisive battle." Musharraf countered that "if India insists on launching all-out war to attack Pakistan's support for Kashmiri militants, Pakistan is prepared to go nuclear."[82] The United States, supported by its European allies and Russia, embarked on a new high-level diplomatic initiative to prevent a military confrontation. In early June, Deputy Secretary of State Richard Armitage traveled to Islamabad and elicited a promise from Musharraf to "end cross-border infiltration permanently."[83]

At that point, the triangular relationship between India, Pakistan, and the United States took a significant turn: India and Pakistan were now willing to "rely increasingly on U.S. intervention," which promised both "a buffer against escalation and a third-party channel of communications in crisis." However, both also attempted to manipulate the U.S. perception of the Kashmir dispute, with Pakistan emphasizing its weakness and "need to rely on early use of nuclear weapons" to prevent Indian movement across the border, India stressing Pakistan's instability, unpredictability, and support for terrorism, and using "nuclear rhetoric to remind the US of the danger in the region"—and both fueling U.S. fears of nuclear escalation, "by accident, unauthorized use, or misperception, in a future crisis." At the same time, earlier experience with the United States had taught both not to place too much faith in U.S. support, which had been a disappointment to Pakistan in the Kargil war and to India during the Kaluchak crisis. [84]

Nonetheless, both India and Pakistan were rethinking the role other powers might play in the changed international context. India had traditionally rejected international intervention in Kashmir because of its bitter, decades-old experience at the United Nations. "Internationalization of the Kashmir dispute" and "third-party mediation" were phrases that once sent Indian ruling elites into a rage. Discarding that political baggage, India was beginning to suggest it was ready to accept a discreet American role—which Vajpayee referred to as "facilitation"—in promoting a reasonable settlement of the Kashmir dispute with Pakistan. Formal mediation by the international community was still politically taboo.[85] Some Pakistanis, on the other hand, believed that if only the United States could mediate, it would put its weight completely behind Pakistan. On the contrary, it and others in the international community have little appetite for remapping borders and may well support the option of preserving the status quo by converting the Line of Control into an international border, an option unacceptable to the Pakistani establishment. The army, in particular, is not so sure about the good offices of outsiders such as the United States in helping Pakistan achieve justice for the Kashmiris and doubts Washington's reliability as an ally.[86]

Sensitive to the attitudes on both sides, Secretary of State Condoleezza Rice and her team unveiled a new U.S. "strategic vision" for South Asia in 2004, which sought to expand relations with both India and Pakistan but "in a differentiated way matched to their variation in geostrategic weights."[87] This was an attempt to "de-hyphenate the relationship," Rice later explained, as "India is looking to grow its influence into global influence," and Pakistan "is looking to a settled neighborhood so that it can deal with extremism in its own borders."[88] The administration's bold initiative sought to build on its success with its "Next Steps in the Strategic Partnership" by declaring its resolve to "help India become a major world power in the twenty-first century." By further asserting that "we understand fully the implications, including military implications, of that statement," Washington made it clear that "a strong and independent India represents a strategic asset, even when it remains only a partner and not a formal ally."[89]

At the same time, the Bush administration stood by its resolve to help Pakistan transform itself into a successful, internally stable, and moderate state, though what exactly that meant and how it was to be achieved remained unclear and pointed to the underlying risks and dangers of this strategy. Its central tenet was to continue rewarding President Musharraf by the lifting of sanctions, direct economic assistance, debt rescheduling, and supply of major weapon systems, including F-16 fighter aircraft. In keeping with the strategy, in March 2004 Pakistan was awarded the new status of a "major non-NATO ally." This included a $3 billion package of economic and military aid that was to be disbursed from 2005 to 2009 and a debt write-off of $450 million. Even the shocking disclosures of February 2003 that Pakistan's top nuclear scientist A. Q. Khan had been selling nuclear secrets to Libya, Iran, and North Korea drew a small response from Washington.

The United States has also been reluctant to call Musharraf to task for breaking his promises to restore democracy. Instead he has kept mainstream political parties out of national elections, held a farcical referendum to become president, twisted Parliament's arm to endorse his Legal Framework Order via constitutional amendments, and installed and removed prime ministers at will—all of which has systematically marginalized the democratic forces within the political process in Pakistan. As a result, anti-U.S. sentiments pervade not only the ranks of the ruling elite but also the liberal intelligentsia. Many are particularly incensed by the fact that Pakistan is included in the U.S. National Security Entry-Exit Registration System, which requires visitors and nonimmigrants of certain nationalities, regardless of citizenship, to be registered upon arrival in and departure from the United States. The U.S. policy of considering Musharraf its "best bet" in Islamabad may indeed prove risky.

The dangers of such a policy become clear from the U.S. administration's pursuit of the "war on terror," in which it has followed somewhat conflicting agendas in the subcontinent. In laying out the ground rules of this war before the United Nations in November 2001, President George Bush stated unequivocally: "We must unite in opposing all terrorists, not just one of them. . . . Any government that rejects this principle, trying to pick and choose its terrorist friends, will know the consequences." Yet during its first term the Bush administration focused narrowly on "al Qaeda first," which paved the way for its policy of "differentiated response" toward terror in the subcontinent. This enabled Musharraf to comply with U.S. demands to act against al Qaeda and Taliban forces that were targeting American interests and citizens while avoiding a meaningful crackdown on homegrown extremist groups focused largely on India. A tacit deal seemed to be in place that allowed the Pakistani establishment to keep the infrastructure of anti-India terrorism intact—even though U.S. pressure had ensured that actual military action on this front would remain limited since the 2002 crisis. New Delhi felt that Washington had not exercised "decisive influence" in meeting India's core national interests in ending Kashmir-related sources of terrorism in Pakistan.[90]

Washington's "differentiated response" to terror groups in South Asia over-looked the reality that al Qaeda thrived on a vast, deeply entrenched, and integrated network of more than fifty extremist groups that shared deep bonds of Islamic ideology, common political targets—the United States, India, and Israel—and training facilities and resources that straddled the Afghanistan and Pakistan borders. These groups, unlike states, operated from a radically different worldview.[91] Some had developed their own agenda while others sided with al Qaeda and the Taliban and turned against the Musharraf regime. Washington failed to understand that al Qaeda could not be vanquished with-out simultaneously targeting its support structures—the other jihadi groups—in the region.[92]

As the war on terror progressed, some of these linkages became clearer, with two striking trends. First, global terror is no longer in the hands of the "centralized" and "networked" system of Osama bin Laden's al Qaeda. The new wave is part of a different, broader movement that relies more on "local outfits with regional agendas."[93] Second, most of these outfits spanning the globe have a Pakistani content, using the pillars of Pakistan's jihad factory—the mosque network, the hawala network, and all-powerful, all-pervasive military-intelligence complex—to provide weapons, training, and infrastruc-ture. The arrest of Lashkar operatives near Baghdad in March 2004 showed that the jihadi groups unleashing terror in Kashmir Valley have spread their operations to Iraq against the U.S. military.[94] The 9/11 Commission Report laid bare the role played by Pakistani intelligence officers in introducing Osama bin Laden to Taliban leaders in Kandahar, their main base of power, to help him reassert control over camps near Khost in the hope that "[bin] Laden would expand the camps and make them available for training Kashmiri mil-itants."[95] In the Bush administration's reappraisal of its war on terror, Pakistan was categorized as a country whose administrative and political structure was most conducive to breeding terrorists.

This assessment led to renewed pressure on Islamabad, especially after U.S. Deputy Secretary of State Richard Armitage returned from a visit to Islamabad in May 2003 with satellite images of the three major training camps in Pak-istani Kashmir. Later, at a news conference, he announced that "President Musharraf gave me an assurance that . . . if there were any camps, they would be gone tomorrow."[96] He returned in October that year with a stronger mes-sage that was subsequently beamed at Pakistan from multiple directions: Pakistan must give up jihad as an option.[97] Following assassination attempts on President Musharraf, U.S. officials began seeing "the militant groups [as] an internal danger to Pakistan." Secretary of State Condoleezza Rice then revived the original formulation outlined by President Bush in 2001: "We have been clear with the Pakistan government that terrorism is terrorism in any form. In that sense, there can be no cause that can justify terrorism."[98] At the same time, the Bush administration's policy has remained consistent in heaping praise on President Musharraf for curbing infiltration across the Line of Control and yet admitting in the same breath that "more progress is needed."[99]

Note, too, that for the first time in the post-1947 history of the subcontinent, the United States is enjoying leverage with *both* India and Pakistan: by helping the former become a global power and the latter obtain economic and military aid. However, Washington is still not in a position, perhaps by choice, to use this leverage to forge a final settlement of the Kashmir conflict. While it continues to support the bilateral dialogue process to achieve that goal, it is not in favor of redrawing Kashmir's borders in the long term. There is a widely shared, albeit unspoken, consensus in Washington that a final settlement must, above all, convert the Line of Control into a border between India and Pakistan and award substantive autonomy to the state of Jammu and Kashmir.[100]

That explains Washington's positive attitude toward the state assembly elections of Jammu and Kashmir held in 2002. For years, the United States had argued that a final resolution of the Kashmir dispute had to take into account the wishes of the Kashmiri people, although it failed to make clear how Kashmiri sentiments might be ascertained. On the eve of Colin Powell's visit in July 2002, the Bush administration ruled out a plebiscite as an option, although Powell acknowledged that elections to the assembly in Jammu and Kashmir could be a way to assess the wishes of the people in the state.[101] India, which traditionally rejected outside assistance in the Kashmir dispute, consciously signaled its willingness to let Delhi-based diplomats, including American embassy staff, serve as international observers, if only in their individual capacity, to see for themselves India's determination to hold elections in an open and transparent manner. This brought a new international legitimacy to the state's popularly elected representatives.[102] In his visit to Kashmir after the elections, Ambassador Robert D. Blackwill did not meet the Hurriyat leaders in Srinagar to reinforce the message that India saw the newly elected government in Kashmir as a legitimate representative of the people.[103] As of this writing, the Bush administration continues to support the ongoing peace process, though primarily through back-channel diplomacy.

Although the United States remains by far the most critical international player in South Asia, other important outsiders include Russia, China, the European Union, and perhaps members of the Organization of Islamic Countries, particularly Saudi Arabia. Their role in the Kashmir conflict has also remained confined to counseling restraint in order to prevent a military confrontation between India and Pakistan. None has volunteered a blueprint for resolving Kashmir. The offers of mediation invariably come with the rider that they must be approached by both India and Pakistan.

In the aftermath of the Kargil war and the 2001–02 crisis, many countries have a better appreciation of India's position on cross-border terrorism in Kashmir, mainly because they have also been victims of international terrorism. Chechnya, for example, is bleeding Russia in much the same way that Kashmir is draining India's resources. In extending full support to India in its war on terrorism, Russian president Vladimir Putin has observed that "the same terrorist organizations, extremist organizations are organizing and, very often, the same individuals participate in organizing, in conducting and igniting terrorist acts from the Philippines to Kosovo including Kashmir, Afghanistan and Russia's Northern Caucasus."[104] With the sources of this threat in Afghanistan and Pakistan, New Delhi and Moscow felt it essential to beat back the Taliban, and together with Teheran, they began a coordinated effort to militarily strengthen the Northern Alliance in Afghanistan. During President Putin's visit to New Delhi in December 2002, the two sides declared that "as victims of terrorism having its roots in our common neighborhood, we have particular interest in putting an end to this common threat through preventive and deterrent measures nationally and bilaterally."[105]

In the case of Kashmir, Russia continues to call for bilateral dialogue between India and Pakistan. At the Almaty conference in June 2002, however, President Putin met with General Musharraf and hinted that he might be prepared to mediate on Kashmir and wanted to invite the Indian and Pakistani leaders to Moscow to promote a peace process. India moved quickly to deny any interest in such mediation.[106] In a joint statement with Russia, it underlined the importance of Islamabad fully implementing its obligations and promises to prevent the infiltration of terrorists across the Line of Control as a prerequisite for the renewal of peaceful dialogue between the countries.

China's position on Kashmir has clearly shifted over the years. In the 1970s, China took an aggressively pro-Pakistani stance on self-determination for Kashmiris but subsequently emphasized Indo-Pakistani bilateralism. By 1996 it had decided that if the Kashmir issue could not be resolved immediately, then it should be put on a back burner and South Asia should concentrate on economic cooperation. Coming amid an intense Pakistani campaign to internationalize the Kashmir dispute, China's new position surprised Pakistan. China's neutrality in the Kargil conflict and its reluctance to bail Nawaz Sharif out from his misadventure reflected its own concerns about the potential

234 / T H E   I N T E R N A T I O N A L   A R E N A

effects of the "Taliban syndrome" on the political stability of its Xinjiang Province, where Uighur Muslims are seeking to win independence. China was also perturbed by Pakistan's deep involvement with the Taliban regime and by the specter of Islamic militant and fundamentalist groups using Kashmir as a launching pad for activities in Xinjiang. It is therefore not favorably inclined toward Pakistan's cultivation of jihadi groups whose outreach beyond Kashmir is well proven. During Premier Wen Jiabao's visit to Islamabad in April 2005, the two countries signed twenty-two agreements, including a treaty of friendship, cooperation, and good neighborly relations as well as pacts on combating terrorism, separatism, and extremism. Significantly, China's relationship with India has also changed dramatically, as is evident from the fact that China now supports India's claim to a permanent seat in the UN Security Council, albeit without veto power.

Pakistan's credentials among the members of the OIC are also not what they used to be. Conservative rulers, particularly the unaccountable monarchies, consider extremist organizations a threat to their control over their own countries, while radicals disapprove of Pakistan's support of America's war on Iraq. As for progressives, they dislike the backward-looking conservatism of some Islamist parties in Pakistan, such as the newly formed but potentially powerful Muttahida Majlis-e-Amal (MMA). In April 2000, the presidents of Kazakhstan, Kyrgyzstan, Uzbekistan, and Turkmenistan signed an agreement to conduct joint operations to combat terrorism, political and religious extremism, multinational organized crime, and other security threats. President Musharraf, well aware of OIC complaints, not to mention Western concerns about Pakistan's nuclear program, has vowed to ensure that Pakistan will not become the next target after Iraq. In the same breath, he has admitted: "Should the situation turn ugly, the country could not even expect assistance from other Muslim countries."[107]

Conclusion

Throughout Kashmir's history, the world's great powers—most notably the United States, the former Soviet Union, and China—have accorded the state a place in their strategic agendas only insofar as it served their global interests or concerned their respective regional partners. However, none were willing to be dragged into the Kashmir issue by those partners.[108] Furthermore, despite Indian and Pakistani expectations, outside support for either side has been limited. The Soviet Union, for example, provided India with an automatic veto in the United Nations on Kashmir-related resolutions and backed New

Delhi diplomatically for many years. Although the United States offered Pakistan political and military support, it failed to provide security assurances against India, precisely because Washington was afraid of being sucked into the Kashmir impasse. Washington and Moscow made several inconclusive efforts to mediate the dispute but found that neither pressure nor persuasion worked. They therefore became wary of trying to resolve the Kashmir issue. The mantra of bilateralism at the heart of the Simla Agreement provided them a way out. Their fundamental positions have not changed. Since the end of the cold war, their involvement in the dispute has been confined to managing each crisis as it arises in order to avoid a fourth war between India and Pakistan over Kashmir.

All in all, no global power has high enough stakes in the Kashmir conflict or the leverage to arrive at a solution acceptable to *all* the principal players. More to the point, the complex character of the Kashmir conflict does not make it amenable to an externally driven peace process. Although it is essential for the international players, especially the United States, to continue engaging the top leaders on both sides, outsiders must rely on strictly low-profile and quiet diplomacy. In the long run, Washington could play the critical role of a catalyst in supporting and sustaining the ongoing peace process, though much of the groundwork and ideas must emanate from within the region.

CHAPTER EIGHT

THE PEACE PUZZLE

THE CURRENT PEACE PROCESS between India and Pakistan, formally known as the "composite dialogue," has begun a new chapter in Kashmir's conflict-ridden history. The meeting between India's prime minister Atal Bihari Vajpayee and Pakistan's president General Pervez Musharraf at the South Asian Association for Regional Cooperation summit in Islamabad in January 2004 restarted the process. With Vajpayee's successor Manmohan Singh carrying it forward and President Musharraf coming up with some new (for Pakistan) proposals, the debate on the dynamics and future prospects of the peace process is expanding in its policy parameters and the set of players with a stake in and commitment to the dialogue.

Policy Parameters

The most challenging aspect of the Kashmir peace process is to think beyond the narrow conceptions of the three parameters along which this conflict is traditionally viewed: ideology, nationalism, and self-determination. Each has proved to be a serious impediment to its resolution.

IDEOLOGY

With the partition of India and the creation of Pakistan in 1947, Kashmir became entangled in a dispute arising in part from two mutually exclusive ideologies. On the one hand, there was Pakistan arguing that including a Muslim-majority state such as Jammu and Kashmir in India repudiated the two-nation theory responsible for its identity; on the other hand, there was India insisting that Kashmir's accession validated the theory of secular nationalism on which it was founded. Nearly sixty years later, Kashmir is still being treated as a test of each state's legitimizing ideology.

At the outset of this long period of turmoil, as argued in chapter 1, Kashmir's fate was neither preordained nor decided on ideological grounds. Being part of the subcontinent's princely order, the Dogra state of Jammu and Kashmir lay outside the domain of British India, which in 1947 was divided on the basis of the two-nation theory. At that point, Kashmir was not yet considered an inalienable part of either Pakistan or India but an important asset from the standpoint of geographical consolidation and the defense needs of the respective dominions. Hence the battle between India's Congress and the Muslim League over Kashmir's accession was fundamentally political in nature.

Since independence, the two ideological rationales at the heart of the dispute have not gone unchallenged, both within and outside Kashmir. Pakistan, some argue, has not yet arrived at a clear formulation of its foundations, which are rooted in Islam. That is to say, the meaning, content, and relationship of Islam and state have never been systematically established.[1] Pakistan has remained suspended between the ambiguity of the call for a Muslim homeland by its founder, Mohammad Ali Jinnah, and the varying expectations of the majority of the religious establishment and populace for an Islamic state. The continuing debate between modernist and orthodox interpretations of Islam within Pakistan mirrors this dilemma.

Modernists reject the notion that a state founded on Islamic principles must operate as a theocracy; rather, they identify Islamic ideals and principles with democracy, freedom, equality, tolerance, and social justice for all, including minorities. Orthodox opinions, most notably those of the Jamaat-i-Islami school of thought, equate the state with Islam and therefore would apply its guiding principles in all matters—legal, constitutional, and political—to the point of establishing Nizam-i-Mustafa (the Rule of Islam) throughout Pakistani society. Jihadi groups such as Lashkar-e-Taiba place yet another interpretation on Islam, emphasizing the integration of *tabligh* (education) and *jihad* (holy war) needed to acquire the military skill essential for wielding political power.[2] Others seek to impose the Taliban version of sharia laws and a puritanical form of Islam in Pakistan.

From the earliest demands for a separate state and the creation of Pakistan in 1947, Islam has been both a rallying force and a legitimizing ideology for a wide array of political and religious leaders. After Jinnah, almost all of Pakistan's leaders, including those with secular leanings, suppressed ethnic, regional, and economic discontent, using Islam to justify their coercive and authoritarian actions. According to one scholar, "the official discourse of inclusionary nationalism far from contributing to the evolution of a collective ethos" has impeded the accommodation of local and regional social formations.[3] The secession of East Pakistan on the basis of Bengali nationalism in 1971 proved this point. Moreover, the demographic fact that India has nearly as many Muslims as either Pakistan or Bangladesh raises serious questions about the necessity of searching for nationhood in religious terms. Despite being an independent state for fifty-nine years, Pakistan has yet to evolve an identity that does not hinge on the inclusion of Kashmir.

The ideological debate in India, which is just as heated and transcends the Kashmir issue, centers on secularism. Indian secularism, critics argue, has failed to achieve its original objectives of deterring the persecution of religious minorities and "imposing limits on the political expression of cultural or religious conflicts between Hindus and Muslims."[4] There is perhaps as much, if not greater religious bigotry today as before independence, and it is still markedly though not exclusively Hindutva-driven. Some attribute it to the peculiar characteristics of Indian society, such as the blind loyalty to caste and religious community, which can easily slide into communal rivalry and more dangerously into communal conflict.[5] The state's policy of making separate laws for religious communities also contravenes the fundamental principle of the separation of religion and state. Some even argue that secularism is "culturally inappropriate" for India partly because "it is much too much a public matter to be privatized."[6] Not indigenous to the religious cultures of India and imported from the West, secularism continues to sit uneasily with homegrown worldviews. Nehru's concept of a secular state did not negate religion, however; it meant equal protection for all faiths. The state did not establish any official religion but reserved for itself the right to intervene in matters of religion in the interest of necessary social reforms.[7]

The biggest challenge to Nehruvian secularism was mounted by the Hindu nationalist political party Jan Sangh (JS) and its successor, the Bharatiya Janata Party (BJP). The JS/BJP sought to subsume different cultural, linguistic, and caste layers of community identity under a single overarching category of religion as well as to transform the multifaceted religious system of Hinduism into a monolithic one. From this standpoint, "*Hindutva* acts as an exclusionary force in the Indian society rather than [being] universalistic and open to the values of other cultures."[8] The real testing ground of Indian secularism has not been Kashmir but developments such as the demolition of the Babri mosque in 1992 and the anti-Muslim riots in the BJP-ruled state of Gujarat in 2003.

Interestingly, Kashmir provides a rallying point to all shades and hues of this ideological debate on both sides of the border. In India, it is not only the secularists but also the Hindu nationalists who seek to appropriate the Kashmir issue to their cause.[9] In Pakistan, Kashmir becomes a unifying force for the modernists, the orthodox, and the jihadis. Yet not one of these groups has yielded critical space to Kashmiri voices. That is why, in the triangular relationship between India, Pakistan, and Kashmir, it is important to distinguish between "religion as faith" and "religion as ideology." Religion as faith may be defined as "a way of life, a tradition that is definitionally non-monolithic," whereas religion as ideology denotes a "sub-national, national or cross-national identifier of populations contesting for or protecting non-religious, usually political or socio-economic interest."[10]

Ideology in this sense is a modern construct that is deeply uncomfortable with the inherent plurality of faiths. When appropriated by a state as a legitimizing tool, it invariably acquires a majoritarian character whatever its specific form, whether Hindu nationalism/secularism, Islamic principles, or even a Kashmiriyat-based ideology. As Jammu and Kashmir's history has proven, the Kashmiri identity, once appropriated by its political masters (initially, Sheikh Abdullah), also acquired an exclusivist character representing only the majority community of "Kashmiri-speaking Muslims of the Valley," and leaving others outside its boundaries.[11] The fact that those boundaries are limited may seem to explain why the insurgent movement of the 1990s seeking Kashmiri self-determination foundered when it was turned into an Islamic jihad. The real source of Kashmir's various problems is not so much the limiting boundaries of an Indian, Pakistani, or Kashmiri ideology but the fact that ideology, with its homogenizing tendencies, is being applied at all to a deeply plural community. This plurality must be the uppermost consideration in formulating an appropriate policy framework for the peace process.

Since the early 1940s, however, most suggestions for settling Kashmir's problems have actually managed to fuel the debate by using regional or religious affiliations as a basis for territorial divisions. This has been the central failing of the cease-fire line (1949), the redrawing of district boundaries within Jammu and Ladakh regions, the Dixon plan for a regional plebiscite, a proposed trifurcation of the state, and the Ladakh demand for union territory status. General Musharraf, for one, weighed in with regional-based options, ostensibly in deference to "Indian sensitivities": "Take Kashmir in its entirety . . . it has seven regions. Two are in Pakistan and five in India. In my view, identify a region, whether it is whole of seven or part, I do not know. Demilitarize it forever and change its status."[12] The problem is, the dividing lines between the religious and regional frontiers within the Indian part of Kashmir are very thin. Thus far, it has been possible to come up with not *one* but at least *four* formulations of regions within the former princely state, the current one consisting of Jammu, Ladakh, and the Valley. The other three formulations would actually deepen the communal fault lines under the guise of carving out new regions.

In the current setup, Kashmir Valley is the only Muslim-majority region, with a prominent, albeit small, minority of Kashmiri Pandits; Jammu has a Hindu-majority populace with a substantial Muslim minority; and in Ladakh the Buddhists outnumber the Muslims. Under General Musharraf's proposed setup, Kashmir would be divided into seven regions, five of which would have a Muslim majority. The National Conference's formulation, as discussed in chapter 4, would establish eight provinces along similar lines in that six (Maraz, Kamraz, Nundabad, Chenab Valley, Pir Panjal, and Kargil) would have a Muslim majority. The Chenab formula would place the Line of Control (LOC) along the riverbed, with Muslim areas on the right side of the river being absorbed into Pakistan and the Hindu- and Buddhist-majority regions into India. This formula self-confessedly partitions Kashmir on religious lines.[13] None of these formulas recognizes that Kashmir's plurality is an asset and not a liability and must therefore be firmly embedded in the peace process.

NATIONALISM

Nationalism, with its hegemonic attributes, has added another problematic dimension to the Kashmir dispute. Both India and Pakistan assign a central place to Kashmir in their respective nation-building strategies. Paradoxically, the two parts of Kashmir have paid a heavy price for holding this position. Kashmiri nationalism became stifled by Indian nationalism, while the adult franchise was altogether absent from Azad Kashmir and the Northern Areas until as late as 1974 and 1994, respectively.

Indeed, the national question is the driving force behind most secessionist movements in South Asia—whether Assamese, Tamil, Sikh, Baluch, or Chakma. Though they might differ in their character, support base, and dynamics, these movements share an uncompromising opposition to a centralized political authority, and unequivocal rejection of the legitimacy of the nation-state as constituted at present. As argued earlier, this centralized authority is a defining feature of the modern nation-state organized around a single national coordinate. Even in a diverse society governed through electoral democracy, organizing the state around only *one* identity is inherently problematic in that the dominant majority becomes the sole repository of political power, while minority communities tend to feel alienated and marginalized. Those left out seek to construct their own identity and create alternative spaces within or without existing state boundaries. But they do so without questioning the basic logic behind the modern nation-state and hence merely reproduce the kind of hierarchical and monolithic social and political organizations from which they seek to escape. For example, India's interventionist and centralized structure alienated the Kashmiris by appropriating their autonomous status. But while fighting those integrative pressures, they replicated the same unitary power structure, thereby alienating the people of Jammu and Ladakh.

Moreover, the nationalist discourse, whether Indian or Pakistani, with its core values of sovereignty and sacred and inviolable territorial borders, makes it difficult to arrive at a creative political solution for a complex community such as Kashmir. Those involved in the peace process must rethink the concepts of state sovereignty, borders, and boundaries and contend with the reality that "sovereignty today is an extraordinarily flexible, manipulative concept."[14] Furthermore, "divided sovereignty may be essential to [a] polity's survival in a period of . . . ethnic assertiveness."[15] Perhaps they should take a cue from the precolonial concept of "suzerainty" and explore the meaning, form, content, and viability of "layered" or "shared" sovereignty in the context of Kashmir. Diverse sets of sovereign-suzerain state structures would better respond to the needs of the individuals and groups within each state who are theoretically the repositories of ultimate sovereign authority. Clearly, the leadership in New Delhi and Islamabad needs to view the conflict from the people's perspective.

SELF-DETERMINATION

The doctrine of national self-determination postulates that "any people, simply because it considers itself to be a separate people has the right, if it so desires, to form its own state."[16] The fundamental problem here, however, is that ethnographic boundaries almost never coincide with political ones. More important, the creation of a Westphalian state—the ultimate goal of most self-determination movements—may simply compound the problem by failing to address the more important question of political rights. There is a close relationship between self-determination and popular sovereignty: "National consciousness was a *necessary* but not a *sufficient* condition for the advent of national self-determination. Popular sovereignty—the notion that ultimate political authority rests with the people—was the other necessary part of the equation."[17] It is important, therefore, to distinguish between the territorial and political dimensions of the right to self-determination.

Kashmiri demands for self-determination have always been viewed in a territorial light, being demands for sovereign rights over an independent territory.

Popular sovereignty or the political rights of the people have been much neglected, although Kashmiris (on the Indian side) were able to secure popular sovereignty for a very brief period in the early 1950s during which they had a separate constitutional assembly to determine the future of the Dogra rule and drew up a state constitution. The political goals and territorial ambitions of the National Conference, however, eroded the state's autonomy when Sheikh Abdullah began exploring the option of a sovereign, independent state of Jammu and Kashmir. After three decades of this erosion, through the imposition of New Delhi's political choices in Srinagar and the blatant manipulation of the electoral process, the idea of azadi (freedom) reemerged in the early 1990s. Although the violent militant movement that inspired it fizzled out, the idea has survived.

The challenge for political leaders engaged in the peace process is to segregate the political and territorial dimensions of the demand for self-determination and work toward safeguarding the political rights of the people of Jammu and Kashmir. A territorial vision of the right of self-determination is entirely the wrong point of departure. For one thing, New Delhi and Islamabad will not allow their respective parts of Kashmir to secede, and the idea violates the "territorial integrity norm" of the late twentieth century.[18] For another, the international context has changed since September 11, 2001, with few willing to believe the myth of the "freedom-struggle" used to justify jihadi terrorism in Kashmir. Most important, territorial independence for Jammu and Kashmir state will not "resolve" the Kashmir problem because it is not supported by *all the people of the state*.

Having failed to recognize that the different communities living in Jammu and Kashmir interpret the right to self-determination differently, Kashmiri leaders allowed their thinking to become enmeshed in contradictions. Sheikh Abdullah, for instance, argued that self-determination was the inherent right of all peoples and demanded it for Kashmiris, yet denied the same to the people of Jammu and Ladakh. Jammu and Ladakh in turn demanded full and unconditional accession to India, but this acted as a countervailing force to the Valley's demand for independence. The current separatist leadership, including the Hurriyat Conference, faces the same dilemma. While it claims to speak on behalf of the "people of Jammu and Kashmir," it represents the political interests of only a part of the majority community—Kashmiri Muslims in the Valley. Meanwhile, the minority social groups in Jammu and Ladakh seek autonomy from the Kashmir Valley. Clearly, the secessionist agenda underlying the demand for the right to self-determination lacks an inclusive character. The collective and consistent opposition of the state's linguistic, regional, and religious minorities has checkmated the demand for secession by the majority community of the Kashmiri Muslims. A just, viable, and lasting peace in Kashmir must involve *all* the communities and nationalities living in the state, not just the Kashmiri Muslims who resorted to the gun and thus became the real victims of the political violence in the state. If the political demands of the nonviolent mobilizations in Jammu, Ladakh, and the Northern Areas are not addressed through the peace process, it will send a message that violence pays, defeating the very purpose of that process.

Players

It is essential for various local, national, and international players to lend their support to a sustained dialogue on Kashmir if there is to be any hope of reaching a mutually acceptable and negotiated solution to the conflict.

LOCAL PLAYERS

Thus far, popular representatives of both parts of Jammu and Kashmir have not been directly involved in bilateral negotiations mainly because it is *wrongly assumed* that only two seats are available at a single negotiation table, one for New Delhi and one for Islamabad. Who, then, speaks for the people of Jammu and Kashmir? The deep pluralities of its society and diverse nature of political demands—ranging from affirmative discrimination to more autonomy to a separate constitutional status within the Indian or Pakistani states or a sovereign independent state—preclude the possibility that a "single spokesperson" will do. The answer lies in augmenting the levels of dialogue so that exchanges occur between the Indian government and representatives of Jammu, the Valley, and Ladakh; between various representatives of Jammu, the Valley, and Ladakh themselves; between Indian and Pakistani parts of Kashmir across the LOC; between representatives of Azad Jammu and Kashmir and the Northern Areas; and between the Pakistani government and representatives of Azad Jammu and Kashmir and the Northern Areas. In other words, negotiations should take place at *several high tables* in layered fashion.

JAMMU AND KASHMIR STATE. A first step of the process should be to identify the political forces in the state. They can be divided into four sets: traditional political parties such as the National Conference, People's Democratic Party (PDP), Congress, BJP, and other elected representatives; separatist groups—mainly but not only—the Hurriyat; the militants; and the leaders of the minority communities in the Indian part of Kashmir.

Elected representatives generally associate the Kashmir conflict with the insurgent movement of the 1990s and think the key to a just and lasting peace is to end the violence, initiate a dialogue with the separatists (including militants), and most important, develop new political and constitutional arrangements to meet popular aspirations for self-governance. People's faith in the electoral process as a legitimate instrument of political change is already on the upswing following the 2002 assembly elections, which ended twenty-seven years of dynastic rule through the ballot box. That faith has been reaffirmed in the high voter turnouts in the 2005 municipal elections and the April 2006 by-elections. The National Conference continues to be the single largest political party with the biggest voter share in the state assembly and has a strong support base, especially in rural Kashmir.[19] It will play an important role in building a domestic political consensus and is unlikely to act as a spoiler in the peace process. The PDP, a three-year-old regional party, represents the new class of political leadership in the state whose pro-Kashmiri stance is trying to appropriate the Hurriyat's political agenda without the latter's secessionist overtones. Now that Ghulam Nabi Azad, a Congress leader from the Doda region, occupies the chief minister's post, the myth that the state government should not be led by a non-Kashmiri also stands discredited. As the mandate for political parties across the state becomes increasingly fragmented, coalition governments are likely to continue replacing one-party rule (of the National Conference).

The greatest challenge for elected representatives pursuing peace is to deepen and broaden the political process by holding panchayat (village council) elections and reinstating constituencies alienated from mainstream politics.[20] Changes are already under way, though slow and arduous: the 1997 assembly elections brought "surrendered militants" into the electoral fray and the next elections saw the breakaway factions of Hurriyat constituents campaigning as "independents." In the 2006 by-elections, youth outnumbered middle-aged and elderly voters at every polling station. To strengthen these processes further, parties across the political spectrum need to reinvigorate their respective organizational networks at the grassroots level.

The separatist groups believe that Kashmir's final future remains to be decided along the lines of their ideological leanings, political strategies, and goals, but they have become a divided lot. The largest political body representing the separatist agenda and thus an important player is the Hurriyat Conference, but it is sharply divided between moderate and hard-line factions. Growing differences with other centrist leaders such as Yasin Malik have also depleted its already limited political capital.[21] Jammu and Ladakh have never been represented in Hurriyat's executive council, and by the same token the political leadership in Azad Kashmir and the Northern Areas does not recognize its leaders as their representatives. Soon after Hurriyat's first public foray across the Line of Control in 2005, Azad Kashmir's prime minister, Sardar Sikander Hayat Khan, questioned its credentials: "How can we accept any decision (on Kashmir) by those who live under compulsions, do not have unity among themselves and are not representatives of all regions?" Hurriyat continues to grapple with a crisis of legitimacy in attempting to be the "sole representative" of Kashmiris. That is because it has always sought this status from the "top leadership" of Pakistan and India rather than earning it through a popular mandate.

For its part, Pakistan has obliged, but on its own terms and at the price of controlling the Hurriyat agenda. As explained in chapter 2, if Hurriyat leaders did not toe the line, they were threatened, marginalized, or eliminated. The lesson has yet to sink in that if "sole-representative" status is bestowed from above, it can also be *taken away* by its patrons. On the Indian side, too, Hurriyat has hoped the central government would acknowledge it as the representative of a de facto nation, something that no political authority in New Delhi is likely to concede. Hurriyat exercises no leverage over militants, either, as is evident from the United Jihad Council's public refusal to even meet Hurriyat leaders during their visit to Azad Kashmir and Hizb-ul-Mujahideen's outright dismissal of a Hurriyat plea to stop the violence and give peace a chance.

Significantly, the Hurriyat has not yet decided on a new agenda after Pakistan's dismissal of the old proposal for a plebiscite, which was also rejected as obsolete by the international community. And the idea of an independent Kashmir is ruled out by both India and Pakistan. The mirwaiz-led centrist faction of the Hurriyat is now being coaxed into supporting Musharraf's proposal for an autonomous Kashmir, although the idea of self-governance or self-rule is far from a new one in the Valley's context. Much older and traditional players such as the National Conference, which have championed this cause since 1947, are clearly better equipped with the political skills needed to fight this battle. If Hurriyat were to abandon its separatist agenda, it would not only run the risk of being eclipsed as a political force but might also invite the wrath of Kashmiris for having misled a generation of young men and women and for sacrificing thousands of lives. Hurriyat's most important challenge, as Mirwaiz Umar Farooq rightly states, is to redefine its goals, which in turn would shape the role it might play in the peace process.

Most of the active militant groups—including Lashkar-e-Taiba, Jaish-i-Mohammed, al Badr, and Harkat-ul-Mujahideen in its original as well as splinter formations—are Pakistan based. Therefore this "jihadi" factor is not influenced by developments in the Kashmir Valley but in Pakistan, as discussed in the next section. Suffice it to say that injecting jihadi groups in the Valley proved to be counterproductive in that they obliterated the indigenous character of the separatist movement and alienated Kashmiris from Pakistan. Kashmiri society, with its deep-rooted Sufi traditions, rejected not only the jihadis' puritanical version of Islam but also the sheer ruthlessness of their practices, such as the beheading of their victims and mutilation of their bodies. This only deepened Kashmiri abhorrence of the foreign militants. Although jihadi attempts to liberate Kashmir are doomed, these groups will continue to act as a spoiler in the peace process.

Hizb-ul-Mujahideen is the only militant group with a substantial Kashmiri cadre. Since its chief led an unprecedented hunger strike in Muzaffarabad in protest of the Musharraf regime's betrayal of the jihad in Jammu and Kashmir, it seems to be wavering on the question of giving up the path of violence. Its dilemma is twofold. First, it clings to Pakistan's *old* political line—being the only player to insist that New Delhi formally recognize that all of Jammu and Kashmir is a disputed territory—yet seeks the status of the principal interlocutor, which only India can concede (though precisely for that reason is not likely to do so). Second, like Hurriyat, the Hizbul expects to be rewarded, although it has little to offer in terms of ending the violence because in the past decade it has been marginalized by none other than its patron—the Pakistani establishment—in favor of Lashkar-e-Taiba and Jaish-i-Mohammed, which have been at the forefront of the Kashmiri jihad. New Delhi is not likely to hand political power to the Hizbul leadership on a platter; if the latter were to join the peace process, however, its best offer might include an amnesty for the Hizbul cadre, a seat (*not* the only one) at the negotiating table, and a level playing field in the political arena, where Hizbul will have to compete with traditional political parties—all rather uncertain and incommensurate rewards. The field commanders of the Hizb-ul-Mujahideen also feel that "the wages of war are greater than any payouts that may come with peace," albeit for different reasons, which, as discussed in chapter 5, make jihad a lucrative proposition. Such entrenched vested interests in continued violence need to be taken into account in any new government initiative that seeks to bring Hizbul, especially its Valley-based leadership (of both factions), into the peace process.

Finally, the political leaders of the minority communities—the Kashmiri Pandits, Ladakhi Buddhists, Shia Muslims (of Kargil), Gujjars, Paharis, and Dogras—must be involved in the internal dialogue between representatives of

Jammu and Kashmir state and the Indian government. However, this must not become yet another top-down process, which is what happened when the State Autonomy Committee (SAC) and the Regional Autonomy Committee (RAC) appointed by Farooq Abdullah's government in 1996 began their deliberations. The merits of the SAC's recommendations for restoring maximum political autonomy to Jammu and Kashmir, as specified in Article 370 of India's constitution, were overshadowed by the fact that the formation and deliberations of the two committees were neither inclusive nor participatory. All their members (except their respective chairpersons, Karan Singh in the SAC, who resigned in July 1997, and Balraj Puri in the RAC, who was dismissed in January 1999, barely three months before the submission of the report) belonged to the ruling party, that is, the National Conference. The opposition had no voice in devising the future rules of the game for power sharing. No formal or informal talks were held with active or former militants, including their political leadership such as the Hurriyat Conference. The RAC report, as pointed out in chapter 4, was not endorsed by half of its members, including its working chairman, Balraj Puri, and the lone minority (Ladakhi Buddhist) member, Pinto Norbu. Prominent minorities, including the Kashmiri Pandits, Gujjars, and Dogras and Shia Muslims, did not figure on the committee's panel. Not surprisingly, its recommendations were never acted upon, although both were important consultative mechanisms and could have been used as an effective medium to seek the opinion of those at the grassroots level. However, their weak representativeness marred their prospects.

It is imperative for the central government to reach out to the minority communities in the peace process and ensure that their political interests are safeguarded in any final settlement. Prime Minister Manmohan Singh's decision to hold the first roundtable conference in Kashmir in February 2006 was the first important step in this direction. Though it is too early to predict the outcome, this move has the potential to recast the long-established hierarchies of power, spreading some of it to religious, ethnic, and linguistic groups as well as regions in Jammu and Kashmir. Gujjar and Bakkarwal leaders hope to see that the special needs of their communities are met, for example, through traveling panchayat systems that will move with their livestock across mountains, more funding for schools and colleges, and efforts to overcome backwardness in their communities.[22] Ladakh's representatives hope to use the dialogue both to address specific regional issues and to free their region from events in Kashmir and Jammu. And politicians in both Leh and Kargil hope the opening of trans-LOC routes to Gilgit and Skardu will help diminish the region's economic dependence on Srinagar.

AZAD KASHMIR AND THE NORTHERN AREAS. Three sets of political forces in Azad Kashmir need to be taken into account in the peace process. One set is controlled by traditional players such as the Muslim Conference and Pakistan People's Party (PPP), which believe the Kashmir conflict revolves around the "other (the Indian) Kashmir" and hope to bring it into Pakistan's fold. Azad Kashmir's leaders across the political spectrum have severely criticized General Musharraf's shift in Kashmir policy. The leader of the Jammu and Kashmir Liberation Front (JKLF), Amanullah Khan, charged Pakistan with "complete surrender," while Sardar Ejaz Aslam, the Azad Kashmir amir of the Jamaat-i-Islami, condemned Pakistan for "stabbing the Kashmiri martyrs in the back."[23] Sardar Attiq, chairman of the ruling Muslim Conference, complained that the "talk of initiating trade relations with India is like trading off the blood of freedom fighters." Pakistan's latest position has also perplexed the former president and chairman of Pakistan's Kashmir Committee, Sardar Abdul Qayum, who believes that Musharraf is inadvertently admitting to charges of terrorism and cross-border infiltration.[24] Others go so far as to suggest that Musharraf's turnaround amounts to intellectual and political abandonment of the Indian part of Kashmir.

Subjugated by Pakistan's overbearing bureaucratic control, the leadership in Muzaffarabad has traditionally pursued the agenda of uniting Kashmir—within and without—with great passion because it has proven to be an unblemished means of seeking political legitimacy. In reality, however, their attempts to organize border crossings from the 1960s right up to the 1990s were driven more by their desire to defy Islamabad than by a clearly thought-out strategy to unite the two parts of Kashmir. Beyond this public posture, however, most constituents in Azad Kashmir do not aspire to unite Kashmir because they have very negative memories of Valley-centric rule and also because their ethnocultural, linguistic, and religious lineage is very different from that of the Valley-based Kashmiri Muslims. Even those who demand a sovereign Kashmir do so because they resent Pakistan's exploitative policies and not because they consider themselves to be part and parcel of a unique Kashmiri identity. Their dilemma is that while they seek to break loose from the hegemonic embrace of Islamabad, they would be loath to yield the leadership role to Valley-based political forces in a united Kashmir. Hence they may consider supporting the peace process worthwhile provided they could use the opportunity and platform provided by the dialogue to negotiate a truly autonomous political status for themselves within Pakistan.

The JKLF is another important political force to reckon with. Over the years, it has sought a united, sovereign, and independent Kashmir. Its political goal, which is to achieve azadi, continues to find popular support in both parts of Kashmir, but JKLF is becoming increasingly marginalized. While it is important to include the group in the dialogue process, especially in the talks between the Indian and the Pakistani parts of Kashmir, it is unlikely to play a determining role in the larger peace process.

Finally, there are the jihadi forces, with the strength of more than one hundred organizations in Azad Kashmir. They are not much different in their character, goals, and strategies from the jihadi groups based in Pakistan, to be discussed shortly.

In the Northern Areas, political forces are broadly organized in two clusters. The first contains sectarian Sunni and Shia organizations, which are politically very active with a substantial support base, though confined to their respective communities. While many sectarian organizations have been banned in the post-9/11 period, their political dynamics in the Northern Areas is very different from that in the rest of Pakistan. First, the entire spectrum of political issues ranging from school curriculums to fundamental rights, representation, and the constitutional and legal status of the region is framed and debated along the Shia-Sunni divide. In 2004–05, the controversy over the Islamiat curriculum in schools was explained as the administration's attempt to divert attention from the issue of representation. Second, in the absence of traditional political parties, which were not allowed to operate there before 1994, the majority Shia community does not have access to any well-established, alternative political platforms to voice its grievances. Because Islamabad is afraid that the local demand for a separate province—a Shia-majority province—is gaining ground, it is unlikely to reverse its policy of encouraging a Sunni influx in order to change the area's demographic character or seriously crack down on the Sunni sectarian organizations, which the administration relies on to undercut the Shias as well as to keep the population divided.

Meanwhile the Shia populace in the Northern Areas labors under oppressive state structures that have deprived this group of a constitution, fundamental rights, normal political channels of mobilization such as political parties (until 1994), and a locally accountable government. Not surprisingly, the "toothless" Northern Areas Legislative Council (NALC) drew a dismal voter turnout of 31 percent in the October 2004 elections, and local bodies less than 25 percent. As explained in chapter 6, the NALC has no powers to address popular aspirations for better development, infrastructure, or jobs. People must therefore look to sectarian parties such as Tehrik-e-Jaffria Pakistan (TJP) to voice their grievances. That is precisely why the government finds it easy to dismiss them as "sectarian" demands of the Shias rather than recognize them as "political" demands of the people of the Northern Areas. This, in turn, explains why the government has failed to see that the violence emanating from the region since the mid-1980s is politically inspired. Painted as sectarian agitators, the Shia parties may find it difficult to get their voices heard even in the peace process.

This problem does not affect other political groups in the Northern Areas, such as the All-Parties National Alliance, the Gilgit-Baltistan National Alliance, and the Balawaristan National Front (BNF). However, most such groups are just beginning to mobilize a large base of support. Each seeks to represent a deeply alienated constituency, and the BNF, in particular, is attempting to fashion a new, common identity with somewhat open and broadly based boundaries that accommodate not only the linguistic, religious, cultural, and social groups of the Northern Areas but also reach out to their historical "kin" in Chitral and Ladakh. While their voices are beginning to be heard in select international forums such as the UN human rights organizations, their key challenge lies in politically mobilizing the masses at home.

Traditionally, Islamabad has taken it for granted that Azad Kashmir and the Northern Areas support accession to Pakistan. It does not even recognize the need for a dialogue with its own constituents. Although General Musharraf's acknowledgment, for the first time in many years, that the Northern Areas' political future remains to be decided has given their people hope, Islamabad is most reluctant to allow their leaders to be formally involved in the dialogue process. Yet Pakistan expects the Indian government to allow the Hurriyat to consult with the leadership in Muzaffarabad as well as Islamabad.[25]

NATIONAL PLAYERS

At the bilateral level, three factors will be critical to sustaining the momentum of the peace process: the political will of the top leaders, the political parties that cut across the political spectrum, and the backing of the armed forces, albeit in different ways, in both New Delhi and Islamabad.

INDIA. Important political stakeholders include the Congress, the United Progressive Alliance (UPA) government led by Prime Minister Manmohan Singh, the BJP (the main opposition party, which started the peace process), and the smaller coalition partners of the Congress and the BJP that favor a deeper federalization of the Indian polity. The UPA government is committed to the peace process. Prime Minister Singh has sought to secure India's vital concerns by laying out the broad parameters of a possible final solution: no redrawing of boundaries on religious grounds, and in the domestic context, maximum autonomy short of secession. With General Musharraf's publicly expressed willingness to engage with these propositions, Singh has been remarkably successful in bridging the gap between the traditionally irreconcilable positions of New Delhi and Islamabad. Even though these moves are declaratory in nature, they signal an important political shift in the right direction. Singh's government's ability to locate the peace process in a much-transformed global context in which India is expected to become a global player has strengthened its position.

At home, the Congress party is showing signs of developing political acumen in balancing national and local interests, as reflected in its decision, much before it came to power in New Delhi, to allow its junior coalition partner, the PDP, to take the lead in running the show in Srinagar by making Mufti Mohammed Sayeed chief minister of Jammu and Kashmir for the first half of the coalition government's tenure. The consultative process launched through the institutionalized mechanism of the roundtable conference involving all the local stakeholders in Jammu and Kashmir is another important initiative. Manmohan Singh's government also needs to pursue a proactive strategy in steering the dialogue with Pakistan in a focused and structured manner.

The BJP's Hindutva philosophy, as argued earlier, does not seem to augur well for the Kashmiri peace process. Kashmir has always been central to the Hindu notion of *rashtra-rajya* (nation-state), and the BJP has traditionally advocated that Article 370 be abolished since Kashmir, by virtue of its Muslim majority, needed to "prove" its loyalty to India by abandoning all claims to special treatment. In practice, however, pragmatism has been the hallmark of its Kashmir policy.[26] The BJP's decision to drop the proposal for abrogating Article 370, first from the National Democratic Alliance's election manifesto in the 1999 elections and then from its own party election manifesto in the 2004 national elections, is a case in point. The Vajpayee government's readiness to break from the mold was also reflected in its response to the Hizb-ul-Mujahideen's unilateral cease-fire in the Valley that "*insaniyat* (humanism), not necessarily the Constitution, [should] provide the framework for the talks." The BJP has also desisted from supporting the Rashtriya Swayamsevak Sangh demand for the trifurcation of Jammu and Kashmir along Hindu-Muslim lines. Despite persistent setbacks such as the Kargil war shortly after the breakthrough at Lahore in 1999 and then the failure of the Agra summit in 2001, followed by the 2001–02 military crisis, the Vajpayee government had doggedly pursued the path of peace.

However, the BJP-in-opposition is acting and thinking differently from the BJP-in-power. In June 2005, Vajpayee complained that the UPA government did not handle the Hurriyat's visit to Azad Kashmir appropriately in allowing its members to travel (without passports) to Islamabad, thus violating the bilateral understanding on the Srinagar-Muzaffarabad bus service. Furthermore, it had allowed the peace process to become Kashmir-centric, let Musharraf slip up on Pakistan's commitment on terrorism, and did not contest his statement that the Hurriyat visit attested to Kashmir's disputed status. A closer analysis of the Singh government's policies shows that such criticisms do not withstand scrutiny and were perhaps fired off to deflect attention from the BJP's growing internal crisis.[27] Overall, the BJP is unlikely to become a spoiler in the peace process.

The smaller coalition partners of the Congress as well as the BJP at the center constitute important players in their own right. They signify a trend that points to the historical widening and deepening of regionalization in the Indian polity. In the 12th Lok Sabha, about 200 seats went to parties with local or regional support. The fact that the Congress-dominated single-party system is giving way to multiparty coalitions at the center and in the states reflects this profound transformation. With the regional forces taking precedence over the national players and states emerging as new pathways to power, the evolving confederate character of the Indian state is better suited to meet the varying political demands of the people of Jammu and Kashmir for self-governance.

The security forces (including the army, various paramilitaries, and the state police) constitute another significant player because of their role in keeping the peace at the borders, stemming the jihadi violence, and minimizing human rights violations within the state—all important ingredients of the peace process. Unlike the military in Pakistan, the armed forces in India are not going to shape the political contours of the peace process, but their inputs are fully taken into account in operational matters such as cease-fire agreements or demilitarization of certain parts of the Valley.[28] When the security forces suspended offensive operations against the militants between December 2000 and April 2001 in the hope of bringing Hizb-ul-Mujahideen to the negotiating table, civilian casualties increased and militant fatalities declined. Therefore New Delhi is unlikely to decide upon demilitarization or redeployment of security forces without the concurrence of security forces.

PAKISTAN. On Pakistan's side, General Pervez Musharraf controls the negotiating process almost single-handedly. Perhaps that is why a shift in his public stand triggered a full public debate in India on whether he should be trusted again, especially after he arrived in New Delhi in April 2005, saying he had "come with a transformed heart." Musharraf embodies a paradox. On the one hand, he is known to be a master tactician who lacks a strategic vision, as was evident from the Kargil operation. His speech on January 12, 2002, was obviously another tactical concession to ward off American pressure and thwart an Indian military attack, for shortly thereafter 90 percent of the arrested jihadis were released and their organizations allowed to resume their operations under new names. On the other hand, Musharraf is the first leader who has questioned many long-held sacred truths of Pakistan's Kashmir policy by abandoning its original stand on the plebiscite option. When Nawaz Sharif, a democratically elected leader with a two-thirds majority in the National Assembly, tried to merely reinterpret the plebiscite option by adding the independence option, he was forced to retract. General Musharraf has taken an important step forward in publicly acknowledging that Kashmir's political future cannot be decided on religious grounds, which his critics argue knocks out the basic rationale of Pakistan's Kashmir policy. This shows that General Musharraf is certainly capable of taking the political risks needed to radically alter Pakistan's impossible calculus built over almost six decades. As the Pakistan army's chief, he is perhaps best placed to deliver a peace deal on Kashmir. Prime Minister Manmohan Singh appreciates this, as he described the general as "frank, forthright and forward looking" and as "a leader we can do business with."[29]

The paradoxical nature of General Musharraf's Kashmir policy persists, however. While he is willing to look for options outside the UN resolutions, including soft borders and joint control of the Valley, he has yet to politically pull the plug on the jihad option for good. Even though some jihadi groups have targeted army and political leaders of Pakistan, the establishment continues to be selective in its crackdowns because it believes the jihadis have strategic value in securing the national objectives in Kashmir. The jihadis remain Musharraf's only leverage with India, while at home he continues to seek the support of their political masters—the Muttahida Majlis-e-Amal (MMA)—safeguarding his own position within the political power structure of Pakistan.

At the same time, the jihadi groups may not be willing to follow the dictates of the Pakistani establishment. Not only are they totally committed to the cause of jihad, but they have also developed sufficient wherewithal—a reservoir of ideologically motivated men, weapons, and a vast terrain straddling the Pakistan-Afghan border with large pockets of sympathetic populations—to continue waging jihad with or without state protection.[30] There is some truth in General Musharraf's statements recognizing this independent dynamic of the jihadi phenomenon: "If there is an agreement, up to a point one can try and do something [on cease-fire]. But I can't give a guarantee that there will be no bullet fired. Absolutely not, that's clear. I don't hold a whistle which when I blow it will end all militancy."[31] And that is precisely why the violence unleashed by jihadis—in Kashmir, India, and lately in Pakistan—will continue to hang like a sword over the peace process. The devastating bomb blasts in Mumbai in July 2006 led to temporary suspension of the composite dialogue process.

Even if General Musharraf were to make the difficult political decision to permanently dismantle the jihadi infrastructure, it might not suffice because the malaise runs much deeper. Cleansing Pakistani society of its jihadi elements is indeed a gigantic agenda. This entails a huge undertaking of deweaponizing a country that is awash with small arms, a substantial portion of which were ironically funded with the U.S. taxpayers' money. Furthermore, it requires demobilizing powerful jihadi groups and sectarian militias that have had two decades to expand their numbers and operations.[32] Their future presents a complex challenge. As General Talat Masood points out, it is such a big industry that "we have to now look at the re-employment of these militants and engage them in other activities."[33] An equally important step would be to overhaul the madaris and government and private schools whose textbooks incite militancy and violence and inculcate the values of jihad and *sahadat* (martyrdom) in children.[34]

Unfortunately, Kashmiri jihad is the goose that lays the golden egg. Too many interest groups ranging from the power brokers in Islamabad and rulers in Azad Kashmir to jihadi leaders and civil-military officials who have enjoyed access to unaudited funds have a direct stake in the industry of violence. They can reportedly "take a lull in business for some time, but few seem ready to wind it up."[35] Finally, as explained earlier, religious extremism and jihadi culture are part of the social dynamic emanating from the Deobandi beliefs and practices of Islam that have seeped deep into Pakistan's body politic since the onset of the Afghan jihad. A mere reshuffling of Pakistan's intelligence agencies and the army's top personnel or banning of the militias may not be enough to recast Islamabad's domestic and foreign policies unless accompanied by a rolling back of this social change, which is indeed a tall order.

Pakistan's polity, deeply divided between military and democratic forces, would make it difficult to arrive at a consensus on Kashmir. Whenever a democratically elected government has attempted a rapprochement with New Delhi on the Kashmir issue, it has had to backtrack under the establishment's pressure. Just as Benazir Bhutto began talking about resolving the Kashmir issue in light of the Simla Agreement, for example, President Ghulam Ishaq Khan was reintroducing the agenda of "unfinished business of partition" and the accession of Kashmir.[36] Likewise, the Pakistan army's Kargil operation completely scuttled the Lahore process initiated by Prime Minister Nawaz

Sharif with his Indian counterpart, Atal Bihari Vajpayee, not to mention the back-channel dialogue on the Kashmir issue.

Currently, the tables are turned, with the Pakistani establishment backing the peace process initiated by General Musharraf while the divergent streams of political forces are unable to reach a consensus on this issue. The Islamists totally reject any compromise with India and insist that jihad is the only viable strategy to get Kashmir. Hafiz Hussain Ahmed, vice president of the MMA, debunked the entire peace process as a "one-man show." The party has rejected Musharraf's proposals as "a U-turn," a rollback of Pakistan's policy on Kashmir since independence, and has lambasted the New Delhi summit meeting as a "national humiliation." Both mainstream political parties—the Benazir Bhutto–led PPP and the Nawaz Sharif–led Muslim League (PML-N)—are keeping aloof. This raises serious questions about how far General Musharraf can sell a Kashmir settlement to the domestic constituencies in Pakistan. Though dissenting voices underlining the costs of Pakistan's Kashmir policy are, for the first time, being heard in the public discourse, whether they or General Musharraf will succeed in bringing about a paradigm shift remains open to question.[37]

INTERNATIONAL PLAYERS

The key international powers—the United States, Russia, China, and to a lesser extent the European Union (especially Britain) and Japan—do not have a direct stake in the resolution of the Kashmir conflict. Although they have been involved from time to time, their main objective has been to avert the risk of a nuclear war over Kashmir and to encourage bilateral India-Pakistan negotiations. The George W. Bush administration, for example, helped secure a cease-fire—for the first time in fourteen years—along the Line of Control in November 2003. India's prime minister Vajpayee had hinted that the idea of a cease-fire was born outside Pakistan and that a "third party" was involved in the backdoor diplomacy between Islamabad and New Delhi. That it was all perhaps a coordinated exercise became evident when New Delhi welcomed the cease-fire initiative and proposed extending it to the Siachin glacier—a suggestion quickly accepted by Pakistan and shortly thereafter implemented on both sides.[38] American, and perhaps British, officials also exercised quiet diplomacy in persuading both New Delhi and Islamabad to give up their respective conditions on starting the Srinagar-Muzaffarabad bus service. Pakistan must make further difficult choices if the Kashmir issue is ever to be resolved, but it may be unable to reach that point without being nudged in this direction by the United States and its other allies, especially China.

Changing relations between India, Pakistan, and these international players—inside and outside the subcontinent—may impinge on the peace process. First and foremost, the triangular relationship between India, Pakistan, and the United States is poised to undergo a major transformation. The 2005 U.S.-Indian agreement, which built upon a number of other bilateral agreements, is set to pave the way for India's membership in the nuclear club, but there is very little prospect that Pakistan will follow suit. Whereas U.S. ties with India are developing the parameters of a "strategic partnership," its relations with Pakistan continue to be dominated by considerations of the latter's usefulness in the war on terror. President Bush clearly indicated that a part of his mission in visiting Pakistan in March 2006 was to ensure that Pakistan's commitments on this account had not wavered—especially in view of attacks on U.S. military personnel in Iraq by Pakistan-based jihadi groups and in Afghanistan by the Taliban. These attacks finally awoke U.S. analysts to the fact that "there is a tremendous overlap" between bin Laden, al Qaeda, Pakistan-based jihadi groups, Pakistani authorities, and Kashmiri groups.[39] The growing evidence of Pakistan's footprints in the London blasts of July 7, 2005, corroborated their assessment that some powerful Pakistani military and intelligence officials are well aligned with radical fundamentalist groups.[40]

General Musharraf's record since 9/11 shows that more than tactical maneuvering may be needed to elicit a strategic shift. Such maneuvering did have some impact when India (and some U.S. officials) asked Pakistan to dismantle the jihadi infrastructure. However, it was only when U.S. forces, citizens, or interests became the target and the United States was forthright with intense pressure that President Musharraf was forced to make many politically unpalatable decisions that put Pakistan's strategic interests at risk. At tremendous political, monetary, and human cost, Musharraf abandoned the Taliban, lost long-nurtured strategic depth by anointing a client regime in Kabul, and unleashed large-scale military operations in the Federally Administered Tribal Areas (FATAs), especially Waziristan. If the United States were to demand a complete, thorough, and verifiable dismantling of jihadi infrastructure, General Musharraf might be left with little option but to comply. This might have a positive side effect on the peace process by way of *finally* clamping down on the most critical "spoiler element" in the peace process. On the other hand, the Bush administration's increasing pressure may boost the anti-Americanism percolating throughout Pakistan because its people resent the Iraq war and might be further inflamed if the United States or Israel were to launch preemptive strikes against Iranian nuclear facilities. This would not only strain U.S.-Pakistan relations but would also strengthen the jihadi groups, which, along with al Qaeda, have assumed the mantle of challengers of American might in the region.

Policies

The principal defects of past policies are that they either froze the issue, sanctioned the use of *force*, or adopted a *formulaic* approach. Following the Simla Agreement, India consistently sought to freeze the status quo, and Pakistan seemed resigned to it throughout the 1970s and 1980s. Zulfiqar Ali Bhutto never raised the matter in bilateral negotiations but made several attempts to integrate Azad Kashmir and the Northern Areas fully into Pakistan. General Zia suggested putting Kashmir on the back burner while the two countries tackled other issues.[41] Initially, Benazir Bhutto did not mention the right of self-determination of Kashmiris in her meetings with India's prime minister Rajiv Gandhi in January 1988 and July 1989.[42] When the Kashmiri insurgency resulted in increasing violence and bloodshed in the Valley, however, her government's position changed. Meanwhile, the Indian government insisted that Kashmir was an "internal matter" and the only issue to discuss was that Pakistan should vacate Azad Kashmir and the Northern Areas. This did not work.

Pakistan, on the other hand did attempt to alter the status quo in Kashmir, using force to this end. Despite relying on the entire spectrum of violence from terrorism to threats of war and the use of nuclear weapons, Pakistan also failed to deliver Kashmir. The last military crisis, in 2001–02, reinforced the unheeded lesson of past armed conflicts over Kashmir (in 1948, 1965, and 1999) that this issue cannot be settled by force. Jihadi violence without the political support of the local populace can and perhaps will continue to bleed India, but it cannot liberate Kashmir.

This realization is most acute among Kashmiris themselves. A decade of violence, criminalization of the militant ranks, the prevailing "gun culture," and the growing presence of mercenary mujahideen has left people in the Valley disillusioned. For Kashmiri youth, the much-anticipated Pakistani attack following the mass movement of the early 1990s never materialized. On the contrary, by the time the goal of azadi caught the people's imagination, the JKLF had been marginalized and replaced by the pro-Pakistan Hizb-ul-Mujahideen. When the latter began to lose momentum and failed to recruit Kashmiri militants in large numbers, they, too, were superseded by the Pakistan-based jihadis of the Harkat-ul-Ansar, Lashkar-e-Taiba, and Jaish-i-Mohammed. Kashmiris, including the separatist political leadership as well as the ethnic-Kashmiri militant groups, realize Pakistan has neither the means nor the political will to liberate them by fighting a war with India. The gun has become redundant, at least for the purposes of *delivering* Kashmir.

In the aftermath of the terrorist attacks against the Indian Parliament in December 2001, New Delhi threatened Pakistan with war unless it abandoned its support for cross-border terrorism. One million troops remained deployed on the borders for six months, yet India did not attack Pakistan, despite the hit on Parliament and the Kaluchak massacre in May 2002. Many realized that a conventional war—either limited or an all-out attack—was not an effective instrument for ending cross-border terrorism. New Delhi could, at best, ask the army to destroy the training camps across the Line of Control to send a political message. But rebuilding them was not difficult. Limited surgical strikes (without the seizure of territory) would not permanently block the cross-border flow of militants and arms.

The military crisis also called Pakistan's nuclear bluff over Kashmir. Pakistan's strategy thus far had been to wage a proxy war under the assumption that its nuclear weapons would deter any Indian retaliation. India's decision to up the military ante in December 2001 indicated that Pakistan's support for cross-border terrorism would not go unpunished, for India was prepared to bear (or disregard) the risk of a nuclear war. Pakistan's defiant response was to conduct three missile tests while Pakistan's ambassador to the United Nations, Munir Akram, threatened to open the war with nuclear weapons if India crossed the Line of Control. This set off alarm bells worldwide. Britain's foreign secretary, Jack Straw, said, "We can understand but cannot tolerate Pakistan's nuclear strategy."[43] Under mounting international pressure, President Musharraf was forced to backtrack, saying that "no one is that insane to contemplate the use of nuclear weapons." The ultimate threat—the use of nuclear weapons—had become a blunt instrument. The battle for resolving Kashmir therefore had to shift from the field to the negotiating table.

Proposals with a *formulaic* approach to resolving the Kashmir conflict have not worked either. Dozens, if not hundreds, of seemingly rational and logical solutions of this kind have been put forth, some calling for an independent state, others for an international border along the LOC or even a soft border, still others for internal trifurcation of the state, and so on.[44] However, most official and nonofficial peace proposals have bypassed the "process" to arrive at the "content" of the solution, disregarding the need for inclusiveness and participation by local stakeholders.

Leaders on all sides are now becoming more cautious about backing any particular formula. After General Musharraf talked about dividing Kashmir into seven regions, for instance, a Foreign Office spokesman indicated that the

"President's 'proposal' was meant to invite a debate to resolve the issue. Nothing is final and it is open for alterations and changes." Musharraf himself emphasized that he had not spelled out "any solutions to the Kashmir issue" but "had only asked the media to identify the options and start a meaningful debate on them."[45] While suggesting the restoration of "all traditional economic, cultural, linguistic pre-partition linkages that existed in the region" may lead to "a new sense of interdependence," Prime Minister Manmohan Singh was also cautious to add, "I do not know what the ultimate solution will be."[46]

Strategic Options

As the peace process moves forward, the players—the Indian and Pakistani governments, various representatives of the people of Jammu and Kashmir on both sides of the LOC, and key international entities—will be examining various strategies for addressing this conflict. The menu of options available to them is quite broad, and only a few can be examined in the short space of this discussion.

INDIA'S POLICY CHOICES

In essence, New Delhi's options are to stick to its "go-slow" and evolutionary approach, go on the offensive against Pakistan, or actively explore a mutually acceptable *final* resolution of the Kashmir issue.

"Go-Slow" while Sustaining the Dialogue Process. Without significantly correcting course, but also without putting Kashmir on the backburner, New Delhi could adopt military confidence-building measures aimed at avoiding a war and promoting economic cooperation and people-to-people contacts. Specific dialogue on Kashmir should exclude any efforts to change the map. New Delhi could ask the international community to keep up the pressure on Islamabad to end cross-border infiltration, dismantle camps, and get rid of other jihadi infrastructure in Pakistan. At home, the UPA government along with the PDP-Congress alliance in Srinagar could continue to "wear down" the militants, provide better and more humane governance, stop human rights violations, and engage Hurriyat and other separatists in dialogue, along with its elected representatives.[47] Militant violence would be controlled through an amalgam of border-management strategies and "weaning away" of the ethnic Kashmir cadre from the militants' ranks with a "no-holds-barred" approach toward eliminating non-Kashmiri jihadis.

This is a time-tested, no-risks, no-new-costs strategy. Its central thesis is that if, despite Kashmir, the Indian economy is consistently growing at 8 percent a year and the country is emerging as an important international player, New Delhi's best bet is to simply stay the course and seek to resolve the dispute in the true spirit of the Indian ethos of favoring an evolutionary rather than a revolutionary approach. On the other hand, such an approach may be castigated for its short-term thinking. History shows that a simmering Kashmir can smolder again if there is too long a hiatus in addressing people's aspirations. Until New Delhi puts its house in order, Islamabad will continue to fish in troubled waters. Kashmir will also hold India back from realizing its global aspirations.

Go on the Offensive. India's second option is to punish Pakistan for waging a proxy war or to toughen its stance in bilateral negotiations. It could go on the offensive in three ways. First, it could reply in kind by waging an all-out covert war against Pakistan, supporting the Baluch rebels, restarting the "civil war" in Karachi, aiding nationalist groups in the Northern Areas, fanning the flames of tribal warfare in Waziristan, and fomenting internecine war between the Sunni and Shia communities with the overall objective of keeping the Pakistani establishment, especially its army, bogged down in coping with challenges to its internal security.[48] This would demonstrate that waging a jihad against India is far from a low-cost option, as Islamabad has long believed. However, India would have to overcome its characteristic defensive approach, radically alter its political objectives for destabilizing Pakistan, and develop a deeply penetrative capacity for this kind of covert action in the long term. This is not only a high-risk strategy but its very success (which could mean the breakup of Pakistan and destabilization of the subcontinent) could spell doom for India's larger national interests. As India's support for the Liberation Tigers of Tamil Eelam and Pakistan's for the Taliban shows, such strategies usually backfire. It is virtually impossible to calibrate and control such groups to ensure they will work for only the sponsoring state's goals.

India's control over the Indus River system—the backbone of Pakistan's agricultural economy—provides a second alternative. The bilateral disputes over the Tulbul Barrage in Wullar Lake and the Baghlihar project on the Chenab River are not about treaty technicalities but about the political implications of allowing India to control Pakistan's water supply. Pakistan argues that India will be able to use these projects as a strategic weapon by inundating its low-lying areas or by cutting it off at will. While this issue has already been referred to the World Bank for arbitration, New Delhi, it may be argued, needs to seriously debate the pros and cons of this policy option in the long term.

Alternatively, India could use the growing Kashmiri complaints against the "iniquitous water-sharing arrangements" to reopen the Indus Water Treaty, as demanded by the Jammu and Kashmir State Assembly's resolution passed on March 2, 2003.[49] This could alter the political equations between different Kashmiri players and Pakistan. Islamabad has already revived old resentments among Mirpuri villagers who received poor compensation and no alternative connectivity when displaced by the Mangla Dam in Azad Kashmir in the 1960s: in 2003 the government decided to raise the dam's height by 30 feet, displacing another 44,000 persons. In the Northern Areas, Islamabad is proposing to build a giant Skardu dam on the Indus at Katzara that is likely to submerge the entire Skardu bowl and Shigar Valley—the grain basket of Baltistan. This scheme is not only considered "technically preposterous" but will obliterate the Baltis civilization by displacing possibly half the Balti population (nearly 300,000 persons) and inundating the famous Buddhist and Bon archeological and historical sites.[50] If New Delhi played its cards well, it could skillfully mobilize such diverse grievances for political purposes, suggesting that the Indus Treaty needs to be renegotiated because of a conflict of interests between Pakistan and Kashmiris across the LOC divide. Traditionally, Pakistan is viewed as championing the cause of Kashmiris against India; this perception could be reversed if water instead of religion became the keystone for shaping Kashmir's political future.

At the same time, reopening or abrogating the Indus Water Treaty after it has withstood forty-five years of wars, military crises, and proxy wars of every kind might unleash a whole new set of unpredictable dynamics. It might become a double-edged sword that Pakistan could use to gratuitously revive its "lifeline" argument for laying claim to Kashmir.[51] It could also use the treaty to redirect the ire of its smaller provinces over sharing water with Punjab toward India by suggesting that it is the "enemy" for usurping their water rights. Within India too, the burgeoning irrigation needs of Jammu and Kashmir's neighboring states—Haryana, Punjab, Rajasthan, and Himachal Pradesh—might persuade them to press for revisions to the Indus Treaty. This might restrict India's options for using this line of action as leverage and perhaps force it in a particular direction, without any hope of retraction. New Delhi's record—in not pursuing this option even in the face of the most serious provocations such as the terrorist strike on the parliament in December 2001 (though the cabinet, for the first time, discussed this possibility), in abiding by the bilateral understanding of suspending the construction on the Tulbul Barrage despite a seventeen-year deadlock, and in agreeing to submit the Baghlihar dispute to international arbitration—clearly demonstrates its reluctance to pursue this course of action.

India could also fight this battle on Pakistan's own turf without muddying the bilateral waters by exacerbating its deep divisions on issues of water sharing. These have been freshly revived by President Musharraf's campaign launched in December 2005 to build the controversial Kalabagh Dam on the Indus River. This issue, since the proposal was first aired in 1989, has divided Pakistan's political elites into two sharply opposed camps, with Punjab lined up against Sindh, Baluchistan, and the North-West Frontier Province.[52] Musharraf's threat that Punjab would topple any provincial government that opposes the construction of Kalabagh Dam has galvanized and united an otherwise disparate opposition. Even government allies such as the Mohajir Quami Movement (MQM) in Sindh are prepared to oppose the dam at the cost of losing power. With such divisive politics being fomented by the Pakistani establishment itself, it may not take much for New Delhi to augment Pakistan's troubles. Irrespective of Kalabagh's fate, the increasingly assertive voices of the smaller provinces may well ignite a political debate among the people of Azad Kashmir and the Northern Areas about their own water rights, which, as mentioned earlier, could alter the political equations with the Pakistani establishment.

India's third alternative is to go on the diplomatic offensive and change the negotiating parameters within the peace process. In this case, it would have to aggressively defend its original thesis that the entire state of Jammu and Kashmir belongs to India by citing the Indian Parliament's unanimous resolution of 1994 mandating that the government bring Pakistan-controlled Kashmir back into its fold. This would be necessary for two reasons. First, it is important to correct the popular perception that India, from Nehru onward, has been willing to convert the LOC into an international border, because that is why Pakistan has made India's best offer its starting point of negotiations and feels encouraged to demand more territorial concessions in Kashmir. Second, India needs to temper the international community's expectations that it can make *more* concessions inasmuch as India itself demands very little of Pakistan and is willing to simply let go of the areas already under Pakistan's control. New Delhi must bridge this *perceived* gap between its *official* stand and popular perceptions by reverting to its original demand, which would then allow more room for negotiating a final deal with Islamabad. In other words, India's decision to forgo its claims on Azad Kashmir and the Northern Areas needs to be perceived as the maximum territorial concession it can agree to, rather than as a right of Pakistan that is taken for granted. This strategy calls for astute diplomatic skills deployed over a long period in order to maintain the fine balance required to keep Pakistan within the peace process.

CLINCH A FINAL DEAL. India's third broad strategic option is to join Jammu and Kashmir and Pakistan in exploring ways to reach a final resolution of the Kashmir conflict. This entails making peace with and among the diverse domestic constituents, mobilizing broadly based diplomatic support for a peace deal that does not compromise India's vital interests, and clinching a settlement with Pakistan.

The first roundtable conference on Kashmir established two critical principles of a prospective peace deal: the propositions of self-rule and autonomy should be reworked through constitutional means, and there should be a shared vision of regional federalism while maintaining the unity of the state.[53] The conference provided a valuable format, first, because of its more or less inclusive character (the Hurriyat stayed away) and, second, because it "signalled New Delhi's resolve, for the first time in J&K's post-independence history to directly engage in a dialogue with the state's peoples rather than to cut a backroom deal with powerful political actors."[54] To continue along this path, the dialogue must be sustained systematically, the separatists persuaded to join the process, and a more concrete agenda formulated to debate the nitty-gritty of critical issues. What, for example, should be the specific features of self-rule in Jammu and Kashmir? Does the instrumentality of Article 370 offer an appropriate methodology with which to address these issues? What kind and how many levels of federal structures does it envisage? How are proposals for state autonomy to be reconciled with demands for regional autonomy? This exercise needs to be buttressed by an independent strategy for ending violence in the state because the jihadi groups perpetrating it are determined not to join the peace process. And precisely because their loci are *outside* the state, a purely domestic approach that does not eliminate their external support bases will not work.

India is most favorably poised in the emerging international equations to grasp a rare opportunity to decisively settle this issue with Pakistan because it can negotiate from a position of strength.[55] A twin-track approach is required in the international domain. On one hand, international support must be mobilized for two key objectives: an end to violence (Washington, Beijing, and other important players need to lean more heavily on the Musharraf regime in this regard), and no redrawing of India's borders. While important international players may implicitly support these propositions, New Delhi underestimates the groundwork needed to bring the collective force of international legitimacy behind them. Second, New Delhi needs to mobilize international investment for infrastructure and development projects that would make Kashmir part and parcel of India's unfolding economic success story, the benefits of which must percolate down to the masses in a visible manner.

To clinch a bilateral deal, New Delhi must engage Pakistan in much more serious, sustained, and substantive negotiations on Kashmir. The central guiding principle of these discussions should be to protect core interests that lie in ending violence, safeguarding India's secular principles, and preserving the plural character of Jammu and Kashmir state without any radical alterations of its territorial boundaries. Prime Minister Manmohan Singh has put it aptly: "Short of secession, short of re-drawing boundaries, the Indian establishment can live with anything. Meanwhile we need soft borders, then borders are not so important."[56] Given President Musharraf's spate of ideas on resolving Kashmir in the past two years, discussed in the following section, it may be possible to find a meeting ground between Manmohan Singh's vision of autonomy for Jammu and Kashmir, regional federalism, and self-governance and Musharraf's seven-region proposal for self-rule. Perhaps borders can indeed become irrelevant. A sustained dialogue on different aspects of these issues may yield an answer to the ultimate puzzle of the peace process: what can India offer, without compromising its core interests, that Pakistan may find acceptable, or vice versa?

This is perhaps an ideal policy option, but it is also the most difficult to pursue and may not necessarily work out as envisaged. In the short term, New Delhi must reckon with the spoiler element of jihadi groups because any peace deal poses an existential threat to them. They will therefore try their best to scuttle the peace process at any cost. The Indian state has no option but to develop a much more effective coercive strategy to deal with the jihadi element. Just as Washington does not negotiate with al Qaeda, India cannot reason with the jihadis, who must be brought to justice. The political battleground poses a much bigger challenge. On India's side, it requires an extraordinary convergence of political consensus at the national as well as the state level under a leadership in New Delhi that is determined to carry it through to its logical end; on Pakistan's side, it calls for a radical transformation of state dynamics.

PAKISTAN'S POLICY CHOICES

Pakistan, too, has three broad strategic choices regarding the future of Kashmir: not to rock the boat and wait for a more opportune moment, invigorate and intensify jihad throughout India, or pursue a negotiated settlement.

DON'T ROCK THE BOAT. As one option, Pakistan could avoid a course-correction and allow jihadis to operate in Kashmir and elsewhere in India while restraining them, as far as possible, from executing any spectacular and high-risk terrorist strikes (such as the Parliament attack) that might trigger a military confrontation with India. The purpose would be to "maintain a relatively stable yet unpredictable peace where Pakistan retains the initiative" for turning on the terror tap or abandoning the peace process if it is not delivering results to Pakistan's satisfaction.[57] With a heavy deployment of Pakistani troops on the Afghan border, the army fighting against its own jihadis aligned with al Qaeda in the Waziristan area, and the need to contend with armed rebels in Baluchistan, Pakistan may want to keep its powder dry where India is concerned, at least until the situation stabilizes at home. Meanwhile, Islamabad will continue to protect jihadi assets for any future use to achieve its ultimate goal of getting Kashmir.

The pitfalls of this course of action are already evident as not all jihadi groups read from the same page written at army headquarters in Rawalpindi. Some are already fighting the Pakistan army and targeting foreign, especially U.S. interests, while others are busy fomenting sectarianism in Pakistan. Growing differences between the jihadi groups and the Musharraf regime, evident from the hunger strike of eighteen top commanders in March 2006, could unleash an unpredictable dynamic, especially if they were to collectively turn against their hosts (there have already been five assassination attempts on Musharraf).[58] Continued support for the jihadi groups is proving to be a case of diminishing returns: dogged pursuit of this strategy for the past decade and a half has not delivered Kashmir, and there have been no radical material changes in Pakistan's favor that warrant a different outcome in the future.

INTENSIFY JIHAD THROUGHOUT INDIA. Pakistan could step up the jihad in India with renewed vigor. This course of action would be in keeping with Pakistan's strategic culture and its past record of consistently waging covert war while invoking the principle of plausible deniability; with its dogged determination to make the entire state of Jammu and Kashmir a part of Pakistan; and with its larger objective of seeking parity with India. Its imperatives emanate from two recent developments: first, the gap between India and Pakistan's military might, economic power, and global influence is growing wider; and second, the old instruments for counterbalancing India through military assistance from the United States and China and thereby securing its Kashmir objectives are no longer available. In the past, too, the United States and even China extended little military help for the purpose of annexing Kashmir; in fact, its attempt to obtain that help led to its complete diplomatic isolation during the Kargil crisis. That is why Pakistan would have to pursue this goal on its own by vigorously implementing the policy of bleeding India through a thousand cuts. There are small, albeit powerful lobbies within the Pakistani establishment that favor continuing jihadi warfare against India.

The perils associated with this course of action may be greater for Pakistan than India. The one common factor that explains Pakistan's strained foreign relations with its neighbors and allies alike, as well as the increasing turmoil at home—in Waziristan and Baluchistan—is its support and sponsorship of jihadi groups. That strain can be seen in the constant American pressure on Pakistan to prove its commitment to the war on terror, differences with China over the jihadi linkages with Uighur Muslims in Xinjiang Province, Afghan president Hamid Karzai's accusations that the Taliban-led insurgency is being launched from bases in Pakistan with the support of its government, and India's long-standing charge that Pakistan is waging a proxy war in Kashmir. The Pakistani establishment has yet to come to terms with the threat jihadis pose to its own power at home as they seem to be stealthily working toward capturing political power within Pakistan. Clearly, this Pakistani option has not only failed to weaken India but poses risks for Pakistan's own political future.

Few in Pakistan seem to recognize that jihad as an instrument of state policy is not only discredited but also unsustainable. Pakistan has bled because of radical Islamic groups no less than India. Furthermore, jihad contravenes Musharraf's professed goal of ending the sectarian violence and ridding Pakistani society of extremist elements, not to mention the objectives of the war on terror to dismantle the terrorist networks in the region.

Pursue a Negotiated Final Settlement of Kashmir. Pakistan's third broad option is to seriously pursue the peace process and negotiate a settlement to the Kashmir dispute. This does not imply giving up the cause of Kashmir unilaterally, though it would entail several strategic shifts in Pakistan's Kashmir policy. The rationale for negotiation might be the establishment's realization that the military and the jihad option had run its course or that it is simply not worth risking Pakistan for Kashmir. The rationale could easily be embedded in the larger and positive redefinition of President Musharraf's formulations of "Pakistan first." This course of action would require painstaking negotiations with India, international support, and a reshaping of Pakistan's relationship with Azad Kashmir and the Northern Areas. Above all, it would have to be sold to Pakistan's diverse domestic stakeholders.

A negotiated settlement would require Pakistan to redefine its core position on Kashmir, which in official circles is that a UN plebiscite would settle the dispute but in reality is that Kashmir must be brought into Pakistan through coercive means. In the past two years, President Musharraf has indicated several politically significant shifts in Pakistan's formulation of a prospective final deal on Kashmir and its expectations. For example, Pakistan would set aside the UN resolutions and give up the demand for a plebiscite; it would carefully and publicly articulate its decision not to make communal criteria Pakistan's central guiding principle in deference to India's secular sensitivities; and it would shift the discourse from demanding territory to making borders irrelevant, from Kashmiris' right to self-*determination* to their aspirations for self-*governance*, and from seeking Kashmir's inclusion in Pakistan to envisaging an autonomous Kashmir.

In fact, President Musharraf has taken several steps toward Prime Minister Manmohan Singh's vision of a deal on Kashmir, which includes a division of the state but not independence, an open border, some form of self-governance, and joint management. In Musharraf's view, some subjects should be "devolved" and others under joint management. Sovereignty could be reduced by the grant of self-governance but not be undermined. And both parts of Kashmir could be granted self-rule, with Pakistan and India overseeing it together, each "having a stake in guaranteeing the situation in the other side of Kashmir."[59] These are important first steps in the right direction, though the precise nature of the *core* elements of Pakistan's new formulation must be made clear, especially what points it will not compromise on, as distinct from what is "not acceptable," such as conversion of the present LOC into an international border.

In the international domain, Pakistan needs to retrieve lost ground. It has paid dearly in terms of diplomatic support of its key allies and friends because of its perceived adventurism (in Kargil), brinkmanship in raising the specter of a nuclear war during the 2002 military crisis, and characterization of violence in Kashmir as a jihad and not terrorism. The consistent American and Chinese support for bilateral talks may have contributed to a small, but significant, shift in Pakistan's own stand from insistence on international mediation to agreeing to "facilitation" of the bilateral peace process.[60] Pakistan's best bet is to seek international support for accelerating Kashmir-specific negotiations within the overall dialogue process as well as for its core interests (somewhat undefined at present) in a prospective peace deal. On the domestic front, Islamabad would have to finally settle the issue of the Northern Areas' political status in terms of their relationship with Azad Kashmir, on the one hand, and the Pakistani state, on the other. New and much more substantive power-sharing arrangements need to be worked out in order to realize the promised goal of self-governance.

This course of action poses multiple and monumental challenges for Musharraf's or any successor's regime. What is most difficult is that it would have to transform Pakistan's structural imperatives in order to stay on course to the logical end. Even if Pakistan were to succeed in negotiating a final deal on Kashmir, its fate would ultimately depend on Islamabad's ability to sell it to various domestic stakeholders. Deep schisms between Pakistan's political forces (that is, the mainstream political parties) and the military establishment will make it extremely difficult to arrive at a political consensus on a volatile issue such as Kashmir. Paradoxically, the political forces are better placed to mobilize public opinion and bestow legitimacy to a final settlement, yet they cannot negotiate the deal as such on their own. On the other hand, the army may have the power to directly negotiate a deal, and its support may be crucial to any final solution, but this alone is not the clinching factor. Unless the peace process and the final settlement are also supported by the democratic political forces, a political backlash or subsequent crisis of legitimacy may nullify the gains made thus far. And as long as both military and political forces remain at loggerheads, which is the situation at present, a consensus on Kashmir may remain elusive.

Pakistan's establishment may face a united opposition to a peace agreement. The PPP, the PML-N, and the MMA might well criticize the deal as a sellout and use it in their own confrontation against President Musharraf, hoping to oust him from power. More important, while Musharraf is backed by the Pakistan army, there is no clear evidence that its top hierarchy would also agree to finally let go of its territorial claims on Kashmir. Pakistan's corps commanders, although loyal to their chain of command, have demonstrated the will to remove leaders who threaten their corporate interests.[61] Hence the possibility of a revolt by General Headquarters cannot be ruled out. Whether General Musharraf could ward off such a challenge would depend on his ability to chalk out a strategy to de-link the Pakistan army's corporate interests from the Kashmir issue, promise to protect these, *and* deliver the goods.

Although Musharraf has shown a penchant for taking political risks, he has yet to demonstrate the necessary political skills for negotiating a deal in which the most important challenge is to devise new mechanisms for realizing the Kashmiris' goal of self-governance. His statement, "Let's work out self-governance and *impose the rules*" on both parts of Kashmir, betrays a top-down approach, which has repeatedly failed. There is also concern that, if granted, self-rule in Azad Kashmir and the Northern Areas may provide an impetus to similar demands by the smaller provinces, with Baluch leading the way. This could unleash a much larger dynamic for radically reworking Pakistan's federal structures wherein Punjab may lose its hegemonic position within Pakistan's power structures.

Finally, despite Islamabad's much-acclaimed resolve to fight terrorism, the Musharraf regime has yet to foreclose the jihad option in a firm and *final* manner. Understandably, this is the only stick or leverage Pakistan has to force India to sustain the negotiating process on the Kashmir issue, but the jihadi groups are gradually turning into a double-edged sword. At best, jihad would be a spoiler element for Pakistan: it could derail the peace process through major terrorist strikes in India or through the assassination of Musharraf himself. However, much more serious consequences follow from Islamabad's acceptance of a final deal on Kashmir (without bringing it into Pakistan's fold), as it would deliver a body blow to the raison d'être of jihadi groups and would delegitimize a critical component of their agenda—the liberation of Kashmir. As a result, they may collectively mobilize their forces— an amalgam of Islamist political parties like the MMA, Pakistan's homegrown jihadi groups like Jaish-i-Mohammed and Lashkar-e-Taiba, and al Qaeda's supporters fighting in the Waziristan areas—and even join hands with Baluch armed groups to confront the Musharraf regime, which, in turn, could raise the specter of a civil war in Pakistan. While most of these scenarios are contingent on several ifs and buts, the bottom line is that disturbing the status quo in Kashmir—with Pakistan abandoning the idea of reclaiming the Indian part of Kashmir as part of a final settlement—has the potential to unleash a series of unpredictable internal challenges and crises, which the Musharraf regime must take into account. The cause of Kashmir has long been used as an ideological bond by successive Pakistani regimes, making it absolutely imperative for Islamabad to work out an alternative strategy for keeping its diverse populace united.

JAMMU AND KASHMIR'S POLICY CHOICES

To the degree they can act independently, the people of Jammu and Kashmir on both sides of the LOC have three broad strategic choices. They might be able to join hands and create a pan-Kashmiri identity, fighting for a sovereign state; they could separately revive the insurgency and demand their political rights; or they could carve their political futures out separately, with those on the Indian side participating in the peace process for negotiating alternative power-sharing arrangements with India, and the people in Azad Kashmir and the Northern Areas engaging in a similar dialogue with Pakistan. The intrinsic plurality of Kashmiri players and their different, often sharply divergent, interests must be kept in mind while considering any of these options.

Coalition Building for the Creation of a Pan-Kashmiri Identity and a Sovereign State. To secure the new coalitions that could create a pan-Kashmiri identity, various internal leaders would have to come together and undertake a truly all-inclusive dialogue—embracing all ethnic, religious, regional, and linguistic identities, down to the grassroots level. This extraordinarily ambitious option is the only political means of creating a sovereign Jammu and Kashmir state. It requires visionary leadership not just in Srinagar and Muzaffarabad but in every corner of the state. Those at the helm must also be able to rise above the narrow political interests of their respective communities, mobilizing the masses for this larger cause and resolving their internal battles for turf through democratic methods. Furthermore, the task of coalition building must not stop at the physical borders of the Jammu and Kashmir state but must extend to political parties in the rest of India and Pakistan, as well as to the international realm. Kashmiri leaders could then collectively negotiate with New Delhi and Islamabad.

Realities in both parts of Kashmir offer little hope for realizing this policy option. The entire populace—on both sides of the LOC—is deeply divided along multiple ethnic, religious, regional, and linguistic lines with no unanimity on political objectives. No leader has mass support in either part of Kashmir, let alone both parts together. The enormous difficulties in pursuing this course of action may be judged from the fact that no headway has yet been made in rehabilitating internally displaced Pandits despite broad agreement among the Valley leaders across the entire political spectrum. Across the LOC, the leaders of Azad Kashmir and the Northern Areas do not see eye to eye on most important political issues.

Reverting to the Path of Violence. The different communities of Jammu and Kashmir could separately or collectively resort to violence to demand their political rights, especially since central and state leaders have consistently failed to fulfill people's aspirations for democracy and development. On the Indian side, the past record of Kashmiri Muslims suggests they may take the lead, though the communal flare-up in Ladakh in February 2006 shows that the propensity for resorting to violence is not restricted to the Valley. Across the LOC, the sectarian violence between Shias and Sunnis has claimed more than 100 lives in Gilgit alone since June 2004.[62] Violence may also accelerate for other reasons, such as weakening of the security grid or complacency among the security forces and the Jammu and Kashmir state police in the long term because of their operational limitations or inability to eliminate external sources of violence. There is no dearth of ideologically motivated, well-trained cadre armed with weapons and funds in Pakistan, which cannot be stopped from infiltrating into the Indian part of Kashmir to wage a jihad.

On the other hand, refashioning a political rationale that justifies reverting to violence may prove to be a difficult task. The prevailing consensus among Valley leaders and the populace is that violence has backfired and not helped their cause. And in the international scenario, terrorism as a means of achieving political objectives stands delegitimized. Though the jihadis may continue to operate in part because of the "fear factor" and in part because it has become a lucrative business, they are unlikely to achieve their ultimate goal—which is to include the Indian part of Kashmir in Pakistan's territory.

NEGOTIATE FRESH POWER-SHARING ARRANGEMENTS FOR SELF-RULE. Another alternative for Kashmiris is to give up their demand for a sovereign and territorially independent state and separately, though simultaneously, negotiate political deals with the governments of India and Pakistan that provide for a highly porous, preferably open, border, between the two parts of Kashmir. The *process* the parties follow in negotiating a peace deal will be absolutely critical in determining the lasting value of its *content*. It must be an open, inclusive, and multidimensional dialogue addressing the political, sociocultural, and economic aspects of the peace deal, which must also institutionalize constitutional safeguards against any unilateral misuse. Furthermore, they must check the growing religious radicalization of various kinds, especially that of the Valley's populace, and refrain from strengthening the communal fault lines within the state.

Although this may be the only realistic option open to the people of Jammu and Kashmir, it involves difficult choices and several impediments. On the Indian side of Kashmir, those willing to explore a political solution within the framework of the Indian constitution (the entire spectrum of political parties) and those excluding this possibility (the separatists, especially the Hurriyat) need to find a way to sit across the same negotiating table. In order to make the dialogue truly inclusive, no player must insist on excluding others. All need to debate in detail the kind of state structures envisaged as part of the new peace deal. Different propositions for self-rule or autonomy by the PDP and the National Conference need to be fleshed out and discussed in every detail, while the Hurriyat need to crystallize their own blueprint for negotiations on this issue. Also, the gaps between Hurriyat expectations and claims and their ability to deliver need to be taken into account. There is little evidence to support Mirwaiz Umar Farooq's claim that "the Hurriyat can influence the militants" and that it "vouches for" the militants to fall into line if India were to move toward a settlement.[63] The long-standing position that Hurriyat alone ought to speak for the people of Jammu and Kashmir is another "representational claim that it has long refused to legitimize through any kind of democratic test."[64] Last but not least, an intraregional dialogue between Jammu, the Valley, and Ladakh is necessary and critical to prepare the ground for negotiating a peace deal with New Delhi. Across the LOC, there may be a greater need for self-rule, as argued earlier, but there is much less pressure on Islamabad from the local players in Azad Kashmir and the Northern Areas to negotiate fresh power-sharing arrangements.

The International Community

For the most part, the international community has stood by as the conflict over Kashmir has waxed and waned. Its members, especially the key international powers—including the United States, Russia, China, Britain, and to a lesser extent Europe and Japan—may want to consider other options as well, in their individual or collective capacities.

Adopt a Minimalist Stand with No Mediation and Bilateralism.
This option does not require a new policy initiative as all the states involved support bilateral negotiations between India and Pakistan as the best mechanism for addressing the Kashmir conflict. There is a broad consensus—endorsed by the UN secretary general—that the UN resolutions on Kashmir no longer provide a relevant framework for resolving the dispute and that post–cold war realities preclude the use of force as a means of changing borders. No countries are willing to offer mediation unless it is sought by both India and Pakistan. A minimal yet important policy objective for most international powers is to avoid a war over the Kashmir conflict in the nuclearized environment of South Asia. Since the early 1990s, therefore, the United States, often with the support of Russia, China, and Britain, has actively sought to manage the recurring military crisis between the two neighboring states.

This is a time-tested, low-cost, and low-risk policy testifying that the stakes for any of the key international powers are fairly small, and hence they are content to leave Kashmir's fate to the decision of the principal parties. Their intervention would become necessary only during a crisis between India and Pakistan, with the sole objective of avoiding another war between them. However, the growing frequency of such crises and the shorter intervals between them (from nine years in the period 1990–99 to five months between December 2001 and May 2002) shows that a crisis-management strategy alone will at best deliver limited dividends with increasingly diminishing returns.

ACTIVELY BROKER A FINAL DEAL ON KASHMIR. Theoretically, the United States, Russia, and China could pursue this option alone or in a coalition of like-minded states. International participants would play an activist, perhaps third-party role, with or without the consent of both parties, and their over-all objective would be to clinch a final settlement of the Kashmir dispute. The rationale here may be that Kashmir will be a nuclear flashpoint, the risk of nuclear war hovering in the background, as long as the dispute is not resolved. Hence the international community has a stake in ending this conflict once and for all.

There are many pitfalls in pursuing this course of action. An external push to forcibly end the Kashmir conflict may create more problems than it may resolve. From the past record of mediation in Kashmir, it is clear that unless such initiatives are supported by *both* principal players, they have no hope of success. And with India's consistent and categorical rejection of any third-party mediation in Kashmir, the fate of future such attempts is also sealed. Moreover, none of the key international players think their national interests would be jeopardized by a lingering Kashmir conflict, nor do they have suffi-cient leverage with *both* sides to broker or impose a final settlement. The U.S. administration is preoccupied with fighting the war in Iraq, combating al Qaeda in Afghanistan and elsewhere, and dealing with the Iranian nuclear threat. Resolution of the Kashmir conflict does not figure in the Chinese or Russian priorities, either. More important, with India emerging as an impor-tant player in the global arena, none of these powers are likely to antagonize it on an issue of vital interest.

On the other hand, if they were to wholeheartedly support the Indian posi-tion and force Pakistan to accept the LOC as the international border, for example, it would not result in a stable peace as Pakistan would continue to try to use jihad as an instrument of terror. The move might also strengthen the hand of religious parties and jihadi groups in discrediting the Musharraf regime for having "surrendered" Pakistan's core national interests. Not only would it be well-nigh impossible to forcibly broker a final deal on Kashmir, but the end result would be a no-win situation for all concerned: India, Pakistan, and most of the international players.

CREATING SUPPORTIVE STRUCTURES THROUGH LOW-KEY DIPLOMATIC EFFORTS. The key international powers, especially the United States, could play an active, albeit low-profile, role in creating supportive structures that would serve as building blocks for the bilateral peace process. Washington could—on its own or joined by others—support intellectual as well as grassroots efforts aimed at identifying the silent stakeholders, giving them a voice through public platforms to actively participate in the peace process; promoting cross-cultural, interethnic, interreligious, intraregional, and intra-Kashmiri dialogues at different levels; and strengthening grassroots democratic institutions such as panchayats (village councils) and other alternative substate structures that could fulfill the popular aspirations for self-governance. The United States and Europe, in particular, could also convey a clear and firm message to the separatists, especially the Hurriyat, encouraging them to establish their representative credentials by entering the electoral arena rather than currying public favor through photo opportunities with diplomatic officials. The international community could also play an important role in encouraging local communities to gain an economic stake in the peace process, for example, by financing development schemes such as power-generation projects, helping them make new trade routes to China and Central Asia economically viable, aiding post-earthquake rebuilding efforts in Azad Kashmir, and, most important, boosting private enterprise in both parts of the state through investments.[65] Last, but certainly not least, the United States and China could do a great deal more to lean on the Musharraf regime to destroy the jihadi infrastructure on its soil and to abandon its jihadi pursuits forever. Otherwise the peace process is bound to run into problems, as it has in the past.

Overall, the best course of action for the international powers, especially America, is to devote their energies to developing supporting structures that generate and institutionalize a new set of shared interests and stakes among various local players that can help sustain the peace process. Their modus vivendi in undertaking these tasks must remain low key as that will be crucial for the success of any such venture.

Prognosis

At this very early stage of the peace process, when the issues are just being defined and the stakeholders identified, only one thing seems certain: resolving the Kashmir conflict is bound to be a long-drawn-out affair, and it is hazardous to predict outcomes. No one involved appears to have clearly thought through any scenarios that might offer a win-win solution for all. Hence one can easily be optimistic or pessimistic about the prospects for peace. Is the process, as it is unfolding, merely an exercise in futility, Kashmir being so rife with complexities that the dispute can never be resolved peacefully or to the satisfaction of all concerned? Or have India and Pakistan actually started traversing a road that is likely to lead to a final solution, albeit in the due course of time?

Skeptics on the Indian side would be quick to raise the question of trust. General Musharraf, they say, cannot be trusted: not as an *individual,* for he is still remembered as the mastermind of Kargil; not as the *representative* of the Pakistani establishment, whose primary constituency is the army and whose fundamental interests are served by continuing enmity with India; and not as *head of a country* whose structural imperatives are entwined with annexing Kashmir at any cost. Before Pakistan could even approach the negotiating table in all seriousness, it would have to undergo a total and radical transformation, which amounts to pursuing a nearly impossible agenda. Some believe the apparent change in Musharraf's current thinking is a tactical ploy, devised to cope with the tremendous pressure he is experiencing from within and without. Waziristan and the Federally Administered Tribal Areas on the Pakistan-Afghan border remain very unstable. Baluchistan is in turmoil, and sectarian clashes and suicide attacks against the Shia community, foreign interests, and some members of the establishment itself continue. Resentment is on the rise in the smaller provinces under Punjabi domination. And Pakistan's middle class is clamoring for greater economic opportunities. Under the circumstances, the new geostrategic thinking of the military establishment should not be so surprising. Since Pakistan is on a weaker footing, its best bet is to buy time and live to fight another day, as it did at Simla in 1972. In other words, Musharraf needs to temporarily douse the fires in Kashmir, hence the peace rhetoric. The jihadis continue to have a safe sanctuary in Pakistan, and the jihadi infrastructure remains intact. Since Pakistan remains capable of turning on the terror tap, intentions can change quickly, as indeed has been the case time and again in the past.

Pakistanis, on the other hand, could complain that despite all the turn-arounds on Musharraf's behalf, India has not yielded an inch. The peace process is expected to be a one-sided surrender on Pakistan's part. Both sides agree that all the developments thus far have been mainly verbal commitments, with no substantial changes on the ground. There has been no breakthrough on an assortment of contentious issues, such as demilitarization and disengagement in Siachin, the demarcation of Sir Creek, and the Wullar Barrage–Tulbul navigation project. "Soft" measures such as the Srinagar-Muzaffarabad bus service, permission for divided families to meet at common points, the opening of new routes for more buses connecting Poonch and

Rawalkot and Kargil and Skardu are deemed inconsequential. The road to peace is littered with pitfalls of vast and complex proportions. Another big terrorist strike in India, in Mumbai in July 2006, has led the Manmohan Singh government to suspend the peace process until Pakistan decides to abide by its commitments on terrorism. In Pakistan, the assassination of General Musharraf could result in yet another U-turn or, at best, an unstable period.

At the same time, some would say there is room for optimism, as attested by the many *firsts* in the peace process. The Pakistani establishment has, for the first time since the early 1950s, acknowledged that a plebiscite is not an option and that religion cannot be the basis for deciding Kashmir's future. Musharraf's assertions about making borders irrelevant is considered to be a gentle way of coming to terms with the reality that the Kashmir Valley may never become part of Pakistan. The rhetoric of Indian leaders has taken on a softer tone as well. After the 1972 Simla Agreement, many in India considered Kashmir to be a closed issue, or at best an internal matter in which Pakistan had no right to be involved, while Islamabad strove hard to make New Delhi concede that Kashmir was in dispute between the two of them. Vajpayee's decision to engage General Musharraf at Agra in 2001 and then at Islamabad in 2004 validated Pakistan's rightful place in resolving the Kashmir conflict. At the summit meeting in April 2005, the leaders issued a joint statement pledging to address the issue of Jammu and Kashmir in a "sincere and purposeful and forward-looking manner for *a final settlement.*"

A consensus is also emerging among all the international players, who for the first time are not practicing gamesmanship but are conveying the same message to both sides: namely, that the world cannot run the risk of a nuclear confrontation and hence they must resolve their differences peacefully. Borders cannot be changed by force, and terror as a tool stands delegitimized. Most significantly, leaders on both sides are trying hard to find common ground by agreeing that borders must be made irrelevant, forging people-to-people linkages across the LOC, and framing the Kashmir issue in terms of self-rule and self-governance. As Prime Minister Manmohan Singh has pointed out, "History obliges us to seize all opportunities to pursue peace. We cannot change borders, but in a globalized world, borders do not matter."[66] Musharraf, too, has recognized that the world has moved from an era of geopolitics to one of geo-economics, with trade and commerce now the defining factors. He has also agreed that boundaries cannot be altered forcibly, that the LOC is not a final solution, and that boundaries must be made irrelevant. The challenge, he believes, is to "take the three stands together and discuss the solution," which may ultimately lie in "boundaries becoming irrelevant."[67] Though Musharraf and others are unclear about how to accomplish this in practical terms, the peace process seems to be moving slowly but decidedly in the right direction. This is all the more evident from Musharraf's new focus on "maximum self-governance," which is a significant departure from Pakistan's traditional demand for a plebiscite and is much closer to Indian views about offering Jammu and Kashmir maximum political autonomy. Most important, it provides a common political space for India, Pakistan, and the people of Jammu and Kashmir on both sides of the Line of Control to negotiate a mutually acceptable agreement.

On the whole, a healthy dose of skepticism helps keep the mind alert and cautious, reminding players to maintain low expectations in the roller-coaster environment of India-Pakistan relations, especially where Kashmir is concerned. At the same time, some element of trust is necessary, despite all the risks involved, if the various parties are to break out of the cycle of conflict, violence, and distrust that has impeded the peace process for so long. An optimistic approach is also helpful in developing a more nuanced and far-sighted perspective of the peace process, which is the long rope much needed to negotiate mutually beneficial trade-offs concerning a variety of complex issues. Being optimistic also means that one is not likely to underestimate the political significance of subtle shifts in the deeply entrenched positions of the key players.

At the same time, it is important not to lower one's guard, especially on the terror front, because the changes occurring at present are still of a short-term nature in that they are *declaratory* and therefore reversible. Thus the way forward may lie in the dictum: "Trust but verify." The key players need to resolve to make the peace process irreversible, and the shifts in their publicly articulated political positions need to be given their due. But any commitments thus made must also be verifiable and must match actions on ground. To move forward, both India and Pakistan must learn to withstand pressure from the vested interests and the spoiler elements such as the jihadis, who are not amenable to *any* negotiated solution. In addition, they and the Pakistani leadership—at the moment dominated by the army and led by President Musharraf—must resist pressure to show immediate results to their domestic constituents. The very nature of this conflict does not invite quick remedies. The task is indeed enormous, but the future of South Asia in this millennium depends precisely on the willingness to see it through.

GLOSSARY

ahimsa Nonviolence

akhoots Depressed castes

amali Practical

aquida Common belief

Arya Samaj Reformist school of thought founded by Swami Dayananda Saraswati

avatars Forms

awaam People

Azad Kashmir Free Kashmir

azadi Independence

bandh Shutdown strike

Bharat India

Bharatiya Indian

biradaries Clans

Brahmin The first and foremost of four castes in traditional Hindu society

darbar The court of a ruler

desh Country

Devanagari Indian script during post-Gupta era

dewan Minister of state

dharna Sit-down strike

Dukhtaran-e-Millat Daughters of the Faith

farz Obligation or religious duty

gompas Buddhist place of worship

Hindutva Spirit of Hinduism

Hizb-ul-Mujahideen The army of the holy warriors

iman Faith

insaniyat Humanism

izhar-e-latalugee Declaration of disassociation

jagirdar Big landlord; one who holds a jagir

janata Public

jeziya Tax

jihad Holy war

jihadi Holy warrior

kabar-i-shaheed Martyrs' graveyards

kardars Taxpayers

khudmukhtar Independent

kisan sabha Peasant assembly or conference

kufr Disbelief

lashkar Tribal army

lok parishads People's councils

Lok Sabha Lower House of Indian Parliament

madrasa Religious school

maharaja Hindu ruler of an Indian state

majlis-i-shoora Advisory council

mantra Incantation

margdarshan Supervision

masla ka hal The solution of the problem

maulvi Muslim priest or teacher

mirs Rulers

Meghdoot God's messenger

mirwaiz Title of head of Kashmiri Muslim sect

Moe-e-Muqaddas The Hair of the Prophet

mohalla Colony or locality

morcha Front
mujahideen Soldiers of the holy war; holy warriors; freedom fighters
mukti morcha Freedom front
Mussalmans Urdu word for Muslims
namaz Prayer congregation
namaz-e-janaza Funeral prayer
nawab Muslim ruler of an Indian state; also used by big Muslim landlords
naya New
nizam Government; also title of the ruler of state of *Hyderabad*
panchayat Village council
Pandit Prefix to a name; generally denotes members of the Brahmin caste; learned or wise man
parakram Valor
patwaris Village official who maintains land records
Pir Muslim saint
Poorna Swaraj Complete Independence
praja mandals Public Committee
Praja Parishad People's Council
quam Community
Rajputs Old and high caste of Rajasthan
rashtra-rajya nation-state

rashtriya National
roti Indian bread
sadar-i-riyasat Governor
sahadat Martyrdom
saheb Gentleman
sahukar Money lender
shaheed Martyr
shudra A member of the lowest of four *varnas*/classes in traditional Hindu society in Vedic age
shura Advisory council
tabligh Education
tehsil Subdivision of an administrative district
tehsildars Presiding officer of administrative subdivision of district
tonga Two-wheeled horse-drawn carriage
urs A birth or death anniversary of a saint
watan dosti Love for one's country
watan parasti Nation worship
wazir-i-azam Prime minister
yome-i-nijat Day of deliverance
yome-i-siaht Black day

NOTES

Chapter One

1. Mohammed Ayoob, "Defining Security: A Subaltern Realist Perspective," in *State, People and Security: The South Asian Context*, edited by Navnita Chadha Behera (New Delhi: Manohar, 2002), pp. 75–77.

2. V. P. Menon, *The Story of the Integration of the Indian States* (Bombay: Orient Longmans, 1956), p. 88.

3. Cited in Sisir Gupta, *Kashmir: A Study in India-Pakistan Relations* (Bombay: Asia House, 1966), p. 36.

4. Cited in ibid., p. 37.

5. Ibid., p. 39.

6. Urmila Phadnis, *Towards the Integration of Indian States, 1919–1947* (New Delhi: Asia House, 1968), pp. 135–37.

7. Gupta, *Kashmir: A Study in India-Pakistan Relations*, p. 42.

8. Menon, *The Story of the Integration of the Indian States*, p. 75.

9. In July 1946, Nehru had decided to personally defend National Conference leader Sheikh Abdullah in his sedition and treason case against the Dogra maharaja Hari Singh in the princely state of Jammu and Kashmir.

10. Gupta, *Kashmir: A Study in India-Pakistan Relations*, p. 42.

11. Menon, *The Story of the Integration of the Indian States*, p. 117.

12. Wayne A. Wilcox, *Pakistan: The Consolidation of a Nation* (Columbia University, 1963), p. 94.

13. Ibid., p. 28.

14. Gupta, *Kashmir: A Study in India-Pakistan Relations*, p. 45.

15. Cited in ibid., p. 47.

16. Jamil-ud-din Ahmed, ed., *Recent Speeches and Writings of Mr. Jinnah* (Lahore: Sh. Mohammad Ashraf, 1943), p. 281.

17. Wilcox, *Pakistan: The Consolidation of a Nation*, pp. 29, 94.

18. Ibid., p. 32.

19. For a concise statement of the Sikh dilemma, see Panderel Moon, *Divide and Quit* (University of California Press, 1962), pp. 29–41.

20. Gupta, *Kashmir: A Study in India-Pakistan Relations*, p. 49.

21. Cited in ibid., p. 48.

22. Cited in Menon, *The Story of the Integration of the Indian States*, p. 88.

23. Gupta, *Kashmir: A Study in India-Pakistan Relations*, p. 45.

24. Wilcox, *Pakistan: The Consolidation of a Nation*, p. 47.

25. Ibid.

26. Gupta, *Kashmir: A Study in India-Pakistan Relations*, p. 49.

27. The maharaja of Jodhpur, after a series of meetings with Jinnah, almost agreed to join Pakistan in return for the use of Karachi as a free port, the free import of arms, jurisdiction over the Jodhpur-Hyderabad (Sindh) railway, and a large supply of grain for famine relief on the condition that Jodhpur would declare its independence on August 15, 1947, and subsequently accede to Pakistan. See H. V. Hodson, *The Great Divide: Britain-India-Pakistan* (Oxford University Press, 1969), pp. 379–80.

28. Junagarh acceded on August 15.

29. Wilcox, *Pakistan: The Consolidation of a Nation*, p. 34.

30. Menon, *The Story of the Integration of the Indian States*, pp. 136–37.

31. Wilcox, *Pakistan: The Consolidation of a Nation*, p. 66.

32. Ibid., p. 48.

33. Jinnah was arrested just once in his life, for disorderly conduct at the 1893 Oxford-Cambridge boat race. See Stanley Wolpert, *Jinnah of Pakistan* (Oxford University Press, 1984), p. 13.

34. Cited by Sheikh Abdullah, *Flames of the Chinar*, translated from Urdu by Khushwant Singh (New Delhi: Viking, 1993), p. 60.

35. Some striking examples of the respective share of Muslims and Hindus in civil employment in 1931 were as follows: in the press, 5 versus 66 percent; public works, 3 versus 194 percent; electricity, 3 versus 194 percent; telegraph, 7 versus 73 percent; customs, 14 versus 195 percent; revenue, 9 versus 85 percent; finance, 19 versus 368 percent; and the judiciary, 21 versus 162 percent. See F. M. Hassnain, *Freedom Struggle in Kashmir* (New Delhi: Rima, 1988), p. 31.

36. In 1930 the Reading Room Party had presented a memorandum to the state government demanding reservation of state services for Muslims according to their population, relaxation of qualifications of Muslim aspirants for state services in view of the general educational and economic backwardness, grant of scholarships to Muslim students for education, appointment of a separate Muslim Directorate to supervise the education of Muslim students, and appointment of Muslim teachers in government schools to protect the educational interests of Muslim children.

37. Punjabi Muslims led by Allama Iqbal formed the Kashmir Committee, which celebrated August 14, 1931, as Kashmir Day in different parts of the country, including Delhi, Ferozepur, Gorakhpur, Simla, Deoband, Jhelum, Gurdaspur, Bhagalpur, Sargodha, Jhang, Shahjahanpur, Bombay, Calcutta, Rangoon, Cuttack, Layalpur, Dera Ghazi Khan, Jaremwala, Mussori, Arwal, Panipat, Kalanoor, Bhani, Khaniwan, Hoshiarpur, Talwandi, Shahabad, Karnal, Patiala, Mansera, Rangpur, Kalicut, and

Lahore. The Ahrars, a militant organization, sent armed volunteers to Kashmir. The Ahmadiyas provided financial support. The Punjabi Muslim press was extremely critical of the policies of the Dogra state.

38. For details, see Syed Jamal Uddin, "From Communal to National Politics: Kashmir during 1930–1940," in *History of the Freedom Struggle in Jammu & Kashmir,* edited by Mohammad Yasin and A. Qaiyum Rafiqi (New Delhi: Light and Life, 1980), pp. 63–68; G. H. Khan, *Freedom Movement in Kashmir 1932–1949* (New Delhi: Light and Life, 1990), pp. 168–72, 200–15; and, Abdullah, *Flames of the Chinar*, pp. 27–34.

39. Cited in Hassnain, *Freedom Struggle in Kashmir,* p. 88.

40. The Bill of Rights guaranteed the right to freedom, conscience and worship, free speech, a free press, free assembly, free street processions and demonstrations, and the right to association (including the right to constitute trade unions, cooperative societies, women and youth organizations, self-defense organizations, political parties, and cultural, scientific, and technical societies). Santosh Kaul, *Freedom Struggle in Jammu and Kashmir* (New Delhi: Anmol, 1990), p. 122.

41. Ibid., p. 53.

42. For a detailed discussion of the agitation, see Navnita Chadha Behera, *State, Identity and Violence: Jammu, Kashmir and Ladakh* (New Delhi: Manohar, 2000), pp. 55–56.

43. These included Chowdhary Ghulam Abbas, Chowdhary Hamidullah, and Mian Ahmed Yar. In Kashmir, Qureshi Mohammed Youssuf and Ghulam Nabi Gilkar led them.

44. Chowdhary Ghulam Abbas wrote in his biography that they had agreed "only to permit the Hindus to join the Conference and nothing beyond." Cited in Kaul, *Freedom Struggle in Jammu and Kashmir,* p. 54.

45. Ibid., p. 154.

46. Sheikh Abdullah, *Flames of the Chinar*, p. 82.

47. Muslim leaders of the National Conference opposed the government's policy of introducing two scripts because that would work against educated Muslim youth not conversant with Devanagari and alleged that the Arms Act sought to arm Hindu Rajputs while divesting Muslims of their right to possess arms. Hindu leaders accused the former of taking a communal stand and supported the introduction of Devanagari and regulation of arms in the state. Chowdhary Hamidullah's proposed legislation in the Praja Sabha, mooting retrenchment of Hindus and reservations for Muslims in the state, also divided the ranks. Muslim leaders demanded employment in proportion to the population of communities, a stand strongly condemned by the Hindu leaders.

48. Cited in Gupta, *Kashmir: A Study in India-Pakistan Relations,* p. 58.

49. I wish to thank Commodore Jasjit Singh for making this point.

50. Menon, *The Story of the Integration of the Indian States,* p. 394.

51. Akbar Khan, *Raiders in Kashmir* (Islamabad: National Book Foundation, 1970), pp. 9–10.

52. Jasjit Singh, *Kargil 1999: Pakistan's Fourth War for Kashmir* (New Delhi: Knowledge World, 1999), p. 3.

53. Khan, *Raiders in Kashmir,* p. 10.

54. After his visit to Kashmir, Gandhi wrote to Nehru: "Both [the maharaja and the maharani] admitted that with the lapse of British paramountcy, the true paramountcy of the people will commence. However much they might wish to join the Union, they would have to make the choice in accordance with the wishes of the people. How they could be determined was not discussed at that interview." Pyarelal, *Mahatma Gandhi: The Last Phase* (Ahmedabad: Navjivan House, 1958), p. 357.

55. Cited in Rajmohan Gandhi, *Patel: A Life* (Ahmedabad: Navjivan House, 1990), p. 434. He also quotes Patel's letter written on September 13, 1947, indicating that if Kashmir decided to join the other dominion, he would accept the fact.

56. Menon, *The Story of the Integration of the Indian States*, p. 377.

57. See *Gandhi-Jinnah Talks* (New Delhi: Hindustan Times, 1944). Earlier, delivering his presidential address at the annual session of the Muslim League in 1943 in Delhi, Jinnah had said: "Whatever may have been the meaning of the word [Pakistan] at the time, it is obvious that the language of every civilized country invents new words. The word 'Pakistan' has come to mean Lahore resolution." Ahmed, *Recent Speeches and Writings of Mr. Jinnah*, p. 485.

58. Khan, *Freedom Movement in Kashmir*, p. 5. See also Owen Bennett Jones, *Pakistan: Eye of the Storm* (Yale University Press, 2002), p. 56.

59. In a speech at Hazratbal on October 5, 1947, Abdullah asserted that "our aim is to establish a people's government in Jammu & Kashmir State. The old regime of the Dogra Maharaja must go and should be replaced by the people's *raj* [rule]. Our first demand is complete transfer of power to the people. It will be the representatives of the people who will decide as to whether we should join India or Pakistan." Cited in Hassnain, *Freedom Struggle in Kashmir*, p. 148.

60. Sheikh Abdullah, *Flames of the Chinar*, p. 83.

61. Ibid., p. 83.

62. "Kashmir Muslims Not to Tolerate Autocratic Rule," *Dawn*, May 22, 1947. p. 4.

63. "Kashmir Ruler Urged to Set Up State Constituent Assembly," *Dawn*, May 11, 1947, p. 7.

64. See M. C. Mahajan, *Accession of Kashmir to India: The Inside Story* (Sholapur: Institute for Public Affairs, 1950), p. 2.

65. Cited in Sheikh Abdullah, *Flames of the Chinar*, p. 60.

66. Pakistan sent two envoys of Kashmiri stock, Mohammad Din Tasir and Sheikh Sadiq Hasan, to Srinagar to negotiate with the National Conference. Sheikh Abdullah told them that their first objective was to break "our chains of slavery." He assured them that past attitudes would not affect the National Conference's decision. "If after independence, we found it in the interest of forty Lakh Kashmiris to join Pakistan, we would certainly do it, but we will, at the same time, refuse to be dictated to by others. Although Dr. Tasir pressed us to join Pakistan, I firmly told him that the time to decide had not yet arrived." Abdullah, *Flames of the Chinar*, pp. 87–88. Ghulam Mohammad Bakshi corroborated this belief that "the Pakistani leaders were unwilling to let the Kashmir issue be decided by a referendum. The Pakistani leaders were reported to have said that unless Sheikh Abdullah pledged to Pakistan that the National Conference

would solidly vote for the state's accession to Pakistan, they could not agree to referendum." Cited in Gupta, *Kashmir: A Study in India-Pakistan Relations*, p. 108.

67. An underground coordinating committee, called the Pakistan Council, was formed to launch Direct Action to compel the maharaja to accede to Pakistan. Kaul notes that several Muslim tribal chieftains with huge fiefdoms in Muzaffarabad and Baramulla had established a secret liaison with their counterparts across the border in order to seek help in overthrowing the Dogra dynasty. Kaul, *Freedom Struggle in Jammu and Kashmir*, pp. 199–200.

68. Ayesha Jalal, *The State of Martial Rule* (Cambridge University Press, 1990), p. 44.

69. Sheikh Abdullah, *Flames of the Chinar*, p. 86.

70. At this meeting, Liaquat Ali Khan argued that if Junagarh belonged to India because of its Hindu majority (even though its Muslim leaders had acceded to Pakistan), then Kashmir surely belonged to Pakistan. Sardar Patel replied: "Why do you compare Junagarh with Kashmir? Talk of Hyderabad and Kashmir and we could reach agreement." See Chaudhuri Mohammad Ali, *The Emergence of Pakistan*, 10th printing (Lahore: Pakistan Research Society, 1998), p. 299. Patel was not alone in this view. On October 29, 1947, officials at the U.S. embassy in Delhi had told the U.S. State Department: "The obvious solution is for the government leaders in Pakistan and India to agree [to the] accession of Kashmir to Pakistan and the accession of Hyderabad and Junagarh to India." British officials in London concurred. Cited in Jones, *Pakistan: Eye of the Storm*, p. 69.

71. Cited in Gupta, *Kashmir: A Study in India-Pakistan Relations*, p. 36.

Chapter Two

1. Ashutosh Varshney, "Three Compromised Nationalisms: Why Kashmir Has Been a Problem," in *Perspectives on Kashmir: The Roots of Conflict in South Asia*, edited by Raju G. C. Thomas (Boulder, Colo.: Westview Press, 1992), p. 197.

2. Interview with Michael Brecher, cited in S. Gopal, *Nehru: An Anthology* (Oxford University Press, 1980), p. 217.

3. Mountbatten handed Jinnah a composite formula for settling differences over Kashmir, Junagarh, and Hyderabad that consisted of an impartial reference to the will of the people. Chandrashekhar Dasgupta, *War and Diplomacy in Kashmir: 1947–48* (New Delhi: Sage, 2002), pp. 72–73. Later, Pakistan's pime minister, Liaquat Ali Khan, accepted the plebiscite principle with regard to Kashmir and Junagarh but *not* as a general principle, clearly with Hyderabad in mind. See Sisir Gupta, *Kashmir: A Study in India-Pakistan Relations* (New Delhi: Asia House, 1966), p. 133.

4. Cited in Prem Shankar Jha, *Kashmir 1947: The Origins of a Dispute* (Oxford University Press, 2003), p. 202.

5. Ibid., p. 137.

6. Ibid., p. 136. General S. K. Sinha, who was posted at the army headquarters in the 1947–48 war, corroborates the view that until December 1947 military operations in Kashmir were perceived along the lines of earlier tribal turmoil in the North-West Frontier Province that was put down within six weeks.

7. Cited in ibid., p. 34.

8. The referendum there took place in extraordinary circumstances, and despite the call for a boycott by the Khudai Khidmatgars, the Muslim League won the referendum by only a 1 percent vote. The Muslim League had propagated the view that the Congress government was a creature of the Hindus and an agent for securing Hindu domination of the North-West Frontier Province; and that the Khudai Khidmatgars' support of the Congress during the freedom struggle was tantamount to cooperating with infidels. Ibid., pp. 60–61.

9. Nehru's remark at the Defense Committee meeting held on October 25, 1947. The minutes of this meeting are reproduced in ibid., app. IV, p. 200.

10. Cited in Victoria Schofield, *Kashmir in Conflict: India, Pakistan and the Unending War* (London: I. B. Tauris, 2003), p. 61.

11. Ghulam Mohammad Bakshi corroborated the belief that "the Pakistani leaders were unwilling to let the Kashmir issue be decided by a referendum. The Pakistani leaders were reported to have said that unless Sheikh Abdullah pledged to Pakistan that the National Conference would solidly vote for the state's accession to Pakistan, they could not agree to [a] referendum." Cited in Gupta, *Kashmir: A Study in India-Pakistan Relations*, p. 108.

12. Liaquat Ali Khan's statement cited in ibid., p. 133.

13. Cited in Dasgupta, *War and Diplomacy in Kashmir*, p. 98.

14. Cited in H. V. Hodson, *The Great Divide: Britain-India-Pakistan* (Oxford University Press, 1969), p. 468.

15. Ibid., p. 465.

16. Cited in Dasgupta, *War and Diplomacy in Kashmir*, p. 100.

17. *Selected Works of Jawaharlal Nehru*, vol. 19 (New Delhi: Teen Murti House, 1996), p. 323.

18. Hodson cites Nehru's letter to Mountbatten stating that from the standpoint of international law, "we can in self-defence take any military measures to resist . . . [the invasion], including the sending of our armies across Pakistani territory to attack their bases near the Kashmir border." Hodson, *The Great Divide*, p. 467. India's reference to the United Nations also noted that "this active aggression against India entitled the Indian government, in law, to take military action against Pakistan."

19. Cited in Jha, *Kashmir 1947*, p. 130.

20. B. N. Rao had made these points in a speech to the Security Council on February 7, 1950. Gupta, *Kashmir: A Study in India-Pakistan Relations*, p. 206.

21. Ibid., p. 140.

22. The Security Council was approached to (1) ask the government of Pakistan to prevent its government personnel, military and civil, from participating or assisting in the invasion of Jammu and Kashmir state; (2) call upon its nationals to desist from taking part in the fighting in the state; and (3) deny the invaders access to and use of its territory for operations against Kashmir, military and other supplies, and all other kinds of aid that might tend to prolong the present struggle.

23. Jha, *Kashmir 1947*, pp. 142–44.

24. In a telegram to the Commonwealth missions dated January 12, 1948, the Com-

monwealth relations officer, Sir Philip Noel-Baker, acknowledged that "these proposals are similar to those made by [the] Pakistani Prime Minister in [a] public statement on 16 November." He insisted, however, that "they are the right solution." For further details, see ibid., pp. 143–62.

25. Ibid., p. 152; and Hodson, *The Great Divide*, p. 469.

26. Described as a "bombshell" by Josef Korbel, *Danger in Kashmir* (Princeton University Press, 1966), p. 121. Jha cites correspondence between the U.S. State Department and the British Foreign Office between May 8 and July 13, 1947, to show that both were aware of the presence of Pakistani troops in Kashmir but deliberately withheld this information from the UNCIP. The "Stand Down" instructions for the British army officers had also been diluted for the benefit of Pakistan. This was evident from the fact that nearly 10,000 Pakistani troops had entered Kashmir when British army officers were still commanding the Pakistani army. Jha, *Kashmir 1947*, pp. 163–65; Hodson, *The Great Divide*, p. 472.

27. In his conversation with Korbel, Nehru insisted that "Pakistan must be condemned. I do not require any solemn, final verdict, but a clear declaration about the Pakistan army's presence in Kashmir and its withdrawal." That was because "as things now stand, the presence of her army is not publicly known and we instead are thought of as aggressors." Korbel, *Danger in Kashmir*, p. 129.

28. Cited in ibid., p. 124.

29. Korbel notes that to one delegate, Nehru "displayed a map on which [the] Indian border stretched far west towards Pakistan, including the crucial Valley of Kashmir and even parts of west Jammu." Ibid., p. 131. Citing the governor-general's report, Hodson points out that before leaving India in June 1948, Mountbatten, too, had made a last attempt to resolve the Kashmir dispute by proposing its partition. At Mountbatten's request, Gopalaswami Ayyangar and V. P. Menon had worked out a partition plan they said the Indian cabinet would accept if Liaquat Ali Khan put it up. Hodson adds that the partition maps were all marked up and discussed between Pandit Nehru and the chief of army staff. In the event, Liaquat Ali Khan fell ill and never came to Delhi. Hodson, *The Great Divide*, pp. 471–72.

30. Cited in Korbel, *Danger in Kashmir*, p. 147.

31. *Selected Works of Jawaharlal Nehru*, p. 323.

32. Nehru believed that if Pakistan did clear out of the whole of Kashmir and a plebiscite could be held soon, so much the better, for with Sheikh Abdullah opting for India, there was little likelihood of the state as a whole voting to join Pakistan. But if Pakistan did not vacate "Azad Kashmir," it would be no great loss, for the parts that the cease-fire would cut away would be those that were not reconciled to union with India. Jha, *Kashmir 1947*, pp. 175–76.

33. Cited in Gupta, *Kashmir: A Study in India-Pakistan Relations*, p. 381.

34. For a more detailed text of Sheikh Abdullah's speech, see Navnita Chadha Behera, *State, Identity and Violence: Jammu, Kashmir and Ladakh* (New Delhi: Manohar, 2000), app. IV, pp. 315–23.

35. Seeing that Maharaja Hari Singh was reluctant to transfer administrative control of the Jammu and Kashmir state army to the Indian army, Sheikh Abdullah insisted

that their separate identity should cease and all should be taken over by the Indian army. But after the maharaja was removed, Abdullah claimed that "when the present emergency is over and the Indian forces are withdrawn, the state will be left with an army of its own to fall back upon." See Karan Singh, *Autobiography* (Oxford University Press, 1994), p. 84; and Ajit Bhattacharjea, *Kashmir: The Wounded Valley* (New Delhi: UBSPD, 1994), p. 177.

36. Cited in Gupta, *Kashmir: A Study in India-Pakistan Relations*, p. 380.

37. Balraj Puri notes that Sheikh Abdullah had claimed that "under the provisions of [the] international agreement, we can sever our relations with India even today, if we wish to do so. This right is given to our state and not to others." Balraj Puri, *Jammu and Kashmir: Triumph and Tragedy of Indian Federalization* (New Delhi: Sterling, 1981), p. 116.

38. Nehru told Sheikh Abdullah that he "would rather give Kashmir to Pakistan on a platter than allow international intrigue to dangle Kashmir over the heads of India and Pakistan like a sword of Damocles." Mir Qasim, *My Life and Times* (New Delhi: Allied, 1992), p. 61. Much earlier, in a note to Sheikh Abdullah written on August 25, 1952, he had explained the "impracticability of an independent Kashmir." *Selected Works of Jawaharlal Nehru*, pp. 322–30.

39. Sheikh Abdullah recognized that Kashmir's accession to India would strengthen Indian secularism. Having seen this link, however, he developed some apprehensions and dithered. Should Hindu nationalists triumph in the struggle for power in Delhi, Abdullah wondered whether Kashmir would be secure in India: "Abdullah was not sure of the longevity of secularism; his unequivocal faith was, however, required for imparting longevity to secularism. Abdullah was unsure of what would happen in Delhi; the leadership in Delhi was unsure what Abdullah's strategy was going to be. Both deeply wanted a secular dispensation, but without a guarantee that a secular future would obtain, they lost each other's trust. And a sub-optimal outcome—an unresolved Indian State problem—resulted." Varshney, "Three Compromised Nationalisms," p. 205.

40. Balraj Puri observed that during Abdullah's tenure (1948–53) he pleaded with Nehru to allow disgruntled elements of the National Conference to form an opposition party; Nehru conceded the "theoretical soundness of [my] argument but maintained that India's Kashmir policy revolved around Abdullah and nothing should be done to weaken him." After Abdullah's arrest, Puri repeated the request. Nehru agreed that Bakshi used unscrupulous methods but argued that "India's case . . . now revolved around him and despite all shortcomings the Bakshi government had to be strengthened." Behera, *State, Identity and Violence*, p. 110.

41. Sumantra Bose, *The Challenge in Kashmir: Democracy, Self-Determination and a Just Peace* (New Delhi: Sage, 1997), pp. 39–40.

42. Cited in Singh, *Autobiography*, p. 267.

43. Sheikh Abdullah, *Flames of the Chinar*, translated from Urdu by Khushwant Singh (New Delhi: Viking, 1993), p. 147.

44. Cited in Behera, *State, Identity and Violence*, p. 117.

45. *Times of India*, May 10, 1964.

46. Y. D. Gundevia, *Sheikh Abdullah's Testament* (Dehradun: Palit & Palit, 1974), p.

82. For details of this proposal, see Y. D. Gundevia, *Outside the Archives* (Hyderabad: Sangam Books India, 1984).

47. Prem Nath Bazaz, *Kashmir in the Crucible* (New Delhi: Pamposh, 1967), pp. 233–34.

48. There were some dissident voices among the Plebiscite Front leaders. Munshi Mohammad Isahaq, president of the Plebiscite Front, resigned soon after Pakistani raiders infiltrated the state. He complained of being let down by his colleagues for not honoring the commitment with Pakistan to collaborate with the infiltrators and regretted that "on account of selfishness and cowardice of the leaders of Kashmir who were outside the jail, we missed a golden opportunity of liberation of Kashmir." Puri, *Jammu and Kashmir*, p. 160.

49. According to Mirwaiz Farooq, the Simla accord had fundamentally weakened Pakistan's position and ruled Pakistan out as a significant factor in the dispute, possibly forever. G. M. Karra announced that "accession is final." The leaders from the Plebiscite Front and the Awami Action Committee joined the District Citizens Defense Councils and condemned the "Pakistani junta" for disturbing the peace on the border. Front leaders such as Syed Mubarak Shah, Ghulam Rasool Kochak, and Mohammad Yakub Beg openly denounced Pakistan. *Link* 14, no. 21 (January 1972): 21.

50. Sheikh Abdullah, *Flames of the Chinar*, p. 164. In his autobiography, Abdullah glosses over the shift in objectives after Bangladesh: "I assured my Indian friends that we had no differences with them over accession. We only wanted Article 370 to be maintained in its original form." Yet later he said: "Our readiness to come to the negotiating table did not imply change in our objectives but a change in our strategy." Ibid., p. 325. Abdullah apparently told Jayaprakash Narayan and Sarvepalli Radhakrishnan that he would be prepared to accept the status of full internal autonomy for Kashmir provided that history was not allowed to repeat itself—that is, provided that the autonomy was not gradually whittled down and the center did not interfere in the state's internal affairs. Cited in "JP's Secret Letter to Mrs. Gandhi on Kashmir," *Sunday*, March 4–10, 1984, pp. 24–27.

51. Hari Ram, *Special Status in Indian Federalism: Jammu and Kashmir* (New Delhi: Seema, 1983), p. 106. For Mrs. Gandhi's statement in the Lok Sabha on the Kashmir Accord, see M. J. Akbar, *India: The Siege Within* (New Delhi: UBSPD, 1996), p. 188.

52. The accord curtailed the powers of the state assembly in specified matters of importance, including elections, the appointment of governors, and terms of office. Parliament retained jurisdiction to legislate on the union list of subjects, and the provisions of the Indian constitution already applied to the state remained unaltered. It would also continue making laws relating to the "prevention of activities directed towards disclaiming, questioning or disrupting the sovereignty and territorial integrity of India or bringing about secession of a part of the territory from the Indian Union or causing insult to the Indian National Flag, the Indian National Anthem and the Constitution." For the full text of the Kashmir Accord, see Behera, *State, Identity and Violence*, app. V, pp. 324–25.

53. S. S. Anand, *Development of the Constitution of Jammu and Kashmir* (New Delhi: Light and Life, 1980), pp. 112–43.

54. Puri, *Jammu and Kashmir*, p. 187.

55. Sumit Mitra, "Farooq's Fierce Fight," *India Today*, June 15, 1983.

56. Cited in Behera, *State, Identity and Violence*, p. 140.

57. Tavleen Singh, *Kashmir: A Tragedy of Errors* (New Delhi: Viking, 1995), p. 30.

58. Mrs. Gandhi exploited the anger of the people against the Resettlement Act, claiming that it would be nothing short of disaster for poor neglected Jammu; Muslims who had left in 1947 for Pakistan would be allowed back, and Jammu would continue to be treated like a stepchild. In the Valley, Mrs. Gandhi projected herself as *Kashmir ki Beti*' (Kashmir's daughter). She avoided criticizing the Resettlement Act there and agreed that genuine cases of permanent "state-subjects" estranged from hearth and home should be sympathetically considered. Ibid., p. 25; and Mitra "Farooq's Fierce Fight," p. 18. See also Arun Shourie, "Eighty or One Thousand," *India Today*, July 31, 1983, pp. 82–87.

59. Mrs. Gandhi had not allowed the ban of the Jamaat-i-Islami because it did not accept the finality of the state's accession to India, whereas a secular though politically competitive Plebiscite Front was declared an illegal organization and barred from contesting the 1972 assembly elections on the same grounds. Mir Qasim corroborates that in order to deter any political challenge to the Congress in the 1972 elections, it had "enlisted the services of Jamaat-i-Islami to fill the vacant political space" and allegedly guaranteed its success in five constituencies. "Crossfire: Kashmir, Drift to Disaster," *India Today*, August 31, 1991. Mrs. Gandhi also used this strategy in Punjab by giving unpublicized support to the extremist wing of the Sikh leadership in order to weaken the more moderate but politically competitive Akali Dal. Henry C. Hart, "Political Leadership in India," in *India's Democracy: An Analysis of Changing State-Society Relations*, edited by Atul Kohli (New Delhi: Orient Longman, 1988), p. 41.

60. Balraj Puri, *Kashmir: Towards Insurgency* (New Delhi: Orient Longman, 1993), p. 34.

61. Cited in Singh, *Kashmir: A Tragedy of Errors*, p. 87.

62. Puri, *Kashmir: Towards Insurgency*, p. 52.

63. Other constituents of the Muslim United Front—such as the Islamic Study Circle, the Muslim Education Trust, the Muslim Welfare Society, the Islamic Jamiat-ul-Tulba, the Majlis Tahafazul-ul-Islami, the Jamiat-ul-Hadis, the Shia Rabita Committee, and the Idara Tahquiqat—were essentially Jamaat-i-Islami outfits.

64. P. S. Verma, "Muslim United Front," in S. Bhatnagar and Pradeep Kumar, eds., *Regional Political Parties in India* (New Delhi: Ess Ess, 1988), pp. 192–95.

65. My conversations with militants, political activists, intellectuals, and journalists lend credence to this assessment.

66. Ved Marwah, *Uncivil Wars: Pathology of Terrorism in India* (New Delhi: Harper Collins, 1995), pp. 60–63.

67. Jagmohan was instrumental in engineering defections in the National Conference MLAs, which were then used to dismiss Farooq Abdullah's government in 1984. Jagmohan never allowed him to test the majority of his government on the floor of the house. Farooq therefore took strong exception to New Delhi's decision to bring back Jagmohan as a governor.

68. See Jagmohan's interview in *Current*, May 26–June 1, 1990.

69. Riyaz Punjabi's statement in "Crossfire: Kashmir, Drift to Disaster," *India Today*, August 31, 1991, p. 84.

70. Over several decades, such concessions have included creating new ethnopolitical territories, giving tribes the legal rights to mineral resources, and offering protection (such as requiring inner-line entry permits and prohibiting outsiders from buying properties in tribal regions). Weapons were not "surrendered" but "handed over" to be stored in safe houses, often under the eye of peace councils led by tribal elders. On striking a deal, the government generally avoided claims of victory, and the militants did not have to admit defeat. See Shekhar Gupta, "India Redefines Its Role: An Analysis of India's Changing Internal Dynamics and Their Impact on Foreign Relations," *Adelphi Paper* 293 (1995), p. 27.

71. While no militants had been killed in 1989, 552 died in engagements with Indian security forces in 1992. The number of militants killed rose steadily until 1994, and then tapered off. Thereafter attacks on security forces, which peaked in 1992, declined steadily until 1998, mirroring the forces' success in hunting down militants. For details, see Praveen Swami, "Terrorism in Jammu and Kashmir in Theory and Practice," *India Review* 2 (July 2003): 63.

72. Statement by JKLF leader Javed Mir, as cited in Behera, *State, Identity and Violence*, p. 180.

73. Of eighty-four persons who disappeared, twenty were found in their homes; six had joined the militant groups, while two were forcibly taken away by the militants; five others had been killed in militancy, and one was lodged in the central jail with family members visiting him. *Tribune Chandigarh*, September 10, 2003.

74. The Jamaat-i-Islami leaders were unnerved and went into hiding for weeks, and the Hizbul militants were literally on the run in Anantnag, Shopian, Pulwama, and Kulgam, fearing people's wrath.

75. Statement by Khaled Ahmed, spokesman of the Hizb-ul-Mujahideen. Yasin Bhatt, chief of Ikhwan-e-Muslemeen, also reiterated, "We will support them only if their program is in the interest of the Kashmiri cause." Harinder Baweja, "Kashmir: A Calculated Gamble," *India Today*, April 30, 1992, p. 147.

76. Home Minister S. B. Chavan had formed a committee to consider the forum's proposals for building confidence by releasing all detainees (especially those who were not charged with specific crimes), restraining the security forces, calling off offensive operations, and disarming the renegade militants. *Hindu* (Chennai), March 16, 1996.

77. Praveen Swami, "Peace and War," *Frontline*, November 8–21, 2003.

78. Of the APHC's seven executive council members, just one—the near-defunct People's League and two individuals (the People's Conference's Ghulam Mohammad Hubbi and the Muslim Conference's Ghulam Nabi Sumji) expelled from other groups represented them in the Executive Council. Geelani could also rustle up only eleven of the twenty-seven members of the APHC General Council, mainly small Islamist groupings such as the Islamic Students League, the Muslim Khawateen Markaz, the Kashmir Mass Movement, and the Jammu Freedom Movement.

79. Praveen Swami, "Danger Signals from the Valley," *Frontline*, October 10, 2003, p. 36.

80. Praveen Swami, "A Meaningful Course," *Frontline*, February 13, 2004, p. 26.

81. Praveen Swami, "Jammu and Kashmir: Breaking the Stalemate," *South Asia Intelligence Review* 2 (November 21, 2003) (www.satporg@satp.org). See also Ajay Darshan Behera, "LTTE, Hurriyat and Self-Determination," *Hindu* (Chennai), October 1, 2002.

82. Even the centrist JKLF has decided against participating in the dialogue with the central government.

83. Praveen Swami, "Conflict, Cash and Search for Peace," *Hindu* (Chennai), March 28, 2006.

84. Prime Minister Shaukat Aziz spent nearly six hours with the APHC leaders during his visit to New Delhi in November 2004, meeting them individually and collectively, apparently to persuade them to put up a united front. John Cherian, "An Uneasy Truce," *Frontline*, December 17, 2004, p. 17. The same was done during Musharraf's visit to Delhi in April 2005. The sharp divisions in the separatist camp were evident from the fact that they called on Musharraf in three separate delegations. Raj Chengappa and Syed Talat Hussain, "Has the General Really Changed?" *India Today*, May 2, 2005, p. 21.

85. Pakistan divested the Tahreek-e-Hurriyat of international recognition through representation at the Organization of Islamic Countries (OIC) meetings, where Hurriyat has observer status; at home, Pakistan Television suspended its daily bulletins on "Geelani-speak."

86. Praveen Swami, "Kashmir Maha Panchayat: Learning from History," *Hindu* (Chennai), February 23, 2006.

87. See http://in.rediff.com/news/2006/apr/25jk.htm.

88. Farooq Abdullah had demanded an autonomy package, restoring the pre-1953 status, before the polls. Congress's prime minister P. V. Narasimha Rao made a half-hearted offer to reexamine the Kashmir Accord (1974) and announced from Burkina Faso, in western Africa, belied hopes of earlier promises of "maximum autonomy short of *azadi*." The National Conference dismissed it as "too little, too late."

89. Jagmohan's strategy was to put strong and sustained pressure on the terrorists and their collaborators, treat the situation as a low-intensity war, organize counterguerrilla groups, effectively block the supply line of the adversaries, prevent the flow of state resources to terrorists, identify and remove subversive elements from government organizations, provide an honorable line of retreat and route to power through fair and free elections to all except pro-Pak fanatics, and prosecute terrorists speedily through the designated courts. In contrast, Fernandes offered compassionate understanding of militants with a healing touch for the Kashmiris. He explored different options of starting a political process through a revamping of the National Conference under Farooq Abdullah; amalgamation of the JKLF, the MUF, the People's Conference, and the People's League into a new political party led by Shabir Shah; and dialogue initiated with Mirwaiz Maulvi Farooq. See Jagmohan, "Past, Present and Future," *Seminar* 392 (April 1992): 24; and Jagmohan interview in *Current*, May 16–June 1, 1990.

90. Author's interviews with senior Kashmiri police officers. The divisions ran so deep that a false rumor of JKAP personnel being shot by the CRPF resulted in a police revolt on January 22, 1990.

91. Under the corps, the divisions were to be responsible for antimilitary operations in their territorial jurisdictions, and all paramilitary forces meant for antimilitary operations were to be under the operational control of the divisional commanders. See V. K. Sood and Pravin Sawhney, *Operation Parakram: The War Unfinished* (New Delhi: Sage, 2003), p. 53.

92. In the aftermath of the Kargil war in 1999, the director-general of the Rashtriya Rifles, Avatar Singh Gill, who took charge of the army's internal security operations, demanded that paramilitary organizations such as the Border Security Force (BSF) and the CRPF be placed under his operational command. The BSF director-general E. N. Ram Mohan contended that this would disrupt the functional relationships among the security forces in the state and help escalate internecine feuds and rivalries. He argued that the Rashtriya Rifles, which, strictly speaking, is not part of the army, was in effect a central police organization, just like the BSF and the CRPF.

93. Praveen Swami, "An Offensive Strategy," *Frontline*, February 18, 2000, p. 23.

94. Praveen Swami, "A Growing Toll," *Frontline*, November 26, 1999, pp. 39–41; and Praveen Swami, "Mufti's Turn," *Frontline*, November 22, 2003, p. 8.

95. Swami, "Terrorism in Jammu and Kashmir in Theory and Practice," p. 65. Raw data are available at the South Asia Terrorism Portal, www.satp.org/satporgtp/countries/india/states/jandk/data_sheets/response_cease_fire.htm.

96. Praveen Swami, "A Widening Network," *Frontline*, January 3, 2003, p. 35.

97. For a detailed discussion on Farooq's performance in power, see Behera, *State, Identity and Violence*, pp. 248–76.

98. In 1998, 30 percent of the Srinagar electorate voted in the Lok Sabha election; this figure dropped to 11.9 percent in 1999. In the votes polled in the three parliamentary constituencies in the Kashmir Valley, turnout in Srinagar, Anantnag, and Baramulla was 35, 50, 41 percent, respectively, in 1996, but it dropped to 12, 12, and 28 percent, respectively, in the 1999 elections. Among the Muslim-majority segments in the Jammu region, the turnout at the polls during these elections was 7 percent in Banihal, 21 percent in Surankote, 23 percent in Inderwal, 24 percent in Kishtwar, and 26 percent in Mendhar. In the assembly elections of 1996, the respective figures were 52.26, 74.26, 62.54, 69.46 and 66.79 percent. Balraj Puri, "Alienation and the Revival of Militancy," *Frontline*, February 4, 2000, p. 24.

99. Interviews with Babar Badr, Imran Rahi, and Bilal Lodhi of the Forum for Peaceful Resolution of Jammu and Kashmir, and Shabir Shah in August 1997.

100. Farooq Abdullah, interview in *Asian Age*, September 18, 1996.

101. *State Autonomy Committee Report*, Jammu, April 1999, pp. 111–12. It also suggested substituting the word "temporary" with "special" in the title of Part XXI of the Constitution of India and also in the heading of Article 370. For a summary of its recommendations, see Behera, *State, Identity and Violence*, app. X, pp. 340–43.

102. Abdul Ghani Lone, interview with Ramesh Vinayak, *India Today*, June 3, 2002, p. 31.

103. Tariq Naqash, "Hurriyat Does Not Represent J&K, Says PoK PM," *Tribune* (Chandigarh), June 26, 2005.

104. Swami points out that the plan to merge SOG into the state police instead of shelving it is purely notional as the SOG since its outset was made up of state police personnel and operated within its command structure. Praveen Swami, "An Outrage in Jammu," *Frontline*, December 20, 2002, p. 122.

105. Venkitesh Ramakrishnan, "A Promising Start," *Frontline*, December 17, 2004, pp. 4–5.

106. In this case, the army had already deployed two new battalions (each comprising six companies with 125 men) of Rashtriya Rifles under the command of the Romeo Force in the Thana Mandi-Kandi area of Rajouri district, from which the 73rd Mountain Brigade had been withdrawn. *Hindu* (Chennai), February 10, 2006.

107. For a detailed debate on these issues, see George K. Tanham, "Indian Strategic Thought: An Interpretive Essay," in *Securing India: Strategic Thought and Practice,* edited by George K. Tanham, Kanti Bajpai, and Amitabh Mattoo (New Delhi: Manohar, 1996); Jaswant Singh, *Defending India* (New York: St. Martin's Press, 1999); T. V. Paul and Baldev Raj Nayar, *India in the World Order: Searching for Major-Power Status* (Cambridge University Press, 2003); Kanti Bajpai, "India: Modified Structuralism," in *Asian Security Practice: Material and Ideational Influences,* edited by Muthiah Alagappa (Stanford University Press, 1998); Ashley J. Tellis, *Stability in South Asia: Prospects of Indo-Pak Nuclear Conflict* (Dehra Dun: Natraj, 2000).

108. In 1971, while open war began with a Pakistani air attack on Indian air force bases, Indian units had in fact been in East Pakistan for some time, and had supported a Bangladeshi separatist movement.

109. India's gains included areas in Shyok Valley, Kargil, Northern Gallies, Uri, and Tithwal sectors, including parts of Lipa Valley and Kaiyan. A few commanding heights across the cease-fire line in the Poonch, Rajouri, and Naushera sector and Chicken's Neck in Jammu sector were also occupied by India. *History of Bangladesh War*, edited by S. N. Prasad (New Delhi: Ministry of Defence, 1992), p. 758.

110. Dasgupta, *War and Diplomacy in Kashmir*, p. 50.

111. Bucher even offered to send a secret signal to his counterpart in Rawalpindi in case the Indian government double-crossed him by changing his plans. Ibid., p. 184.

112. Singh, *Defending India*, p. 160.

113. S. N. Prasad and Dharm Pal, *Operations in Jammu and Kashmir 1947–48* (New Delhi: Ministry of Defence, 1987); Lieutenant General (Retired) M. L. Chibber, *Pakistan's Criminal Folly in Kashmir* (New Delhi: Manas, 1998).

114. Sinha pointed out that the army could have sorted out the angularities in the cease-fire line had they even got one week's notice that a cease-fire was in the offing. Nehru too admitted it as a "past mistake"; that is, India "could have got the ceasefire line on a somewhat better line if we had given more thought to it." *Selected Works of Jawaharlal Nehru*, p. 324.

115. Sumit Ganguly, *Conflict Unending: India-Pakistan Tensions since 1947* (Oxford University Press, 2002), p. 38.

116. Ibid., p. 46.

117. The full text of the Simla Agreement of July 2, 1972, is available at www.jammu-kashmir.com/documents/simla.html.

118. The original cease-fire line is a rough arc running 800 kilometers north and then northeastward to a point (NJ9842) 20 kilometers north of the Shyok River at the foot of the Saltoro Range. Beyond the delineated grid point, the Karachi Agreement said that the line continues "thence northwards to the glaciers." Siachin glacier lies well east of that line. The Tashkent Agreement only reaffirmed the cease-fire line without attempting to extend it. The 1972 Simla Agreement too left it vague: "From Chorbatla in the Turtok sector the line of control runs north eastward to Thang (inclusive India) thence eastward joining the glaciers." See Robert G. Wirsing, "The Siachin Glacier Dispute-I: The Territorial Dimension," *Strategic Studies* 1 (Winter 1988): 51; and A. G. Noorani, "Fire on the Mountains," *Illustrated Weekly of India*, June 30, 1985, pp. 40–41.

119. General Mirza Aslam Beg's press briefing on September 13, 1989, in *Defence Journal* 6–7 (1991): 43.

120. Lieutenant General M. L. Chibber, "Siachin: The Untold Story (A Personal Account)," *Indian Defence Review Digest*, vol. 3, 1989, p. 93. See also his article, "Siachin Solution Will Help India and Pakistan," *Times of India* (New Delhi), July 13, 1988.

121. General Mirza Aslam Beg, in a press briefing, acknowledged that "in 1983, GHQ decided to send a Special Service Group team into the Siachin glacier. A[n] SSG company was moved in August 1983. This company crossed the Sia la and went into Siachin." See Beg's press briefing, September 13, 1989, pp. 43–44.

122. The army has acknowledged that its formations and senior commanders were so involved in counterinsurgency operations that when the first reports of an incursion came in, few believed that this was a Pakistani gamble to "take possession of the strategic heights." Saikat Datta, "War against Error," *Outlook,* February 28, 2005, p. 39. For a detailed critique of the intelligence failures, see *The Kargil Review Committee Report* (New Delhi: Sage, 2000).

123. Raj Chengappa, Zahid Hussain, and Sujatha Shenoy, "Face-Saving Retreat," *India Today*, July 19, 1999, p. 24.

124. Tellis, *Stability in South Asia,* pp. x–xi.

125. Ibid., pp. 29–30. See also Sood and Sawhney, *Operation Parakram*, pp. 145–70.

126. Cited in Sood and Sawhney, *Operation Parakram*, p. 145.

127. Sunderji's conversation with Devin T. Hagerty as reported in "Nuclear Deterrence in South Asia," *International Security* 20 (Winter 1995–96). On Indian leaders, General Sunderji said, "The reason why they have hesitated to take recourse to their stated, avowed strategy of reacting in the plains conventionally is because of the nuclear equation . . . I have got no doubt in my mind at all."

128. Tellis, *Stability in South Asia,* p. 76

129. Ashley J. Tellis, *India's Emerging Nuclear Posture: Between Recessed Deterrent and Ready Arsenal* (Santa Monica, Calif.: Rand, 2001), p. 146.

130. Pravin Sawhney, *The Defense Makeover: 10 Myths That Shape India's Image* (New Delhi: Sage, 2002), pp. 143–44.

131. Swami, "Terrorism in Jammu and Kashmir in Theory and Practice," p. 69.

132. For details, see ibid., p. 70.

133. Praveen Swami, "Peace on the Guillotine, Again," *Hindu* (Chennai), July 19, 2004. He reported that three militants shot dead near the Line of Control in the Mandi-

Loran area in June 2004 were carrying plastic pipes designed to penetrate the fencing. For more details on the militants' tactics to bypass the fence, see Raj Chengappa, "General Mischief," *India Today*, September 13, 2004, pp. 38–44.

134. Swami, "Terrorism in Jammu and Kashmir in Theory and Practice," p. 71.

135. C. Rajamohan, "Fernandes Unveils 'Limited War' Doctrine," *Hindu* (Chennai), January 25, 2000. The possibility of "proactive" Indian counterresponses is discussed widely in New Delhi under the rubric of "limited war," and the following sources either advocate or describe a variety of actions consistent with this policy: M. D. Nalapat, "No More Waffling," *Times of India* (New Delhi), January 18, 2000; Satish Nambiar, "Make the Army Fighting Fit, Paddy," *Hindustan Times* (New Delhi), August 20, 2000; and C. Raja Mohan, "Jawing about War," *Times of India* (New Delhi), January 29, 2000.

136. V. P. Malik, "Indo-Pak Security Relations: Kargil and After," *Indian Express*, June 21, 2002.

137. Ashley J. Tellis, speech to the India Today Conclave, *India Today*, March 23–29, 2004, pp. 64–65.

138. Raja Menon summed it up as a strategy of "huff and bluff." See Raja Menon, "War against Terrorism," *Times of India* (New Delhi), October 6, 2001, and "Hot Pursuit, Cold Turkey," *Outlook*, December 31, 2001.

139. Cited in Sood and Sawhney, *Operation Parakram*, p. 62.

140. Swami, "Terrorism in Jammu and Kashmir in Theory and Practice," pp. 69–70.

141. Perhaps that is why former prime minister Atal Bihari Vajpayee, in a reflective moment, later wished he had acted immediately, possibly with punitive military action or air strikes rather than by deploying the military machine for an unlikely war. V. R. Raghavan, "Through the Prism of Nuclear Weapons," *Hindu* (Chennai), April 17, 2005.

142. Sood and Sawhney, *Operation Parakram*, p. 172.

143. Sawhney, *The Defense Makeover*, pp. 143–44.

Chapter Three

1. Cited in Wayne A. Wilcox, "India and Pakistan," in *Conflict in World Politics*, edited by Steven L. Spiegel and Kenneth N. Waltz (Cambridge, Mass.: Winthrop, 1971), pp. 257–58.

2. Ahmad Faruqi, *Rethinking the National Security of Pakistan: The Price of Strategic Myopia* (Hampshire, England: Ashgate, 2003), pp. 41–66; and Ashley J. Tellis, *Stability in South Asia: Prospects of Indo-Pak Nuclear Conflict* (Dehra Dun: Natraj, 2000), pp. 58–70.

3. Michael P. Fischerkeller, "David versus Goliath: Cultural Judgments in Asymmetric Wars," *Security Studies* 7 (Summer 1998): 1–43.

4. Pakistan's share of the movable assets was to come from ordnance depots in India, in 300 trains containing 170,000 tons of army stores. Only 3 trains carrying 6,000 tons of ordnance reached their destination, and most contained trash. Faruqi, *Rethinking the National Security of Pakistan*, p. 42; Sumit Ganguly, *Conflict Unending: India-Pakistan Tensions since 1947* (Oxford University Press, 2002), p. 19. For more

details, see Ayesha Jalal, *The State of Martial Rule: The Origins of Pakistan's Political Economy of Defence* (Lahore: Vanguard Books, 1991), pp. 25–48.

5. Owen Bennett Jones, *Pakistan: Eye of the Storm* (Yale University Press, 2002), p. 64.

6. Akbar Khan, *Raiders in Kashmir* (Islamabad: National Book Foundation, 1970). Also Jalal, *The State of Martial Rule*, pp. 56–60; Ibrahim Khan, *The Kashmir Saga* (Mirpur: Verinag, 1990), pp. 102–44. The British archives also show Pakistan's involvement in designing the raiders' plan. See Prem Shankar Jha, *The Origins of a Dispute, Kashmir 1947* (Oxford University Press, 2004), pp. 27–37.

7. Jalal, *The State of Martial Rule*, p. 58.

8. Ibid., p. 59.

9. Cited in Sisir Gupta, *Kashmir: A Study in India-Pakistan Relations* (Bombay: Asia House, 1966), p. 136.

10. Ibid., p. 130.

11. Alan Campbell-Johnson, *Mission with Mountbatten* (London: Robert Hale, 1951), p. 229.

12. V. R. Raghavan, "Limited War and Nuclear Escalation in South Asia," *Nonproliferation Review* 8 (Fall–Winter 2001): 91.

13. Gauhar presents a trenchant critique of these biases. See Altaf Gauhar, "Four Wars, One Assumption," *Pakistan Link* (www.pakistanlink.com/opinion/99/Sep/10/0l.html).

14. Khan, *Raiders in Kashmir*, p. 191. Also Ibrahim Khan, *The Kashmir Saga*, pp. 134–35.

15. Jalal, *The State of Martial Rule*, p. 59.

16. He wrote that at almost every step volunteers met with discouragement from the Pakistan army as well as from many high-placed Muslim civil officers. The attitude of many senior Pakistani officers was not only unhelpful but also enigmatic. See A. H. Suharwardy, *Tragedy in Kashmir* (Lahore: Wajidalis, 1983), p. 209.

17. Ayub Khan, *Friends, Not Masters: A Political Autobiography* (Oxford University Press, 1967), p. 38.

18. Jalal, *The State of Martial Rule*, p. 58.

19. Ibid., p. 44.

20. Pervaiz Iqbal Cheema, "Pakistan, India, and Kashmir: A Historical Review," in *Perspectives on Kashmir: The Roots of Conflict in South Asia*, edited by Raju G. C. Thomas (Boulder, Colo.: Westview Press, 1992); and G. W. Choudhury, *Pakistan's Relations with India 1947–66* (New York: Praeger, 1968), p. 111. See also Zafarullah Khan's statement in Josef Korbel, *Danger in Kashmir* (Princeton University Press, 1966), pp. 138–39.

21. Chaudhri Muhammed Ali, *The Emergence of Pakistan* (Columbia University Press, 1967), p. 305.

22. Cheema, "Pakistan, India, and Kashmir," p. 104. See also Lars Blinkenberg, *India-Pakistan: The History of Unresolved Conflicts* (Copenhagen: Danskudenrigspolitisk Institute, 1972), p. 108.

23. Ganguly, *Conflict Unending*, p. 31; also T. V. Paul, *Asymmetric Conflicts: War Initiation by Weaker Power* (Cambridge University Press, 1995), pp. 115–17.

24. Mohammad Musa Khan, *My Version: India-Pakistan War 1965* (Lahore: Wajidalis, 1983), pp. 35–37.

25. Ganguly, *Conflict Unending*, p. 40.

26. Cited in Jones, *Pakistan: Eye of the Storm*, p. 77.

27. Iqbal Akhund, *Memoirs of a Bystander: A Life in Diplomacy* (Oxford University Press, 1997), p. 104.

28. Brian Cloughley, *A History of the Pakistani Army: Wars and Insurrections* (Oxford University Press, 1999), p. 64.

29. Cited in ibid., p. 71.

30. T. V. Paul and Baldev Raj Nayar, *India in the World Order: Searching for Major-Power Status* (Cambridge University Press, 2003), p. 166.

31. Asghar Khan, *The First Round* (Ghaziabad: Vikas, 1979).

32. A Pakistani account given by Mohammad Musa Khan states that his objections against the infiltration strategy were overruled by Foreign Minister Z. A. Bhutto, Defence Secretary Aziz Ahmed, and ultimately by President Ayub Khan. Musa disclosed that the objectives of Operation Gibraltar included sabotage of military targets, disruption of communications, and distribution of arms to the Kashmiris and initiation of a guerrilla movement to eventually start an uprising in the Valley. Mohammad Musa Khan, *My Version*, pp. 35–37.

33. Faruqi, *Rethinking the National Security of Pakistan*, p. 57.

34. Ibid.; Jones, *Pakistan: Eye of the Storm*, p. 266.

35. He knew that Lahore was extremely vulnerable. The commander in charge of the city's defense, Major General Sarfraz Khan, had been specifically ordered to put no defensive measures in place. When a junior officer implored him to deploy troops in defensive positions, he replied: "Sorry, GHQ has ordered no move, no provocative actions." Jones, ibid., p. 79.

36. Cloughley, *A History of the Pakistani Army*, p. 125.

37. Ibid., p. 6.

38. Several people were killed under police fire, and hundreds, mainly students, were arrested. Fourteen Pakistani navy officers were reportedly sentenced to life imprisonment in consequence of their opposition to the Tashkent Declaration. Robert G. Wirsing, *Kashmir in the Shadow of War: Regional Rivalries in a Nuclear Age* (London: M. E. Sharpe, 2003), p. 175.

39. Cited in Faruqi, *Rethinking the National Security of Pakistan*, p. 44.

40. Ibid., p. 134.

41. This description occurs in the textbook on Pakistan studies, a compulsory subject for students of the higher secondary or intermediate classes in all groups: arts, humanities, premedical, and preengineering. Mohammad Abdullah Malik, *Tarikh-i-Pakistan: 1708–1977* (Lahore: Qureshi Brothers, 1988–89). Another textbook notes that in the 1965 war India "suffered great losses" and "her casualities (dead, not just wounded) were ten times those of Pakistan." Abdul Ghafur Chaudhri and others, *Mu'ashrati Ulum (Tarikh wa Shariat)* (Lahore: West Pakistan Textbook Board, 1968), pp. 158–59.

42. Cited in Faruqi, *Rethinking the National Security of Pakistan*, p. 60.

43. K. M. Arif, *Working with Zia: Pakistan's Power Politics, 1977–1988* (Oxford University Press, 1995), p. 36.

44. Cited in Ganguly, *Conflict Unending*, p. 73.

45. Cited in Faruqi, *Rethinking the National Security of Pakistan*, p. 134.

46. In Zarb-i-Momin, the exercise area was divided into the "Blue-land" (the Pakistani territory) and the Fox-land (the enemy areas). Blue-land forces were to launch an offensive on the excuse that there was supposedly domestic political turmoil in Fox-land. Notably, the Zia regime had indeed provided support to the Sikh secessionist movement in the 1980s. Siddiqa notes that the plan of supporting turmoil in Punjab was primarily the brainchild of the then Pakistani army chief, General Mirza Aslam Beg. See Ayesha Siddiqa-Agha, *Pakistan's Arms Procurement and Military Buildup, 1979–1999: In Search of a Policy* (New York: Palgrave, 2001), pp. 24–25.

47. Ibid., p. 25.

48. Ajay Darshan Behera, "On the Edge of Metamorphosis," in *Pakistan in a Changing Strategic Context*, edited by Ajay Darshan Behera and Joseph C. Mathew (New Delhi: Knowledge World, 2004), p. 7. See also excerpts from General Mirza Aslam Beg's press briefing in *Defence Journal* 6, no. 7 (1991): 39–50.

49. Tellis, *Stability in South Asia*, p. 66.

50. Author's interviews with a cross section of militants.

51. Faruqi, *Rethinking the National Security of Pakistan*, p. xvi.

52. Robert Wirsing, *India, Pakistan and the Kashmir Dispute* (New Delhi: Rupa, 1994), pp. 122–23.

53. Zaigham Khan, "Inside the Mind of the Holy Warrior," *Herald* (Karachi), July 1999, p. 43.

54. Hafeez R. Khan, "The Kashmir Intifada," *Pakistan Horizon* 43 (April 1990): 87–104.

55. This information was relayed by I. D. Swami, minister of state for home in the BJP-led NDA government, in a television program, *We, the People . . .*, Star News Channel, December 16, 2001.

56. Arun Shourie, *Will The Iron Fence Save a Tree Hollowed by Termites?* (New Delhi: Rupa, 2005), p. 169.

57. For a detailed account of the astronomical multiplication of madaris and maulanas in Pakistan, see the International Crisis Group, *Pakistan: Madrasas, Extremism and the Military*, Asia Report 36, July 29, 2002 (www.crisisgroup.org/). Over a million and a half students at more than 10,000 seminaries are being trained, in theory for service in the religious sector. In 1950, the group reports, Baluchistan had only seven and Karachi, four madaris. By 2003, the former had 1,045 and the latter 979.

58. Tariq Rahman, "The Madrassa and the State of Pakistan," *Himal* 17 (February 2004): 19.

59. Chris Smith, *The Diffusion of Small Arms and Light Weapons in Pakistan and Northern India* (London: Brassey's, 1993); Tara Kartha, *Tools of Terror: Light Weapons*

and India's Security (New Delhi: Knowledge World, 1999); and Jasjit Singh, *Light Weapons and International Security* (New Delhi: Indian Pugwash Society, 1995).

60. In an interview with the Arab daily, *Asharaq Al-Aswat* (Jeddah), the Pakistani high commissioner in London (and later foreign secretary), Shahryar Khan, stated that "independence of Kashmir is not part of the game." Similarly, the Pakistani foreign affairs and national security adviser under Prime Minister Benazir Bhutto, Iqbal Akhund, told the *Herald* (Karachi) in 1990 that Kashmir's choice is limited to accession to India or Pakistan. Independence is ruled out. Foreign Minister Sahabzada Yaqub Khan pointedly recalled on March 11, 1990, that under the UN resolutions, "the third option [of an independent Kashmir] is not mentioned." A. G. Noorani, "The Betrayal of Kashmir: Pakistan's Duplicity and India's Complicity" in *Perspectives on Kashmir*, edited by Thomas, p. 262.

61. The total number of incidents related to militant violence, as reported by the Jammu and Kashmir police, rose from 5,163 in 1990 to 5,606 in 1991, 7,315 in 1992, 7,987 in 1993, and 8,784 in 1994, then dropped to 8,731 in 1995, 6,633 in 1996, 4,702 in 1997, and 4,150 in 1998. This downward trend was slightly reversed in 1999, with 4,326 incidents of militant violence. See K. P. S. Gill, "Tackling Terrorism in Kashmir: Some Lessons from Recent History," paper presented at the Indian Council of Social Science Research seminar, "Terrorism: An Unending Malaise," March 2–3, 2000.

62. C. Raja Mohan, *Crossing the Rubicon: The Shaping of India's New Foreign Policy* (New Delhi: Viking, 2003), p. 188.

63. V. R. Raghavan, "A Turning Point in Kashmir," *Frontline*, June 18, 1999, pp. 16–17.

64. Naziha Ghazali, "Down from the Peaks," *Newsline*, July 1999, p. 28.

65. Shireen Mazari, who defended the Kargil operation as "necessary and legitimate," also concedes that the Pakistan army "got sucked incrementally into a larger military operation by India with the latter's induction of reinforcements, the Bofors guns and use of [its air force]. Pakistan had not anticipated this." Shireen M. Mazari, *The Kargil Conflict 1999: Separating Fact from Fiction* (Islamabad: Ferozsons, 2003), p. 44.

66. Raj Chengappa, Zahid Hussain, and Sujatha Shenoy, "Face-Saving Retreat," *India Today*, July 19, 1999, p. 24.

67. Faruqi, *Rethinking the National Security of Pakistan*, p. 7.

68. Ibid., p. 15.

69. Security analysts in Pakistan did try to use this principle of "deniability" after the fact. Ikram Sehgal openly wrote that there was direct Pakistani involvement: "The Kashmiri mujahideen in Kargil blamed the establishment [for] making the 'cardinal mistake' of stating that the mujahideen have gone across the LOC, and said it should have maintained that the fighting was taking place in 'no-man's land.'" Zaffar Abbas, "Whodunnit?" *Herald* (Karachi), July 1999, p. 66. Mazari, on the other hand, justified the use of Northern Light Infantry to point out that Pakistani military planners saw the Kargil operation simply as a tactical operation to preempt further Indian adventurism in the Dras-Kargil sector and attributes the troop crossing of the Line of Control to the "nature of the terrain." Mazari, *The Kargil Conflict*, p. 64.

70. Mazari, *The Kargil Conflict,* p. 14. For what is described as the complete verbatim record of two nearly back-to-back conversations between Musharraf and his deputy, see Ashok Krishna and P. R. Chari, eds., *Kargil: The Tables Turned* (New Delhi: Manohar, 2001), app. 10, pp. 315–20.

71. Michael Krepon, "Pak's Pact with Blood," *Outlook,* June 28, 1999, p. 16.

72. Nawaz Sharif along with his army chief, General Pervez Musharraf, also met the leaders of the United Jihad Council, an umbrella organization representing fifteen militant groups. See Navnita Chadha Behera, *State, Identity and Violence: Jammu, Kashmir and Ladakh* (New Delhi: Manohar, 2000), p. 269.

73. Maleeha Lodhi, "Anatomy of a Debacle," *Newsline,* July 1999, p. 32.

74. Ibid.

75. In June 1999, the powerful House Relations Committee had approved a resolution by an overwhelming 22-5 vote, calling for "the withdrawal of Pakistani forces" and urging the administration to consider opposing loans to Islamabad from the international financial institutions. Hassan Ali Shahzeb, "Clueless in Washington," *Newsline,* July 1999, p. 23.

76. Lodhi, "Anatomy of a Debacle," pp. 31–36. Also, Ayaz Amir, "A Fiasco in the Making," *Dawn* (Karachi), June 26, 1999.

77. Jones, *Pakistan: Eye of the Storm*, p. 268.

78. Jones notes that Pakistani officers attending courses at the Military Academy, the Staff College, and the National Defence College routinely analyze and discuss every war, battle, and skirmish in the history of the Pakistani army, but they still do not talk about Kargil. The usual explanation given by instructors is that "not all the details have yet been collected." Ibid., p. 100. Baig wonders how the army could be blamed for the Kargil fiasco: "It is outrightly tragic and a myopic view, because no government can even be viable and can sustain itself if the armed forces are discredited and their morale is sacrificed at the altar of expediency." Zaffar Abbas, "Whodunnit?" *Herald* (Karachi), July 1999.

79. Shireen Mazari insists that Nawaz Sharif panicked even though he had the upper hand: "Had the Kargil tactical operation been allowed to sustain itself for a few more weeks (till the end of August 1999) most military analysts I spoke to felt it would have led to a Pakistan-India dialogue, if Sharif had not dashed to Washington and given in to U.S. pressure." Mazari, *The Kargil Conflict,* pp. 53–54.

80. Shireen Mazari largely blames all the political leadership for its various acts of omission and commission during the Kargil crisis. See ibid., pp. 22–27.

81. Ashley J. Tellis, C. Christine Fair, and Jamison Jo Medby, *Limited Conflicts under the Nuclear Umbrella: Indian and Pakistani Lessons from the Kargil Crisis* (Santa Monica: Rand Corporation, 2000), p. 80.

82. Ibid., p. x.

83. Ibid., p. 7.

84. Swami notes that this explains how the top Inter-Service Intelligence officials could attend the Lashkar-e-Taiba convention in November 2002, despite international condemnation of the organization. Praveen Swami, "Terrorism in Jammu and Kashmir in Theory and Practice," *India Review* 2 (July 2003): 86.

85. Brigadier S. K. Malik, *The Quranic Concept of War* (Lahore: Wajid Ali, 1979), p. 59.

86. The Muslim components of Dinia included a "Pakistan" consisting of the Muslim-majority provinces in the northwest, "Bangistan" or "Bang-i-Islamistan" (Bengal), and several innovatively named Muslim sovereign states. While it confined "Hindoostan" to a shrunken space in northern India with a vengeance, it allowed for non-Muslim countries like "Sikhia," "Akhoostan," "Dravidha," and such sovereign linguistic states as Andhra, Karnatar, and Maharashtar. See Ayesha Jalal, "Conjuring Pakistan: History as Official Imaging," *International Journal of Middle East Studies* 27 (February 1995): 75.

87. Stanley Wolpert, *Zulfi Bhutto of Pakistan: His Life and Times* (Oxford University Press, 1993), p. 162. A Pakistani expert in geopolitics writes that "as undivided and one, expansionist, nuclear and hegemonic 'Akhund Bharat' is a total menace to Afro-Asian and world peace. The world may realize the blessing of the Balkanization of Bharat one day." Ikram Azam, *Pakistan's Geopolitical and Strategic Compulsions* (Lahore: Progressive, 1980), p. 141.

88. Praveen Swami, "A Widening Network," *Frontline*, January 3, 2003, p. 35.

89. The Lashkar-e-Taiba was renamed Jamaat-al-Dawa (Party of Preachers) and its magazine *Jihad* was retitled *Ghazwa* (Battle). The Jaish-i-Mohammed and the TJP renamed themselves Khuddam-ul-Islam and Millat-i-Islami, respectively. The Jaish-i-Mohammed Bookstore was now called the Reformatory Library, and its magazine *Jaish-e-Muhammad* was now *al-Islah* (Reform). For details, see Behera and Mathew, *Pakistan in a Changing Strategic Context*, p. 30. General Musharraf's comments were made in a January 12 speech, which Mazari describes as "basically a tactical operational shift in Pakistan's Kashmir policy." Shireen Mazari, "Pakistan in the Post-9/11 Milieu," *Strategic Studies* 22 (Autumn 2002): 7. Also, Karl Vick, "Sceptics Question Sincerity of Crackdown by Musharraf," *Washington Post*, April 28, 2002; "Pak Advises Militant Outfits to Keep Low Profile," *Indian Express* (New Delhi), December 17, 2001.

90. President Musharraf, interview with Malini Parthsarthy, *Hindu* (Chennai), April 1, 2002.

91. The United Jihad Council, an umbrella organization for fifteen militant groups, had announced that it was cutting down the number of parties to between seven and nine for coordinating their activities in a more organized manner. See "Pak Plugging for Swadeshi Kashmir Movement?" *Indian Express* (New Delhi), January 3, 2002; and "Kashmir Militant Groups Merging," *News* (Lahore), March 8, 2002. For more details, see Behera and Mathew, *Pakistan in a Changing Strategic Context*, pp. 37–38.

92. Cited from Kamran Khan, "Army Believes Kashmir Freedom Is Near," *News* (Lahore), May 2002 (www.jang.com.pk/thenews/may2002-daily/29-05-2002/main/main4.htm). Earlier, General Javed Nasir, writing about the Indian motives for the cease-fire in Kashmir in 2001, stated that the Indian leadership is convinced that Kashmir is a lost cause. The army's morale in Kashmir is on the brink of total collapse. And if India does not withdraw troops from Kashmir, it would lead to India's disintegration. See Javed Nasir, "Ceasefire, Indian Motives and Pakistan's Response," *Nation*

(Lahore), January 23, 2001 (www.syberwurx.com/nation/daily/today/editor/opi4.htm). See also Javed Nasir, "Calling the Indian Army Chief's Bluff," *Defence Journal* (February–March 1999) (www.defencejournal.com/feb-mar99/chief-bluff.htm).

93. Quoted from "Musharraf: 'There Is Nothing Happening on the Line of Control,'" *Washington Post*, May 25, 2002 (www.washingtonpost.com/wp-dyn/articles/A10049-2002May25.html).

94. Lieutenant General Javed Hassan, presentation at the Brookings Institution. Also discussed in Ayesha Siddiqa-Agha, "Another Round of War Hysteria?" *Friday Times* (Lahore), May 24–30, 2002 (www.thefridaytimes.com/news7.htm).

95. Khan, "Army Believes Kashmir Freedom Is Near." A Pakistani army mountain division was also reported to have conducted exercises across the Line of Control with about 3,000 jihadis. See Rahul Bedi, "The Military Dynamics," *Frontline*, June 8–21, 2002.

96. See "Pak Amassing Militants for Aid in Case of War," *Indian Express* (New Delhi), May 29, 2002; Vishal Thapar, "Militants Get Night Vision Devices, Better Weapons," *Hindustan Times* (New Delhi), May 31, 2002; and, K. P. Nayar, "Western Intelligence Spots Ranks of Saboteurs behind Enemy Lines," *Telegraph* (Kolkata), June 2, 2002 (www.telegraphindia.com/front_pa.htm).

97. Raj Chengappa and Indrani Bagchi, "Gambling on Peace," *India Today*, January 19, 2004, pp. 26–27.

98. "India and Pakistan: Good Neighbors but Going Where?" *Economist*, June 24, 2004 (www.economist.com/world/asia/PrinterFriendly.cfm?story_id=2792524).

99. Rehana Hakim, "Kashmir's Endless Autumn," *Newsline*, November 2004, p. 50. For a detailed discussion on this issue, see chapter 5.

100. Zaffar Abbas, "The Pakistani Al-Qaeda," *Herald* (Karachi), August 2004, p. 57.

101. Behera and Mathew, *Pakistan in a Changing Strategic Context*, p. 13.

102. Khaled Ahmed, "*Jihad* and the Price It Extracts," *Lahore Friday Times*, June 14–20, 2002 (www.thefridaytimes.com/news10.htm).

103. Abbas, "The Pakistani Al-Qaeda," p. 55.

104. Lieutenant General Safdar Hussain, interview by Qwais Tohid, *Newsline*, April 2005, p. 53.

105. Azmat Abbas, "Death Wish," *Herald* (Karachi), July 2003, p. 47. A midlevel official belonging to the political administration agrees: "Even after the government ditched the Taliban, security agencies in Pakistan continued to welcome these militants in Waziristan." M. Ilyas Khan, "Mixed Signals," *Herald* (Karachi), March 2004, p. 64.

106. The latter was banned on September 29, 2001, in compliance with UN Security Council orders to crack down on terrorist outfits. The ban ostensibly led to the creation of al-Aalami, whose name was first heard in June 2002. Amir Mir, "Terror's Allies," *Herald* (Karachi), August 2004, p. 59.

107. On May 8, 2002, there was a suicide bombing on Club Road, in front of the Sheraton Hotel. On June 14, 2002, the U.S. Consulate on Abdullah Haroon Road was targeted. The ringleader of this suicide squad told the authorities about Maulana Jabbar, who is believed to have brought together Pakistan's first group of suicide bombers. Subsequent attacks took place on the Christian School at Gharial, in Jhika Gali near

Murree, on August 5, 2002, and the chapel of the Taxila Christian Hospital on August 9, 2002. Azmat Abbas, "Standards," *Herald* (Karachi), January 2005, pp. 38–42; and Abbas, "Death Wish," pp. 45–46.

108. Tim McGric, "The Monster Within," *Time Asia*, January 16, 2004.

109. Ayaz Amir, "Grow up, Pakistan," *Newsline*, January 2004, p. 17–18.

110. Khaled Ahmed, "Tragic Fallout of the Doctrine of `Strategic Depth,'" *Friday Times* (Lahore), October 25–31, 2002.

111. Abdus Sattar Ghazali, "Pakistani Suspect Denied Bail in U.S.," *Dawn* (Karachi), June 12, 2005 (www.dawn.com/2005/06/12/top10.htm [August 10, 2006]).

112. Intikhab Amir, "One Step Forward, Two Steps Back," *Herald* (Karachi), December 2004, p. 30.

113. "*Jihadi* Rate of Growth: No Quick-Fix for Pakistan's Economy," *Financial Express*, June 18, 2002.

114. Akmal Hussain, "Is GDP Growth Sustainable?" *Daily Times* (Lahore), May 1, 2006.

115. Vali Nasr, interview by Asim Butt, *Herald* (Karachi), January 2003, p. 92.

116. Aamer Ahmed Khan, "Art of the Possible," *Herald* (Karachi), January 2005, p. 33.

117. M. Ilyas Khan, "Waziristan Descent into Anarchy," *Herald* (Karachi), March 2004, p .62. "The locals have developed social, economic, and religious relations with foreign elements and were in fact encouraged to do so by past governments. Now, they are being asked to hand these foreigners over to the authorities. This makes no sense to them." Amir, "One Step Forward, Two Steps Back," p. 32.

118. Pervez Musharraf, "Kashmir Is the Central Issue," *India Today*, March 23–29, 2004, p. 27.

119. Husein Haqqani, "Behind the Mask of Enlightened Moderation," *Nation* (Lahore), June 15, 2005. In December 2003, there were reports that Pakistan was, once again, playing the same deadly game of bleed-thy-neighbor as the Taliban regrouped, rearmed, and reorganized on Pakistani territory for a future jihad. Afghan foreign minister Abdullah Abdullah, during his visit to the United States, told the Congress that the Taliban leaders were brazenly announcing their plans from mosques and madaris in Quetta, their new headquarters. Pakistan also tried to "pull a Kargil" on Afghanistan as Pakistani militias crossed the Durand Line in the summer, occupying positions 5 kilometers inside Afghan territory. The Americans were summoned and told of the incursions: "Musharraf admitted and said it won't happen again." Secretary of State Colin Powell reportedly assured Afghans that the United States "won't tolerate any breach of the Durand Line." Seema Sirohi, "Strategic Depths," *Outlook*, December 8, 2003, p. 24.

120. Haqqani, "Behind the Mask of Enlightened Moderation."

121. On November 15, some twenty months after the ban on these groups in their previous incarnations, the government suddenly realized they were flouting the antiterrorism act by operating under new names. A brief order was issued to reinforce the ban. The groups proscribed under the fresh directive were the Tehrik-e-Islami Pakistan, earlier known as the Tehrik-e-Jaffria; the Millat-e-Islami, which was previously working as the Sipah-e-Sahaba Pakistan; and Khuddam-ul-Islam, the new face of the

Jaish-i-Mohammed. The police were now familiar with the drill, and more than 130 party offices all over the country and beyond were sealed within forty-eight hours. Zaffar Abbas, "Inaction Replay," *Herald* (Karachi), December 2003, p. 56.

122. Ibid.

123. Maulana Jabbar is believed to have brought together Pakistan's first group of suicide bombers, which carried out at least three successful attacks. Jabbar was also a member of the Harkat-ul-Mujahideen until 1999. He then joined the Jaish-i-Mohammed, the Harkat-ul-Mujahideen splinter formed by Maulani Masood Azhar after he was freed on December 31, 1999, from an Indian prison in exchange for the passengers of a hijacked Indian airliner. Abbas, "Standards," pp. 38–42.

124. Stephen Philip Cohen, "The Nation and the State of Pakistan," *Washington Quarterly* 25 (Summer 2002): 111.

125. This was part of the "mullah-military deal" whereby Musharraf agreed to relinquish the post of Pakistan army chief in December 2004, a commitment he never abided by; the MMA supported parliamentary ratification of his position as president. Najam Sethi, "Playing Tactical Games," *Indian Express* (New Delhi), January 17, 2004.

126. The National Security Council is headed by the president. Other members include the Joint Chiefs of Staff and the three service chiefs. The civilians are represented by the prime minister, the chief ministers of the four provinces, leader of the opposition in the National Assembly, and the leader of the Senate. The constitution of the National Security Council is incongruent in that unelected members outweigh the elected members. Amir Mir, "Coup de Grâce," *Herald* (Karachi), May 2004, p. 75.

127. International Centre for Peace Initiatives, *The Future of Pakistan* (Mumbai: Strategic Foresight Group, 2002), p. 82.

128. *The Way Out: Interviews, Impressions, Statements and Messages, Benazir Bhutto* (Karachi: Mahmood, 1988), p. 150.

129. General Pervez Musharraf, President of Pakistan's Address to the Nation, April 5, 2002.

130. Jalal develops this thesis in her seminal work, *The State of Martial Rule*.

131. For a classic study on this issue, see Rounaq Jahan, *Pakistan: Failure in National Integration* (Columbia University Press, 1972).

132. Of the 1.48 million acres of land made cultivable by the Ghulam Muhammad Barrage, 0.87 million acres were allocated to defense personnel, tribesmen of Quetta and the Frontier, and settlers from East Pakistan. Of the 0.64 million acres of the Guddu Barrage land, 0.32 million acres were allocated to defense personnel, civil bureaucrats, and families displaced by the construction of the new capital, Islamabad (in Punjab), and the Tarbela and Mangla dams (in Punjab and North-West Frontier Province). Of the 0.28 million acres of Sukkur Barrage land, 0.13 million acres were given to army personnel. In most instances "defense personnel" were Punjabis. See Abbas Rashid and Fardia Shaheed, *Pakistan: Ethno-Politics and Contending Elites* (Geneva: United Nations Research Institute for Social Development, June 1993), p. 16.

133. Shaheen Sardar Ali and Javaid Rehman, *Indigenous Peoples and Ethnic Minorities of Pakistan, Constitutional and Legal Perspectives* (Surrey: Curzon Press, 2001), p. 162.

134. B. Muralidhar Reddy, "Islamabad Looks to Calm Domestic Tension," *Hindu* (Chennai), May 5, 2005.

135. M. Ilyas Khan, "Back to the Hills," *Herald* (Karachi), September 2004, pp. 52–53.

136. International Centre for Peace Initiatives, *Future of Pakistan*, p. 88. Also, Ian Talbot, "The Punjabization of Pakistan: Myth or Reality," in *Pakistan: Nationalism without a Nation*, edited by Christophe Jaffrelot (New Delhi: Manohar, 2002), pp. 51–62.

137. Nawabzada Baloch Marri, interview by Shahzada Zulfiwar, *Newsline*, September 2004, pp. 38–39.

138. Clive Dewey's empirical historical research has fruitfully traced the "military-ethnic equation" in Pakistan to the colonial legacy of recruitment from a handful of "martial-caste" communities and reigns of Punjab. The British recruiting policy was so narrow that 75 percent of the Pakistan army came from three districts of the Punjab (Rawalpindi, Jhelum, and Campbellpur) and from two districts of Sarhad (Mardan and Kohat). Cited in Talbot, "The Punjabization of Pakistan," pp. 53–54.

139. Rashid, "Pakistan: Ethno-Politics and Contending Elites," p. 10.

140. Tahir Amin, *Ethno-National Movements of Pakistan: Domestic and International Factors* (Islamabad: Institute of Policy Studies, 1993), p. 88.

141. Ali and Rehman, *Indigenous Peoples and Ethnic Minorities*, p. 2.

142. Mehtab Ali Shah, *The Foreign Policy of Pakistan: Ethnic Impacts on Diplomacy* (London: I. B. Tauris, 1997), p. 196.

143. Ibid., p. 146.

144. Ibid., p. 68. Shah also cites an interview with a young Sindhi leader, Asif Baladi, who interpreted the slogan of Kashmir becoming a part of Pakistan as a "Punjabi ploy to impose centralization on Sindh under the guise of confronting India over the Kashmir issue" (p. 67).

145. Cited in ibid., p. 106.

Chapter Four

1. See *Facets of a Proxy War* (New Delhi: Government of India, 1991). *Pakistan's Targets: Punjab and Kashmir* is also an Indian government publication. See also K. Subrahmanyam, "Kashmir," *Strategic Analysis* 13, no. 2 (May 1990): 111–98. His analysis is based on the scenario presented by "Operation Topac," a fictional account of a scheme designed to destabilize Jammu and Kashmir that was supposedly hatched in 1988 under the military dictatorship of General Mohammed Zia-ul-Haq of Pakistan. Prem Shankar Jha, *Kashmir 1947: Rival Versions of History* (Oxford University Press, 1996). Jha presents the Indian viewpoint on the issue of the accession of Kashmir to India in 1947.

2. Shaheen Akhtar, *Uprising in Indian-Held Jammu and Kashmir* (Islamabad: Institute of Regional Studies, 1991); Alastair Lamb, *Kashmir: A Disputed Legacy, 1846–1990* (Oxford University Press, 1992). Lamb questions the legality and validity of the Instrument of Accession, as argued by Pakistan. See also Mushtaq Rahman, *Divided Kashmir:*

Old Problems, New Opportunities for India, Pakistan and for Kashmiri People (Boulder, Colo.: Lynne Rienner, 1996).

3. Sumit Ganguly, *The Crisis in Kashmir: Portents of War, Hopes of Peace* (Cambridge University Press, 1997).

4. Sumantra Bose, *The Challenge in Kashmir: Democracy, Self-Determination and a Just Peace* (New Delhi: Sage, 1997).

5. Ganguly's argument in *The Crisis in Kashmir* is linked to the India-Pakistan dimension of the Kashmir conflict, and he does not address the Jammu and Ladakh factor at all. He also does not take into account the deep divide between Kashmiri Muslims and Kashmiri Pandits that emerged in the 1990s. Bose briefly touches on it in *The Challenge in Kashmir* but squarely blames the successive Congress governments in New Delhi for not addressing Jammu's grievances.

6. Cited in F. M. Hassnain, *Freedom Struggle in Kashmir* (New Delhi: Rima, 1988), p. 140.

7. Early attempts to forge Muslim unity and revive the Muslim Conference led by Sardar Guar Lehman did not come to fruition primarily because of Chowdhary Ghulam Abbas's deep distrust of Kashmiri leaders. These differences were resolved only when the two sides agreed to unanimously elect Chowdhary Abbas as the president of the Muslim Conference and Qureshi Mohammad Yousuf from Kashmir as the general secretary.

8. For details, see Sisir Gupta, *Kashmir: A Study in India-Pakistan Relations* (New Delhi: Asia House, 1966), pp. 110–55.

9. Balraj Puri, *Jammu and Kashmir: Triumph and Tragedy of Indian Federalization* (New Delhi: Sterling, 1981), p. 116.

10. Balraj Puri, "Jammu and Kashmir," in *State Politics in India*, edited by Myron Weiner (Princeton University Press, 1968), p. 219. Korbel remarked that "no dictator could do it better." Joseph Korbel, *Danger in Kashmir* (Princeton University Press, 1966), p. 222.

11. Puri points out that communal considerations have officially been a part of the recruitment of government employees ever since the Glancy Commission, appointed after the mass Muslim upsurge of 1931, recommended that "due regard should be paid to the legitimate interests of every community in the matter of recruitment to government services and the grant of scholarship for training." Balraj Puri, *Simmering Volcano: Study of Jammu's Relations with Kashmir* (New Delhi: Sterling, 1983), p. 81.

12. Gupta, *Kashmir*, p. 378. The Praja Parishad supported the "land to the tiller" policy in principle, with some specific changes. These included: "fix the economic unit according to productive capacity of the land; grant full proprietary rights to beneficiaries; exempt lands held by religious institutions and trusts from application of such laws; rehabilitate suitable persons displaced from lands under the scheme; exempt from assessment of revenue all uneconomic holdings; and, same compensation policy to be pursued as in the rest of India." *Programme: All Jammu and Kashmir* (Jammu: Praja Parishad, n.d.).

13. Cited by Ashutosh Varshney, "Three Compromised Nationalisms: Why Kashmir Has Been a Problem," in *Perspectives on Kashmir: The Roots of Conflict in South Asia*, edited by Raju G. C. Thomas (Boulder, Colo.: Westview Press, 1992), p. 213. This debate

was carried out between three eminent political leaders—Sheikh Abdullah, Pandit Nehru, and Syama Prasad Mookerjee—through correspondence. It has been published as *Integrate Kashmir: The Mookerjee-Nehru-Abdullah Correspondence* (Lucknow: Bharat Press, n.d.).

14. Mookerjee's letter to Abdullah, dated February 13, 1953, *Integrate Kashmir*, p. 77.

15. The small relief provided by the government of India never reached Zanskar; it was distributed among the Muslims of the Suru Karste area in Kargil tehsil. See Shridhar Kaul and H. N. Kaul, *Ladakh through the Ages: Towards a New Identity* (New Delhi: Indus, 1992), p. 183.

16. Ibid., p. 195.

17. Cheewang Rigzin, president of the Buddhist Association, Ladakh, Memorandum to the "Prime Minister of India on behalf of the people of Ladakh." The full text is reprinted in Navnita Chadha Behera, *State, Identity and Violence: Jammu, Kashmir and Ladakh* (New Delhi: Manohar, 2000), pp. 311–14.

18. Kushak Bakula, as cited in Kaul and Kaul, *Ladakh through the Ages*, p. 185.

19. Prem Nath Bazaz, *The History of Struggle for Freedom in Kashmir* (New Delhi: Kashmir, 1954), p. 553. The main demands of Ladakhis included the formation of a Ministry of Ladakh Affairs headed by a popularly elected Ladakhi member of the Legislative Assembly, adequate representation in the legislature and civil service, the establishment of Panchayat and Rural Development Departments, development funds for constructing roads and canals and promoting agriculture and horticulture, and replacement of Kashmiri police by local personnel. They wanted Bodhi, the mother tongue of the Ladakhis, to be made the medium of instruction for school education, and special provisions made for facilitating higher education and training in medicine, law, engineering, agriculture, and forestry. See ibid., pp. 203–04.

20. Syama Prasad Mookerjee, letter to Pandit Nehru, dated February 17, 1953. *Integrate Kashmir*, pp. 88–94.

21. Under this plan, three provinces—namely, Kashmir Valley, Jammu, and Poonch-Mirpur-Rajouri—would each have an executive head and council of ministers responsible to the provincial legislature. The regional councils would administer Ladakh and Gilgit. State legislatures would be empowered for altering the area of these autonomous units and for establishing new units. Vidya Bhushan, *State Politics and Government: Jammu and Kashmir* (Jammu: Jaykay Book House, 1985), p. 185.

22. Sheikh Abdullah, letter to Syama Prasad Mookerjee, dated February 18, 1953. *Integrate Kashmir*, pp. 95–107.

23. Abdullah's undelivered speech, as cited in Puri, *Jammu and Kashmir*, p. 231. He admitted that the National Conference had lost its hold on Kashmiri Muslims as their minds had moved from fear to frustration and from frustration to disillusionment. The Muslim middle class realized that while accession to India had opened the doors of progress to Hindus and Sikhs, Muslims had become like the proverbial frog in the well.

24. Ibid., p. 100. Jammu leaders of the National Conference differed with Abdullah on this issue.

25. P. S. Verma, *Jammu and Kashmir: At the Political Crossroads* (New Delhi: Vikas, 1994), p. 42.

26. Karan Singh, *Autobiography* (Oxford University Press, 1994), pp. 153–54.

27. At the All-Kashmir People's Convention in 1968, a more understanding Sheikh Abdullah admitted that "it was fear and suspicions of one region regarding the other which apparently prompted Jammu to opt for merger with India against Kashmiris wanting to join Pakistan" and assured that their regional interests would be safeguarded. *Times of India*, October 25, 1969.

28. This was first introduced in the NEFA after the Chinese aggression in 1962. Under this system, Ladakh was manned by the Indian Frontier Administrative Personnel. The deputy commissioner-cum-development commissioner of the district and the assistant commissioners of Kargil, Nubra, and Nyoma were also drawn from the same service cadres. Kaul and Kaul, *Ladakh through the Ages*, p. 220.

29. In the 1967 Legislative Assembly elections, the Congress nominated Kushak Bakula's nominee Sonam Wangyal for the Leh seat, but unofficially his opponent Kushak Thiksey enjoyed the patronage of the state government. The relations between Ghulam Mohammad Sadiq and Kushak Bakula were further embittered when Sonam Norbu, till then Ladakh's deputy commissioner, was nominated to the legislative council as a prelude to his inclusion in the state cabinet. Bakula's supporters perceived it as an attempt to divide the Ladakhi Buddhists by ignoring the claims of the elected representative, Sonam Wangyal. Ibid., p. 231.

30. Although 84 percent of the population of Leh district is Buddhist, Bodhi teachers were provided in only 32 of the 252 government schools. Despite specific recommendations of the Gajendragadkar Commission, the state government had not set up a degree college for two Lakh inhabitants of the region.

31. The Jammu and Kashmir Secretariat had *only one* Buddhist employee, and there was no Buddhist among 18,000 employees of nine corporate sector units. *Hindustan Times* (New Delhi), May 14, 1992.

32. Rs 25 crore was spent under the World Bank–aided Social Forestry Schemes, but Leh district was ignored. It had no share in the funds disbursed by the Central Land Development Bank and the Khadi and Village Industries Corporation in the state. For tourism development schemes in 1990, the sum of Rs 59 lakh was earmarked for the Valley, whereas Leh was given only Rs 7 lakh, and the neighboring Kargil district Rs 17 lakh. *Hindustan Times* (New Delhi), May 15, 1992, and April 20, 1995.

33. Behera, *State, Identity and Violence*, p. 218.

34. Yoginder Sikand provided an excellent historical account of such ties in an essay, "Inter-Community Relations in Leh, Ladakh," e-mailed to the author on November 22, 2004.

35. Martijn Van Beek, "Dangerous Liaisons: Hindu Nationalism and Buddhist Radicalism in Ladakh," in *Religious Radicalism and Security in South Asia*, edited by Satu P. Kimaye, Robert G. Wirsing, and Mohan Malik (Honolulu: Asia-Pacific Center for Security Studies, 2004), pp. 193–218 (www.apcss.org/Publications/Edited%20Volumes/ReligiousRadicalism/ReligiousRadicalism.htm).

36. *Frontline*, December 30, 1994.

37. Beek, "Dangerous Liaisons," pp. 198, 205.

38. Cited in ibid., p. 205.

39. Interview with the then Ladakh Muslim Association president, Akbar Ladakhi.

40. Beek, "Dangerous Liaisons," p. 206.

41. Based on my conversations with Ladakh Buddist Association leaders, October 1995.

42. See Navnita Chadha Behera, "'Autonomy' in J&K: The Forgotten Identities of Ladakh," *Faultlines* 6 (2000): 49–52. For a detailed account of the working and structural and political problems faced by Leh AHC, see Martijn Van Beek, "Hill Councils, Development and Democracy: Assumptions and Experiences from Ladakh," *Alternatives* 24 (1999): 441.

43. The Kargil Muslims had a meager 5.5 percent representation in the Ladakh Scouts in comparison with their nearly 50 percent share of the population in the region. After the Kargil conflict, the army began a series of initiatives under the Operation Sadbhavna scheme that included the provision of free transport and the establishment of schools and vocational training centers in the villages along the Line of Control. This led to a backlash from the LBA, which repeatedly denounced the government's "pampering" of Muslims. The program was later expanded to central Ladakh and the Tibetan border areas, and more than 2,500 Ladakhi Buddhists were also recruited into the expanding Ladakh Scouts regiment and paramilitary units. The LBA nonetheless saw reason to complain because the Special Security Bureau program training Buddhist villagers in the use of weapons—a program initiated in the wake of the Sino-Indian war of 1962—was discontinued. According to the LBA, the discontinuation was due to Muslim complaints that only Buddhists were given training and weapons. Beek, "Dangerous Liaisons," p. 215.

44. Martijn Van Beek, "Making a Difference? Reflections on Decentralization, Recognition and Empowerment." Paper presented at conference on Global Development in the 21st Century, Polson Institute of Global Studies, Cornell University, September 21–22, 2001.

45. Ibid., p. 12.

46. Ibid.

47. *Kashmir Times* (Jammu), July 10, 1997.

48. According to the Ladakh Autonomous Hill Development Council Act, one of the executive councilors must be a member of the "principal minority" (that is, a Muslim), but this had not been honored since the elections for the second LAHDC in 2001.

49. Beek points to the tense relationship between the two communities as symbolized by a "loudspeaker war" between the Sunni mosque and the Buddhist Chokhang Vihara, on opposite sides of the main bazaar of Leh. From 1996 until 1999, every time the call for prayer would sound from the mosque, the LBA switched on a tape with religious chants or songs. The practice was in retaliation for the fact that several local mosques in the suburbs and villages around Leh had installed loudspeakers. Beek, "Dangerous Liaisons," p. 206.

50. Ibid., p. 208. The UPA government renamed it the Ladakh Singhey Khabab Spring festival. *Hindu* (Chennai), June 1, 2006.

51. Ibid., p. 212.

52. Ibid., p. 218.

53. Praveen Swami, "Snowstorm of Hate," *Frontline*, February 25–March 10, 2006, pp. 42–43.

54. While both have a chauvinistic approach to religious practice, the IKMT embraces reform in matters of education, particularly that of girls. See ibid., p. 43.

55. In the civil secretariat, Jammu's representation was less than 10 percent. Only two of thirty-five secretaries/commissioners were from Jammu region, and its employees from all cadres constituted no more than 8 percent of the total strength. All twelve corporations of the Jammu and Kashmir government had their headquarters in Srinagar, and almost 100 percent of the employees were from the Valley. The headquarters of most central offices were also in Srinagar. According to a statement made in the state assembly in 1988–89, 43,000 out of 69,000 registered unemployed youth belonged to Jammu region alone. Behera, *State, Identity and Violence*, pp. 219–20.

56. In the prime minister's Special Assistance program of 1986, Jammu got only Rs 15.5 crore, about 8 percent of the total assistance of Rs 179.73 crore, as compared with the 40 percent share of Rs 79.06 crore for the Valley. Of the remaining Rs 92.76 crore earmarked for the common development of three regions, more than Rs 80 crore was allocated to the Valley.

57. Only Rs 10 crore had been spent on the Chennai project as compared with Rs 500 crore spent on the projects in Kashmir Valley. Other power projects—Upper Jhelum, Lower Jhelum, Upper Sind, Mohra, and Gandarbal—were in the Valley with a production capacity of 328 megawatts.

58. These included the postgraduate Sher-e-Kashmir Institute of Medical Sciences, the dental college, veterinary college, agricultural university, artificial limb center, and regional engineering college.

59. Based on my interviews with the activists from JMM and its president, Virender Grover.

60. Based on my conversations with intellectuals, journalists, and political leaders in Jammu.

61. Praveen Swami, "A Turning Point," *Frontline*, November 5–18, 2005 (www.flonnet.com/fl2223/stories/20051118004402700.htm [August 7, 2006]).

62. On October 26, 2005, a day before the Congress's central leadership was to announce its decision on who would occupy the chief minister's post in Jammu and Kashmir, twenty-one Congress and Congress-affiliated members of the Legislative Assembly (including key cabinet ministers such as Power Minister Mohammad Sharif Niaz, Health Minister Suman Bhagat, Roads and Buildings Minister G. A. Mir, Minister of State for Finance Babu Singh, Minister of State for Sports Yogesh Sawhney, Minister of State for Revenue Ramesh Kumar, Minister of State for Forests Thakur Puran Singh, Minister of State for Transport Raman Bhalla, Minister of State for Housing Abdul Majid Wani, and Minister of State for Tourism Jugal Kishore) let it be known that they had submitted their resignations to the speaker.

63. "The Veiled Strategy," *Probe India*, May 1991, p. 22.

64. See www.kashmir-information.com/Miscellaneous/slogans.html.

65. I have discussed the Kashmiri Pandit community's attempts to reconstruct their

history in view of their present political interests in detail elsewhere. Behera, *State, Identity and Violence*, pp. 227–29. See also Panun Kashmir Movement, "Destruction of Cultural Symbols and Shrines of Kashmir" (http://207.159.86.9/Atrocities/Temples/); "Kashmiris Demand a Homeland" (www.kashmir-information.com/Miscellaneous/homeland1.html); "Persecution of Kashmiri Hindus: A Historical Evidence" (www.kashmir-information.com/Miscellaneous/ Persecution.html); M. K. Rasgotra, "Slow Eviction of Kashmiri Pandits," reproduced from Koshur Samachar (www.kashmir-information.com/Miscellaneous/homeland1.html). See also Panun Kashmir, *Why Homeland?* (n.d.), p. 6.

66. Rasgotra argues that 1941 marks the beginning of a statistical assault on the Pandit numbers by the junior local Muslim officials, who underestimated the strength of the Pandits by nearly 10–15 percent. The 1981 census had put the Pandit numbers at a little over 124,000 in a total population of 3.1 million, which stood exposed in 1990 when 300,000 Pandits fled the Valley. Rasgotra, "Slow Eviction." For a good account of the politics of numbers, see Alexander Evans, "A Departure from History: Kashmiri Pandits, 1999–2001," *Contemporary South Asia* 11, no. 1 (2002): 23–27.

67. M. K. Teng and C. L. Gadoo, "Human Rights Violations in Kashmir," Kashmiri Smiti Publication (n.d.), p. 3.

68. Committee for Initiative on Kashmir, "*India's Kashmir War*," A Report (New Delhi: March 1990), pp. 43–48.

69. The details are as follows, with the year, constituency, and name of legislator listed in that order: 1957, Amirakadal, Shri Sham Lal Saraf; 1957, Habbakadal, Shri D. P. Dhar; 1957, Kothar, Shri Manohar Nath Koul; 1962, Kothar, Shri Manohar Nath Koul; 1962, Amirakadal, Shri Shamlal Saraf; 1962, Habbakada, Shri D. P. Dhar; 1967, Devsar, Shri Manohar Nath Koul; 1967, Pahalgam, Shri Makhan Lal Fotedar; 1967, Habbakadal, Shri Sri Kanth Kaul; 1972, Pahalgam, Shri Makhan Lal Fotedar; 1977, Pahalgam, Shri Piyarey Lal Handoo; 1983, Pahalgam, Shri Piyarey Lal Handoo; 1987, Habbakadal, Shri Piyarey Lal Handoo; 1996, Habbakadal, Shri Piyarey Lal Handoo (www.kashmir-information.com/Miscellaneous/homeland1.html).

70. See Panun Kashmir, "Homeland Resolution" (http://207.159.86.9/PanunKashmir). The demand for a secure zone with a concentrated Hindu population in the Valley was first raised at a two-day international conference held in Jammu on July 14–15, 1990. It was then modeled after the kind of safe areas created by the United States for the Kurds in Iraq. This was reiterated at a meeting held by the representatives of the Kashmir Overseas Association, the Indo-American Kashmir Forum, and Panun Kashmir on November 14, 1991.

71. K. L. Kaul and M. K. Teng, "Human Rights Violations of Kashmiri Hindus," in *Perspectives on Kashmir*, edited by Thomas, p. 177.

72. Evans, "A Departure from History: Kashmiri Pandits," p. 30.

73. Minister of Revenue, Relief, and Rehabilitation Hakeem Mohammad Yasin had provided this information, drawn from a survey by the Revenue Department. *Times of India* (New Delhi), February 12, 2005. Earlier state legislation against the distress sales of the Pandit properties included the Jammu and Kashmir Migrant's Immovable Prop-

erty (Preservation, Protection and Restraint on Distress Sales) Act of 1997 and Jammu and Kashmir Migrant Proceeding Act of 1997.

74. Anuradha Bhasin, "Pandits: When Will They Return?" *Communalism Combat,* vol. 10, no. 95 (January 2004).

75. *Ministry of Home Affairs, Annual Report 2001–02,* sec. VII. Bhasin, however, reports that during the 2002 state assembly elections, about 59,000 displaced families were listed as voters. Ibid.

76. For a detailed account of these packages, see Internal Displacement Monitoring Report at www.db.idpproject.org/idmc/website/countries.nsf/(httpEnvelopes)/35E3A22ED5B888DB802570B8005A717B?OpenDocument. Also, Bhasin, "Pandits: When Will They Return?"; and M. Mayilvaganan, "Kashmiri Pandits" (www.ipcs.org/nmt_refugees2.jsp? database=1003&country2=Kashmiri%20Pandits).

77. *Greater Kashmir* (Srinegar), May 24, 2006.

78. Riwaz Wani, "Geelani Now Musharraf Baiter," *Indian Express* (New Delhi), February 1, 2006 (www.indianexpress.com/res/web/pIe/archive_full_story.php? content_id=87022 [August 7, 2006].

79. For a discussion of George Grierson's classification in his magisterial *Linguistic Survey of India,* see J. C. Sharma, "Gojri and Its Relationship with Rajasthani," in *Language in India* 2, no. 2 (April 2002).

80. For data on their district distribution, see Behera, *State, Identity and Violence,* p. 234.

81. For details, see ibid., p. 144.

82. Gojri broadcasts over the radio stations at Jammu (1975), and more recently Kathua (1993) and Poonch (1994), along with fortnightly programs on Doordarshan, boosted the morale of Gojri speakers and writers. Private institutions such as Anjuman Taraqqi Gojri Adab, Adabi Sangat Kashmir, Idara Adbiyat, and Gojri Adabi Board, besides dramatic and cultural clubs, were involved in promoting the Gojri language and literature. Gojri journals and magazines such as *Al Insan, Nawai Qoum, Gujjar Desh, Gujjar Gunj,* and *Awaz-e-Gurjar,* published from Jammu, focused on political and economic issues affecting the community. See Rafique Anjum, "Evolution of Gojri Language," *Awaz-e-Gurjar,* January 1996, pp. 6–12.

83. Syed Mushtaq Bukhari, "Pahari, An Ancient, Distinct and Acknowledged Language," *Kashmir Times* (Jammu), January 18, 1992; and "Pahari: A Distinct, Linguistic, Ethnic and Cultural Entity," *Kashmir Times* (Jammu), April 13, 1992.

84. The Paharis include Khatris, Brahmins, and Mahajans among Hindus and the depressed castes of Syed, Qureshi, Manha, Jarals, Dulli, Lohar, Tarkhan, Mochi, Lone, and Dar among Muslims.

85. Three memorandums were submitted to the Regional Autonomy Commission to this effect. These included "Memorandum on Behalf of Poonch-Rajouri Hill Council" by Mohammad Younis Chauhan, President, Poonch-Rajouri Hill Council; "Memorandum for Grant of Regional Council Status for Rajouri and Poonch"; and an individual "Memorandum for Regional Council for Rajouri and Poonch" by Tahir Khurshid Raina.

86. In 1997, out of 4 additional chief secretaries, 10 commissioners/secretaries, 4 sec-retaries, 8 special secretaries, and 14 deputy secretaries, only 1 resident of Rajouri was posted as secretary to the Gujjar and Bakkarwal Advisory Board. Among 38 officers working as heads of departments in the Jammu region, one officer each belonged to Rajouri and Poonch district. Out of approximately 50,000 Group D employees in the civil secretariat, only 2 belonged to these districts. Starred question no. 199 by Mush-taq Ahmad Shah in the Legislative Assembly Budget Session, 1997.

87. "Memorandum for Recommending Statutory Autonomous Hill Development Council for the Chenab Valley Region Consisting of District Doda, Tehsil Gool-Gulabgarh, Dudu Basantgarh of Udhampur District, Lohai Malhar to Bani of Kathua District," submitted to the Regional Autonomy Committee by Sheikh Abdul Rehman, member of the Legislative Assembly from Bhaderwah; Qazi Jalal-ud-Din, member from Inderwal; Mohammad Ayub; Abdul Gani, member from Gool; Abdul Hamid Qazi; Abdul Latif Malik (spokesman); Farooq Ahmed Mir, member from Banihal; Mohammad Ayub Khan and Abdul Aziz; A. R. Fida Kishtwari, chairman, Develop-ment Forum of Kishtwar, and others. Another memorandum to this effect was submitted by G. H. Khan, member from Kishtwar. See Behera, *State, Identity and Vio-lence*, pp. 344–45.

88. Gujjar leader, Masood Choudhary, interview, August 1997.

89. Gujjar leaders Mian Altaf, Masood Choudhary, and Choudhary Talib Hussain, interview, August 1997.

90. Praveen Swami, "Blossoming Mutinies in Kashmir," *Hindu* (Chennai), March 30, 2006.

91. These include Dogri Sanstha, Jammu University Students Federation, Hindu Raksha Smiti, Shree Rajput Youth Federation, Democratic Youth Federation of India, All-India Students Union, Jammu Mukti Morcha, Muslim Federation, and Jammu Maha Sabha.

92. Interviews with political leaders and activists in Kargil, August 1997.

93. *Hindu* (Chennai), May 26, 2005.

94. BalrajPuri, *Simmering Volcano*, pp. 51–52.

95. Ibid., p. 52.

96. *Times of India* (New Delhi), October 25, 1969.

97. *Hindustan Times* (New Delhi), March 14, 1979.

98. Its working chairman, Balraj Puri, was the only exception, and he was uncere-moniously removed in January 1999, barely three months before the submission of its report. Eventually, he released his report separately. See Balraj Puri, *Jammu and Kash-mir: Regional Autonomy (A Report)* (Jammu: Jay Kay Book House, 1999).

99. Praveen Swami, "Towards Greater Autonomy," *Frontline*, July 30, 1999, p. 40.

100. *Indian Express* (New Delhi), May 23, 2006.

101. Praveen Swami, "A Turning Point," *Frontline*, November 5–18, 2005.

102. Praveen Swami, "Through the Looking Glass in J&K," *Hindu* (Chennai), May 29, 2006.

Chapter Five

1. Praveen Swami, "Terrorism in Jammu and Kashmir in Theory and Practice," *India Review* 2 (July 2003): 74–78.

2. Ganguly underlines the phenomenal growth in literacy rates and ranks of the educated, unemployed youth whose political aspirations were choked off by the decaying political institutions in the Valley. See Sumit Ganguly, *The Crisis in Kashmir: Portents of War, Hopes of Peace* (Cambridge University Press, 1997). Swami points to the two near-distinct economies: the reform economy, of small peasants, and the nonreform economy, of artisans, orchard-owners, and small businessmen. The nonreform sector was in some distress in the early 1980s, when the first generation of "tanzeem" leaders would have been forming. Swami, "Terrorism in Jammu and Kashmir," pp. 72–74. A 1994 study reported that 68 percent of trained militants earned between Rs 500 and Rs 1,000 a month, and that another 11 percent earned between Rs 1,000 and 2,000. Only 19 percent were classified as dependents. Forty-two percent worked as laborers, while 19 percent were students, 22 percent farmers, and 14 percent petty traders. Major General Afsir Karim, *Kashmir: The Troubled Frontiers* (New Delhi: Lancer, 1994), pp. 311–12, 254.

3. Mustapha Kamal Pasha, "Beyond the Two-Nation Divide: Kashmir and Resurgent Islam," in *Perspectives on Kashmir: The Roots of Conflict in South Asia*, edited by Raju G. C. Thomas (Boulder, Colo.: Westview Press, 1992, pp. 373–74; Charles Krauthammer, "This Islamic Arc of Crisis Traces a Global Intifada," *International Herald Tribune*, February 17–18, 1990, p. 4; and Akbar S. Ahmed, "Kashmir 1990: Islamic Revolt or Kashmiri Nationalism," *Strategic Studies* 15 (Autumn 1992): 22–29.

4. Yasin Malik, *Our Real Crime* (Srinagar, Jammu and Kashmir, India: JKLF, 1994), pp. 93–98.

5. The Station House Officer at the Police Station Maisooma, Srinagar, was killed in broad daylight outside the Hazratbal shrine on December 1, 1989. For two hours, no one dared remove his body from the road for fear of annoying the militants, who later put it on a garbage cart and left it outside a police station. In another such incident, a police officer and JKLF leader Hamid Sheikh shot at each other in a crowded market area in Srinagar. While Hamid's supporters immediately took him to a hospital, the injured police officer remained bleeding on the road for a few hours. Such attacks were accompanied by warnings to the "traitors" that they would be given exemplary punishment if they were found to be "collaborating with the enemies," meaning the government and the security forces. Ved Marwah, *Uncivil Wars: Pathology of Terrorism in India* (New Delhi: Harper Collins, 1995), p. 61.

6. On January 2, 1990, R. N. P. Singh, assistant central intelligence officer, was shot dead in Anantnag. A subinspector of the Intelligence Bureau (IB), Gopal Chauhan, was killed on January 8, 1990. On the same day, Inspector Hamidullah Bhatt of the state's Counter-Espionage Cell in Srinagar, and Head Constable Ghulam Mustafa Jatoi working in the Criminal Investigation Department's counterintelligence wing, were shot down. Of thirty-two officers in the Valley, the IB had decided to pull out the totally unprotected operatives, numbering twenty-six.

7. Shekhar Gupta, "Kashmir Valley: Militant Siege," *India Today*, January 31, 1990, p. 27.

8. Cited in Tavleen Singh, *Kashmir: A Tragedy of Errors* (New Delhi: Viking, 1995), p. 113.

9. Cited in A. G. Noorani, "The Betrayal of Kashmir: Pakistan's Duplicity and India's Complicity," in *Perspectives on Kashmir*, edited by Thomas, p. 260.

10. Based on my interviews with JKLF militants.

11. Some officials felt it was a failure in correctly *reading* intelligence information rather than gathering information. Interviews with senior Army and Border Security Force (BSF) and police officials. One officer told about a peculiar and sharp rise in the theft of gumboots from shops and houses. In retrospect, he felt that no one suspected that they were being used by the youth for crossing the snowbound mountain passes on the Valley's border with Pakistan.

12. Jagmohan started the first day in office with 35 dead in police shootings and over 400 arrested. During his first week in office, about 90 people, including a dozen security officials, fell to bullets. Prabhu Chawla, "J&K: A Formidable Challenge," *India Today*, February 15, 1990, p. 40.

13. An Asia Watch Report in 1991 stated that the Kashmiri militants did not deny receiving support from Pakistan, and Kashmiri officials acknowledged the existence of training camps inside Pakistan. *Tribune* (Chandigarh), August 1, 1991. This is corroborated by my interviews with JKLF leaders. For details on the structure of the JKLF organization that extended to both sides of the Line of Control, see Tahir Amin, *Mass Resistance in Kashmir: Origin, Evolution, Options* (Islamabad: Institute of Policy Studies, 1995), pp. 94–95.

14. *Nation* (Lahore), November 1, 1991; *Pakistan Times* (Islamabad), October 31, 1991.

15. Conversations with a cross section of active and former militants.

16. The doctors had addressed an open letter to the "Medical Fraternity of the World" on June 26, 1990, protesting the atrocities of the security forces. The All-Kashmiri Engineering Department Employees Union, about 3,000 engineers and 70,000 unskilled laborers including the Kashmiri Pandit chief engineers, staged a *dharna* (sit-down strike) at the district headquarters in the Valley and issued a letter to the administration asking it to release thousands of innocent Kashmiris, including their colleagues, from prisons within and outside Kashmir; direct the security forces to stop harassing engineers and other government employees; and immediately reinstate all dismissed government employees. Lawyers in the Valley struck in protest against the detention of their colleagues and formed a committee challenging the government notification (of May 1, 1990) abolishing the functioning of the designated court in Srinagar related to cases under the Terrorist and Disruptive Activities (Prevention) Act and extended the jurisdiction of the related court in Jammu to the entire state. *Sunday Mail* (New Delhi), July 8, 1990.

17. Interview with a JKLF leader, August 1995.

18. Riyaz Punjabi's statement in "Crossfire: Kashmir, Drift to Disaster," *India Today*, August 31, 1991, p. 84.

19. Based on my interviews with a cross section of people.

20. Swami, "Terrorism in Jammu and Kashmir in Theory and Practice," p. 75.

21. JKLF, "Our Ideology, Aims and Objectives" (shell.comsats.net.pk/~jklf/i2.htm). Also, Amanullah Khan, *Free Kashmir* (Karachi: Central Printing, 1970).

22. Swami, "Terrorism in Jammu and Kashmir in Theory and Practice," pp. 74–75.

23. Farooq Ahmad Dar, widely known by his nom de guerre, Bitta Karate, admitted in a *Newstrack* interview on television that several Kashmiri Pandits had been killed on the orders of top JKLF leader Ishfaq Majid Wani. Cited in Swami, ibid., p. 75.

24. See Amaunullah Khan's interview with Harinder Baweja, *India Today*, December 31, 1992. Also Noorani, "Betrayal of Kashmir," p. 261.

25. Governor Jagmohan had listed 44 active "terrorist organizations' in January 1990. In 1991, Amanullah Khan put their number at 60 to 70. At one point, the army authorities had listed 177 militant outfits.

26. Robert Wirsing, *India, Pakistan and the Kashmir Dispute* (New Delhi: Rupa, 1994), p. 132.

27. When Pakistan cut off the weapons supply and harassed the JKLF cadre to join pro-Pakistan groups, one rebel leader changed the name of his outfit from the Jammu and Kashmir Students Liberation Front to the Islamic Brotherhood. He admitted a little shamefacedly that "we had to do this to stay on the good side of the Pakistanis." See Edward W. Desmond, "Himalyan Ulster," *New York Review*, March 4, 1993.

28. Geelani's major writings include *Nava-i-Hurriyat* (Srinagar, India: Mizan, 1992); *Rudad-i-Qafas*, vol. 1 (Srinagar: al-Huda House, 1993); and *Hijrat-Shahadat* (Srinagar: Tulu, 1998).

29. Geelani, *Hijrat-Shahadat*, pp. 3–4.

30. He writes that nation-worship based on the principle of "my nation, right or wrong" leads to group prejudice, a quality of the pre-Islamic period of *jahiliya*, an age of utter darkness. Geelani, *Rudad-i-Qafas*, p. 3.

31. Yoginder Sikand, "Changing Course of Kashmiri Struggle: From National Liberation to Islamist *Jihad*?" *Economic and Political Weekly*, January 20–26, 2001, p. 221.

32. Ibid., p. 220.

33. Geelani, *Hijrat-Shahadat*, p. 72.

34. Geelani, *Nava-i-Hurriyat*, p. 227.

35. Ibid.

36. Geelani, *Rudad-i-Qafas*, p. 29.

37. *Sunday Mail* (New Delhi), July 8, 1990. The supreme commander of Al Jehad, Sheikh Abdul Aziz, laid down three conditions for the Pandits' return: "First, that India accepts that Kashmir is disputed. Second, India requests the UN to convene a General Assembly session to discuss Kashmir. And, third, that Amnesty International and other human rights organizations be allowed to visit Kashmir."

38. Ibid.

39. Amin notes that each wing of the organization had a leader for military and ideological training, intelligence, supplies, logistics, and finances. All positions together formed the nucleus of the larger body, the *Majlis-i-Shoora*, which was the central command of the Hizb-ul-Mujahideen. See Amin, *Mass Resistance in Kashmir*, p. 92. Also Alifuddin Tarabi, *Hizbul Mujahideen: The Principles and Struggle*, translated from Urdu

(n.d.); and Shamshul Haq, *Hizbul Mujahideen: Its Background and Struggle,* translated from Urdu (Rawalpindi: Markaz Matbruit Kashmir, May 1994).

40. Tarabi, *Hizbul Mujahideen.*

41. Haq, *Hizbul Mujahideen,* p. 24.

42. As translated and cited in Jagmohan, *My Frozen Turbulence* (New Delhi: Allied, 1991), p. 396.

43. Ibid.

44. Khaled Ahmed, "Re-assertion of the Barelvis in Pakistan," *Friday Times* (Lahore), September 8, 2000. For details about the doctrinal roots of major Islamic parties, see Mushahid Hussain, "Among the Believers," *Herald* (Karachi), September 1992, p. 38.

45. Asim Butt, interview with Vali Nasr, *Herald* (Karachi), January 1, 2003, p. 92.

46. Abu Fattada, "Open the Lock with the Key," *Siratul Mustaqeem,* June 1995, p. 22.

47. The last point identifies such lands that must be reclaimed. It includes Andalusia (Spain), Palestine and the whole of India (including Kashmir, Hyderabad, Assam, Bihar, Junagarh), and Nepal and Burma. It also mentions other countries such as Bulgaria, Hungary, Sicily, Russian Turkistan, and Chinese Turkistan. Abdul Salam bin Mohammad, *Why We Do Jihad?* (Department of Communication and Publications of Al-Dawa, May 1999).

48. Mohammad Amir Rana, *A to Z of Jehadi Organizations in Pakistan,* translated by Saba Ansari (Lahore: Mashal, 2004), p. 41.

49. Ibid., p. 42.

50. Riyaz Punjabi, "The Concept of Islamic Caliphate: The Religious and Ethnic Pulls of Kashmir Militant Movement," *United Kashmir Journal,* May–June 1994, p. 2.

51. A political pamphlet of Harkat-ul-Ansar (n.d.). See also Kamran Khan, "Harkat-ul-Ansar: Pakistan's Islamist Commandos Engaged in *Jihad* Worldwide," *News* (Lahore), February 13, 1995. According to Abu Jindal, a Harkat-ul-Ansar member apprehended by the army at Charar-i-Sharif, "*Jihad* means to kill all those who are not Muslims. Only Muslims who practice the religion truly should live, [and the] rest [of] all the people should be put to death." An army officer's conversation with Abu Jindal as told to the author. See also his interview in *Kashmir Times,* May 17, 1995.

52. Cited in Rana, *A to Z of Jehadi Organizations in Pakistan,* p. 299. The Lashkar-e-Taiba claims to have first entered Kashmir in 1990, and then to have upgraded its jihad in 1993, when its militants attacked an army base in Poonch. In 1994, it began sending a large number of its fighters into Kashmir, most of them non-Kashmiris, and by 1995 its fighters had been "engaged properly and striving hard" against the Indian forces. See Ijtima Congregation: Zaki-ur-Rehman Lakhvi, Amir, Mujahideen-i-Lashkar-e-Taiba (www.dawacenter.com/ijtimah/zaki-e.html). Also "Are the Talibans Coming?" (www.kashmir.force9.co.uk/editorials.htm).

53. Geelani, as cited in Sikand, "Changing Course of Kashmiri Struggle," p. 243.

54. See www.dawacenter.com/kashmir/kashmir.html.

55. Hafiz Muhammad Saeed, "No More Dialogue on Kashmir" (www.dawacenter.com/magazines/voiceofislam/sept99/editorial.html).

56. *Daily Srinagar Times,* August 30, 1993.

57. Cited in Praveen Swami, "Terrorism: A Widening Network," *Frontline*, January 3, 2003, p. 35.

58. Statement by Tehrik-e-Khilafat-e-Islamia (The Movement for Islamic Caliphate), in Punjabi, "The Concept of Islamic Caliphate," p. 4.

59. See Yasin Malik's interview with Ramesh Vinayak in *India Today*, October 15, 1995, p. 80.

60. *Indian Express* (New Delhi), May 6, 2002.

61. *Times of India* (New Delhi), November 23, 2001. For some interesting interpretations of the Hizbul feud, see Praveen Swami, "The Rage of the Doves," *Frontline*, January 31–February 13, 2004, pp. 27–28.

62. Praveen Swami, "Danger Signals from the Valley," *Frontline*, September 20–October 10, 2003, p. 35.

63. Rehana Hakim, "Kashmir's Endless Autumn," *Newsline* (Karachi), November 2004, p. 50.

64. Zaffar Abbas, "Endgame Begins," *Herald* (Karachi), February 2004, pp. 51–53.

65. K. P. S. Gill, "Tackling Terrorism in Kashmir: Some Lessons from Recent History," paper presented at Indian Council of Social Science Research seminar, "Terrorism: An Unending Malaise," March 2–3, 2000, p. 1.

66. Azmat Abbas, "The Making of a Militant," *Herald* (Karachi), July 2003, p. 58.

67. Syed Salahuddin's briefing to the Hizbul cadres as reported to the author.

68. Dar suggested a broad linkage with criminal organizations elsewhere in the country by contacting underworld kingpins to get assigned weapons and ammunition through other possible ways. He added that a cell of three persons would work to develop relations with the underworld and try to start a project of counterfeiting currency. As noted in Swami, "Terrorism in Jammu and Kashmir in Theory and Practice," p. 82.

69. "Hizbul against U.S. Mediation in Kashmir," *Indian Express* (New Delhi), December 10, 1998.

70. Swami, "Terrorism in Jammu and Kashmir in Theory and Practice," p. 79.

71. Ibid.

72. Riyaz Punjabi, "Charar-i-Sharif Tragedy: The Ideological Complexities," in *Charar-i-Sharif: Crisis, Complexity and Tragedy*, Occasional Paper (New Delhi: Centre for Peace Studies in Conflict, n.d.), p. 4.

73. Ibid., and P. N. Jalali, "Charar-i-Sharif: Destruction and Resurgence of Kashmiriyat," in *Charar-i-Sharif: Crisis, Complexity and Tragedy*, p. 13.

74. Some residents told stories of Mast Gul desecrating the shrine by walking around it with shoes. When the imam of the adjoining mosque protested, he was beaten. A few admitted reluctantly that if Mast Gul did not intend harming the shrine, he would not have planted improvised explosive devices all around it and the mosque. A Pakistani national, Abdul Rahman, confirmed in an article in *Urdu Digest* of Lahore that the shrine of Charar-e-Sharif was destroyed by Mast Gul. Cited in the *Hindu* (Chennai) and *Indian Express* (New Delhi), March 2, 1998.

75. Harinder Baweja, "Kashmir: People Turning against the Militants," *India Today*, May 31, 1992, pp. 70–71.

76. Ibid.

77. Ramesh Vinayak, "Kashmir: New Straws in the Wind," *India Today*, June 30, 1994, p. 64.

78. "Shah: Self-Determination An Inalienable Right," *Kashmir Times*, October 15, 1994.

79. See his interview in the *Herald* (Karachi), April 1995, p. 65.

80. In April 2002, Lone and Mirwaiz Farooq had traveled to Sharjah to meet with the leader of the Pakistan-based Kashmir Committee, Sardar Abdul Qayyum. During this meeting, Lone reportedly asked the Pakistan-based militant groups to stop their activity and allow the Hurriyat to negotiate with India independently. Some observers have speculated that Lone may also have been interested in participating in upcoming elections for the Jammu and Kashmir state assembly and asked that he be allowed to survive a boycott by the militants. Reportedly, the director of Pakistan's Inter-Services Intelligence, Lieutenant General Ehsan-ul-Haq, denounced Lone during the meeting and warned him to stop supporting participation in elections. For more details of this meeting, see interview with Sardar Abdul Qayum, June 24, 2002 (www.rediff.com); and Selig Harrison, "As Kashmir Boils, Keep Heat on Pakistan," *Los Angeles Times*, August 7, 2002.

81. O. N. Dhar, "No Longer a Kashmiri Insurgency," *Hindu* (Chennai), January 18, 1996. Dhar adds that Hurriyat leaders like Mirwaiz Umar Farooq and Abdul Ghani Lone—who had at first attributed the assassination to the Indian security forces but failed to carry conviction with the mass of people who knew how and why the young Maulvi had been liquidated—were forced to promise an impartial public investigation and punishment to those found responsible.

82. The son of a well-respected forest ranger, Abdul Rasheed, Inqalabi made his debut in politics as a second- year science student in 1965. After delivering a fiery anti-India speech, he was arrested and imprisoned for three months. Five years later, on a trip to Pakistan, he met the late Maqbool Butt, founder of the JKLF, who was a great source of inspiration to him. After less than two years, he returned to India again. In 1988, after the death of President Zia-ul-Haq, Inqalabi departed for Pakistan and in 1990 set up an organization called Operation Balakote (named after a Muslim saint who set out for Jehad and was murdered).

83. Mohammad Azim Inqalabi, *Quest for Friends, Not Masters* (Rawalpindi: Jammu Kashmir Mahaz-e-Aazadi, 1993), pp. 23–24, 34.

84. B. Muralidhar Reddy, "We Will Stay the Course, Say Hurriyat Leaders," *Hindu* (Chennai), June 4, 2005.

85. Ibid., p. 41.

86. Ibid., pp. 41–43.

87. Maleeha Lodhi, "Anatomy of a Debacle," *Newsline*, July 1999, p. 35.

88. An *India Today* report cited a study by army psychologists that probed the motivating factors of militants. Harinder Baweja, "In the Mind of a Militant," *India Today*, December 31, 1994, pp. 120–22.

89. Muzamil Jameel and Shishir Gupta, "PM Calls for Army and Civilian Reforms in Valley," *Indian Express* (New Delhi), May 25, 2006 (www.indianexpress.com/story/5108.html).

90. Mubashir Zaidi, "The Himalayan Implosion," *Herald* (Karachi), June 2003, p. 59.

91. Shujaat Bukhari, "Hizb Leader Rejects Mirwaiz's Offer," *Hindu* (Chennai), June 13, 2005 (http://www.hindu.com/2005/06/13/stories/2005061305441200.htm [August 11, 2006]).

92. Praveen Swami, "Hizb, LeT Leaders on Hunger-Strike," *Hindu* (Chennai), March 13, 2006 (http://www.hindu.com/2006/03/13/stories/2006031306441200.htm).

93. Cited in Praveen Swami, "Mayhem in the Menagerie," *Hindu* (Chennai), March 13, 2006.

94. Cited in Praveen Swami, "Through the Looking Glass in J&K," *Hindu* (Chennai), May 29, 2006.

95. Cited in Ahmad Faruqi, *Rethinking the National Security of Pakistan: The Price of Strategic Myopia* (Hampshire, England: Ashgate, 2003), p. 134.

Chapter Six

1. The term "intellectual silence" is used by Riffat Hussain, "Pakistan's Relations with Azad Kashmir," *Regional Studies* 21 (Autumn 2004): 82.

2. This concept was first applied to study the secession of Bangladesh from Pakistan in 1971. See Ali Riaz, *State, Class and Military Rule: Political Economy of Martial Law in Bangladesh* (Dhaka: Nadi New Press, 1994), chap. 3, pp. 72–115. For another important study on this issue, see Rounaq Jahan, *Pakistan: Failure in National Integration* (Columbia University Press, 1972). Also K. P. Misra, "Intra-State Imperialism as a Factor in Conflicts within and between States," *International Studies* 14 (January 1975): 39–52.

3. Victoria Schofield, *Kashmir in Conflict: India, Pakistan and the Unending War* (London: I. B. Tauris, 2003), p. 183.

4. Azad Kashmir leader Shaukat Ali cited in "PoK Leader for Free, United Kashmir," *Times of India* (New Delhi), November 1, 1993.

5. Many scholars have made this point. See Vernon Hewitt, *Reclaiming the Past: The Search for Political and Cultural Unity in Contemporary Jammu and Kashmir* (London: Portland Books 1995) p. 87; Leo E. Rose, "The Politics of Azad Kashmir," in *Perspectives on Kashmir: The Roots of Conflict in South Asia*, edited by Raju G. C. Thomas (Boulder, Colo.: Westview Press, 1992), p. 236; Roger Ballard, "Kashmir Crisis: View from Mirpur," *Economic and Political Weekly*, March 2–9, 1991, p. 513.

6. "Take Gilgit Violence Seriously," *Daily Times* (Lahore), editorial, April 30, 2005.

7. Cited in Rose, "The Politics of Azad Kashmir," p. 236.

8. Sardar M. Ibrahim Khan, *Kashmir Saga* (Azad Kashmir: Verinag, 1990), p. 129.

9. Cited in ibid., p. 126.

10. Ibid., p. 127.

11. Rose, "The Politics of Azad Kashmir," p. 238.

12. Nawaz Khan Naji, Balawaristan leader, interview by Rediff, March 16, 2004 (www.rediff.com/news/2004rachi/mar/17inter.htm).

13. A. H. Dani, *History of Northern Areas of Pakistan* (Islamabad: National Institute of Historical and Cultural Research, 1991), p. 426.

14. Iffat Malik, *Kashmir, Ethnic Conflict, International Dispute* (Oxford University Press, 2002), p. 219.

15. Bhashyam Kasturi, *Situation in Pakistan-Occupied Kashmir: An Analysis*, Report prepared for Observer Research Foundation (April 2004), p. 12.

16. Hussain, "Pakistan's Relations with Azad Kashmir."

17. They offered the following reasons in support of their stand: (a) the Northern Areas were historically a part of the state of Jammu and Kashmir; (b) according to the government of India census for the years 1911, 1921, 1931, and 1941, Ladakh, Gilgit, and Gilgit Political Agency were included in the state of Jammu and Kashmir; (c) the erstwhile maharaja of Kashmir had leased the areas to the British in March 1935 for sixty years—the agreement ceased to exist owing to the coming into force of Section 7 (1)(b) of the Indian Independence Act, whereupon the maharaja took over the possession of the Northern Areas and appointed Governor Ghanshara Singh, who took over from British Resident Lieutenant Colonel Becon; (d) in July 1947, elections to Kashmir State Assembly were held, and Raja Jagmat Dadool Nano, Chewing Rinchin, Raja Fateh Ali Khan, Ahmed Ali Khan, Raja Raza Khan, and Mohammad Javed Ansari were the members of the state assembly from the Northern Areas; (e) in 1949 the Azad Kashmir government was not in a position to look after the areas because of a lack of communication facilities, so the administration of the Northern Areas was transferred *temporarily* to the government of Pakistan in April 1949; (f) under Clause 6 of the March 1963 Sino-Pakistan Agreement, the Northern Areas were part of Jammu and Kashmir, but when the Indian government lodged a protest in the United Nations, the Pakistan Foreign Minister categorically stated on the floor of the United Nations that the Northern Areas were a disputed territory, being part of the state of Jammu and Kashmir.

18. A. A. Salaria, "AJK HC Ruling on N. Areas Status," *Dawn* (Karachi), April 14, 1993, p. 7.

19. Shaheen Sardar Ali and Javaid Rehman, *Indigenous Peoples and Ethnic Minorities of Pakistan: Constitutional and Legal Perspectives* (Surrey: Curzon Press, 2001), p. 128.

20. Cited in Sanjay Suri, "J&K Is Better Off" (www.outlookindia.com/full.asp? fname=gilgit&fodname=19980420&sid=1[March 12, 2002]).

21. Arif Shamim, "A 'Political Question' That Must Be Answered," *News* (Lahore), December 14, 1997.

22. Rose, "The Politics of Azad Kashmir," p. 238.

23. Khan, *Kashmir Saga*, p. 130; and Hewitt, *Reclaiming the Past*, p. 111.

24. Khan, *Kashmir Saga*, p. 130.

25. Rose, "The Politics of Azad Kashmir," p. 238.

26. Ibid., p. 246.

27. Cited in I. Rammohan Rao, "POK in Fetters," *Hindustan Times* (New Delhi), May 18, 1996.

28. Khan, *Kashmir Saga*, p. 206.

29. In an interview with *Nawai-i-Waqt*, March 25, 1992.

30. M. H. Askari, "Kashmir through the Looking Glass," *Herald* (Karachi), August 1991, p. 86.

31. Hewitt, *Reclaiming the Past*, p. 111

32. Ali and Rehman, *Indigenous Peoples*, p. 137. For details, see Dani, *History of Northern Areas*, pp. 414–20.

33. Rose, "The Politics of Azad Kashmir," pp. 249–50.

34. Ali and Rehman, *Indigenous Peoples*, p. 139.

35. See excerpts from *Report for Human Rights Commission of Pakistan*, in Kamran Arif, "What Is Wrong in the Northern Areas?" *Friday Times* (Lahore), October 15–21, 1992.

36. "Northern Areas Need Urgent Attention by Islamabad," *Muslim* (Islamabad), January 8, 1993.

37. Kamran Arif, "What Is Wrong in the Northern Areas?"

38. Ishtiaq Ahmad, "Do Something about Northern Areas," *Nation* (Lahore), June 30, 1996, p. 7.

39. Cited in Rose, "The Politics of Azad Kashmir," p. 252.

40. Cited in Kasturi, *Situation in Pakistan-Occupied Kashmir*, p. 23.

41. Farman Ali, "The Puppet Show," *Herald* (Karachi), November 2004, p. 30.

42. Zaigham Khan, "Northern Exposure," *Herald* (Karachi), December 1997, p. 74.

43. Cited in B. Raman, "Musharraf's Visit to POK & NA," Paper 307 (South Asia Analysis Group, September 3, 2001).

44. Cited in M. Ilyas Khan, "The Pariahs of Pakistan," *Herald* (Karachi), October 2002, pp. 74–75.

45. Ali, "The Puppet Show."

46. Nawaz Khan Naji, interview, March 16, 2004.

47. Rose, "The Politics of Azad Kashmir," p. 241.

48. Ibid., p. 242.

49. See her interview in *India Today*, September 15, 1991.

50. Nasir Mallick, "Trouble in Paradise," *Herald* (Karachi), July 1991.

51. Brigadier (retired) Saleem Zia, "What's Wrong with our Kashmir Cause?" *Pakistan Times*, August 11, 1991.

52. Zaffar Abbas, "Elective Affinities," *Herald* (Karachi), July 1996, p. 59.

53. *News* (Lahore), July 1, 1996. See also the editorials in *Dawn* (Karachi), *Nation*, and *News*, July 3, 1996.

54. Syed Shoaib Hasan and Intikhab Amir, "The New Fault Line," *Herald* (Karachi), November 2005, p. 57. *Newsline* noted that "even in normal times, the [Azad Kashmir] government is a mere formality as every vital decision is taken in consultation with the GoC Murree." See Naveed Ahmad, "Hell on Earth," *Newsline* (Karachi), November 2005, p. 40.

55. Scores of army bunkers were buried beneath the landslides in Neelam and Jhelum Valleys, as well as in the Bagh region, killing hundreds of troops. These included positions near Chattar, Rairra, and Doli villages in the Bagh sector; Simarri, Kuri Patika, Naseeri, Chalyanla, Dhanyal, Jura, and Kel in the Neelam Valley along with substantial military casualties in Reshian and the Lipa Valley region. In Bagh, Muzaffarabad, Ath-

muqam, and Kel, the local military headquarters were wiped out. The army's Nisar Camp and the Combined Military hospital in Muzaffarabad, the brigade headquarters, was also left in ruins. Hasan and Mir, "The New Fault Line."

56. Amir Mir, "Militant Philanthropy," *Newsline*, November 2005, pp. 65–71.

57. Cited in Khan, *Kashmir Saga,* p. 193

58. Ballard, "Kashmir Crisis," p. 514.

59. Ibid.

60. Ibid., p. 515.

61. Ibid.

62. Ibid.

63. B. Raman, "Virtual Military Rule in POK," Paper 297 (South Asia Analysis Group), August 20, 2001.

64. Ajai Shukla, "Gilgit-Baltistan: A Potential Problem for Pakistan," September 24, 2003 (http://balawaristan.net/ndtv.html).

65. Tariq Hussain, "The Last Colony," *Herald* (Karachi), April 1990, pp. 112–17; and Arif, "What Is Wrong in the Northern Areas?"

66. The agreement stated: "The two parties have agreed that after the settlement of the Kashmir dispute between Pakistan and India, the sovereign authority concerned will reopen negotiations with the Government of the People's Republic of China on the boundary, as described in Article II of the present agreement, of Kashmir so as to sign a boundary treaty to replace the present agreement."

67. *Times of India* (New Delhi), January 20, 1990.

68. In an interview with *Time* magazine, April 16, 1990. See also *Frontier Post* (Lahore), April 16, 1990.

69. Zaffar Abbas, "Whodunnit?" *Herald* (Karachi), July 1999. See also B. Raman, "Unrest in Gilgit-Baltistan," Paper 1241 (South Asia Analaysis Group, February 3, 2005) (www.saag.org/papers13/paper1241.html).

70. Kasturi, *Situation in Pakistan-Occupied Kashmir*, p. 15.

71. Kargil and Northern Scouts (http://balawaristan.net/KargilNS.html).

72. The narrative account of the Northern Areas' religious, caste, and linguistic pluralities relies heavily on the excellent exposition provided by Ali and Rehman, *Indigenous Peoples* , pp. 133–35.

73. Ballard, "Kashmir Crisis," p. 513.

74. Sumantra Bose, *The Challenge in Kashmir: Democracy, Self-Determination and a Just Peace* (New Delhi: Sage, 1997), p. 68.

75. Adil Zareef, "The Northern Areas: Roots of Sectarianism," *Friday Times* (Lahore), October 15–21, 1992; and Arif, "What Is Wrong in the Northern Areas?" Also Shukla, "Gilgit-Baltistan: A Potential Problem for Pakistan"; and Shabir Choudhry, "A Ceasefire Within May Help" (http://balawaristan.net/shabir.html).

76. Shujaat Bukhari, "Voices of Dissent," *Newsline* (Karachi), January 2005, p. 39.

77. Choudhry, "A Ceasefire Within May Help."

78. Arif, "What Is Wrong in the Northern Areas?"

79. Zareef, "The Northern Areas: Roots of Sectarianism."

80. Arif, "What Is Wrong in the Northern Areas?" and Sardar Attiq Ahmad Khan, "Pakistan Lacks Locus in Gilgit and Baltistan," *Voice of Millions: Jammu and Kashmir*, Special Issue, 1995, p. 40.

81. Strategic Foresight Group, *The Future of Pakistan* (Mumbai: International Centre for Peace Initiatives, 2003) p. 60.

82. Hussain, "The Last Colony," p. 114.

83. Abubaker Saddique, "Paradise Lost?" *Newsline* (Karachi), February 2005.

84. The Holy Prophet (PBUH, Peace Be Upon Him) is quoted as saying that God chastised the Jews because they began to worship their prophets' graves. "Therefore, you should not worship my grave after my death." This excerpt clearly provokes the Barelvis and the followers of saints like Bari Imam, says Shia scholar Amin Shaheedi. Furthermore, one of the textbooks carries a sketch of a boy offering prayers in the Sunni way. "The picture can mislead a Shia student about his/her religious rituals. Shia scholars also say the textbooks utterly ignore Hazrat Ali, the fourth caliph, which the Shias revere. Moreover, while the books speak highly of the sahaba (companions of Holy Prophet [PBUH) they ignore important figures from Ahle-Bait [family of the Prophet (PBUH)]," says Shaheedi.

85. Mohammad Shehzad, "Textbook Controversy in Gilgit," sikhspectrum.com Quarterly, 13 (August 2003).

86. Hewitt, *Reclaiming the Past*, p. 120.

87. Ibid., p. 88.

88. Khan, *Kashmir Saga*, p. 206.

89. Ibid., p. 207.

90. Hewitt, *Reclaiming the Past*, p. 113.

91. Ibid., p. 114.

92. Ibid., p. 120.

93. Shujaat Bukhari, "Breaking the Barriers," *Newsline* (Karachi), January 2005, p. 32.

94. Ibid.

95. Ballard, *The Kashmir Crisis*, p. 513.

96. Ibid.

97. Ibid., p. 515.

98. Ibid.

99. Ibid.

100. Kasturi, *Situation in Pakistan-Occupied Kashmir*, p. 25.

101. Sultan Shahin, "Free Balawaristan Movement Gains Momentum" (www.-jammu-kashmir.com/insights/insight20000206b.html).

102. Bukhari, "Voices of Dissent," p. 39.

103. Abdul Hamid Khan, chairman of Balawaristan National Front, "An Interview,"Paper 614 (South Asia Analysis Group, February 24, 2003) (www.saag.org/papers7/paper614.html).

104. Shabir Choudhry, "Gilgit Is on Fire Again," January 10, 2005 (http://balawaristan.net/shabirGlt.html).

105. Ibid.
106. Ibid.
107. Abdul Hamid Khan, "Islam and Interfaith Relations in South Asia" (www.islaminterfaith.org/july2002/interview.html).
108. Nawaz Khan Naji, interview, March 16, 2004.
109. Ibid.
110. Khan, *Islam and Interfaith Relations.*
111. Nawaz Khan Naji, interview, March 16, 2004.
112. Zaigham Khan, "Turning the Tide," *Herald* (Karachi), November 1994, p. 55.
113. Ibid.

Chapter Seven

1. For a detailed discussion of the Gurdaspur Award, see Prem Shankar Jha, *Kashmir 1947: The Origins of a Dispute* (Oxford University Press, 2003), pp. 86–94.

2. Lawrence Ziring, *Pakistan in the Twentieth Century: A Political History* (Oxford University Press, 1997), pp. 62–63.

3. Chandrashekhar Dasgupta, *War and Diplomacy in Kashmir: 1947–48* (New Delhi: Sage Publications, 2002), pp. 10–12. For a lucid exposition of the Anglo-American strategic rethinking at this stage, see Sir Olaf Caroe's statement cited in Girilal Jain, "India, Pakistan and Kashmir," in *Indian Foreign Policy: The Nehru Years,* edited by B. R. Nanda (New Delhi: Vikas, 1976), p. 53.

4. Dasgupta, *War and Diplomacy in Kashmir,* pp. 10–18; Ayesha Jalal, *The State of Martial Rule: The Origins of Pakistan's Economy of Defence* (Lahore, Pakistan: Vanguard, 1991), p. 52.

5. Jalal, *The State of Martial Rule,* p. 55; Dennis Kux, *The United States and Pakistan, 1947–2000: Disenchanted Allies* (Washington: Woodrow Wilson Center Press, 2001), p. 120. See also Mountbatten's interviews with Liaquat Ali Khan on April 11, 1947, and with Jinnah on April 26, 1947, as cited in Dasgupta, *War and Diplomacy in Kashmir,* p. 15.

6. Kux, *The United States and Pakistan,* p. 23.

7. Cited in Dasgupta, *War and Diplomacy in Kashmir,* p. 111.

8. Ibid., p.119. Delegates of China and Colombia showed greater appreciation of India's viewpoint. China did not think that an entirely new regime in Pakistan was necessary to secure a free plebiscite; it also felt that the Security Council directive to Pakistan in regard to putting a stop to the fighting might be more specific.

9. For details on the differences between the American and British approach, see the exchange between their officials as noted in the State Department records. Cited in Dasgupta, *War and Diplomacy in Kashmir,* p. 121.

10. Ibid., p. 205. Dasgupta gives details of correspondence between Attlee and Noel-Baker as well. See pp. 128–30.

11. Cited in Dennis Kux, *India and the United States: Estranged Democracies, 1941–1991* (Washington: National Defense University Press, 1992), p. 61. Earlier, on

February 15, 1948, he had remarked that "instead of discussing and deciding on our reference in a straightforward manner, the nations of the world sitting in that body [were] lost in power politics." Cited in A. Appoadorai and M. S. Rajan, *India's Foreign Policy and Relations* (New Delhi: South Asian, 1985), p. 83.

12. This pattern of thinking was indicated by an early memorandum of September 1949 from Deputy Assistant Secretary of State Raymond A. Hare to Ambassador-at-Large Phillip C. Jessup, which stated that while "India has emerged from World War II as the strongest power in Asia . . . [w]e have *no great assurance that India in the future will ally itself with us* and we have some reason to believe that it might not. Pakistan, if given reasonable encouragement, might prove the more reliable friend. In certain circumstances, therefore, *a strong Muslim bloc under Pakistan leadership could provide a very desirable balance of power* in Asia." Cited in Baldev Raj Nayar and T. V. Paul, *India in the World Order: Searching for Major-Power Status* (Cambridge University Press, 2003), p. 147.

13. Cited in Jalal, *The State of Martial Rule*, p. 125.

14. Ibid., p. 127.

15. Cited in Kux, *The United States and Pakistan*, p. 20.

16. Stephen P. Cohen, "U.S. Weapons and South Asia: A Policy Analysis," *Pacific Affairs* 49 (Spring 1976): 49–69. Liaquat Ali Khan sent the deputy chief of the army, General Walter Joseph Cawthorn, on a top secret mission to London with a proposal for a military alliance. See Dasgupta, *War and Diplomacy in Kashmir*, pp. 71–73.

17. Cited in Rajendra K. Jain, ed., *U.S.–South Asian Relations, 1947–1982* (New Delhi: Radiant, 1983), p. 23; and Kux, *India and the United States*, p. 89.

18. Kux, *India and the United States*, p. 62.

19. For a detailed account of these debates in the Security Council, see Sisir Gupta, *Kashmir: A Study in India-Pakistan Relations* (Bombay: Asia House, 1966), pp. 110–254, 310–42.

20. See Secretary of State John Foster Dulles, memorandum to the president, March 24, 1953, cited in Kux, *The United States and Pakistan*, p. 64.

21. Ibid., p. 55.

22. Nayar and Paul, *India in the World Order*, p. 149; Kux, *The United States and Pakistan*, p. 61. Of equal importance is the fact that the weapons mix Pakistan received from the United States was, as Ambassador Chester Bowles pointed out, meant for use against India in the plains of the subcontinent rather than against the Soviet Union or China in the mountainous areas. Chester Bowles, *Ambassador's Report* (New York: Harper & Brothers, 1954), p. 478.

23. Sarvepalli Gopal, *Jawaharlal Nehru: A Biography,* vol. 2, (Harvard University Press, 1976), p. 182; Kux, *India and the United States*, p. 117; and Kux, *The United States and Pakistan*, pp. 66, 55.

24. Kux, *The United States and Pakistan*, p. 58.

25. According to Harold Gould, the method Dulles adopted "was to try to diplomatically isolate India to cut it off as much as possible from Western sympathy and support in the context of the United Nations and other international bodies." Nayar and Paul, *India in the World Order*, p. 73.

26. Gopal, *Jawaharlal Nehru*, p. 185. He also mentions that Nehru believed the United States was diplomatically coercing India by promoting its encirclement through a ring of alliances. See p. 254.

27. For details, see Gupta, *Kashmir*, pp. 244–45. Taken aback by the Soviet support, Bajpai called in the American chargé d'affaires and stressed that India had not asked the Soviet Union to intervene; Bajpai emphasized that India did not want Kashmir to become embroiled in the cold war. Kux, *India and the United States*, p. 66.

28. For a detailed discussion of China's fear of encirclement, see A. Doak Barnett, *China and the Major Powers in Asia* (Brookings, 1977).

29. Samina Yasmeen, "The China Factor in the Kashmir Issue," in *Perspectives on Kashmir: The Roots of Conflict in South Asia*, edited by Raju G. C. Thomas (Boulder, Colo.: Westview Press, 1992), p. 323.

30. Kux, *The United States and Pakistan*, p. 130.

31. Ibid., p. 144.

32. Memorandum of conversation between Ayub Khan and Duncan Sandys and Harriman on November 28, 1962, as cited in ibid., p. 134.

33. Memorandum of conversation between Dean Rusk and Aziz Ahmed, February 23, 1963, as cited in ibid., p. 139. During Eisenhower's second term, too, the U.S. administration's view on Kashmir was that "any reasonable solution" was acceptable, whether a plebiscite, partition, or some other arrangement (ibid., p. 96).

34. Ibid., 140.

35. Sarvepalli Gopal, *Jawaharlal Nehru: A Biography*, vol. 3 (London: Jonathan Cape, 1984), p. 259.

36. Kux, *The United States and Pakistan*, p. 142.

37. Ibid., p.138.

38. Kux, *India and the United States*, p. 210.

39. Cited in Kux, *The United States and Pakistan*, p. 146.

40. The aide-mémoire had stated that "the Government of the United States of America reaffirms its previous assurances to the Government of Pakistan that it will come to Pakistan's assistance in the event of an aggression from India." Cited in ibid., p. 132.

41. In a meeting with U.S. ambassador McConaughty, Pakistan's foreign minister, Z. A. Bhutto, charged Washington with badly treating an ally dependent on U.S. military equipment. Accusing India of "naked aggression," the foreign minister stated, "It is our honor we have to safeguard." McConaughty retorted, "Was this realized when guerrilla operations were started in Kashmir? . . . It was a fateful decision you took to plan, organize, and support the Mujahid [freedom-fighter] operations." Kux, *The United States and Pakistan*, p. 162.

42. K. Arif, ed., *China–Pakistan Relations 1947–80* (Lahore: Vanguard Books, 1984), Document 49, p. 47.

43. Altaf Gauhar, *Ayub Khan: Pakistan's First Military Ruler* (Lahore: Sang-E-Meel, 1994), pp. 351–53. G. M. Choudhury also notes that Ayub secretly visited China before announcing Pakistan's acceptance of the cease-fire. G. M. Choudhury, *India, Pakistan, Bangladesh and the Major Powers* (New York: Free Press, 1975), pp. 190–91.

44. Choudhury, *India, Pakistan, Bangladesh and the Major Powers,* p. 165.

45. Jack Anderson of the *Washington Post* released secret documents revealing the administration's wholly one-sided approach. Jack Anderson, *The Anderson Papers* (New York: Random House, 1973), pp. 203–69. Although the United States formally suspended the shipment of all military supplies to both India and Pakistan upon the outbreak of the war, the U.S. administration was complicit in the transfer of F-104 aircraft to Pakistan from Libya and Jordan. The Nixon administration then stunned India by warning it not to expect any U.S. help in case China decided to intervene in any war between India and Pakistan. Nayar and Paul, *India in the World Order,* p. 177.

46. For differing interpretations on Simla, See P. R Chari , Pervaiz Iqbal Cheema, and Stephen Philip Cohen, *Perception, Politics and Security in South Asia: The Compound Crisis of 1990* (London: Roultedge, 2003).

47. J. N. Dixit, *My South Block Years* (New Delhi: UBS Publishers, 1997), p. 223.

48. J. Mohan Malik, "India Goes Nuclear: Rationale, Benefits, Costs and Implications," *Contemporary Southeast Asia,* August 20, 1998, pp. 194–95.

49. This position was enunciated by U.S. Assistant Secretary of State for Near East and South Asia John Kelly, during testimony before Congress on March 6, 1990. See Mushahid Hussain, "The Kashmir Issue: Its New International Dimensions" in *Perspectives on Kashmir,* edited by Thomas, p. 343. For a discussion of the American view of Kashmir, see Mushahid Hussain, "U.S. now Opposes Plebiscite in Valley," *Nation,* April 23, 1990; and Mowahid H. Shah, "U.S. Considers Kashmir a Time-Barred Issue," *Nation,* April 27, 1990.

50. The first public expression of the revised Chinese approach to the Kashmir problem was made by Deng Xiaoping in an interview with an Indian journal, *Vikrant,* in June 1980. He described Kashmir as a bilateral problem between India and Pakistan, which the two countries needed to settle amicably. See R. K Jain, ed., *China-South Asian Relations 1947–88,* vol. 1 (New Delhi: Radiant, 1981), document 492, p. 544; also pp. 542–44.

51. "Kashmir Solution on Basis of Simla Pact," *Dawn* (Karachi), October 28, 1992, p. 1.

52. "Germany Should Be Even Handed," *Frontier Post* (Lahore), October 29, 1992, p. 10.

53. *Muslim* (Islamabad), March 23,1992; and Shahid M. Amin, "A Re-evaluation of the Kashmir Dispute," *Pakistan Horizon* 56, no. 2 (2003): 37–53 .

54. Shaheen Akhtar, "Nuclearization of South Asia and the Kashmir Dispute," *Regional Studies* 17 (Summer 1999): 3–70.

55. Kux quotes U.S. Undersecretary of State for Political Affairs Arnold Kanter, warning the new Pakistan ambassador, Abida Hussein, that "if you get hit with this on top of Pressler, that will end the U.S.-Pakistan relationship." He further cites Nicholas Platt, who replaced Robert Oakley as U.S. ambassador in Islamabad later in 1991, as saying: "I raised this issue at every level from the prime minister on down." Kux, *The United States and Pakistan,* p. 316. James Woolsey, the new director of the Central Intelligence Agency under Clinton, took a hard line, warning publicly that Pakistan stood "on the brink." Douglas Jehl, "Pakistan Is Facing Terrorist Listing," *New York Times,* April 25, 1993. For a Pakistani point of view, see Maleeha Lodhi, "Removing the Noose

of Terror," *News* (Lahore), May 15, 1993.

56. Hasan Askari Rizvi, "China and the Kashmir Problem," *Regional Studies* (Islamabad), XII, no. 3 (Summer 1994): 97–99.

57. Of the OIC's fifty-two members, only six countries—Saudi Arabia, Nigeria, Turkey, Albania, Gambia, and Bosnia and Herzegovina—were willing to back Pakistan's resolution. Some members of the Contact Group told Pakistan that a resolution was not needed since India had already initiated the process of holding elections in Kashmir, and India had more than adequate votes to support its stand. See Navnita Chadha, "Pakistan's Stonewalling Tactics," *Pioneer* (New Delhi), December 11, 1994.

58. Farzana Shakoor, "UN and Kashmir," *Pakistan Horizon* 51 (April 1998): 65.

59. According to Timothy Hoyt, the idea that the Kashmir dispute is somehow fundamentally connected with nuclear danger is pervasive in U.S. policy circles. A search of the Internet for the phrases "Kashmir" and "nuclear flashpoint" brought up 998 references. See Timothy D. Hoyt, "Politics, Proximity and Paranoia: The Evolution of Kashmir as a Nuclear Flashpoint," *India Review* 2 (July 2003): 117. See also Akhtar, "Nuclearization of South Asia and the Kashmir Dispute," pp. 3–70.

60. Kanti Bajpai and others, *Brasstacks and Beyond: Perception and Management of Crisis in South Asia* (New Delhi: Manohar, 1995), p. 74.

61. Ibid., p. 81.

62. The nuclear deployment report came from Seymour Hersh, "On the Nuclear Edge," *New Yorker*, March 29, 1993, pp. 55–73, and was repeated in William E. Burrows and Robert Windrem, *Critical Mass* (New York: Simon & Schuster, 1994), pp. 60–90. It was also supported by Mary Anne Weaver, *Pakistan: In the Shadow of Jihad and Afghanistan* (New York: Farrar, Straus & Giroux, 2002), p. 206. According to the U.S. ambassadors in New Delhi and Islamabad at the time, however, the U.S. government was unaware of any nuclear deployment or even of the evacuation of nuclear materials from Kahuta. See Michael Krepon and Mishi Faruqee, eds., *Conflict Prevention and Confidence-Building Measures in South-Asia: The 1990 Crisis,* Occasional Paper 17 (Washington: Henry L. Stimson Center, April 1994).

63. Chari and others, *Perception, Politics and Security in South Asia*, pp. 97–98.

64. Ibid., p. 97.

65. Ibid., p.103.

66. For reports that Pakistan prepared "nuclear-tipped missiles," see Bruce Riedel, *American Diplomacy and the 1999 Kargil Summit at Blair House,* Policy Paper Series 2002 (Philadelphia, Pa.: Center for the Advanced Study of India, 2002). For reports that India placed its nuclear arsenal at "Readiness State 3" (ready to be mated with Prithvi and Agni missiles and Mirage 2000 aircraft for delivery), see Raj Chengappa, *Weapons of Peace* (New Delhi: Harper Collins India, 2000), p. 437.

67. The principal secretary to the prime minister, Brajesh Mishra, in a background briefing to Indian reporters in early June 1999, at the height of the Kargil crisis, talked about the "paradigm shift" in Indo-U.S. relations. He based his comment on the emerging signals of unprecedented American support to India during the Kargil War.

68. Raj Chengappa, "Face-Saving Retreat," *India Today International*, May 31, 1999,

p. 20; Thomas W. Lippman, "India Hinted at Attack in Pakistan; U.S. Acts to Ease Tensions on Kashmir," *Washington Post*, June 27, 1999, p. A26. See also Seema Guha, "Brajesh on Secret Mission," *Times of India* (New Delhi), June 18, 1999.

69. Raj Chengappa, "Will the War Spread?" *India Today International*, July 5, 1999, p. 14; and John Lancaster, "U.S. Defused Kashmir Crisis on Brink of War," *Washington Post*, July 26, 1999.

70. Transcript of the "Joint Statement by President Clinton and Prime Minister Sharif of Pakistan," Office of the Press Secretary, *White House Web Service*, July 4, 1999.

71. M. Ehsan Ahrari, "China, Pakistan, and the 'Taliban Syndrome,'" *Asian Survey* 50 (July–August 2000): 669–70.

72. C. Raja Mohan, *Crossing the Rubicon: The Shaping of India's New Foreign Policy* (New Delhi: Viking, 2003), p. 100.

73. For text of the prepared remarks by Secretary of State Madeleine Albright at the Asia Society in Washington on March 14, 2000, see *Washington File*, March 16, 2000.

74. In his televised address to the people of Pakistan during his brief stay there on March 25, 2000, Clinton added: "I have listened carefully to General Musharraf and others. I understand your concerns about Kashmir. But a stark truth must also be faced. There is no military solution to Kashmir. International sympathy, support and intervention cannot be won by provoking a bigger, bloodier conflict. On the contrary; sympathy and support will be lost. And no matter how great the grievance, it is wrong to support attacks against civilians across the line of control." *Dawn* (Karachi), March 25, 2000.

75. Bill Clinton, interview with Peter Jennings, *ABC World News*, March 21, 2000.

76. See Council on Foreign Relations, *After the Tests, U.S. Policy toward India and Pakistan*, Task Force Report 18 (Washington, February 1998), p. 19. See also Council on Foreign Relations, *A New U.S. Policy toward India and Pakistan*, Task Force Report 10 (Washington, January 1997), pp. 38–39; Selig S. Harrison and Geoffrey Kemp, *India and America, After the Cold War: Report of the Carnegie Endowment Study Group on U.S.-Indian Relations in a Changing International Environment* (Washington: Carnegie Endowment for International Peace, 1993), p. 34; and Asia Society, *South Asia and the United States, After the Cold War: A Study Mission Sponsored by the Asia Society* (New York, 1994).

77. Condoleezza Rice, "Prompting the National Interest," *Foreign Affairs* 79 (January–February 2000): 45–62. See also Barbara Leitch LePoer, "The Kashmir Dispute: Recent Developments and U.S. Policy," Report 96-730F (Washington: Congressional Research Service, August 30, 1996), pp. 4–5.

78. Robert D. Blackwill, "An Action Agenda to Strengthen America's Alliances in the Asia-Pacific Region," in *America's Asian Alliances*, edited by Robert D. Blackwill and Paul Dibb (Cambridge, Mass.: MIT Press, 2000), p. 124.

79. Pakistan was asked to stop al Qaeda operatives at the border, intercept arms shipments through Pakistan, and end all logistical support to Osama bin Laden; provide blanket overflight and landing rights; give access to naval and air bases and borders; provide immediate intelligence and immigration information; condemn the 9/11

attacks and curb all domestic expression of support for terrorism against the United States, its friends, or allies; cut off all shipments of fuel to the Taliban and stop Pakistani volunteers from going into Afghanistan to join the Taliban; and break diplomatic relations with the Taliban should evidence strongly implicate Osama bin Laden and the al Qaeda network and should the Taliban continue to harbor him and his network. These demands were conveyed on September 13 by Richard Armitage to the then chief general of Inter-Services Intelligence, Mahmud Ahmad, who was in Washington at that time. Secretary of State Colin Powell then called up General Musharraf, who agreed to all the U.S. demands. Ajay Darshan Behera, "On the Edge of Metamorphosis," in *Pakistan in a Changing Strategic Context*, edited by Ajay Darshan Behera and Joseph C. Mathew (New Delhi: Knowledge World, 2004), pp. 4–5.

80. Before September 11, Pakistan under General Pervez Musharraf was largely in diplomatic isolation, not merely because of its nuclear tests but also because of the overthrow of legitimate democratic government by the military in 1999 and the lack of a definitive promise on the holding of fresh elections. Pakistan had been suspended from membership in the British Commonwealth while important officials from the major powers except China avoided making a side trip to Pakistan when visiting India. Pakistan's economy was also in deep trouble, in part because of the sanctions, and the international financial institutions were being rough with the regime on conditionalities.

81. Devin T. Hagerty, "U.S. Policy and the Kashmir Dispute: Prospects for Resolution," *India Review* 2 (July 2003): 104.

82. Steve Coll, "Between India and Pakistan, A Changing Role for the U.S.," *Washington Post*, October 17, 2002. See also Munir Akram, Pakistan's ambassador to the United Nations, "At UN, Pakistan Defends First-Strike Nuclear Policy," Agence France-Presse, May 20, 2002.

83. Rahul Bedi and Anton La Guardia, "Pakistan Steps Back from Brink," *Kolkatta Daily Telegraph* (Kolkatta), June 8, 2002.

84. Hoyt, "Politics, Proximity and Paranoia: The Evolution of Kashmir as a Nuclear Flashpoint," p. 135.

85. In response to a direct question from *Newsweek* correspondent Lally Weymouth on America's role in Kashmir, Vaypayee said, "That of a facilitator." Asked if it went against the traditional Indian rejection of third-party roles in Kashmir, Vajpayee added, "No, that's why I said a facilitator, not a mediator." For a text of the interview, see the website of the Ministry of External Affairs (http://meadev.nic.in/govt/pm-newsweek-july2002.htm).

86. Chari and others, *Perception, Politics and Security in South Asia*, pp. 29, 32.

87. Ashley J. Tellis, "South Asian Seesaw: A New U.S. Policy on the Subcontinent," Policy Brief 38 (Washington: Carnegie Endowment for International Peace, May 2005), pp. 1–2.

88. Ibid., p. 1.

89. Tellis, "South Asian Seesaw," pp. 1–2.

90. National Security Adviser Brajesh Mishra spoke about India's coercive diplomacy after December 13 and its consequences in an interview on the BBC: "We are happy with what Washington and London have done but not happy with the results

which have come because we were promised much more. We were told that General Musharraf will have to carry out his promises because these promises are to the U.S. and UK." See "Talking with Brajesh Mishra," *Indian Express* (New Delhi), November 29, 2002. See also his statement in *Hindu* (Chennai), December 12, 2002. Others argued that the United States seemed to have given Pakistan's military establishment considerable freedom to continue its support to officially authorized jihadis operating in the Indian part of Kashmir. See Praveen Swami, "Riding the Jihadi Tiger," *South Asia Intelligence Review* 2, no.38, April 5, 2004 (satporg@satp.org).

91. Jaish-i-Mohammed supreme commander Saifur Rehman Saifi had told interrogators in Pakistan that "the mujahideen brotherhood is beyond your understanding. All mujahideen are brothers." Azmat Abbas, "Death Wish," *Herald* (Karachi), July 2003, p. 48.

92. Navnita Chadha Behera, "Kashmir: Redefining the U.S. Role," Policy Brief 110 (Brookings, November 2002).

93. Indrani Bagchi, "Beyond Control," *India Today*, December 8, 2003, pp. 36–38.

94. Praveen Swami, "Lashkar-e-Taiba Activists Arrested Near Baghdad," *Hindu* (Chennai), April 1, 2004; Abdus Sattar Ghazali, "Pakistani Suspect Denied Bail in U.S.," *Dawn* (Karachi) (www.dawnarchive/calberarst/art/net.html). Also, C. Rajamohan, "The War: Pakistani Stamp on International Terrorist Acts Post 9/11," *Indian Express* (New Delhi), September 10, 2006.

95. Anil Padmanabhan, "Not Guilty as Charged," *India Today*, August 9, 2004, p. 53.

96. Mubashir Zaidi, "The Himalayan Implosion," *Herald* (Karachi), June 2003, pp. 58–60.

97. Richard Armitage had flatly told the general's men that the United States could not afford the risk of a nuclear conflict in South Asia, so militants had to be reined in. Armitage repeated the blunt message to Foreign Secretary Riaz Khokhar, who visited Washington in early November. Khokhar was apparently told Pakistan had not done enough to stop cross-border terrorism in Kashmir. Within days of Khokhar's return, U.S. ambassador to Pakistan Nancy Powell urged Pakistan to increase its efforts to stop unauthorized movement across the Line of Control. Seema Sirohi, "Good Cop, Bad Cop," *Outlook,* December 15, 2003, p. 52; and Mubashir Zaidi, "Desperately Seeking Options," *Herald* (Karachi), February 2003, pp. 26–29.

98. See Rice's interview in *India Today*, March 22–28, 2005, p. 64.

99. Ibid., p. 65. In the same interview, Rice said, "We have talked to them about the situation in Kashmir and the importance of undoing the terrorist infrastructure there. I understand some progress has been made. I believe there is less activity across the LOC. But more progress is needed." Two years before, U.S. Assistant Secretary of State Christina Rocca, in a deposition before a House Subcommittee on International Relations in October 2003, had singled out Musharraf for effusive praise: "The government of Pakistan has taken many steps to curb infiltration, but we are asking it to redouble its efforts." Praveen Swami, "Peace and War," *Frontline*, November 21, 2003, p. 30.

100. Tellis, "South Asian Seesaw," p. 5.

101. In response to a question on Kashmir elections, Powell said, "I think we'll have to wait and see how the election goes, whether it truly is free and fair and whether there is a broad participation. There are some groups now who say they won't participate so I think it is one step forward in a process of determining the will of the Kashmiri peo-

ple." *Washington File,* July 29, 2002.

102. Rajamohan, *Crossing the Rubicon,* p. 106.

103. For an assessment of Blackwill's visit to Srinagar at the end of 2002, see Shujaat Bukhari, "U.S. Envoy Takes a Different Track," *Hindu* (Chennai), December 8, 2002. The Bush administration continued to insist, however, that free and fair elections alone would not be enough to resolve the Kashmir dispute, and it required negotiations between India and Pakistan.

104. Ministry of External Affairs, "Visit of the President of the Russian Federation to India, October 2–5, 2000" (New Delhi: Ministry of External Affairs, 2000), p. 48.

105. For the text of the Delhi declaration issued by President Vladimir Putin and Prime Minister Atal Bihari Vajpayee on December 4, 2002, see "No Double Standards in Fighting Terrorism," *Hindu* (Chennai), December 5, 2002.

106. For reports on the disconcerting Russian-Pakistani diplomatic pas de deux in Almaty, see "Serious and Positive Signals from Musharraf: Putin," *Hindu* (Chennai), June 5, 2002; Atul Aneja, "Putin Has Invited Us: Musharraf," *Hindu* (Chennai), June 5, 2002; Vladimir Raduhin, "India Grateful to Russia for Support," *Hindu* (Chennai), June 6, 2002. The First Summit of the Member States of the Conference on Interaction and Confidence Building Measures in Asia (CICA) was convened in Almaty, Kazakhstan, on June 3–5, 2002. First CICA Summit, Press Release, June 5, 2002 (http://missions.itu.int/~kazaks/eng/cica/cica08.htm).

107. Zaidi, "Desperately Seeking Options," p. 27.

108. Chari and others, *Perception, Politics and Security in South Asia,* p. 62.

Chapter Eight

1. For an excellent discussion on the Constituent Assembly debates on this issue, see Anwar Hussain Syed, *Pakistan: Islam, Politics and National Solidarity* (New York: Praeger, 1982), pp. 86–92. See also Ayesha Jalal, *Democracy and Authoritarianism in South Asia: A Comparative and Historical Perspective* (New Delhi: Foundation Books, 1995); Mohammad Waseem, *Politics and the State in Pakistan* (Lahore, Pakistan: Progressive, 1985), pp. 129–32; and John L. Esposito, "Pakistan: Quest for Islamic Identity," in *Islam and Development: Religion and Sociopolitical Change,* edited by Esposito (Syracuse University Press, 1980), pp. 139–62.

2. Saeed Shafqat, "From Official Islam to Islamism: The Rise of Dawat-ul-Irshad and Lashkar-e-Taiba," in *Pakistan: Nationalism without a Nation?* edited by Christophe Jaffrelot (New Delhi: Manohar, 2002), pp. 143–45. Lashkar's chief, Hafiz Saeed, argues that it is "playing a major role in transforming Pakistani society: through its educational institutions . . . producing a new breed of Pakistanis. These men are semi-educated but motivated to wage 'holy war'" (p. 145).

3. Jalal, *Democracy and Authoritarianism in South Asia,* p. 223.

4. Rajeev Bhargava, "Introduction," in *Secularism and Its Critics,* edited by Rajeev Bhargava (Oxford University Press, 1998), p. 1.

5. D. E. Smith, "India as a Secular State," in *Secularism and Its Critics,* edited by

Bhargava, pp. 225–28.

6. Bhargava, *Secularism and Its Critics*, p. 22. Some proponents of this school of thought include Ashis Nandy, T. N. Madan, and Partha Chatterjee, although their reasoning as to why secularism is inappropriate in the Indian context is quite different. See T. N. Madan, "Secularism in Its Place"; Ashis Nandy, "The Politics of Secularism and the Recovery of Religious Tolerance"; and Partha Chatterjee, "Secularism and Tolerance"—all in ibid., pp. 297–379.

7. Nehru's reluctance to adopt a uniform civil code and the debate on the Hindu Code Bill (1951), withdrawn under pressure and reintroduced as the Hindu Succession Bill (1955) and the Hindu Marriage Bill (1956), catering to and limited to the majority community, are cited as some examples. Gautam Navlakha, "Invoking Union: Kashmir and Official Nationalism of Bharat," in *Region, Religion, Caste, Gender and Culture in Contemporary India*, vol. 3, edited by T. V Sathyamurthy (Oxford University Press, 1996), p. 85.

8. Yogendra K. Malik and V. B. Singh, *Hindu Nationalists in India: The Rise of the Bharatiya Janata Party* (New Delhi: Vistaar, 1994), p. 15.

9. At the time of the formation of the Jan Sangh, Syama Prasad Mookerjee drew the attention of delegates to two issues: the special relationship of Kashmir with India and the condition of the Hindus in East Bengal. Its manifesto focused on Bharatiya (Indian) culture, Hindi as the link language, full integration of Jammu and Kashmir, and the denial of safeguards to minorities. Navlakha, "Invoking Union," pp. 102–03. See also Navnita Chadha Behera, "Kashmir: A Testing Ground," *South Asia* 25 (December 2003): 343–64; and Gautam Navlakha, "Defending National-Cultural Identity," *Economic and Political Weekly* 25 (March 3, 1990), p. 423.

10. Nandy, "The Politics of Secularism," p. 322. He explains that it was religion-as-faith that prompted 200,000 Indians to declare themselves to be Mohammedan Hindus in the census of 1911. It was religion-as-ideology, on the other hand, that prompted a significant proportion of the Punjabi-speaking Hindus to declare Hindi as their mother tongue, thus underlining the differences between Sikhism and Hinduism and sowing the seeds for the creation of a new minority.

11. For a detailed exposition of the changing character of Kashmiri identity, see Navnita Chadha Behera, *State, Identity and Violence: Jammu, Kashmir and Ladakh* (New Delhi: Manohar, 2000), pp. 58–61.

12. Smita Gupta, "A Doc Disposes . . . While a General Proposes," *Outlook*, November 29, 2004, p. 49.

13. Zahid Hussain, "Kashmir: The Long Road to Peace," *Newsline*, November 2004, pp. 23–27.

14. Ashis Nandy, "Pluralism as the Politics of Cultural Diversity in India," in *Making a Difference: A Collection of Essays*, edited by Rukmini Sekhar (New Delhi: SPICMACAY, 1998), p. 54.

15. P. Richard Nathan and Eric P. Hollman, "Modern Federalism," *International Affairs*, May 1991, p. 35.

16. Walker Connor, "Nationalism and Political Illegitimacy," in *Ethnonationalism in the Contemporary World: Walker Connor and the Study of Nationalism*, edited by Daniele

Conversi (London: Routledge, 2004), p. 26.

17. Ibid., p. 29.

18. This implies the growing respect for the proscription that force should not be used to alter interstate boundaries. See Mark W. Zacher, "The Territorial Integrity Norm: International Boundaries and the Use of Force," *International Organization* 55 (Spring 2001): 215–50.

19. In the 2002 State Assembly elections for eighty-seven seats, the National Conference polled 28.18 percent of the vote, while the PDP took 14.64 percent in the seats it contested, and just 9.28 percent statewide. Congress won 24.24 percent of the votes in the seats it contested and 24.24 per cent statewide. Praveen Swami, "The Question of Power" (www.flonet.com/fl2220/stories/20051007004602900.htm).

20. At present, just 1,659 of the state's 2,700 panchayats exist even on paper, and fewer still provide anything resembling grassroots democracy. Praveen Swami, "Blossoming Mutinies in Kashmir," *Hindu* (Chennai), March 30, 2006.

21. *Hindu* (Chennai), June 16, 2005. The JKLF chief publicly disagreed with the mirwaiz that their visit to Azad Kashmir amounted to Kashmiri involvement in the peace process or that the visit marked the beginning of a triangular process toward a resolution of the Kashmir issue. See also the mirwaiz's statement in *Times of India* (New Delhi), June 18, 2005; and interview with Yasin Malik in *Hindu,* June 21, 2005.

22. Swami, "Blossoming Mutinies in Kashmir."

23. Zaffar Abbas, "Great Expectations," *Herald* (Karachi), January 2004, p. 37.

24. Mubashir Zaidi, "The Himalayan Implosion," *Herald* (Karachi), June 2003 p. 60.

25. Raj Chengappa and Syed Talat Hussain, "Has the General Really Changed," *India Today*, May 2, 2005, p. 19.

26. For details, see Behera, *Kashmir: A Testing Ground*, pp. 360–63.

27. Navnita Chadha Behera, "Has the Government Handled Hurriyat's Pak Visit Properly?" *Times of India* (New Delhi), June 26, 2005.

28. Just before his first visit to the Valley, Prime Minister Manmohan Singh announced a reduction in troop levels in the state. An army battalion numbering 3,000 soldiers was deinducted from the Khannabal area of Anantnag district in south Kashmir, followed by another battalion in the Sunderbani area of Rajouri district and 1,200 soldiers from Uri in Baramulla district. In February 2006, India's defense minister Pranab Mukherjee announced the redeployment of another brigade-sized formation of 5,000 troops to the northeast.

29. Chengappa and Hussain, *Has the General Really Changed*, p. 19.

30. Hassan Abbas, *Pakistan's Drift into Extremism: Allah, the Army and America's War on Terror* (London: M. E. Sharpe, 2005), pp. 212–16.

31. Simon Cameron-Moore and K. J. M. Varma, "India Okayed Hurriyat Trip, Its Breakthrough, Let's Get Started: Gen," *Indian Express*, May 25, 2005 (www.indianexpress.com/res/web/pIe/archive_full_story.php?content_id=71036).

32. In 2001–02, Pakistan was home to fifty-eight religious political parties and twenty-four armed religious militias. Shafqat, "From Official Islam to Islamism," p. 133.

33. Cited in V. Sudarshan, "K for Conciliation," *Outlook*, May 2, 2005, p. 45.

34. Sustainable Development Policy Institute (*SDPI*), *Bulletin*, January-February 2004.

35. Iliyas Khan, "The Waiting," *Herald* (Karachi), July 2003 p. 41.

36. Satish Kumar, *Yearbook on India's Foreign Policy 1990–91* (New Delhi: Sage, 1992), p. 169. See her statement at the joint press conference with French president François Mitterrand in Islamabad on February 21, 1990, as quoted on p. 170. She also said that Pakistan was not interested in internationalizing the issue and was prepared to settle it through bilateral negotiations.

37. Samina Yasmeen, "Pakistan's Kashmir Policy: Voices of Moderation?" *Contemporary South Asia* 12 (June 2003): 187–202; Shahid M. Amin, "A Re-evaluation of the Kashmir Dispute," *Pakistan Horizon* 56, no. 2 (2003): 37–51; Ayaz Amir, "There Is No Kashmir Solution," reprinted from *Dawn* (Karachi) in *Sentinel*, January 7, 2001; Ayaz Amir, "Kashmir and Power of Illusion," *Dawn* (Karachi), January 19, 2001; I. Sehgal, "Untangling the Kashmir Knot," *Nation* (Lahore), January 20, 2001. For details on costs of conflicts for both India and Pakistan, see Mahmud Ali Durrani, *India and Pakistan: The Cost of Conflict, The Benefits of Peace* (Washington: Johns Hopkins School of Advanced International Studies, 2000); and Strategic Foresight Group, *Cost of Conflict between India and Pakistan* (Mumbai: International Center for Peace Initiatives, 2004).

38. B. Muralidhar Reddy, "Softening Stances," *Frontline*, December 6, 2003, p. 19.

39. Josh Meyer, "Terror Camps Scatter, Persist," *Los Angeles Times*, June 20, 2005, p. A1. Recent arrests in Lodi, California, illustrate what authorities say is the failure of Pakistan to halt elusive militant training groups.

40. Luke Harding and Rosie Lowan, "Pakistan Militants Linked to London Blasts," *Guardian* (London), July 19, 2005.

41. In an interview with B. G. Verghese in 1983, he said: "If we involve Kashmir in our [bilateral] dialogue, we will never be able to proceed further. Let us leave Kashmir for the time being. Let there be a *status quo* for the time being." *President of Pakistan General Mohammad Zia-ul-Haq: Interviews to the Foreign Media*, vol. 6 (Islamabad: Directorate of Films and Publications, Ministry of Information and Broadcasting, January–December 1983), p. 167. See also his interview with Partha Chatterjee in the same volume, p. 40. On another occasion, he said: "We have suggested to India . . . for the time being, let us keep [the] Kashmir issue aside and settle other issues first. Let us create a better atmosphere, build up more confidence between each other; and once there is an environment of mutual trust then we will take up the Kashmir dispute."

42. After their July meeting, Rajiv Gandhi made it clear in a press conference that the plebiscite was a dead issue as the Indian government had held a number of elections in the state of Jammu and Kashmir and therefore Kashmir was a closed issue. The only response Benazir Bhutto gave was that the Simla Agreement records the recognized position of both sides. Significantly, there was still no mention of the Pakistani demand that India must hold a plebiscite and grant the right of self-determination to Kashmiris.

43. Straw's remarks are quoted in *News International* (Karachi), June 7, 2002 ([August 9, 2006]).

44. For a succinct summary of more than forty proposals to resolve the Kashmir

issue, see Joseph E. Schwartzberg, "Proposals for Resolving the Kashmir Dispute," unpublished paper, available from the author. For a contemporary debate on this issue, see Sumantra Bose, *Kashmir: Roots of Conflict, Paths to Peace* (New Delhi: Vistaar, 2003); and the report of the Kashmir Study Group, "*KASHMI–A Way Forward*," available at www.kashmirstudygroup.org.

45. Gupta, "A Doc Disposes," p. 49.

46. Sudarshan, "K for Conciliation," p. 43.

47. Complaints of human rights violations have been on a steady decline, from 142 in 2001 to 74 in 2002, 25 in 2003, 16 in 2004, and just 7 in 2005. Seventy Border Security Force personnel and 134 soldiers received sentences of up to life imprisonment for human rights violations between 1990 and 2004. Praveen Swami, "The Politics of Death," *Hindu* (Chennai), March 4, 2006.

48. Bharat Karnad, "A Strategy to Counter Pakistan-Supported Terrorism," in *Pakistan in a Changing Strategic Context*, edited by Ajay Darshan Behera and Joseph C. Mathew (New Delhi: Knowledge World, 2004), p. 314.

49. Rajesh Sinha, "Two Neighbours and a Treaty," *Economic and Political Weekly*, February 18, 2006, p. 608.

50. *News* (Lahore), January 10, 2006.

51. In the early 1950s, Pakistan justified its claims on Kashmir on the grounds that India would otherwise control its "lifeline" as its economy is dependent on rivers that originate in the Himalayas. For details, see B. G. Verghese, "From Indus-I to Indus-II," *Mainstream*, July 1–7, 2005.

52. At least three resolutions in the Sindh assembly and two each by provincial assemblies of Baluchistan and North-West Frontier Province have already been passed unanimously opposing the construction of the Kalabagh Dam. The Senate Standing Committee and the Council of Common Interests also rejected the plan for this dam. For a detailed discussion, see Massoud Ansari, "Storm over the Indus," *Newsline*, July 1998, pp. 42–45; Adnal Ali, "The Great Water Divide," *Newsline*, February 2001, pp. 57–58; Seemi Kamal, "Apocalypse Now," *Newsline*, April 2001, pp. 57–60; Massoud Ansari, "The Water Divide," *Newsline* (www.newsline.com.pk/NewsJan2006/news1sp2006.htm).

53. Prime Minister Manmohan Singh's statement at the roundtable conference. *Hindu* (Chennai), February 26, 2006.

54. Praveen Swami, "Kashmir Maha Panchayat: Learning from History," *Hindu* (Chennai), February 23, 2006.

55. Shekhar Gupta, "New Pitch, Front Foot Forward," *Indian Express*, March 4, 2006 (http://www.indianexpress.com/res/web/pIe/archive_full_story.php?content_id=88925 [August 9, 2006]).

56. Ibid.

57. Ayesha Siddiqa's expression, though her definition of what this means, is somewhat different. In a conversation with the author, February 2006.

58. For details, see "Musharraf Assassination Plot Failed" (www.cnn.com [September 18, 2002]). See also "Musharraf Faces Threat to Life, Says Moin," *Dawn* (Karachi),

July 23, 2002; Anwar Iqbal, "Musharraf Tightens Personal Security," *Washington Times*, August 19, 2002; "Musharraf Convoy Escapes Bomb Blast," *Dawn* (Karachi), December 15, 2003.

59. For a complete text of President Musharraf's interview with Karan Thapar in which he made these points, see (www.ibnlive.com/article.php?id=3492&section_id=3&single=true). For a detailed analysis of these points, see A. G. Noorani, "A Working Paper on Kashmir," *Frontline*, February 25–March 10, 2006, pp. 44–47.

60. See Musharraf's remarks at a joint press conference with President Bush, press release, "President's Meeting with U.S. President Bush," New York, September 14, 2005, at the Pakistan president's website (www.presidentofpakistan.gov.pk/prpressreleasedetail.aspx?nprpressreleaseid=1388&nyear=2005&nmonth=9 [August 9, 2006]).

61. General Yahya Khan, General Ayub Khan, and General Mohammed Zia-ul-Haq were deposed by palace coups. See Praveen Swami, "Mayhem in the Menagerie," *Hindu* (Chennai), March 13, 2006.

62. Sarmad Abbas, "The Unending War," *Herald* (Karachi), November 2005, p. 33.

63. Mirwaiz Umar Farooq, interview with Riyaz Wani, *Hindu* (Chennai), February 26, 2006.

64. Swami, "Kashmir Maha Panchayat: Learning from History."

65. See Teresita C. Schaffer, *Kashmir: The Economics of Peace Building* (Washington: CSIS Press, 2005).

66. John Cherian, "A New Momentum," *Frontline*, April 22, 2005, p. 5.

67. General Pervez Musharraf, speaking to a conference of members of parliament from across South Asia, as cited in Ghazi Salahuddin, "Dreams for South Asia," *News* (Lahore), May 22, 2005 (www.jang.com.pk/thenews/may2005-daily/22-05-2005/oped/o4.htm [August 14, 2006]).

INDEX